revisiting women's cinema

a Camera Obscura book

REVISITING WOMEN'S CINEMA

LINGZHEN WANG

feminism,
socialism, and
mainstream culture
in modern china

duke university press   durham & london   2021

© 2021 Duke University Press
All rights reserved
Printed and bound by CPI Group (UK) Ltd, Croydon, CR0 4YY
Designed by Aimee C. Harrison
Typeset in Minion by Westchester Publishing Services

Library of Congress Cataloging-in-Publication Data
Names: Wang, Lingzhen, author.
Title: Revisiting women's cinema : feminism, socialism, and
mainstream culture in modern China / Lingzhen Wang.
Other titles: Camera obscura book (Duke University Press)
Description: Durham : Duke University Press, 2021. | Series: A
camera obscura book | Includes bibliographical references and
index.
Identifiers: LCCN 2020017609 (print)
LCCN 2020017610 (ebook)
ISBN 9781478009757 (hardcover)
ISBN 9781478010807 (paperback)
ISBN 9781478012337 (ebook)
Subjects: LCSH: Motion pictures—China—History—20th century. |
Women motion picture producers and directors—China. |
Feminist films—History and criticism. | Women in motion
pictures. | Motion pictures—Political aspects—China—20th century.
Classification: LCC PN1993.5. C6W364 2020 (print) |
LCC PN1993.5.C6 (ebook) | DDC 791.430820951—dc23
LC record available at https://lccn.loc.gov/2020017609
LC ebook record available at https://lccn.loc.gov/2020017610

Cover art: Photograph of Wang Ping, circa 1958–1959.
Photographer unknown.

To my parents, Wang Yaobing and Fang Ya

CONTENTS

ILLUSTRATIONS

ACKNOWLEDGMENTS

This book, more than a decade in the making, has gone through several significant revisions, and my desire to continue revising it remains strong even on the eve of publication. My anxiety over completing the book not only indicates the level of complexity of the project but also, and more importantly, reflects the ceaseless transformations that have occurred in China, in the greater world, and in feminist, media, and cultural studies since the book's original conception. This book records an ongoing dialogue with all these changes as it reviews socialist feminist history in China from the 1920s to the 1960s; retraces mainstream feminist cultural practice from Mao's socialist period to the post-Mao promarket era (1950s–1980s); reengages with Western feminist theories from the 1970s forward along with a set of influential English-language scholarship on Chinese socialist women's liberation produced in the 1980s; and reimagines a transnational feminist future with a mass-oriented cultural practice. Both the book's significance and limitations, as a result, lie in this open-ended and continuing dialogic engagement. I sincerely hope that this book, despite its unavoidable incompleteness, invites scholars from diverse generations, disciplines, and geographic regions to reflect continuously and critically on the geopolitical and socioeconomic underpinnings of current and emerging research paradigms and to forge new frameworks that promote a transnational emancipatory vision, endorse political-economically and socioculturally integrated approaches, and revitalize historical materialism in the studies of feminist movements, mainstream culture, and women's cinema.

I am indebted to many kinds of support and endorsements received over the years that have enabled me to complete this book. Fellowships offered by Johns Hopkins University, the National Endowment for the Humanities, and the Pembroke Center for Teaching and Research on Women at Brown University provided me invaluable time to conduct research in China and to write the manuscript. I presented many of the book's ideas at conferences, symposia, research seminars, and invited talks. Responses from participants at these academic events, organized particularly by the following universities and programs, helped me adjust my arguments to have both broader implications and more details: the Hopkins-Nanjing Center, the Gender Workshop at Harvard University's Fairbank Center for East Asian Studies, the Pembroke Center at Brown University, the Institute for Advanced Studies in Social Sciences and the Humanities and the School of Liberal Arts at Nanjing University, the Heyman Center for the Humanities and the Weatherhead East Asian Institute at Columbia University, the Center for Chinese Studies at the University of Michigan, the Institute for World Literatures and Cultures at Tsinghua University, the Center for East Asian Studies at the University of Chicago, the Shanghai Film Academy and the College of Liberal Arts at Shanghai University, the Guangqi Center for International Scholars at Shanghai Normal University, Renmin University, the Humanities Institute at the State University of New York at Stony Brook, Concordia University in Canada, the Communication and Performing Arts Department at Roma Tre University in Italy, Fudan University, Xiamen University, Shanxi Normal University, the Center for Language and Culture and the Department of East Asian Studies at Oberlin College, the Department of East Asian Studies and the China Institute at the University of Alberta, and the Jinling Women's College at Nanjing Normal University. My thanks to all the event organizers and participants for creating a space in which to present this work.

Dialogues with feminist, film/media, and Chinese studies scholars over the course of my work have greatly inspired me, helping me sharpen my intellectual vision and situate my project closer to the most innovative, critical, and transnational scholarship in these academic areas. I especially value and treasure my conversations and exchanges of ideas with the following colleagues and friends: Li Xiaojiang, Jane M. Gains, Patricia White, Veronica Pravadelli, Tina Mai Chen, E. Ann Kaplan, Haiping Yan, Tani Barlow, Dong Limin, Lynne Joyrich, Mary Ann Doane, Ellen Rooney, Lisa Rofel, Song Shaopeng, Xueping Zhong, Wang Zheng, Xiaobing Tang, Chengzhou He, Tze-Lan Debra Sang, Tamara Chin, Yingjin Zhang, Philip Rosen, Ban Wang, Ellen Widmer, Gail Hershatter, Gao Xiaoxian, Jin Yihong, Christopher Lupke, Paola Iovene, Kathleen Anne McHugh, S. Louisa Wei, Rossana

Maule, Gina Marchetti, Zhang Zhen, Hsiu-Chuang Deppman, Shuqin Cui, Zhang Ling, Luo Liang, and Lin Shaoxiong.

Additionally, I want to thank several academic editors. Elizabeth Weed and Ellen Rooney supported projects of the Nanjing-Brown Joint Program in Gender Studies and the Humanities by publishing a special issue titled "Other Genders, Other Sexualities: Chinese Differences" (summer 2013) in *differences: A Journal of Feminist Cultural Studies*, where my research on 1980s post-Mao Chinese feminism and Li Xiaojiang appeared. Then, the editors of a special issue of *Signs: Journal of Women in Culture and Society*, "Feminist Sinologies: A Thematic Cluster" (spring 2015), Nan Z. Da and Wang Zheng, invited me to publish an article on mainland China's first female director, Wang Ping, and her film practice in the socialist era. John Belton and Jennifer Crewe at Columbia University Press included my edited volume, *Chinese Women's Cinema: Transnational Contexts* (2011), which contained my initial discussion of the socialist female director Dong Kena, in their Film and Culture series. Finally, thanks to the Camera Obscura editorial collective for their enthusiasm in publishing my writing on Zhang Nuanxin, a pioneer of post-Mao film theory and experimental cinema, in *Camera Obscura: Feminism, Culture and Media Studies* (34, no. 2 [2019]).

Special appreciation goes to Patricia White, editor of *Camera Obscura: Feminism, Culture and Media Studies*, who invited me to submit my book manuscript to their Camera Obscura series for review, and the acquisitions editor Elizabeth Ault at Duke University Press. Their transnational feminist vision and professional dedication most significantly moved me to complete the project. In addition, two anonymous readers at Duke University Press offered insightful comments, great support, and constructive suggestions.

I send gratitude also to Min Ruixin, a conscientious and dedicated editor working for the most influential feminist and gender studies journal in China, the *Journal of Chinese Women's Studies*, for her abundant enthusiasm and energy, which have made the publication of my articles in the Chinese context especially meaningful. Wang Qinwei at Shanghai Sanlian Press greatly supported the publication of *Chinese Sex/Gender: Historical Differences* (2016), a critical Chinese anthology I edited, which is based on the special issue of *differences*, "Other Genders, Other Sexualities: Chinese Differences." Song Zhao (daughter of Wang Ping), Meng Hui (daughter of Zhang Nuanxin), and Zheng Dasheng (son of Huang Shuqin) have provided me with invaluable historical photographs of their mothers working on various film projects. Thanks to Rosemary Peters-Hill for her valuable editing and important dialogues; Xiao Hua for his tireless effort to translate my articles into Chinese; Kate Chouta for her meticulous editing; Laura Magee for her gifted and beautiful design of the book cover; and Kate Herman at Duke University Press for her wonderful assistance in the final stage of my manuscript preparation.

My most heartfelt gratitude goes to the four Chinese female directors I have studied in this book—Wang Ping, Dong Kena, Zhang Nuanxin, and Huang Shuqin—whose life experiences and cinematic practices in socialist and postsocialist China leave us inexhaustible resources to explore the intertwining relationship between "big picture" phenomena like socioeconomic institutions, geopolitics, feminism, and mainstream culture and the subjective matter of individual creativity. Both their unprecedented achievements and their historical limitations compel us to rethink feminism and women's cinema in the context of the modern world, thus contributing to the formation of a different understanding of gender and history and an alternative imagination for future feminist sociocultural practices.

This book is dedicated to my parents, Wang Yaobing and Fang Ya, who—having devoted their youth to socialist revolution and socialist construction, suffered during the Cultural Revolution, and experienced rapid market transformation in contemporary China—remain hopeful and committed to social justice and equality, better lives for all, and peace in the world.

INTRODUCTION

From the advent of the Maoist era in 1949 to the end of the first decade of the post-Mao economic reform around 1987, Chinese female film directors played a key role in producing popular and mainstream feminist visual culture. Working within the general socialist environment, where gender and class equality were considered institutionally foundational and where the publicly owned studio system promoted women's filmmaking, artistic experimentation, and new socialist values combating patriarchal consciousness, Chinese female directors demonstrated unprecedented individual and social agency. They stood front and center in the formation and transformation of socialist proletarian mainstream cinema, creating films that not only helped articulate socialist vision, ethics, and subject positions but also contributed to diversifying socialist cultural imaginations and aesthetics, reaching a broad mass audience. They exemplified an integrated socialist-feminist approach to cinematic representation during the first seventeen years of socialist China (1949–1966), before the Great Proletarian Cultural Revolution (无产阶级文化大革命, hereafter Cultural Revolution, 1966–1976), and pioneered a socially engaged experimental filmmaking during the first decade of the post-Mao era (1976–1986). They produced many popular, sociopolitically engaged, and artistically experimental films, contributing significantly to global women's cinema and feminist culture.

Their great achievements, however, have long been overlooked and denied in feminist and cinematic studies inside and outside China since the late 1970s. This overall dismissal is neither purely cultural nor simply gender-related. In the late 1970s and 1980s, the world as a whole underwent a series of geopolitical and economic transformations: the launch of the Second Cold War

(1979–1985), the advancement of capitalist globalization and the subsequent decline of the global Left and rise of the new Right, and China's economic reforms. The fall of the Berlin Wall in 1989 and the dissolution of the Soviet Union in 1991 brought an end to the passive-aggressive geopolitics of the Cold War, but this "conclusion" actually represented the ultimate triumph of capitalism over socialism as it not only fanned the flame of capitalist Cold War ideology but also advanced the development of global neoliberalism. Together, these global movements have, by and large, caused a cultural turn in the transnational intellectual world, a shift from both the socioeconomic interrogation of capitalist systems and the insistence on the importance of geopolitical signification of aesthetic values and cultural practice.[1] These global changes also produced a profound impact on feminist movements. Not only was Marxist feminism questioned but the linkage between class and gender, as well as historical materialism, became gradually repudiated in the rise of radical and cultural feminism in the 1970s.[2] "Does socialism liberate women?" This Cold War–enhanced question, which early-1970s Western scholarship on Eastern Europe first raised,[3] was greatly revived in the early 1980s, particularly in Western feminist approaches to socialist China. The proliferating radical as well as liberal definition of feminism as an independent and individualistic endeavor put forward an unwavering negative answer to the question.[4]

In the Chinese context, the Chinese party-state, while implementing economic reform, launched in 1978 the "thought liberation" (思想解放) campaign to reevaluate the Cultural Revolution and to relax the political control of cultural production. Chinese women's autobiographical literature and subjective experimental cinema emerged during this period of diverse sociopolitical imagination and cultural pluralism. As economic reforms solidified around the mid-1980s and more Western liberal theories and Cold War–influenced scholarship entered China, however, discourses promoting Enlightenment modernity (scientific truth, universal rationality, human nature, and individualistic subjectivity), economic development, and sexual difference (as opposed to gender equality) became mainstreamed. In the area of literature and cinema, the dynamic "cultural fever" (文化热) of the early 1980s developed into the "Root-Seeking" Movement (寻根运动) in the mid-1980s, pronouncing the power of the cultural (un)consciousness, masculine vitality, (male) intellectual reflection, and a detached avant-garde aesthetic.[5] Freud's psychoanalysis, Jung's collective unconsciousness and archetypes, Arnold J. Toynbee's philosophy of civilization, and Li Zehou's ancient Chinese thought and culture all worked together influentially to promote an abstract and universal psychocultural structure indifferent to historical and sociopolitical changes.[6] Post-Mao Chinese feminism, which appeared in the early 1980s to address extant gender issues in socialist China, was also implicated in the newly mainstreamed economic and sociocultural trends. In its attempt to catch up with universal feminist values and more "advanced" feminist practice, mostly referring to liberal and post-second-wave feminist developments in the West, post-Mao feminism in the mid- and late 1980s advocated independent female consciousness, essential sexual difference, and a critique of patriarchal culture.[7] This post-Mao official and intellectual turn toward the universal (liberal and apolitical) standard of truth, humanism, and economic development occasioned a retreat from socialism's central endeavor—addressing structural injustice and socioeconomic inequality—and a dismissal of socialist feminism and socialist proletarian mass-oriented culture. Within the newly established framework of the universal market and cultural (post)modernity, Chinese socialism of the Maoist era was often represented and indeed critiqued as backward, feudalistic, abnormal, and patriarchal—a politically, economically, and culturally negative state from which China should depart.[8]

By the late 1980s and early 1990s when feminist and film scholars inside and outside China finally turned their attention to Chinese women's cinema, they had already employed a set of liberal and post-second-wave feminist criteria for measuring women's cultural practice, criteria that center on individual(istic) consciousness, independent female essence/difference, a critique of men, and the significance of artistic marginalization and subversion.[9] Disappointed by the research findings in their studies of Chinese women's cinema, these scholars invariably drew two conclusions. One, female directors of the Mao years had passively conformed to socialist politics, modeled themselves after men by repressing their female essence or difference, and produced mainstream and propagandistic—and thus non-feminist—films.[10] Two, women's experimental cinema of the 1980s, despite its markedly subjective styles and individual consciousness, exhibited serious ambiguity about collective values, the role of the state, and the socialist structure of justice and thus failed to break away from socialist political ideology and mainstream culture.[11]

These joint dismissals of socialism and socialist feminist mainstream culture have raised serious questions about our world today and feminist practice for the future. What kinds of positions, visions, and imaginations have been rejected and lost with this global repudiation of socialist practice, particularly those related to feminism and media? How is rediscovering the legacy of Chinese socialist feminist mainstream culture significant in today's world, where the globalized market and transnational media have marginalized women's cinema and other sociocultural endeavors? And how should we reengage with the history of Chinese socialist mainstream culture and work with renewed transnational and materialist feminism and media theories to forge an alternative and emancipatory vision for contemporary and future feminist film practice?

Indeed, since the early 1990s, when the end of the Cold War showcased the triumph of Western capitalism and when global neoliberalism and marketization caused multilevel sociopolitical crisis including the deterioration of both women's status and the emancipatory vision of women's liberation, feminist scholars and activists around the world have critically probed the dangerous liaison between contemporary (post-second-wave) feminist practices, neoliberalism, and free market fundamentalism.[12] The crisis-ridden situation has particularly spurred feminists to reconsider the socioeconomic insights and international legacies of the second-wave feminism and renew the practices of socialist feminism:[13] its systematic critiques of capitalism, its integrated socialist emancipatory vision of the future, and its promise for a transnational feminist political alliance confronting global neoliberalism.

The rise of transnational feminism in the early 1990s reflected both the "shared or common context of struggle due to common exploration and domination across the north-south divide" and the feminist needs to not only "destabilize . . . hegemonic boundaries of nation, race, and gender" but also remap feminist endeavors with a geopolitical anchor and historical materialist approach.[14] Critically revisiting the theory and practice of socialist feminism at this historical juncture would thus help forge new transnational solidarity among feminists, integrating cultural and ethical concerns with political-economic structural transformation and articulating an alternative feminist model for the post–Cold War world.

This book discusses geopolitical history, feminism, and women's cinema in Maoist socialist and post-Mao China by engaging directly with this revised transnational feminist framework. Carefully reassessing the practice of socialist feminist culture from the 1950s to the 1980s, I reveal the critical relevance of socialist institutionalized feminism and mainstream women's cinema to contemporary feminist media practice, foregrounding its mass-oriented spectatorship, multidimensional agency, and integrated approach to gender and culture. One of the most urgent and important tasks for contemporary feminism and feminist media studies is indeed to reconnect seemingly autonomous areas or subject matters—such as aesthetics, technology, medium, textuality, sex and gender, and individual agency—to the "big pictures" of sociopolitical environments, global market movements, and transnational media and cultural forces. I particularly investigate the structural and institutional linkages between the autonomous matters and the big pictures, thus challenging the implicit beliefs that cultural, technological, or feminist practices could be independent from their political and economic systems and that these supposedly autonomous practices alone could bring significant changes to today's world. Cultural practice, technological innovation, and individual creations contain their respective potentials to challenge the status quo, but my research demonstrates that only an integrated feminist cultural practice can articulate an alternative vision for future sociocultural transformations. Further, only a multidimensional approach can critically probe these autonomous practices' political and institutional constitution, social and aesthetic effects, and historical limitations.

With an emphasis on the geopolitical and integrated approach to socialist revolution, Chinese feminism(s), and women's cinema, this research has the following goals. First, I investigate the political and historical implications of the ways in which socialist feminism and socialist mainstream film practice has been dismissed. In the process I reveal the complicity among seemingly unrelated global forces, including international feminist practices that seek to erase this critical alternative sociopolitical and cultural practice in modern world history. Second, I redefine a set of important concepts—such as socialist feminism, mainstream culture, post-Mao feminism, and experimentalism—in Chinese contexts and offer a new approach to histories of Chinese feminism and socialist film. Third, I provide the first history of Chinese women's cinema: its emergence and development within the socialist institutional remapping of gender, culture, and the audience as well as the socialist collectivization of economic ownership and film studios in the 1950s and early 1960s; its return after the derailed Cultural Revolution; its pluralization in the early and mid-1980s with the state-initiated thought liberation movement and economic reform; and its marginalization and repudiation in the late 1980s and 1990s, when market globalization, universal modernity and postmodernity, and a detached masculine aesthetic became mainstream while post-Mao feminism moved in a combined liberal and cultural feminist direction. This study by no means simplifies or idealizes socialist feminism and its mainstream cinematic practice. Rather, revisiting Chinese socialist feminist history entails a critical reexamination of its theoretical, historical and political problems: the limitations of Marxist theory on gender, the constraints Chinese agrarian and traditional culture—along with modern China's semicolonial and turbulent history—impose on Chinese women's liberation; and the complex geopolitical and socioeconomic causes for which socialist feminism is repudiated in contemporary China. Last but not least, this project focuses on four representative Chinese female directors and their films: Wang Ping (王苹, 1916–1990) and Dong Kena (董克娜, 1930–2016) in the 1950s and 1960s and Zhang Nuanxin (张暖忻, 1940–1995) and Huang Shuqin (黄蜀芹, b. 1939) in the 1980s and early 1990s. Through their work, I demonstrate how an individual woman's artistic agency along with the historical significance of her filmmaking is contingent on and embedded within dynamic interactions among geopolitical, socioeconomic, cultural, and individual forces and thus is by no means constituted exclusively from above or autonomously (independently). The four chapters on these female directors also explore the (trans)formation of gender, aesthetics, and socialist cinematic authorship, emphasizing Chinese women's important role in producing and diversifying mainstream culture and their negotiated imaginations for different feminist cultural practices. To better situate these directors in Chinese cinema from the 1950s to the late 1980s, the four chapters also discuss many other films by contemporary female and male directors.

Chinese post-Mao feminist film criticism emerged and became influential at the turn of the 1990s as China began to expand its market development and Chinese mainstream cinema rested on the cusp of formal privatization and commercialization. Post-Mao feminist film scholars, in their study of women's cinema from Mao's socialist era to post-Mao economic reform times, continued the post-Mao effort of the 1980s, moving further away from integrated socialist feminist practice and gender equality and toward a separatist gender approach and essentialized female difference. They also used Western cine-feminist and poststructuralist theories as major references to promote a marginalized, avant-garde, and subversive women's cinema, questioning socialist women's mainstream cinema as a feminist practice. Although this book is chronologically organized, the four chapters on female directors include discussions of film criticism and feminist scholarship published since the late 1980s in order to address issues raised particularly by post-Mao feminist film scholars and thus to forge a critical dialogue between historical Chinese women's film practice and contemporary feminist and film theories.

Transnational Concepts, Theoretical Issues, and Political Matters

Several major terms and concepts I use in this book require critical retheorization and historical elaborations to elucidate the significance of their important geopolitical, economic, and sociocultural differences. Whereas most critical conceptualizations and theoretical revisions are conducted in individual chapters, the following two terms, *socialist feminism* and *mainstream culture*, demand clarification in this introductory chapter—they either compete with other terms exploring specific geopolitical and sociocultural meanings in the Chinese context, or introduce radically different analytic frameworks when used in different political-economic environments or systems. As these two terms are also crucial to the book's overall structure and argument, I will briefly elucidate why I have chosen to use them and how reconceptualizing them can contribute to the study of Chinese feminism, culture, and women's cinema from the 1950s to the 1980s.

Socialist Feminism

The term *socialist feminism* was not used or circulated in the history of either the Chinese socialist revolution (also called the "new democratic revolution," 1921–1949) or Mao's socialist China (1949–1976). "Women's liberation" (妇女解放) was. I employ socialist feminism as a structuring concept in this book, rather than women's liberation, for two reasons. First, women's liberation, as a modern, progressive concept, refers to movements that aim to eliminate women's oppression and gender inequality in human history. Despite the term's universal appeal and usage, however, the specific framework, goals, and contents of women's liberation movements in different geopolitical locations, historical periods, and political-economic systems are not identical. Women's liberation in the Western capitalist context centers on bourgeois individualism, female independent consciousness, and equal legal rights between men and women. Third-world women's liberation usually ties itself to modern anticolonialism and bourgeois national independence movements. Finally, socialist women's liberation aims to dismantle the capitalist political-economic structure that (re)produces not only gender hierarchy but also class, racial, and regional inequalities. Most critically, the socialist theory of women's liberation does not separate women's issues from other structural inequalities; on the contrary, it argues that women's oppression cannot be resolved as long as other oppressions continue. As an extraordinary feminist movement that helped establish a socialist country where gender and class equality became the norm, the Chinese socialist women's liberation movement distinguished itself by its multidimensional engagements: it participated simultaneously in the national independence movement, the proletarian revolution, and various international socialist anti-imperialist endeavors. Chinese socialist women's liberation, like the Chinese socialist revolution, is a long, complicated, and transnational process that consists of both bourgeois and proletarian revolutionary tasks and aims to achieve a socialist emancipatory vision by ultimately dismantling and transforming capitalist and other forms of patriarchal socioeconomic structures.[15]

Problems arose in the 1970s and 1980s when Western Cold War ideology joined hands with a radical cultural feminist repudiation of both Marxist theory and the left-wing movement to reassert the universal value of Western "women's liberation"—individualism, independence, and essential female difference—(re)orienting Western scholarship on socialist women's liberation in the world. The long dormant question "Does socialism liberate women?" was reinvigorated in the Western feminist scholarship of the 1980s to critically interrogate the practices of socialist countries, including China, by forging an antithetical relationship between socialism and feminism. Since the early 1980s, "much feminist inquiry, both in the United States and in China, has directed itself to this question," and the antithesis of socialism and women's liberation (based on the Western model) has formed and informed most of the feminist research.[16] As I elaborate in my first chapter, scholars who directed their research to the question "Does socialism liberate women?" often ended up searching for answers to the flip side of that question, "Why has socialism *not* liberated Chinese women?"[17] Similarly, scholars who argued that Chinese socialist women's liberation had been subordinated, postponed, or unfinished, also derived their criteria from Western feminist practice, Cold War ideology, and universal capitalist values. In the Chinese context, the new ideology of economic reform the party-state implemented toward the end of the 1970s, in an apparent delegitimization of the Cultural Revolution (1966–1976), swept aside some central socialist principles, including gender and class equality. In mid-1980s China, the state augmented reforms by further endorsing scientific objectivity, economic rationality, and technological progress—values granted the status of "universal truths" due to their place in Western modernity. At the same time, female activists and scholars also began to seek a universal model for feminist movements, embracing particularly post-second-wave, radical, and cultural feminisms. Li Xiaojiang (李小江, b. 1951), one of the best-known post-Mao feminist scholars, once stated, "It was after I compared the Western and Chinese feminist movements that I began to question the assumption that Chinese women were liberated. Following the Western forerunners of women's liberation, I called for the awakening of Chinese women's female consciousness [in contemporary China]."[18] Taking Western women's liberation as the standard reference, post-Mao feminists began, in the 1980s, to either perceive socialist women's liberation in socioeconomic and political realms as an early stage of the feminist movement that must be surpassed and later negated, or pit socialist women's liberation against an essential female difference, consciousness, and cultural expression.[19]

Socialist feminism rather than *women's liberation*, therefore, effectively avoids the geopolitically loaded hegemonic usages of the latter term, highlighting instead the integrated and interdependent relationship between socialism and feminism in the context of Chinese socialist revolution and construction. Furthermore, whereas the term *women's liberation* often provokes ideological debates around criteria and the final point of completion, the term *socialist feminism* prioritizes the historical process of the socialist women's movement, particularly its complicated interactions with major socioeconomic, cultural, and geopolitical forces. Indeed, neither the founding of a socialist nation-state nor the establishment of an official organization of socialist women's liberation marks the end of the historical proletarian and feminist revolution in history. Socialist China of the 1950s and 1960s was only in the beginning stage of socialist transformations, and, as expected, new internal contradictions and international conflicts emerged to both condition and (re)orient its particular movement and process. Attention to the historical and geopolitical course of the socialist women's movement is critical as it helps us recognize the special negotiations and contributions a regional feminist practice has made, and at the same time enables us to probe the limitations shared between socialist feminism and socialist revolution situated in a specific national and international context. Moreover, it also questions the problematic assumption that the ultimate women's liberation should be and can be achieved independently and alone while other political-economic and sociocultural issues persist at local and global levels.

Second, the use of *socialist feminism* foregrounds a transnational feminist framework that highlights not only the socialist women's movement's international origin in the nineteenth century but also a global body of feminist theory developed in relation to Marxist theory, proletarian revolutions, socialist and left-wing movements, and other feminist endeavors across the world. This transnational dimension is crucial when we reevaluate the legacy of the Chinese socialist women's movement and gender policy today in relation to historical feminist revisions of Marxist theory, seeking an alternative vision for future transnational feminism. Indeed, a comparative study of socialist feminism in different parts of the world is long overdue, as is a critical reassessment of Chinese socialist revolution in terms of its potential contribution to transnational feminist theory and political practice. I thus use *socialist feminism* in this book to trace and reflect on the theory, policy, and institutionalized practice of the women's movement and gender equality in the Chinese contexts of socialist revolution and the Mao era, especially from 1949 to the early 1960s, referencing international socialist feminist movements and reenvisioning future transnational feminist theory and politics.[20]

Mainstream Culture

During the post-Mao era, and especially since the early 1990s, China scholars have frequently used "mainstream" (主流) in such compound terms as "mainstream literature" (主流文学), "mainstream cinema" (主流电影), "mainstream culture" (主流文化), "mainstream ideology" (主流意识形态), and "mainstream discourse" (主流话语) to refer to cultural and sociopolitical practices in both Mao's and post-Mao China.[21] The term has also been deployed in English scholarship on Chinese cultural practices (art, literature, and film) in a similar way.[22] Like *socialist feminism*, *mainstream culture* did not circulate in the Mao era. "People's literature and art" (人民文艺) and "worker-peasant-soldier literature" (工农兵文学) were dominant terms at the time. At the turn of the twenty-first century, as China began to play an increasingly important role on the world stage and as commercialism further reconfigured China's cultural practice, "socialist mainstream culture" (社会主义主流文化) emerged as a new political and intellectual discourse to address China's international ambitions and domestic concerns.[23]

My decision to use the term *mainstream culture*, however, was initially prompted by some influential post-Mao feminist publications in the early 1990s on socialist women's cinema. These articles accused Chinese female directors, especially those of the Mao era, of making mainstream rather than marginalized or avant-garde films. Directly influenced by the Western cine-feminist theory of the early 1970s, which used *mainstream* to refer to Hollywood commercial cinema, especially its perpetuation of the dominant capitalist patriarchal ideology and male-centered pleasure, post-Mao feminist film scholars took *mainstream cinema* or *mainstream culture* as universally applicable and intrinsically conservative and patriarchal concepts.

Their radical conclusion that films by Chinese socialist female directors are not feminist because they belong to mainstream rather than marginalized or experimental culture spurred serious questions about the validity and the risk of accepting the concept in an undifferentiated way.

The problems exhibited in post-Mao feminist film scholarship attest to the reasserted global hegemonic power of Western discourses since the late 1970s. At the same time, post-Mao feminism's outrageous conclusions about socialist women's cinema have also inadvertently called for an urgent and critical inquiry into the central characteristics of socialist mainstream culture in the Chinese context. Although *mainstream culture* was not a term historically used in socialist China, it has emerged as a critical concept in the study of transnational culture, gender, and avant-gardism/experimentalism, thus demanding a serious historical analysis and geopolitical redefinition. Indeed, how do we reconceptualize mainstream culture in order to make it critically useful in the study of the Chinese socialist culture of the 1950s and 1960s? How does socialist mainstream culture differ from the mainstream culture mostly critiqued and sometimes reimagined by Western intellectuals in a capitalist system? How can this comparison help us understand the role of socioeconomic institutions in (re)configuring cultural practices? And how does the relationship between women's cinema and the dominant ideology and culture differ across political-economic systems? As scholars in Chinese studies have frequently used the term *mainstream culture* in their research on both Mao-era and post-Mao literature and cinema, it is also time to discern the difference, and the continuity, between the two period's mainstream cultures. How indeed has mainstream culture changed from the Maoist socialist period to the post-Mao market era? How did Chinese female directors fare in this transformation, and how did their filmmaking change in relation to the new mainstream culture in the 1980s and 1990s? This book investigates, among other important topics, the trajectory of Chinese women artists' relationship to the changing mainstream culture and cinema from the 1950s and 1960s to the 1980s and beyond.

Scholars who research on Western mainstream culture have argued that although the term *mainstream* is frequently used in relation to mass or popular culture and mass media, it is "rarely defined in Western literary, media or cultural studies."[24] At the same time, however, in Western intellectual and academic discourses, a general consensus about mainstream culture has long existed. The term usually refers to Western cultural commodification, which is tied to the marketplace or cultural industry, fraught with conservative (e.g., patriarchal and racist) values, marked by conformity and convention, enhanced by mass media and new technology, associated with low taste, and perceived as a vulgar or inferior aesthetic. Mainstream is also often understood negatively as a streamlining of culture, "as a subordination of cultural specificity to one hegemonic cultural strand."[25] True, some Western intellectuals and artists have argued against the idea that mainstream culture is monolithic and have envisioned certain subversive or progressive potentials of mainstream or popular culture, but the liberating and subversive potential of new technology, media, and political movements in the practice of mainstream/mass/popular culture has yet to be realized in a meaningful way, structurally or sociopolitically.[26] For those artists who attempt to mainstream their progressive ideas and art practice and to diversify the mainstream culture, the stakes have been high. They constantly risk being appropriated and having their works commodified and reconfigured in the process. Sometimes, the compromises they have to make to reach a mass audience result in reinforcing rather than challenging existing sociocultural stereotypes and commercial power.[27] Many Western critical thinkers, leftist intellectuals, and feminists have thus continued to hold a negative and pessimistic view of mainstream culture. Instead, they endorse avant-gardism, minor/marginalized literature, and independent filmmaking for political resistance, intellectual nonconformism, individual freedom, and artistic autonomy.

This bifurcation of conservative commercial mainstream culture and radical independent avant-gardism, however, does not necessarily denote a true opposition. Socioeconomic factors, especially, constitute a key shared dimension of both cultural practices. The extant critique of most avant-garde or independent cultural movements concerning their open elitism (class and education) and sustainment of social hierarchy (gender and race) has clearly illustrated that conscious self-marginalization in cultural practice does not necessarily help change sociopolitically conservative values largely embodied in the commercial mainstream culture.[28] Both Western mainstream and marginalized cultural practices have corresponded, in different ways, to the dominant mode of socioeconomic and cultural production in the capitalist system.[29]

Some Western scholars and activists, seeking to bring sociocultural diversity to mainstream culture, have argued that the goal of implementing the principle of diversity (class, gender, race, etc.) in mainstream culture is not to showcase pure differences but to achieve a true state of equity: "A mainstream not based on the principle of diversity is essentially inequitable."[30] It is critically important to link mainstream diversity to the goal of socioeconomic equity, but it seems their relationship should be argued the other way around; that is, not until we address issues of socioeconomic equity across different groups can we imagine and sustain a truly diverse mainstream culture. Diversity remains superficial when detached from the principles of equity and equality. Furthermore, the promotion of this seeming diversity only helps to express the very logic of the market, which works to enhance the capitalist mode of cultural production by tirelessly generating novelty and difference.

Chinese socialist cultural practice, which emerged on the premise of socioeconomic equity and political equality and in accordance with the socialist mode of cultural production, thus offers us an alternative historical model for mainstream cultural practice. My first chapter presents a concentrated discussion of Chinese socialist and feminist mainstream culture in the 1950s and 1960s, and chapters 4 and 5 elaborate on some fundamental changes taking place in mainstream discourses and culture in the economic reform era, especially the 1980s. But before moving into those discussions, I want to briefly highlight several major points concerning the changing trajectory of Chinese socialist mainstream culture.

After the People's Republic of China was founded in 1949, the new party-state working under the principle of "people's democratic dictatorship" (人民民主专政) focused on economic modernization and took steps to transform formally private ownership of the means of production into socialist state and local collective ownerships (1949–1956). It also institutionalized socialist class and gender equality and promoted the spirit of serving the people. The role of literature and the arts was thus redefined in this new system. Socialist culture became an integral part of the overall socialist political and socioeconomic endeavor: serving socialist transformations, propagating socialist values, strengthening socialist international solidarity, and developing a proletarian (worker-peasant-soldier) public cultural space, where the mass population was not only the target audience but, more importantly, also a model figure and active participant in the cultural production.[31] This proletarian mass culture (people's literature and art or worker-peasant-soldier literature), as I discuss in chapter 1, was also feminist. The principles of equity and equality manifested in socialist cultural practice were not only advocated by the party-state but also concretely supported by socialist cultural and industrial institutions. Socialist state film studios and the socialist system of film production, distribution, and exhibition, for example, were key institutional forces in the formation of the socialist proletarian and feminist mainstream cinema. Different from commercially or aesthetically (autonomously) driven culture, socialist mass culture was pedagogically oriented and sociopolitically engaged. It was therefore neither independent of nor separated from the overall socialist political endeavors. At the same time, it also aimed to appeal to and entertain the masses by modernizing and revolutionizing both Chinese traditional popular culture along with foreign aesthetics.

As an essential part of the socialist revolution and construction, socialist mainstream culture played the most critical role in combatting traditional conservative ideas and bourgeois ideology and promoting socialist vision and ethics. Socialist socioeconomic transformations were foundational in establishing proletarian mainstream culture, but they did not automatically eliminate old ideas and influences. The ideological battle was thus perceived as one of the central and long-term tasks of socialist mainstream culture.

Unlike mainstream culture in the capitalist West, socialist mainstream culture did not entail a minor, marginalized culture that functioned as a separate or "ghettoized" domain for critical reflection or aesthetic innovation. As I illustrate in chapters 1, 2, and 3, Chinese socialist mainstream culture in the 1950s and 1960s integrated the political and the aesthetic, exhibiting a trajectory filled with critical revisions, individual creative imprints, varied sociocultural imaginations, international influences, and dynamic political and aesthetic experimentalism. Both Wang Ping's *The Story of Liubao Village* (柳堡的故事, 1957), discussed in chapter 2, and Dong Kena's *Small Grass Grows on the Kunlun Mountains* (昆仑山上的一棵草, 1962), analyzed in chapter 3, are good examples. In the first seventeen years of socialist China, Chinese women not only gained institutional empowerment to make films but also pioneered socialist mainstream cultural practice. The term "nonmainstream" (非主流) appeared in post-Mao scholarship to refer to those cultural works that were criticized or even banned during certain periods of Mao's China.[32] Most of these works, however, such as Wang's *The Story of Liubao Village*, both represented the socialist mainstream and received high recognition when they first appeared. Later criticisms reflect the changing dynamic of socialist mainstream culture, which was indicative of the existence of critical diversity and competing ideas in Mao's socialist China. In addition, as socialist culture during its own formation and development openly culled inspiration and resources from traditional (classical and folk) Chinese cultures and modern world literatures and arts, negotiations with and revisions of these other cultures constituted a critical and productive dimension of the mainstream cultural practice throughout the Maoist period. Indeed, scholars have already forcefully argued that both Chinese socialism in history and Chinese socialist culture of the 1950s and 1960s exhibited a distinctive character of revolutionary cosmopolitanism or transnationalism.[33] Socialist mainstream culture was, therefore, by no means monolithic, fixed, or exclusively managed from the top down, whether from a political or an artistic perspective.

However, while highlighting the sociopolitical and experimental nature of socialist mainstream culture, we should bear in mind that socialist mainstream culture encountered its own share of problems in history. Similar to socialist feminism, as a practice integrated with the overall Chinese socialist endeavor during this period, socialist mainstream culture exhibited problems when China's entire socialist practice either stalled, due to domestic and international political-economic constraints, or suffered from a loss of an integrated vision and strategy for China's socialist development. When socialist practice wrestled with internal divisions concerning areas of priority in development (e.g., the political or economic) and struggled to cope with the global effects of the Cold War and neoliberalism, Chinese mainstream culture exhibited corresponding radical tendencies ranging from dogmatic practice to elitist individualism as well as market commercialism. Chapter 6 explores exactly how Chinese female directors like Zhang Nuanxin critically negotiated the different mainstream cultural trends formed during the Cultural Revolution and in the market-oriented era of the mid-1980s to the early 1990s, respectively, questioning the uniform dogma of the former and resisting the rising individualism and growing social inequality of the latter.

Indeed, since the implementation of economic reform in the late 1970s, China's mainstream culture has undergone some most significant structural transformations, moving toward a depoliticized and masculine aesthetic, which formally turned commercial in the late 1980s and early 1990s. According to some scholars, as early as in 1984 when the Chinese state moved to expand its economic reform and retreated from its previous full support for socialist mainstream cinema, Chinese film production became redefined "as a *cultural industry* rather than a *propagating institution.*"[34] In 1987, as "commodity economy" (商品经济) and the market were officially promoted as part of socialist development in the report of the Thirteenth People's Congress, the first wave of Chinese commercial film production emerged, including films by the Fifth Generation filmmakers, who graduated from the Beijing Film Academy in 1982 and became known for their avant-garde experimentalism and arthouse cinema in the early to mid-1980s. In 1992, "socialist market economy" (社会主义市场经济) was formally circulated during the Fourteenth People's Congress. In 1993, after China embarked on its path to a market economy, the Chinese film system was formally restructured. The Ministry of Radio, Film, and Television moved to decentralize its decades-long monopoly of distribution. This decentralization accelerated the privatization of the film industry and "pushed film production further toward the market economy."[35] To boost theater attendance, the Ministry of Radio, Film, and Television in 1994 issued a document announcing the planned annual importation of ten international blockbusters, mostly big-budget, high-tech Hollywood fare.[36] Chinese mainstream cinema consequently transformed itself along with China's socioeconomic structural changes and became comparable to the mainstream film industry in the capitalist West, although it maintained certain distinctions. Chapters 4 and 5 critically trace and discuss the radical changes taking place in mainstream feminist and cultural discourses in the 1980s. Chapter 7 further explores and illustrates how Chinese women's cinema, represented by Huang Shuqin's *Woman Demon Human* (人鬼情, 1987), responded to the new mainstream culture's demands toward the end of the 1980s, resolutely departing from the women's mainstream cinema practiced in both Mao's times and the early economic reform era. Female directors themselves, however, whether resisting or supporting the new universal market logic of mainstream culture, became significantly marginalized or "disabled" in the mid- to late 1990s, a period when Chinese male directors began to dominate commercial-mainstream, "main melody" (主旋律, officially sponsored), and art-house cinemas. Although the term *socialist mainstream culture* has emerged in contemporary China to defend and renew certain Chinese socialist values at both national and international levels, its significance and effect have yet to be examined as China's participation in the global market and commercial culture increases.

Outline of the Book

Over seven chapters I remap Chinese feminist and mainstream cultural practices in relation to a series of major sociopolitical and economic transformations occurring in both local and global contexts. Particularly, I trace the history of Chinese women's cinema, offering an in-depth study of four Chinese female directors. Chapter 1, "Socialist Feminism and Socialist Culture Reconsidered," tackles the geopolitical ideology and elitist cultural centralism behind three research paradigms entrenched in the study of socialist mainstream culture and women's cinema: the patriarchal character of the Chinese socialist revolution, the political and propagandistic nature of socialist cultural production, and the conception of women's cinema as a marginalized, subversive practice. By resituating socialist feminist and cultural practice in its historical and international contexts, this chapter provides a revisionist history of Chinese socialist feminism, reevaluates the nature and significance of socialist proletarian public space, and retheorizes socialist film practice as a mainstream experimental cinema.

In particular, the chapter offers a critical, in-depth analysis of Judith Stacey's *Patriarchy and Socialist Revolution in China* (1983), one of the most influential English-language books on Chinese women's liberation and socialist revolution. I question the book's Cold War and radical feminist stance, its definition of feminism as primarily individualistic, and its conclusion that Chinese socialist revolution is inherently patriarchal. Through tracing the history of socialist feminism in relation to modern China's anti-imperialist, antifeudalistic, and anticapitalist endeavors, this chapter reconceptualizes socialist feminism as a proletarian, mass-oriented, integrated, and multifaceted practice. I particularly highlight the critical interdependence between socialist revolution and Chinese women's liberation—a nonnegligible factor that contributed greatly to both the Communist victory in 1949 and to subsequent socialist constructions, including the formation of a feminist mainstream culture.

Chinese cinema was dominated by men from its inception in 1905 until the early 1950s, when socialist state film studios actively recruited and helped train women for film directing. My second chapter, "Articulating Embedded Feminist Agency in Socialist Mainstream Cinema," turns to mainland China's first female director, Wang Ping. I examine her life story as a modern woman, left-wing artist, and socialist feminist filmmaker, analyze one of her most representative socialist films, *The Story of Liubao Village*, and reevaluate her multidimensional contributions to socialist mainstream cinema.

The socialist transformation of property ownership, the film industry, and gender, together with socialism's new concept of authorship, worked in the early and mid-1950s to empower Chinese female cultural workers, enabling the emergence of the first generation of female filmmakers in mainland China. An individual woman's historical agency and cinematic authorship, as Wang's case reveals, originates from neither individual autonomy nor an independent experience of gender. Rather, it is contingent on and embedded within the dynamic interplay of political, institutional, cultural, and individual factors. Wang's extensive collaboration with the original story writer and scriptwriter in adapting "The Story of Liubao Village" into film not only reflected the productive socialist collective authorship but also manifested the experimental nature of socialist filmmaking, which involved intense negotiations among different participants and often resulted in distinctive individual imprints in the final product. This chapter particularly studies

Wang Ping's interactive cinematic authorship and her individual initiative in making *The Story of Liubao Village*, a successful socialist mainstream film that exhibited distinctive Chinese national and folk styles, reached a mass audience, and articulated both left-wing intellectuals' sentiments of the 1940s and socialist feminist ideals of the 1950s. This chapter challenges the persistent feminist assumption that feminist cinema should occupy only a counter-, minor, marginalized, or independent position regardless of its specific geopolitical and sociopolitical contexts and the nature of its contemporary mainstream culture.

In the late 1980s and early 1990s, the introduction of radical and cultural feminism, cine-feminism, and Western discourses influenced by Cold War ideology indirectly joined China's embrace of the market economy in reinforcing a universal model for gender, culture, and modernity. Feminist film scholarship singled out Mao-era female directors for making mainstream, propagandist, and masculine films that suppressed female difference and critical consciousness. Chapter 3, "Socialist Experimentalism, Critical Revision, and Gender Difference," addresses these issues by focusing on another important socialist female director, Dong Kena. In studying her popular 1962 film, *Small Grass Grows on the Kunlun Mountains*, I closely analyze her cinematic practice in relation to such theoretical and historical concepts as political conformity, cultural diversity, critical reflection, and gender difference.

This chapter presents close analyses of the film's aesthetic innovation, gendered voice, and critical revision in adaptation. The purpose of foregrounding these aspects of Dong's film is not, however, to prove the *presence* of what feminist scholars from the 1980s forward have claimed absent from Chinese socialist women's cinema. Rather, it is to interrogate the political and artistic binary paradigm underpinning most of the Cold War–influenced research on socialist culture, and challenge the Western middle-class-centric feminist framework often used to measure women's cultural practices across geopolitical locations. Furthermore, this detailed study of the film also aims to illustrate that not only do conformity and critique coexist in integrated socialist cultural practice, but the former also constitutes the very foundation of the latter. Dong's film clearly adheres to the emancipatory vision and pedagogical function of socialist mainstream culture. This commitment, however, enables rather than inhibits the film's critical and creative interventions in the adaptation process. It is with socialist principles and ethics that the film critiques the official (mis)representation of the local situation and targets the implicit prejudice against women among male model workers.

Like Wang Ping's films, Dong's *Small Grass* significantly showcases the diversity and individual creativity in the practice of socialist mainstream culture. Most significantly, the film transforms the story from a fixed, progressive narrative to an overdetermined structure where different temporalities, multiple discourses, and various imaginations are manifested and sustained. In addition, Dong revises the two heroines' relationship in the film, a choice that has enriched the dynamic socialist feminist culture by foregrounding intersubjectivity, female bonding, and individual differences in the context of socialist construction.

Chapter 4, "Feminist Practice after Mao," turns to the economic New Era (新时期, the late 1970s and 1980s) to study the rise and development of post-Mao independent feminism. Resituating post-Mao Chinese feminism in its political-economic, historical, and global contexts, this chapter critically explores three primary aspects of the movement: its personal, institutional, and transnational origins; its initial promises for revising Marxist theory and improving socialist feminism; and its subsequent development in the mid- to late 1980s into a universal and cultural discourse implicated in contemporary capitalist globalization as China marched toward a market economy. These changes in Chinese feminist practice reflected broader transformations: China's expansion and deepening of its economic reform, the rise of global neoliberalism, and the cultural turn of global intellectual movements.

Specifically, this chapter moves from a discussion of the gendered personal, a concept articulated in women's autobiographical literature and culture of the late 1970s and early 1980s, to an examination of post-Mao independent feminism and its central theoretical arguments made by its most influential figure, Li Xiaojiang, around the mid- and late 1980s. It closely examines post-Mao feminism's entanglements with the overall official promotion of economic reform, the newly mainstreamed intellectual discourse on science, Enlightenment modernity, and cultural independence, and Western post-second-wave feminism, particularly radical feminism. In the context of 1980s China, I argue, post-Mao feminism joined other historical forces, contributing to the formation of a separatist-, cultural-, and difference-oriented feminist practice that represented a significant departure from integrated socialist feminism.

As China under Deng Xiaoping (邓小平) began to move away from previous sociopolitical policy and implemented economic reforms toward the end of the 1970s, the cinema of the New Era also critically reacted to the Cultural Revolution, especially its class-struggle ideology and politicized cultural practice. My fifth chapter, "Film Theory, Avant-Gardism, and the Rise of Masculine Aesthetics," discusses the transformation of Chinese mainstream culture, particularly the rise of film theory and masculine avant-gardism in the

1980s. This transformation, combined with the gradual privatization of the film industry, repudiated earlier socialist traditions and endorsed a liberal, humanistic, and aesthetic direction for cultural development. In the hands of the emerging Fifth Generation filmmakers, New Era experimental cinema reached a pinnacle of abstract cultural reflection, stylistic renovation, and masculine reimagination of a teleological future.

This chapter also critically reassesses the global significance of post-Mao Chinese experimental cinema by comparing it with its initial inspiration, the French New Wave, from the perspectives of sociopolitical history and gender. Despite different historical and political situations between France in the 1950s and China in the 1980s, similar concerns emerged in the two countries and led to the rise of cultural elitism, artistic autonomy, a universal aesthetic, and the repudiation of previous left-wing or socialist cultural practices. Drawing on recent feminist scholarship on French New Wave and Chinese experimental cinema, this comparative section also illustrates how female directors became marginalized in both movements and how the claim to the universal value of the aesthetic and artistic genius is not only individualistic and elitist but also male-centered. The chapter concludes with a close examination of avant-garde cinema's rapid commercial turn in the late 1980s, revealing an internal logic that was shared by experimental and commercial cinemas as the market finally gained the upper hand in contemporary China at the turn of the 1990s.

Chapter 6, "Alternative Experimental Cinema," returns to Chinese women's mainstream cinema by focusing on Zhang Nuanxin and her experimental films in the 1980s. Women's cinema flourished in the early post-Mao era, exhibiting intriguing characteristics especially in relation to the changing mainstream film trajectory and the rise of the independent feminist movement. Zhang was a pioneer in both the theory and practice of post-Mao new experimental cinema, but was dismissed later as nonessential when the New Cinema turned abstract, depoliticized, and masculine toward the end of the 1980s. This chapter investigates that dismissal and argues that she was ousted mostly due to her sociopolitically engaged, feminist experimentalism.

This chapter offers a detailed study of Zhang's most representative film, *Sacrificed Youth* (青春祭, 1985). My analysis highlights both Zhang's critique of Cultural Revolution's ideological uniformity and her resistance to the new mainstream discourse that advocated sociopolitically detached individualism, naturalized sexual difference, and rising market value in the mid-1980s. This chapter also introduces post-Mao feminist film criticism formed at the turn of the 1990s, particularly reviewing the most influential publications that, despite their initial interest in 1980s women's experimental cinema, charge Zhang and other female directors with an incomplete break from the socialist mainstream cinema of the Mao era. I end the chapter with a discussion of the trajectory of Zhang's films, particularly her last film, *South China, 1994* (南中国, 1994), a political melodrama centering on the socioeconomic and political struggles of women and migrant workers against transnational capitalists in one of southern China's special economic zones. Zhang's stylistic change from subjective experimentalism to political melodrama over the course of her career exhibits her continued engagement with the changing sociohistorical reality and her consistent refusal either to grant an autonomous status to cinematic style or to separate cinematic form from content.

Only one year after *female consciousness* appeared as a hotly debated topic in a symposium organized by the editorial staff at *Contemporary Cinema* and the Contemporary Film Studies Office in 1986, the concept became crystallized in Huang Shuqin's *Woman Demon Human* (人鬼情, 1987), manifesting the beginning of another important transition in Chinese women's cinema. Huang's film has received critical acclaim, considered by many as the only feminist film in Chinese film history. The last chapter of my book, "The Black Velvet Aesthetic," offers a revisionist study of Huang's film and a close analysis of the general trend of Chinese cinema of the late 1980s, unveiling the underlying logic that ironically links women's cinema and post-Mao feminism to male-centered cultural movements.

A major part of this chapter explores the film's "black velvet aesthetic" (黑丝绒效果), a depoliticized revision of the socialist *xieyi* (写意) aesthetic. This artistic device functions to efface the significance of the sociopolitical transformations in socialist history as the film pursues a universal cultural feminism, transhistorical cultural mentality, an essential female inner world, naturalized sexual difference, and a neotraditional female self-salvation. The chapter also analyzes the relationship between the *xieyi* aesthetic embodied by an ideal patriarchal kinsman in the film and the mainstream revival of Chinese traditional culture in the late 1980s, illustrating how Huang's film redefines women's role primarily through men and the traditional ritual of arranged marriage.

The chapter ends with an in-depth exploration of female consciousness, the central concept in the post-Mao feminist practice of the late 1980s. If sexual difference laid a biological and psychological foundation for the concept's universal legitimacy and appeal, three other forces—namely, universal cultural feminism, the depoliticized liberal discourse of the 1980s, and the restored and modernized Confucian tradition—worked together in China in the late 1980s to signify the layered meanings of female consciousness. Equally important, the global and domestic markets provided the very political and economic conditions that made the rise and articulation of this female consciousness possible.

1 Socialist Feminism and Socialist Culture Reconsidered

Institutionalized Practice, Proletarian Public Space, and Experimental Mainstream Cinema

In the Anglophone academy, the study of socialist women's cinema requires confronting three entrenched research paradigms that posit, first, the political and propagandistic nature of socialist cultural production; second, the patriarchal character of socialist revolution; and, third, women's cinema as a marginalized practice, disruptive or subversive of mainstream patriarchal culture. These paradigms have prolonged Cold War ideology both directly and indirectly, prohibiting a productive assessment of the legacy of socialist culture and the women's movement, especially in today's research on transnational feminist theory and cultural practice. They have also derailed any serious examination of real historical limitations, paradoxes, and problems that existed in the history of the Chinese socialist revolution. Although more nuanced scholarship has emerged from Chinese socialist film studies and gender studies since the end of the 1980s,[1] it has not succeeded in displacing these problematic frames. We urgently need a concentrated critical analysis of the historical, political, and theoretical underpinnings of the rooted paradigms to reconfigure related research areas, making the study of socialist women's cinema meaningful.

I start this chapter with just such a critical reassessment of extant research paradigms, examining especially the roles of Cold War ideology and Western radical feminism in creating and sustaining these frameworks in the study of Chinese socialist women's liberation, socialist culture, and women's cinema. I then join the current scholarly effort to explore the historical dynamics of the socialist women's movement and mainstream socialist feminist culture. Specifically, I explore socialist feminist socioeconomic institutionalization in the Chinese socialist revolution, as well as the formation of socialist proletarian and feminist public space and cultural practice in early socialist China. These socioeconomic and cultural changes directly contributed to the emergence and success of the first generation of female film directors in the 1950s and 1960s. Lastly, I examine the socialist transformation of the film industry, illustrating the diversity of socialist aesthetic values and retheorizing socialist film practice as a mainstream experimental cinema.

Research Frameworks on Socialism and Chinese Women: Cold War Ideology and Western Radical Feminism

The Cold War, which entrenched a seemingly unbridgeable divide between liberal and socialist ideologies, has left deep and lasting impressions in transnational studies. Despite some recent scholarly attempts to revise the extant reductive perspective on socialist culture, Western academics generally show little interest in socialist literature and cinema.[2] Their relative silence indirectly reinforces the stereotype that socialist art is mere propaganda.[3] Certainly, one of Chinese socialist cinema's major functions was to propagate socialist ideas and ideals, but the claim that "political commitment (especially socialist political commitment) is inimical to . . . genuine art" is a complete fallacy.[4] The assertion betrays its own Cold War positionality, associating aesthetics exclusively with capitalist society's individualistic, bourgeois values. The widely promulgated notion that "socialist political commitment is incompatible with the production of genuine art" has led to a sweeping dismissal of Chinese socialist films, including those by women.[5] While studies of Chinese women directors do exist,[6] little serious research has been conducted to date on the socialist female directors of the Mao era.[7]

Within Chinese gender and feminist studies, a collection of social science–oriented scholarship, published in the United States in the 1980s, established today's mainstream perceptions of Chinese socialism and women. Such works include Judith Stacey's *Patriarchy and Socialist Revolution in China* (1983), Phyllis Andors's *The Unfinished Liberation of Chinese Women, 1949–1980* (1983), Kay Ann Johnson's *Women, the Family and Peasant Revolution in China* (1983), and Margery Wolf's *Revolution Postponed: Women in Contemporary China* (1985).[8] All these books—despite their differences in approach and connotation—conclude that the Chinese socialist revolution was patriarchal, the Chinese Communist Party (CCP) simply appropriated women's labor for economic development, production, and war efforts, and the CCP departed from the May Fourth Cultural Movement's (1915–1925) independent and individual feminism and failed to liberate Chinese women. For some of the authors, the liberation of women in socialist China remained either incomplete or perennially postponed as class struggle, national salvation, and other grand projects always took priority;[9] for others, the CCP was never serious about women's liberation, and socialist revolution was simply a series of negotiations among patriarchal forces.[10]

In a revisionist study of China's Marriage Law of 1950, Neil J. Diamant explores why these earlier works became "conventional wisdom" on women and socialist China in Western academia. He suggests four possible causes: "These books addressed the concerns of feminist theory, were guaranteed a high profile by publication with prestigious presses, were all published in paperback, and, most importantly, were frequently assigned for classes whose subject matter covered 'Chinese women,' 'women and development' or 'gender in China'—not a negligible market in the United States."[11] Diamant continues: "Today, one is hard-pressed to find a reference to the 1950 Marriage Law that does not cite one or several of these works."[12] These works have also greatly influenced Chinese cultural studies because of their feminist and theoretical appeals. For example, in the first two English-language essays on contemporary Chinese women's cinema, both authors, Chris Berry and E. Ann Kaplan, cite Judith Stacey when discussing the CCP and women's liberation in socialist China.[13] As another example, in the limited English-language studies on Mao's socialist women's cinema, mainstream socialist culture is automatically understood as a patriarchal erasure of gender differences. Women directors who worked for mainstream socialist cinema are routinely perceived as nonfeminist and lacking in independence, and their films are reduced to a means to help promote socialist state consolidation and nation building.[14]

Since the 1990s, China studies scholars have raised important concerns in response to such dismissive assumptions. Some question the absence of Chinese women's participation, agency, and voice in the study of revolutionary history.[15] Others address the erroneous representation of the Chinese socialist revolution or the CCP as a fixed entity that produced uniform policies and had monolithic control regardless of international, regional, and historical distinctions.[16] While these newer works help generate a more dynamic perspective on gender and the Chinese socialist revolution, the aforementioned studies from the 1980s "[have] remained amazingly resilient."[17] More critically, the conclusions and theoretical framework regarding gender and socialism in those influential works remain largely unchallenged. The persistence of this "conventional wisdom" demands a serious and concentrated analysis of its historical, ideological, and theoretical underpinnings that have sustained and reproduced its influence. In the remainder of this section, I focus on Stacey's *Patriarchy and Socialist Revolution in China* (1983), a popular and influential book in English-language academia, to illustrate the broader political and theoretical bases of the conventional wisdom.

In a study of American views and intellectual discourses on China, Harry Harding traces the trajectory from the 1970s to the 1980s and offered illuminating analyses: "If Americans concluded in the 1970s that Communism had succeeded in China, the most common judgment in the early 1980s [was] that Communism has failed—and failed rather badly."[18] He links the denigration of China in the 1980s to neoconservative criticism of totalitarianism and the renewal of American intellectuals' faith in such "bourgeois" values as individual liberty, privacy, and justice. During the Second Cold War (1979–1985) especially, the United States saw a renewed tendency to assert the universality of Western values and to "apply these values to an appraisal of China."[19] Harding's insightful arguments—that Americans' extreme views on China, whether in the form of idealization or denigration, reflected American politics and that their disparagement of China in the 1980s was at heart a Cold War mentality endorsed by neoconservatives—provide necessary context for the following examination of Stacey's work.

Stacey's own publications on China typify the trajectory Harding has outlined, shifting from an extremely optimistic evaluation of socialist China in her "When Patriarchy Kowtows" (1975) to a totally negative reassessment in her *Patriarchy and Socialist Revolution in China.*[20] Indeed, Stacey's book from 1983 exemplifies the radical change and disillusionment in Western studies of women and the Chinese socialist revolution. After reviving the long-dormant question "Does socialism liberate women?" on the first page of her book, Stacey moves quickly to state that the goal of her current research is to address instead the question "Why has socialism *not* liberated women in China?" (5, 10; my emphasis). This second question not only offers a resolute answer to the first without going through the process of scholarly argumentation but also positions the book to prove a predetermined thesis. As a Western sociologist in family studies without training in either Chinese language or Chinese studies, Stacey uses the discovery of Western sociologists' research on the European peasant family to frame her study of peasant revolution in modern China, particularly in the communist base areas and, later, socialist China (5–8). The European peasant family, according to the sociological study, did not stay passive in the process of Western capitalist industrialization; on the contrary, it actively and strategically worked with capitalist forces to preserve traditional patriarchal values. Stacey argues that Chinese peasants resorted to a similar strategy in their cooperation with the Chinese socialist revolution. Furthermore, she points out that the CCP also strategically worked with rural peasants, helping preserve and democratize rural patriarchy, in order to bring communists to power. The Chinese socialist revolution, according to Stacey, merely replaced Confucian patriarchy with a "new democratic patriarchy" before 1949, and then with "patriarchal socialism" or "public patriarchy" once the CCP established the People's Republic of China (253). Stacey's unidimensional conclusion that "the socialist revolution in China was a patriarchal revolution" (253) proved compelling in the U.S. context of the 1980s and was praised by many at the time for offering a "fresh" and radically new perspective on Chinese socialism.[21]

When read today, *Patriarchy and Socialist Revolution in China* seems to lack some basic, scholarly standards required for research, especially in the social sciences.[22] The point I intend to highlight here, however, is not about the shortcomings of a particular book but the pervasive Cold War ideology and neoconservative values in the production and reception of the aforementioned scholarship of the 1980s as a whole. The book's direct application of Western scholarship on the European peasant family to a drastically different geopolitical context did not provoke any serious questions. Although some China specialists found the book's approach too mechanistic and formulaic, "obscuring what really happened" and thus making them yearn for some concrete sense of Chinese social reality and diverse experiences, these specialists accepted Stacey's conclusion nonetheless.[23] Cold War ideology not only made an assessment of Chinese women and socialism by a scholar not specializing in China an influential mainstream discourse but also compelled China specialists to subdue their criticism or modify their own fieldwork materials in order to reach similar Cold War conclusions.[24] That is to say, Cold War ideology joined by a renewed tendency to universalize Western values actively constructed the direction and conclusion of major English-language scholarship of the 1980s on socialism and Chinese women's liberation.

An equally important factor contributing to the formation of the conventional wisdom on women and socialist China in the 1980s was Western radical feminism. In the 1960s and 1970s, American left-wing feminists confronted male misogyny within the left-wing camp and grew to doubt the utility of Marxist theory on women's liberation. For some, Marxist theory centered on class revolution and could not address women's issues. Their experiences with male counterparts furthered their belief that Marxist theory was gender blind and that the left-wing movement was male-centered. This led to the formation of radical feminism, which took patriarchy as a self-continued, transhistorical, and universal form of domination, arguing that women's oppression (sexual difference) rather than class (private property) was the origin of human inequality.[25] Despite its initial stance against both right-wing and left-wing male domination, and despite its critique of mechanical Marxist theory's inadequate theorization of gender, radical feminism turned conservative when it began to separate women's liberation from class and other sociopolitical structural changes, abandoning the overall left-wing goal to eliminate class oppression and the capitalist system. Indeed, as radical feminism essentialized patriarchy and women's oppression, it delinked gender from economic and sociopolitical forces in history, advancing instead an autonomous sex-gender system.[26] To eliminate women's subordination in history, radical feminists turned to the domain of culture, advocating raising cultural consciousness, leaving the capitalist socioeconomic structure intact. According to Ellen Willis, who experienced this major feminist transformation in the United States in the 1970s, radical feminists began to promote cultural feminism after 1975 and joined forces with individual liberal feminism, developing into a dominant force in Western feminist practice.[27]

Many left-wing feminists participated in this transformation to radical feminism. Stacey was no exception. In her book's introduction, she outlines the rise of an autonomous realm of gender relationships and also lays out feminist debate about it.[28] Although she claims that she will adhere to a feminist historical-materialist analysis in her study of patriarchy and socialism in China, she also makes clear in her introduction and conclusion that she does not discard the concept of an autonomous sex-gender system.[29] Whereas dualism became a problem for left-wing turned radical and socialist feminists in the late 1970s and 1980s,[30] Stacey's approach typifies the radical feminist turn by redefining feminism worldwide as individualistic, independent of or antagonistic to other political and economic movements.[31]

In Stacey's book, radical feminism works intimately with Cold War ideology to discredit the Chinese socialist revolution and its women's movement. Whereas Cold War ideology denied that socialism could in any way liberate women, and neoconservative discourse promoted the universality of Western values, radical and liberal feminism reinforced these views by asserting that urban capitalist individualism be the criterion for measuring all feminisms across different geopolitical locations. According to Stacey, the Chinese socialist revolution was fundamentally a response to rural and traditional family crises in the early twentieth century, and as such the revolution only enacted a radical redistribution of patriarchy to peasant men, forging a "new democratic patriarchy" (86, 116). This reconceptualization of socialist revolution as solely a rural family phenomenon aiming to perpetuate patriarchal values effectively sets the Chinese revolution against all feminist movements redefined according to the Western capitalist model. It also significantly erases the complexity of modern revolutions in non-Western contexts. The Chinese socialist revolution, like the earlier bourgeois republican revolution, was an anti-imperialist national independence movement. Given China's devastated and largely agrarian economy, the Chinese socialist revolution also had to shoulder the responsibility of transforming and modernizing Chinese economic structure, a task usually designated to or accomplished by a bourgeois revolution. But different from other third-world bourgeois nationalism and capitalist development, the Chinese socialist revolution was also a proletarian, anticapitalist, and antitraditionalist revolution. Stacey's reconfiguration of the Chinese socialist revolution thus functions to deny its complexity, especially its socialist vision and characteristics, dismissing the significance of the radical structural transformation brought about in (geo)political, economic, and social realms.

More critically, by focusing exclusively on the rural family, Stacey not only erases the connection between Chinese socialist women's liberation and anti-imperialism, national independence, and class revolution in Chinese history but also produces two disturbing equations that represent socialism and capitalism, respectively: family and patriarchy versus individualism and feminism. "When peasants calculated their interests, as they did, in familial rather than individualistic terms, they applied a patriarchal calculus which assured different costs, opportunities, and benefits to the sexes and generations" (255). These equations and their overt simplifications and erroneous assumptions effectively cancel out the manifold dimensions of socialist revolution, reinforcing the Cold War and radical feminist conclusion that Stacey repeats throughout her book: namely, that capitalism is less patriarchal and thus a better system and that individualism is the foundation for feminism (262).

A critical examination of continued traditional influences in socialist revolution and society is important, but the idea that Chinese socialist women's liberation could and should be discussed according to Western capitalist individualism—leaving intact (semi)colonized conditions, capitalist public patriarchy, and domestic and transnational class exploitation—exposes

Western radical and liberal feminist complicity with capitalist imperialism in transregional and transnational studies.

Throughout her book, Stacey implicitly and consistently places women's interests in opposition to major political, social, and economic movements launched by the CCP. For example, the CCP began land reform in communist base areas in the 1940s, granting all peasants, especially female peasants, property rights to land. Although it is true that the CCP might not have been able to implement the new land law with the rigor and thoroughness it wished given the extremely limited resources available during the war period and given the particular situations in the various liberated areas, including entrenched traditional customs, the land reform was nonetheless an extraordinary and unprecedented movement that raised the economic and political status of rural Chinese women tremendously. However, Stacey argues, the land reform, by not changing the Chinese rural family economic structure, a task that the CCP was in no position or capacity to accomplish during wartime, functioned primarily to "restore patriarchy to the peasantry" and "to establish the economic basis for the new democratic patriarchy" (264).

Such a forced and ahistorical argument illustrates, on the one hand, the author's ignorance of the historical and sociopolitical conditions of the Chinese socialist revolution and Chinese rural women's situation and, on the other hand, her lack of a historical-materialist approach to rural women's liberation. First, rural Chinese working-class women's oppression, from the 1920s to the 1940s, cannot be understood from the singular framework of gender within the rural family. On top of economic imperialism and national instability, "village women of the laboring classes . . . suffered the exploration and oppression of the landlord class just like other peasants, and ha[d] the same demands, the same fierceness."[32] Land reform was by no means a redistribution of patriarchy to male peasants, as Stacey claims; rather, it transformed the material base for the class and gender hierarchy that had lasted in China for thousands of years. As some scholars have forcefully argued, the goals of China's land reform, which became fully accomplished in the early 1950s after the CCP took power in mainland China, were to eliminate the longest-lived ruling class in world history, to bring social equity to the Chinese countryside, and to create an essential base for modern industrial development.[33] Furthermore, the land reform movement motivated oppressed rural women to speak up about their bitter experiences.[34] This "speaking bitterness" (诉苦), a form of telling one's life story in public under communist organization, "turned into a self-conscious political act with concrete, material ramifications."[35] Second, and more importantly, the new legal code established by the CCP that granted women equal rights to land was an important step in building material conditions and institutional support for women's liberation, both theoretically and practically.[36] As other scholars have pointed out, "aside from the women's program against feudal oppression and the struggle for its implementation, the program of most importance to women was land reform."[37] Before the land reform, Chinese women had always been referred to by others as "the wife of her husband" or "the mother of her son." "Now for the first time in their lives they said they heard their names spoken in public. They had acquired a name alongside a share of the land."[38] This institutionalization of women's economic rights was especially critical during periods of war when other changes, such as nationalizing the means of production and collectivizing the rural family economy, were simply out of the question. The failure to recognize the importance of land reform to Chinese rural women shows a nonmaterialist and Western-centered feminist position that refuses to take geopolitical, economic, and social differences among women into consideration. Even Stacey conceded at one point that "women's new de jure rights to land, although easily circumvented, coupled with women's public participation in the process of land redistribution, materially enhanced their status within the newly democratized patriarchal order."[39] The contradiction manifested in Stacey's argument exposes once again the predetermined Cold War and radical feminist nature of major English scholarship of the 1980s on gender and Chinese socialism.

Stacey's redefinition of socialist revolution as an exclusive response to the Chinese rural family's crisis and her exclusive emphasis on the independent or autonomous interests of women seriously distort the historical condition and the complex process of the Chinese socialist revolution, setting up both revolution and socialist feminism to fail from the very beginning. As Stacey herself has argued, agrarian and poor societies "provide a weak basis for the development of an autonomous feminist movement that is strong enough to play an independent role in the revolutionary process."[40] Thus, without even the need to examine what was brought about by socialist revolution in modern China, Stacey reaches the following Cold War and radical feminist conclusion: "Feminism has found more hospitable environments in capitalist than in socialist societies."[41]

The political and research paradigms of the 1980s remain influential today. Discussions of Chinese women and socialism continue to validate individualistic or independent practices, implicitly forging an antagonistic relationship between Chinese women and the CCP, as well as socialist revolution as a whole.[42] This persistent conventional wisdom has effectively contributed to a near total ignorance of socialist China's women film directors, whose works are stamped as non-independent, conformist, and propagandistic, lacking individualistic or feminist significance.[43]

Breaking from these Cold War and liberal feminist research paradigms requires concerted, sustained effort among scholars in Chinese studies, as well as fundamental changes in international politics and the global political culture. The worldwide spread of neoliberal capitalism and governmentality challenges research in feminist and area studies from a different direction. Feminist scholars today are called on to critically reexamine historical legacies and to explore strategies that could address transnational issues arising from both history and the present. In the following section, I turn to the institutional nature of all feminist practices, stressing the inevitable linkage of feminism with the corresponding political-economic system. More specifically, I examine the Western conception of women's cinema as a counter-, minor, or marginalized practice, revealing its implicit and complex reliance on certain institutionalized discourses in a capitalist system. I then offer an alternative account of Chinese socialist feminism as an integrated and institutionalized practice of socialist revolution, tracing the formation of a proletarian and feminist public space that fostered a diverse range of mainstream feminist cultural practices in early socialist China.

Chinese Socialist Feminism: Institutionalized Women's Movement, Mainstream Ideology, and Multidimensional Agency

Institutional Underpinnings of Feminist Practice

The concept of women's cinema emerged in Western cine-feminist film theory in the late 1960s. By the early 1970s, this idea had developed into a political countercinema that challenged mainstream filmmaking by completely resisting its patriarchal language. Claire Johnston, in her essay "Women's Cinema as Counter-Cinema" (1973), envisions a genuinely revolutionary countercinema for women's future struggles. Johnston maintains that women's counterdiscourse can grow from within the ideological contradictions of mainstream Hollywood cinema, as disruptions,[44] but she does not describe how such disruptive cinema could develop into women's countercinema. Laura Mulvey upholds this conception of women's cinema as countercinema but denies the possibility of feminist work emerging from mainstream film. In "Film, Feminism and the Avant-Garde," Mulvey envisages women's countercinema in the tradition of political modernism,[45] and she perceives avant-garde cinema—with its storehouse of feminist aesthetic strategies of defamiliarization, rupture, and reflexivity—as a model for feminist film.[46]

Women's cinema was contested in the 1980s when black and third-world feminism challenged certain tenets of Western feminism, but the countercinema concept remained unquestioned. In her book from 2002, Alison Butler attends to the development of diverse forms and contents in contemporary global women's cinema,[47] proposing to redefine women's cinema as "minor" cinema, a term adapted from Gilles Deleuze and Felix Guattari's concept of minor literature—the literature of a marginalized group written in the major language. Butler argues that key features of minor literature—displacement, dispossession, and deterritorialization—also characterize women's cinema. Like minor literature, women's cinema involves a community's projection rather than its expression, thereby avoiding an essentialist understanding of women.

Butler's reformulation seeks to encompass the diversity of women's film practice around the world, but by positing Anglophone feminist film theory and practice of the 1970s as the source of minor cinema, she conceptualizes contemporary global feminist film production as a natural outgrowth of earlier Western women's cinema.[48] Thus, her concept of minor cinema risks legitimizing Western cine-feminist practice as the origin of all women's cinema practice worldwide. Furthermore, although minor cinema modifies the radical claim about countercinema, which completely resists mainstream language, Butler's notion still defines women's cinema as a marginalized practice, authored by a marginal or deterritorialized group, and, as such, automatically subversive.[49]

The persistent and influential conception of women's cinema as countercinema (or minor cinema), whether emerging from capitalist mainstream or marginalized film practice, suggests an independent or self-generating origin of feminist political practice. This implication obscures the relationship between feminist cultural practices and the political and economic systems within which those practices emerge. Owing to its powerful geopolitical position, Anglophone cine-feminist theory has traveled widely, shaping studies of women's cinema in other political and economic systems. Its influence is palpable in contemporary China, especially since the early 1990s, following a decade of China's economic reform and open-door policy. Chinese scholars, in their critical reassessment of the Cultural Revolution, have turned to the West for a universal model for modernity. Within film studies, analyses of Chinese women's cinema, especially from the Mao era, have largely centered on women directors' failure to produce counter-, minor, or marginalized cinema.

"Almost without exception, contemporary women directors are the makers of mainstream films. They do not experiment with radical, therefore marginal, cinema, nor did they attempt to create works that can be categorized as 'anti-cinema' [countercinema]."[50] Whereas Western feminist film theory targeted the capitalist mainstream commercial film industry, the commercial film industry in the Chinese context did not begin to reemerge until the turn of the 1990s. By situating Chinese socialist film production within the terms of debate set by Western critics in the capitalist system, post-Mao feminist film studies has mistakenly equated socialist mainstream culture,[51] which promoted women's and class liberations, with capitalist market-manufactured mainstream culture, arriving at the problematic conclusion that no feminist films were produced during the socialist period, a conclusion that distorts the history of feminist cinema in China. We therefore need a critical reexamination of the relationship between feminism, socialist mainstream culture, and the economic system to reveal the different institutionalizations and significations of feminism and mainstream culture in various geopolitical locations and political-economic environments.

Before exploring mainstream culture and women's cinema in the context of socialist China, I want to discuss the institutional nature of all feminist practices and then provide a history of the institutionalization of socialist feminism within the Chinese socialist revolution. Two steps of analysis are required to illustrate the institutional foundation of all feminisms. First, we need to study the relationship between those feminist practices that occupy a relatively marginalized position and their respective political and economic systems. A marginalized position does not automatically correlate to a politically subversive or oppositional stance, as many of them are contained and even supported by the broader system. More importantly, marginalized practices often collaborate with central political and economic forces on other social issues or in different political realms. For example, although experimental or avant-garde cinema remains marginalized in the Western capitalist system, it is endorsed by the capitalist discourse of private property and the middle-class ideology of individualism. Its elitist and often male-centered values are also institutionalized in the dominant system. Interestingly enough, the writers that Deleuze and Guattari deem authors of minor literature—including Franz Kafka, James Joyce, Samuel Beckett, and Jean-Luc Godard—are all Western male canonical figures of experimental literature. Although the terms used to define minor literature or cinema no longer appear antithetical to the mainstream language, as Mulvey once claimed, this minor literature refers to the same elitist and male-centered avant-garde practice. Consequently, to envision women's experimental cinema—whether perceived as countercinema (countering the mainstream commercial language) or minor cinema (using and appropriating the major language)—as subversive of Hollywood, or as a challenge to capitalist patriarchy overall, is untenable. Moreover, it masks a much more complicated relationship among Western feminist cultural practice, capitalist institutions, and mainstream discourses. This conflation of the marginal and subversive reveals cine-feminist blindness to its own dependence on the broader political-economic system and to its complicity with the market ideology and institutions in (re)producing other forms of disparities, such as class dominance, racial discrimination, and regional colonialism. In foregrounding the marginalized, independent role of women's cinema in resisting and changing misogyny and patriarchy, feminist theories of countercinema and minor cinema have bypassed questions concerning the institutional forces and powers that both enable and restrain such feminist endeavors.

The second step in this discussion concerns the various ways in which feminist practices integrate themselves into central political, economic, and cultural institutions in different systems. Unlike first-world feminist practices, which were mediated through either liberal bourgeois ideologies of individualism, property, and political rights or marginalized left-wing intellectual discourses, third-world feminist practices were directly linked to central political movements of anti-imperialism, nation building, and economic development. This significant difference compels us to reexamine interactions between feminism and third-world nation-states and the position of feminist practice in third-world mainstream political-economic institutions and culture. Chinese socialist feminism warrants one such reexamination.

A more sophisticated approach to feminist cultural production therefore must investigate the institutionalization of feminist practice in different geopolitical locations and periods; analyze the power dynamics that inform specific feminist practices in established and emerging systems, institutions, and discourses; and demystify claims that feminisms are and could be independent from political, economic, and cultural authorities and institutions—whether imperialist, nationalist, state-based, or market-oriented. Investigating the institutional character of feminist practice also helps us recognize how certain limitations of feminist practice are institutionally bound and so can be addressed only by transforming the broader economic and political structure.

The global spread of Western feminisms, especially across China and other third-world countries, was a direct result of Western imperialism, capitalist expansion, and colonial modernity. Although different schools of Western feminism traveled globally, not all feminist ideas and practices would take root and grow under local conditions. Anarchist, liberal, evolutionary, eugenic, and Marxist theories appeared during China's transition from a dynastic system to a modern nation-state, yet only those feminisms that were institutionalized locally, or sinicized through political, social, and economic practices, became an integrated force in modern Chinese history.[52]

Chinese socialist feminism developed from urban liberal and Marxist feminist discourses of the May Fourth Cultural Movement,[53] embracing both individualist and socialist ideas about women's emancipation. As a critical cultural discourse, Marxist feminism established itself early in the May Fourth Movement, articulating a central set of Marxist views on women's liberation that included women's participation in social production and political governance; the abolition of private property ownership and capitalism; the transition from a middle-class (bourgeois) women's rights movement to working-class women's class and gender liberation; and socialism as the political-economic foundation for women's emancipation.[54] It was, however, not until the establishment of the CCP in July 1921 that Marxist and feminist ideas were adopted by a political organization that unequivocally committed itself to socialist feminist practice.

The CCP, at its Second Congress in 1922, passed a "Resolution on the Women's Movement," formal guidelines for organized feminist activities that highlighted the Chinese women's movement as an integral part of broader proletarian liberation, as well as anti-imperialist and antifeudal struggles.[55] The party continuously pursued this basic policy of uniting struggles for women's liberation with the socialist revolutionary movement.[56] This theoretical and political clarification distinguished Chinese socialist feminism from all other feminist discourses imported into China at the time and paved the way for the institutional integration of Chinese women's liberation into the Communist Revolution. Chinese socialist feminism continued developing throughout the 1920s, directly engaging with the anti-imperialist movements, labor movements, and the Northern Expedition (1922–1927), during which the ruling party of the Republic of China (1912–1949), the Nationalists, formed a united front with the CCP to exterminate regional warlords and reform political and economic institutions. In 1925, at the Fourth

CCP Congress, a new "Resolution on the Women's Movement" was stipulated, stressing the central role of "women workers and peasants" (工农妇女) in party-led women's movements.[57] Xiang Jingyu (向警予, 1895–1928), the most important female leader of the early socialist women's movement, was a crucial figure in formulating the CCP's policies on socialist women's liberation and drafting CCP resolutions on the women's movement.[58]

In 1927, however, the Nationalists and the CCP split violently. The subsequent terror inflicted on the CCP and women activists marked a dramatic turn in the history of socialist feminism in China. The Nationalists' massacring of communist activists drove the CCP underground in all urban centers and also led some of the most dedicated members to retry previous experiments at organizing communist forces among rural peasants. The late 1920s witnessed the party's most significant theoretical and practical transformations, including serious reflections on its feminist policy and affiliations. The CCP repositioned itself in relation to China's large rural populations of women rather than urban-based women workers alone. As part of the general Sinification of Marxist theory, this reflexive change ultimately reoriented Chinese socialist feminism.

Mao Zedong's (毛泽东) "Report on an Investigation of the Peasant Movement in Hunan, March 1927" provided the initial and most important theoretical argument for both peasant revolution and socialist feminism in the Chinese context. In this document, Mao famously described how Chinese men (peasants) are oppressed by political authority, clan authority, and religious authority, while women, in addition to these three authorities, "are also dominated by men [the authority of the husband]."[59] The political authority of the landlord, according to Mao, underpinned three other systems of authority. Therefore, dismantling these economic relations and overthrowing the power of the landlord marked the first step in the process of breaking down the traditional social system. For the first time in Chinese history, peasant women were represented as those most oppressed in China's political, economic, religious, and social systems and were tied explicitly to the Chinese communist revolutionary cause. Moreover, being the most subjugated group, peasant women, together with peasant men, were perceived as historical agents in the proletarian revolution that would bring structural changes to China.

In 1928, the Sixth CCP Congress passed a resolution prioritizing the development of a "peasant women's movement" (农妇运动). According to this resolution, because female peasants remained at the bottom of China's rural system, the CCP must "recognize that peasant women were the most active revolutionary force" and therefore must recruit them into general peasant organizations.[60] Indeed, the potential great contribution of peasant women to the Chinese Communist Revolution was duly recognized during the transformation of the Chinese socialist revolution in the late 1920s and early 1930s.[61] This recognition among CCP leaders helped establish socialist feminism as a core component of future communist revolution.

By the time the Jiangxi Soviet Republic (Jiangxi Soviet hereafter), a Chinese communist base and governing body, was established in southeastern China in 1931, certain CCP members had formed a relatively coherent platform to address the combined issues of nationalism, class, and gender in the Chinese context, while keeping with general Marxist tradition. At this early stage, socialist feminism began to be systematically institutionalized and integrated into the Chinese Communist Revolution. First and foremost, the Chinese Soviet constitution, proclaimed by the first All-China Congress in Ruijin, Jiangxi, guaranteed equal rights for the working masses and the complete emancipation of women:

> All workers, peasants, Red Army soldiers, and all toilers and their families, without distinction of sex, religion, or nationality shall be equal before the Soviet law, and shall be citizens of the Soviet Republic.
>
> It is the purpose of the Soviet government of China to guarantee the thorough emancipation of women; it recognizes freedom of marriage and will put into operation various measures for the protection of women, to enable women gradually to attain the material basis required for their emancipation from the bondage of domestic work, and to give them the possibility of participating in the social, economic, political, and cultural life of the entire society.[62]

In addition to constitutional guarantees and a new political ethic of egalitarianism, the Jiangxi Soviet established concrete laws to enforce equality in status and participation: "These laws marked a break with tradition, reflecting the ideological commitment of the CCP and the influence of Soviet Russia."[63] These new legal codes "specifically affected the position of women in marriage and the family, and in their relationship to the land, the factory and new political institutions."[64] For example, the marriage regulation, granting women freedom to marry and divorce, was pronounced along with other rules promising laborers' equal rights to land allotments irrespective of sex (Land Law of the Soviet Republic, 1931). For the first time in modern Chinese history, women's social liberation was promoted together with their economic and material liberation. The implementation of these newly established laws was particularly emphasized, as the CCP fully understood "it was not enough just to introduce new legislation, it had to be put into practice."[65] Special women's departments were established in all party organizations, along with local women's congresses to preside over women workers. Literacy classes and training courses were provided as well, to coach women activists in leadership techniques as well as to break down traditional, gendered divisions of labor. Such opportunities enabled a significant number of women to step out of their homes and participate in political and economic activities.[66] In short, the CCP's policies of 1931 and their implementation set the course for the institutionalization and development of the peasant women's movement in the soviet areas.[67]

During this same Soviet Republic period, the CCP also developed intensive, periodic campaigns to directly confront local resistance to the women's movement, reinforcing the institutionalization of socialist feminism. The Jiangxi Soviet's circumstances—that is, the establishment of a radically new and modern political power base in an underdeveloped and relatively isolated agrarian area—were extremely irregular. Deeply ingrained Confucian family values rendered certain feminist ideas, especially women's freedom to marry and divorce, completely alien even among peasant women themselves. Nationalist Party military offensives further prevented orderly education regarding feminist policies and their implementation. As a result, short-term, intensive political campaigns and mass mobilizations were adopted for revolutionary practices, especially during politically and militarily unstable periods. This mass mobilization approach gradually became a signature style of CCP leadership and governance, continuing into the socialist period. In the Chinese context, socialist feminist institutionalization was accompanied by a unique mass mobilization approach. Although periodic campaigns might appear temporary and less formal, they played a critical role in disseminating socialist feminist ideas, challenging traditional gender perceptions among the rural masses, and mobilizing women to participate in the party, politics, and production.[68] In the Jiangxi Soviet, both formal and informal institutionalizations of socialist feminism set new precedents for Chinese women's political, economic, and even military participation. Mass campaigns also contributed to the creation of local spaces where women's education and feminist culture were promoted.

Socialist feminist practice in the Jiangxi Soviet was in many aspects experimental, testing an array of ideas, policies, legal implementations, and local conditions in a rural area of southern China. Nevertheless, the republic's multilevel, institutional configuration created a model for feminist practice in later years of socialist revolution, as well as after the People's Republic of China was established in 1949.[69]

Scholars who criticize the CCP for betraying its early May Fourth liberal feminist ideas overlook serious historical limitations of May Fourth feminist practice. Western economic colonialism and China's major agrarian economy precluded the full development of a national capitalism, the formation of a bourgeois class of significant size, and the acceptance of liberal and individualistic values among the majority of the Chinese population. Despite liberal feminism's critical power in the cultural realm, which continued even during and after the revolutionary years, this brand of feminism did not take hold in China because the overwhelming majority of Chinese women were rural peasants and urban laborers. For more than 80 percent of Chinese women, class equality and economic emancipation were as urgent and important as gender liberation. To insist that the CCP should have stuck uncompromisingly to the May Fourth urban middle class's liberal vision of feminism, when working with peasants and the working class to launch a proletarian, anticapitalist revolution,[70] reveals not just a wishful dismissal of Chinese historical and geopolitical conditions but blindness to the transformative nature of the Chinese socialist revolution.

Another critical topic in this examination of Chinese socialist feminism's institutionalization concerns the interdependence and integration of the socialist revolution and the proletarian women's movement in modern China. This interdependence does not simply reflect the Marxist theoretical proposition that women's liberation is part of the overall proletarian revolution; more importantly, it reveals a specific geopolitical and historical material condition that required Chinese socialist revolution and feminism to rely on each other to succeed. Of all the major, modern revolutionary ideas introduced to rural China by the CCP in the late 1920s, feminism and women's liberation appeared most foreign to Chinese peasants, both men and women.[71] In the context of long-standing Confucian traditions, a devastated rural economy, and geographical and social isolation, granting women equal rights to social and public production, political participation, and governance was extremely radical. Local resistance first appeared as early as the beginning years of the Jiangxi Soviet period.[72] Later, when the Red Army was forced to abandon the Soviet Republic in 1934 and move farther inland to more conservative northwestern regions, certain feminist practices, especially women's rights to marry and divorce, encountered waves of resistance from local rural populations. Adjustments to the implementation of socialist feminist policies were not a choice or bargain the CCP negotiated but rather the only option presented by the historical and material reality. This conflict clearly demonstrates how gender issues and feminist questions cannot be addressed in separation from other social, political, and economic conditions. To stress the "independence" and "autonomy" of feminist movements in China from the 1920s through the 1940s, especially in rural areas, would further estrange feminism from local populations, consigning women's emancipation to failure from the start.[73] The integration of feminism into Chinese socialist revolution, and the interdependent relationship forged between Chinese socialist feminism and other components of communist revolution since the late 1920s, particularly class struggle, nationalist revolution, and economic development, proved essential to the survival of feminism in the Chinese context.

The other side of this interdependence also requires emphasis. The success of the Chinese socialist revolution would be inconceivable without the CCP's rigorous feminist policies and practice. Fully aware that Chinese socialist revolution depended on both peasant men and women, rural-oriented CCP leaders at the turn of the 1920s and in the 1930s did not position themselves as external liberators of rural Chinese women. Rather, they redefined Chinese socialist revolution by reenvisioning male and female peasants as its core participants. Throughout the 1930s, the CCP created new policies to recruit women to local leadership positions. As Kathy LeMons Walker points out, "the new direction in the women's movement was an essential part of the Party's general effort to integrate itself with the rural populace."[74] Those who argue that the CCP simply compromised its feminist stance when conflicts arose with (peasant) men have ignored the crucial fact that neither class nor gender was dispensable for the Chinese socialist revolution. Both class revolution and women's liberation constitute the very goal of socialist revolution, and peasant and working men and women served as the central force in carrying out the revolution. A CCP document published in 1930 explicitly argued for the Chinese women's movement as "an indispensable arm of the revolutionary struggle as a whole."[75] Pressured by national crises, the Nationalists' military offensives, and conservative forces in various areas, the CCP sometimes had to compromise on both class and gender issues,[76] but such maneuverings do not suggest fundamental concessions. In practice, it was the CCP's dogmatic faction, which ignored Chinese conditions by stubbornly insisting on Marxist theories of urban working-class struggle and Russian experiences, that risked destroying the revolutionary force in the Jiangxi Soviet.[77]

The recognition of the critical role of rural women in socialist revolution catalyzed the Jiangxi Soviet's integrated institutionalization of socialist feminism and led to the CCP's continued revisions of its policies regarding the practice of the women's movement. To a large extent, Chinese women's liberation became a crucial criterion for the CCP to measure the effect and success of the Chinese socialist revolution. In 1931, the party conducted an extensive assessment of the women's movement in the soviet area and discovered a great number of issues caused mostly by the reluctance of local intermediate and lower-level leadership in promoting peasant women's interests and their political and economic participation. New policies were thus implemented to change the situation, including better organizing and recruiting of women into local leadership positions.[78] In 1934, Mao Zedong, after investigating women's work in the Zhongyang District, criticized the local record. He concluded that women's specific interests were much ignored in the general policy making, and attention to women's education, including how to explain new policies to peasant and working women, was insufficient. Mao then offered concrete suggestions for better attending to local women's needs and connecting their interests to other political goals.[79]

From 1937 to 1941, women's work in the more conservative, less developed northwestern area, the Shan-Gan-Ning Border Region, experienced certain setbacks. With the outbreak of the Second Sino-Japanese War (July 7, 1937) and the subsequent formation of the Second United Front (1937–1941) between the CCP and the Nationalist government, the overall revolutionary policy prioritized the war effort as well as the unification of different social classes and forces.[80] In the late 1930s, however, the CCP had already noticed the stagnation existing in women's work, and a party resolution in 1939 made an urgent request to recruit more women:

> Women constitute half of the population of China. Without women's participation in the revolution, the revolution cannot succeed. The number of women workers in the Party is too small at present, primarily because not enough attention has been paid by the Party. . . . The Party must today emphasize the task of absorbing into its ranks revolutionary peasant women and women intellectuals in great numbers. The Party must regard this as part of its regular activity and see to it that the political consciousness and the cultural level of its women members are enhanced through training and work. (Resolution of the Party, 1939)[81]

By mid-1941, party leaders had discovered more problems in the women's movement, and the elections of 1941 in the Shan-Gan-Ning Border Region were consequently coordinated with a campaign for women's rights. On February 26, 1943, as a part of both the Rectification Campaign (整风运动) against dogmatism within the CCP and the CCP's effort to deploy the mass-line approach to revolution, the Central Committee issued a new policy for women, actively addressing the problems existing in women's work and mobilizing women to advance their liberation through production and war efforts. The new policy of 1943 "fit in well with the goals of the [CCP's] Great Production Drive—a campaign to strengthen the economy and promote social cooperation," when the border region confronted severe military assaults by Japanese troops and economic blockades by the Nationalist government.[82] Whereas some scholars have questioned this "pragmatic" mobilization of women into the economic and war efforts, arguing that women's own interests were subordinated to the revolution, others have pointed out that the need to solve immediate problems in other areas never replaced long-term socialist feminist goals.[83] For example, immediately after the Sino-Japanese War ended in 1945, the CCP was able to turn its focus to class and gender struggles. Land reform, while directly confronting class issues, was also linked to women's rights to land and economic equality. At the same time, direct struggle between the sexes was condoned and encouraged. Although gender issues were placed under the practice of "internal thought struggle," the "backward elements" that wanted to "maintain the old feudal customs and who constantly tormented and oppressed women could now be overtly criticized and reformed."[84] These scholars have demonstrated that although the short-term roles of women might vary, the long-term policy goal did not: "There was a consistent effort throughout the Yan'an period to move women toward equality by bringing them out of the confines of their traditional lives and, in each stage, involving them in larger groups with broader concerns."[85]

More critically, however, women's participation in political and economic activities, in addition to addressing the revolution's needs, also explicitly advanced their own economic interests and sociopolitical status. As scholars have illustrated, women's involvement in various means of social production in the 1940s in the border region—like land cultivation, livestock raising, and particularly spinning and weaving—not only made a great contribution to the war economy but also "revolutionized the economic value of women, contributing to the redefinition of their domestic roles and elevated their status in village society."[86] Furthermore, rural women's organization into social production and cooperation from 1942 to 1945 produced a large group of "new women" who became self-conscious as historical agents in the sociopolitical process and helped build new social communities on the principle of mutual support and equality, the precursors of a socialist society.[87] The binary framework that automatically opposes revolutionary agenda to "women's own interests" has not only ignored historical and material conditions of a given women's movement by essentializing "women" and "interests" across class, race, and geopolitical differences but also imposed individualist separatism and capitalist competition as criteria to measure a socialist revolution. The CCP's continued effort to revise its revolutionary and feminist policy showcased the party's recognition of the indispensability of the women's movement to the overall revolution. The integration of women's work into the socialist revolution was thus key to advancing both women's causes and communist revolution in modern China.

While assessing the interdependence between Chinese socialist feminism and socialist revolution, I do want to highlight Chinese socialist feminism's limitations. Theoretically, international socialist feminism has been both enabled and constrained by Marxist theory on gender, which stipulates that social production is central to women's liberation and that the elimination of private property would automatically address both class and gender issues. As feminist scholars have already pointed out, structural transformation brought about by the capitalist mode of production challenged and shook up the traditional division of labor but, in doing so, generated a new public form of patriarchy and a different gendered division of labor.[88] Even in the socialist period after the completion of nationalization and collectivization, traditional ideas and practices—although much reduced in the urban public and official space—remained active in some private and local rural areas.[89] At the same time, Marxist theory's dismissal of women's roles in reproduction and domestic labor led to gender blindness in its materialist approach to history. This theoretical oversight resulted in Chinese socialist practice's having inadequate policies to address women's double burden in public and domestic spaces. Finally, Marxist theory, based on the European model, provides limited guidelines for the anticolonial, socialist, and feminist revolutions taking place in third-world areas.

In the context of the socialist revolution, the combination of China's underdeveloped agrarian economy, a largely illiterate rural population, and a deeply entrenched Confucian culture, all in a semicolonialized state with endless wars and military conflicts, presented considerable local challenges to feminism in practice. The CCP encountered various obstacles and resistance, including from its own members, when implementing policies to forward the women's movement. Clearly, Chinese feminist practices do not transcend their historical conditions; nor can they be assessed apart from China's overall political, socioeconomic, and cultural transformations. Many of socialist feminism's limitations are tied to the limits of China's socialist revolution and the overall material and geopolitical conditions. The idea that feminism(s) should independently address a universal set of issues across the globe, and the assumption that socialist revolution should solve all "women's questions" raised from the universalized Western perspective regardless of historical conditions, manifest an imperialist and Cold War stance in transnational studies of women and socialist revolution. The frequently asked question "Does socialism liberate women?" exactly presupposes a totalistic understanding of women's liberation as happening once and for all, as if there exists one clear point of completion. This politically charged stance ignores particular historical processes, concrete geopolitical conditions, international politics, and different meanings of "liberation" in various historical moments. By attaching a universal, singular, and yet abstract meaning to such concepts as socialism, liberation, or even "women," this question easily slides into the research query Judith Stacey tackled—that is, "Why has socialism *not* liberated women in China?"[90]—and a discourse on socialism's failures to liberate women in China. A closer examination of the roots and processes of feminist institutionalization in different geopolitical contexts is thus essential to any adequate evaluation of the strengths and limitations of feminist strategies for social transformation.

Formations of Diverse Mainstream Feminist Culture and the Proletarian Public Space in the People's Republic of China

The modern political term *women's rights* was introduced to China from the West via Japan around 1900,[91] and yet Chinese women across class, age, and regional divides did not obtain their legal, political, and economic rights until half a century later. On March 24, 1949, shortly after the CCP took control of Beijing, the First Chinese National Women's Congress convened, and the formation of the All-China Federation of Democratic Women (中华全国民主妇女联合会, ACDWF; changed to ACWF 中华全国妇女联合会 in 1957) was announced. The Marxist materialist view of women's emancipation, which espouses women's direct participation in social production, constituted the central principle of socialist feminist policy.[92] Although private property was collectivized by 1956, China's economy remained seriously underdeveloped and faced enormous Cold War constraints. The CCP considered socialist economic development key to both nation building and women's emancipation.

Radical changes also followed the state's restructuring of gender relationships as egalitarian, the general official implementation of equal pay for equal work, and the redefinition of women's roles as socialist subjects, in the early 1950s.

With the consolidation of the communist victory in mainland China, socialist feminism gradually evolved into a dominant mainstream discourse and practice. In addition to guiding the promulgation and implementation of new marriage laws (1950–1953) and championing gender equality and women's special interests, socialist feminism also integrated itself into other major state movements, such as land reform and collectivization (1950–1953), the Korean War (1950–1953), early industrialization (1950–1955), literacy campaigns (1950–56), and the Great Leap Forward (1958–1960). In 1955, Mao Zedong famously pronounced, "Chinese women can hold up half the sky." Indeed, socialist feminism was a central force in advancing all aspects of the newly established socialist structure, strengthening its own position in the process. This interdependence and reinforcement between feminism and other socialist practices resulted in the emergence of a politically engaged and mass-oriented public space that was essentially and simultaneously feminist and proletarian.

The national institutionalization of socialist feminism and the full-scale promotion of class and gender equality fostered the growth of socialist feminist mainstream culture. This mainstream culture, different from capitalist commercial mainstream culture, was tied not to the market mechanism but to socialist public ownership and the ethics of class and gender equality. It was endorsed by the party-state and participated in by the masses. Mainstream culture became crucial in combating traditional and capitalist patriarchal values, advocating for women's interests, and promoting the socialist proletarian woman subject in the China of the 1950s and beyond. Although the CCP was unable to launch sustained campaigns against patriarchal traditions during the rural revolutionary era (1927–1949) due to various historical constraints, the new socialist party-state in the 1950s sponsored and institutionalized feminist cultural production in ways that targeted patriarchy explicitly. Whereas the socialist political-economic system stressed the development of productive forces and the economic emancipation of all classes and women, socialist feminist cultural practice launched unprecedented (and unmatched) mass campaigns against patriarchal customs in everyday lives. These attacks took a multidimensional and nationwide approach to gender equality and produced impressive results—particularly given early socialist China's socioeconomic and geopolitical condition. The conventional wisdom that assumes Chinese socialist revolution and construction simply subordinated gender to class and ignored patriarchal ideology must be seriously revised in light of China's lived history.

The development of Chinese socialist feminism in the post-1949 era was naturally a complex process, manifesting a geopolitically constrained, socioeconomically conditioned, and culturally negotiated practice. Not all initiatives succeeded. The United States' and other Western countries' severe economic and technological sanctions launched during the Cold War period, combined with a devastated economy after a century of turbulent history, significantly constrained China's overall economic development, producing uneven and unequal development in rural and urban areas and the persistence of certain gendered divisions of labor.[93] Regional economic patterns and local customs also demanded careful reflection and adjustments during various policy implementations. History had already shown that radical campaigns without considerations for local conditions would cause serious negative effects.[94] Furthermore, while conservative views were largely silenced in the socialist public, conventional gender ideas and male chauvinism persisted in private domains, inland rural areas, and among some CCP cadres as well.[95]

It is true that despite the abolition of private ownership and strong ideological campaigns against patriarchy, certain gender and class issues remained in socialist China. But this truth should in no way cancel out the extensive and unprecedented advancement made in Chinese women's and proletarian liberations. Whereas most scholarship focuses on Chinese women's socioeconomic liberation and their participation in social production—whether as liberated subjects or laborers of the party-state—this section foregrounds mainstream socialist feminist culture, which significantly transformed social ethics, gender roles, and the construction of modern women subjects in socialist China.

Contrary to the conventional wisdom that construes all state-sponsored endeavors as dogmatic and totalitarian, Chinese socialist mainstream culture grew from diverse international and domestic influences, changed over time,[96] and produced various representations and aesthetics. As recent scholarship has revealed, Chinese socialist culture in the 1950s embraced and developed a critical new cosmopolitanism.[97] Socialist culture "does not veer from the commitment to worldliness but rather attempts to reconstruct its literary world, to adapt the project of literary transnationalism to new conditions, to the new missions assigned to cultural production by the socialist state and to the evolving sense of identity of writers and readers in socialist China."[98] Socialist cosmopolitanism is highly "critical of the privilege and arrogance of a cosmopolitan idealism born out of an age of colonialism, imperialism, racism, and gendered exclusion."[99] The visible influence of Soviet films on developing Chinese socialist new cinema and fostering socialist internationalist visions for the future has been well studied.[100] Cultural influences from East Asia, Eastern Europe, the third world, and even Western Europe and the United States have also been well documented.[101]

In mainstream feminist discourse and culture, female icons and heroines from the Soviet Union played a significant role in the construction of Chinese socialist women in the 1950s.[102] Feminisms practiced in modern China, including the indigenized liberal trend of the May Fourth Movement and left-wing movements of the 1920s and 1930s, also integrated themselves into the project of socialist feminist culture. In the 1950s, many female cultural workers, including writers, film directors, and popular journal editors, were May Fourth and left-wing feminist figures.[103] Scholarly studies of the most important feminist journal in socialist China, *Women of China* (中国妇女), published by the All-China Federation of Democratic Women, for example, have revealed the contribution of the May Fourth feminist legacy to the formation and development of a socialist feminist cultural front from 1949 to 1966.[104] The editorial board's promotion of women's self-reliance and the journal's concentrated discussions of various gender-related issues showed how different senses of agency and critical concerns emerged in the first seventeen years of socialist China. At the same time, the editorial board's receptivity to readers' suggestions, and their subsequent revisions made to expand the journal's intended audience to include working-class and rural women, also demonstrated the critical transformation of the May Fourth feminist heritage in the socialist era.

Chinese socialist feminist culture's having diverse components, however, does not suggest the lack of a coherent, central agenda. The idea and practice of "proletarianization," to use Tina Mai Chen's term,[105] is what distinguishes Chinese socialist feminism from earlier Chinese feminisms, as well as from socialist feminism in Western countries. Indeed, proletarian women, broadly defined, emerged as a new political, social, and economic subject in socialist China. Chen, in her study of female icons in China in the 1950s, examines how the public representation of new roles for working-class women, such as tractor drivers, train dispatchers, and high-pressure welders, showcased "the arrival of a socialist modernity contingent upon shattering the fetters of Confucian, feudal and capitalist worldviews and their attendant patriarchal forms."[106] The first group of women who embodied socialist gender equality, empowering themselves with modern knowledge of heavy machinery, also brought Chinese women to "the forefront of new national, international, and world orders."[107] The mass-circulated images of female workers as everyday icons, according to Chen, signified the proletarianization of women's emancipation and historical progress in socialist China.[108] At the same time, Chen warns against simplistic conflations of agency and individuality with individualism, illustrating women model workers' multilayered lived experiences and the multifaceted interactions between these women and their official representations in individual, national, and international frameworks. She argues that socialist women's agency must be viewed within the complex negotiations among these dynamic forces and that this situated agency was largely enabled, although sometimes limited, by socialist discourses and state-sponsored feminism.[109]

Mass media representations of working-class women as exemplary socialist subjects constituted a most critical and significant dimension of socialist feminist culture. In addition, proletarian women also became a targeted audience and active participants. The officially endorsed proletarian-oriented public space in socialist China worked hand in hand with the development of socialist feminist mainstream culture. To improve working-class women's education and cultural participation, numerous national and regional literacy classes were designed and taught under the Combat Illiteracy Campaigns (1950–1956). New book genres and magazines were also published targeting working-class people with limited literacy. Many comic books and "picture-story pamphlets" (连环画), like *Li Fengjin: How the New Marriage Law Helped Chinese Women Stand Up* (1950), appeared as part of socialist China's early efforts to educate the populace about gender equality and women's legal rights.[110] Many local pictorial journals published by local women's federations; for example, the *Northwest Women's Pictorial* (later renamed *Shaanxi Women's Pictorial*) served illiterate rural women and grassroots women's cadres.[111] In the area of film production, national mobile projection teams were set up to allow socialist films and feminist messages to reach remote and rural areas. "In 1949 there were over 600 cinemas nationwide but no mobile projection teams. By 1959 the number of projection units, including both movie theaters and mobile projection teams, had risen to 15,400. Films were shown in rural villages and in urban parks, workers' clubs, universities, and factories, in addition to regular theaters."[112] This process of proletarianizing the cultural space, combined with the practice of developing a mass-oriented mainstream culture, is crucial for understanding the outreach and popularity of Chinese socialist feminist culture.

Major points about Chinese socialist feminist culture can be summarized as follows. First, socialist feminist culture, including film production, belonged to the political mainstream, as it was promoted by the state, supported by socialist institutions, and directly engaged with by the masses. Second, despite its mainstream position, socialist feminist culture had diverse historical and transnational origins. In the process of developing itself, it also modernized and revolutionized different cultural productions. Third, Chinese socialist feminist culture, manifesting socialist feminist multidimensional agency, did not represent gender as an isolated category but rather situated gender in relation to other political and social agendas. Fourth, for the first time in Chinese history, proletarian women become not only central characters and national models in the mass media but also audience members and cultural participants. This mass-oriented proletarianization, which was designed to serve the urban working classes and large rural populations, distinguished Chinese socialist feminism from most other feminisms practiced in history. Finally, Chinese socialist feminism, like other third-world feminisms, contained a pronounced nationalist character. Whether in content or artistic form, nationalism was an important component of socialist feminist cinematic practice. But as some scholars have convincingly argued, Chinese socialist nationalism was by no means an isolated practice; it was tied to socialist internationalism, which aimed to critically reconfigure the world. Chinese socialist feminist culture was thus part of the articulation of the new international imaginary. The mutual implication between the socialist national and international was one of the distinctive characteristics of socialist cosmopolitanism.[113] These central features of Chinese socialist feminist culture challenge the prevailing assumptions that socialist culture is an isolated and monolithic practice and that feminist cultural practices like filmmaking should be marginalized endeavors that necessarily resist, disrupt, or subvert mainstream ideology. Chinese socialist feminist culture and the proletarian, mass-oriented public space together provide us an alternative site for remapping transnational feminist and cinematic practices in modern history.

Film Industry Transformations and Experimental Mainstream Cinema in the First Seventeen Years of Socialist China (1949–1966)

In early socialist film production, several major changes took place. With the advent of a radically different economic and political system, cinema—as the most effective mass medium reaching the largest audience, both literate and illiterate, at the time—became an important venue to articulate corresponding world views, promote new social relationships, and envision a revolutionary history partially informed by Marxist theory. From 1946 to 1949, the CCP confiscated the previous foreign (Japanese) and government-run (Nationalist) film facilities and turned them into three major state-run studios, Northeast (1946), Beijing (1949), and Shanghai (1949). The subsequent nationalization of all film studios from 1949 to 1952 transformed the entire film industry from a private, profit-driven commercial enterprise to a publicly owned, mass-oriented pedagogical apparatus working to construct new socialist subjects in line with proletarian revolution and socialist construction. From 1953 to 1965, the party-state significantly expanded film enterprises, setting up new studios in various regions, organizing projection teams to bring films to rural and remote areas, establishing film schools to offer professional training, developing film culture and research, and creating national film awards and competitions.[114] Cinematic subject matter and audience constituted another major concern in early socialist China. Workers, peasants, and soldiers became the main characters as well as the target audience for socialist films.

These industrial, financial, and sociocultural transformations were crucial for the establishment of Chinese socialist film production. Rather than entailing a monolithic development of socialist cinema, these transformations generated a dynamic process of negotiation, a process that was further affected by an unstable political climate (domestic and international), different cultural influences from the past and abroad, and the varying backgrounds of individual authors and artists. Situated in relation to both a radically new political-economic-social system and a confluence of cultural factors, the first seventeen years of Chinese socialist filmmaking manifested itself as highly experimental in nature.

First of all, socialist film experimentation occurred at the conceptual and political levels. "How to Represent the New China" (新中国) in films, for example, posed a challenging question to all early socialist filmmakers; answers to it were seldom unified.[115] Most artists and writers in early socialist China agreed that socialist cinema should represent and serve the proletarian class and promote socialist ideals; still, few filmmakers, including scriptwriters and directors, knew exactly what such cinema should look like. Chinese socialist revolution, particularly its unique proletarian vision, placed its cultural representation at a conceptually vanguard position in world cinema. Chen Bo'er (陈波儿), a Shanghai actress turned Yan'an scriptwriter and director who became a cultural cadre in charge of early socialist film development at the Northeast Film Studio in 1946,[116] wrote a report in 1950 on the challenge of bringing into being Chinese socialist feature films in the 1947–1950 period.[117] She pointed out that because worker-peasant-soldier films were so novel in the late 1940s and early 1950s, all sorts of "obstacles" and uncertainties arose during the filmmaking process. Situated in an unprecedented historical, political, and artistic position, early socialist Chinese filmmakers resorted to high-level experimentalism to represent new China and create socialist aesthetics.

The experimental nature of socialist cinema manifested as well in the tension and constant negotiation between state policies and film practices. Although socialist cinema had been defined as the pedagogical apparatus for general socialist revolution and construction, the specific relationship between state cultural policy and cinematic practice at a given historical juncture was by no means predictable. Film production during this seventeen-year period is said to have experienced four highs (1946–1950, 1953–1957, 1959, and 1961–1963) and four lows (1951, 1957–1958, 1959–1960, and 1964–1966).[118] This seesaw movement of socialist film production indicates the constant remapping of the political and cultural, on the one hand, and the continued exploration of different visions, themes, and styles among film critics and filmmakers, on the other. Political campaigns, such as the 1951 campaign against *The Life of Wu Xun* (武训传, dir. Sun Yu, 1950), the Hundred Flowers Campaign (1956–1957), and the subsequent antirightist movement in the late 1950s, for example, showcased socialist China's changing definitions of the political and the cultural. But even during these moments, the state's position was not fixed but rather changed in reaction to international politics (e.g., the changing situation in the Soviet Union after Stalin passed away in 1953 and the Hungarian Revolution of 1956) and contemporary Chinese film practices and cultural discourses. Some scholars have traced film policies from the 1950s, illustrating the changes in emphasis. If the establishment of the Film Guidance Standing Committee (电影指导委员会, 1950–1952) resulted in lowering the quality of film scripts due to rigid obstructionist guidelines, "Decisions Concerning Strengthening Film Production Work" (关于加强电影制片工作的决定), a corrective policy made in December 1952, reflected the CCP's desire to stimulate screenplay-writing and increase film production.[119] The Central Film Bureau vice minister Chen Huangmei's (陈荒煤) report produced in March 1956 further promoted greater variety in screenplay subjects and greater reflection of China's revolutionary history and struggle, of national minorities, and workers', youth and children's lives, which indeed "raised the number of productions in each of these areas, even after the Anti-Rightist Campaign began in 1957."[120] This back-and-forth movement challenges the assumed existence of a monolithic political and cultural authority and of uniform control of the party. Indeed, even top state policy makers' views on cultural representation and production were far from identical.[121]

The existence of an influential group of expert-officials in the 1950s—including Yuan Muzhi (袁牧之), Chen Bo'er, Xia Yan (夏衍), Yang Hansheng (阳翰笙), Cai Chusheng (蔡楚生), Chen Huangmei, and Zhang Junxiang (张俊祥)—further challenges the assumption of a monolithic political and cultural authority. Members of this important group had worked as filmmakers and film critics in the left-wing film movement in Shanghai, Chongqing, and the communist base area of Yan'an before 1949. Several of these expert-officials had also become CCP members early on and became cultural leaders in the Ministry of Culture, the Central Film Bureau, and the China Federation of Literary and Art Circles. In the 1950s, this group helped establish socialist film discourse and practice and also participated in crafting socialist filmmaking policy.[122] They promoted a new revolutionary aesthetic and a more relaxed environment for socialist film practice—some emphasizing cinema as a special form of visual art,[123] others insisting that art, irreducible to politics, had to reflect the complex socialist transformation and diverse life experiences.[124]

In the area of aesthetic experiments, the socialist exploration highlighted and revitalized national and folk forms. As Chinese socialist cinema developed in the Cold War environment, national forms and styles became central for film practice and theory. The Korean War in the early 1950s directly compelled socialist China to ban Hollywood films and develop a new system of representation, emphasizing *distinctly Chinese* cultural and artistic characteristics manifested in classic, folk, and popular cultures. Then, too, China's split with the Soviet Union in the late 1950s and early 1960s further reinforced the demand for Chinese national cinema in order to reduce Soviet cinema's influence.[125] True, promoting a particular Chinese style of cinema was hardly unprecedented in China before 1949,[126] but it was not until the mid-1950s that national forms became a theoretical, political, and aesthetic priority in making socialist films.[127] Most discussions in the 1950s and 1960s focused on how to transform and integrate traditional Chinese aesthetic expressions into modern, revolutionary, cinematic narrative. Cultural and film critics of the 1950s expressly attributed the following Chinese aesthetic values to the successful formation of a socialist national cinema: the unrestrained conceptualization of time and space (beyond the limits of real time and space) in Chinese popular performing arts; the montage-like use of imagery in Chinese classical poetry; the structured expression of subjective feelings in depicting nature and the external environment;[128] and the idea of art as a staged, essentialized performance (*xieyi*, 写意) rather than an imitation of nature or reality (mimesis and realism).[129] These values were based on both high and popular cultures and thus exhibited diverse characteristics. In particular, the early 1950s launched a modern socialist reform of Chinese opera, and many traditional opera films were created from 1953 to 1966 to appeal to the cultural sensibilities of the mass audience.[130] The demand for national cinematic styles also led to many transmedia or cross-pollination experiments with traditional arts and literature (poetry, opera, painting, folk music and performance, and vernacular fiction). By the early 1960s, after several years of exploration and experimentation, a Chinese revolutionary cinematic aesthetic that drew inspiration from various traditional Chinese arts and literature had not only been articulated but also deployed by many directors in the mainstream filmmaking.

Despite its emphasis on national forms, however, Chinese socialist cinema was not created in isolation from world cinema. Contrary to the conventional view influenced by Cold War ideology, Chinese socialist cinema prior to the Cultural Revolution maintained frequent contact and, indeed, interacted with cinematic traditions from around the globe. From 1949 to 1955, for example, 199 foreign films were introduced and screened in China, a number that significantly outstripped the 63 domestically produced films.[131] While Hollywood films disappeared from public theaters in the 1950s after the outbreak of the Korean War, they remained available to high-ranking cultural personnel and film directors. More importantly, the influence of Hollywood's narrative style and camera work persisted, particularly in the practice of filmmakers with a Shanghai background.[132] Socialist China during its first seventeen years both imported and exported many films from and to the Soviet Union and other socialist countries.[133] Between 1950 and 1966, the Shanghai Dubbing Studio alone introduced 320 foreign films to China: of that number, 179 films issued from the Soviet Union; over 100 came from other socialist countries; and the rest hailed from other Asian and Western European countries.[134] The influences of Russian revolutionary cinema, the theory of montage, and socialist realism on the formation of socialist Chinese national cinema and proletarian internationalism have been well recognized and studied.[135] The specific influence of Italian neorealism and French New Wave cinema on Chinese filmmaking in both Mao's and post-Mao times, though, has yet to be closely examined.[136] Most representative Italian neorealist and French New Wave films—from *Rome, Open City* (Roberto Rossellini, 1945), to *The Bicycle Thief* (Vittorio De Sica, 1948), *Cops and Robbers* (Steno and Mario Monicelli, 1951), *Miracle in Milan* (Vittorio De Sica, 1951), *Rome 11:00* (Giuseppe De Santis, 1952), and *Hiroshima mon amour* (Alain Resnais, 1959)[137]—were introduced to China in the mid-1950s. In addition, Italian neorealism and French New Wave film theories were also systematically translated into Chinese between 1961 and 1963, together with other foreign film theories and movements. In both theory and practice, Chinese socialist cinema in its first seventeen years manifested a much wider transnational influence than the typical view has generally assumed.[138]

Although mainstream socialist cinema refers to all films produced in the state-planned economic system and state-owned film studios, that fact, as history reveals, does not rule out changes, different influences, or even contentions over time and across works. Far from a uniform practice, socialist mainstream film production entailed a process of dynamic political and artistic experimentation, which simultaneously defined and contested the boundaries of a new national cinema. Chinese women's cinema emerged exactly in this highly productive and transformative environment.

Since its inception in 1905, men had dominated Chinese cinema. Never before had women been institutionally and socially supported to produce films;[139] nor had female directors produced any more than one film in mainland China.[140] In the new socioeconomic system, however, a group of women including Wang Ping, Dong Kena, Wang Shaoyan (王少岩, 1923–2018), and Yan Bili (颜碧丽, 1928–1986) rose to prominence and continued to make socialist films. The emergence of the first generation of Chinese women film directors and their unprecedented success remained directly tied to the transformation of gender roles in socialist society, the national institutionalization of gender equality, the collectivization of the film industry, and the formation of an experimental, mass-oriented, and feminist mainstream cinema in early socialist China. This first group of Chinese female filmmakers also experimented with a wide range of genres and styles, significantly diversifying socialist cinema. In the next two chapters, I turn to two influential female directors from this generation, Wang Ping and Dong Kena, exploring their life experiences, cinematic authorship, film styles, and critical interventions. These chapters particularly seek to demonstrate how Wang's *The Story of Liubao Village* and Dong's *Small Grass Grows on the Kunlun Mountains*, emblematic of Chinese socialist cultural practice, made distinctive contributions to the (trans)formation of Chinese socialist feminist and mainstream cinema.

2 Articulating Embedded Feminist Agency in Socialist Mainstream Cinema

Wang Ping and *The Story of Liubao Village* (1957)

Wang Ping (王苹, 1916–1990) was the first female director in modern China. She started making films around 1952 at the age of thirty-six and became one of the most successful, popular, and versatile film directors in Mao's socialist China prior to the Cultural Revolution. Of the fifteen films she independently directed, eleven were produced during the first seventeen years of socialist China, one in the late Cultural Revolution, and an additional four in the late 1970s and 1980s. Her best-known and most popular films include *The Story of Liubao Village* (柳堡的故事, 1957), *The Everlasting Radio Signals* (永不消逝的电波, 1958), *Locust Tree Village* (槐树庄, 1961), and *Sentinels under the Neon Lights* (霓虹灯下的哨兵, 1964). Her musical epic *East Is Red* (东方红, 1965) remains an unprecedented achievement. All these films are now considered socialist classics with individual cinematic styles and varied aesthetic appeals. In 1962, Wang won the Hundred Flower Film Festival's award for best director for *Locust Tree Village*, and in 1986 she received the Golden Rooster's special award for her fourth musical epic film, *The Song of Chinese Revolution* (中国革命之歌, 1985).

In the early socialist era, a small group of women film directors—including Wang Ping, Dong Kena, Wang Shaoyan, and Yan Bili—emerged for the first time in modern Chinese history. These women had neither training nor experience in filmmaking prior to the founding of the People's Republic of China in 1949 yet won national awards for their films of the 1950s and 1960s and contributed greatly to the formation of mass-oriented, mainstream socialist cinema.[1] What did it mean for Chinese women to make mainstream films in socialist China? How should we understand women's cinematic authorship in the socialist context? What is the relationship between female directors' individual agency and the new sociopolitical system, particularly its integrated, institutionalized socialist feminism,[2] its mass-oriented cultural practice, and its collectivized film industry? How can the study of socialist female directors help us recognize not only the experimental nature and diverse aesthetics of socialist mainstream cinema but also different feminist visions and political aspirations? What alternative imaginaries can Chinese socialist women's cinema offer us as we explore ways to break the current worldwide feminist stagnation and to advance transnational feminist media practice? This chapter addresses some of these questions by focusing on Wang Ping's 1957 film, *The Story of Liubao Village.*

Socialist Transformations of Cinematic Authorship and Gender

The socialist ideology of gender equality was nationally promoted and institutionalized in legal, economic, and cultural systems soon after the founding of the People's Republic of China. In the film industry, collectivization was completed in 1952, and the new state studio system implemented gender equality in both filmmaker recruitment and filmmaking opportunities. Early socialist China's lack of professional filmmakers partially accounted for studios' employment of nonprofessionals, but the belief that women could succeed in filmmaking played a more critical role in the hiring of female film directors in the 1950s.

Wang Ping, an actress with extensive performance experience in the left-wing plays and films of Shanghai and Chongqing in the 1930s and 1940s, was appointed in early 1951 to help establish a military education film studio for the People's Liberation Army (PLA), the precursor to the August First Liberation Army Film Studio. Later that year, the head of this emerging film studio approached Wang and entrusted her with directing its first film: *Hechuan Offensive* (河川进攻, 1953), an educational military documentary. With no filmmaking experience and little knowledge of military affairs, Wang hesitated to accept this request. Liu Bocheng (刘伯承), a famous army general of the revolutionary era and then-head of the Nanjing Military Academy, where the film was set, persuaded Wang to agree by promising his full support.[3] The unprecedented trust and endorsement that Wang received, from both film and military institutions, not only enabled her to accomplish the task but also rendered her the first female film director in modern Chinese history. Wang literally learned filmmaking through the process of making films. Her first feature, which was also the first feature of the August First Liberation Army Film Studio, *Darkness before Dawn* (冲破黎明前的黑暗, 1956), took more than two years to produce and ran over eight hours even after the first edit. As Wang herself emphasized many times later in life, she would not have become a film director without the institutional support and "expensive tuition" the state was willing to pay for her experimentation, especially in the 1950s when the socialist film industry was financially precarious.[4] Equally important, the establishment of public day care and boarding schools by state and neighborhood committees in early socialist China provided key structural and concrete support for career women like Wang.[5] Wang had four children, the youngest only nine months old when the new director's husband passed away suddenly in 1956. She relied on public day care and boarding schools to continue her filmmaking career. The emergence of the first generation of Chinese women film directors like Wang was a direct result of the transformation of gender roles in socialist society, the national institutionalization of gender equality, and the establishment of the socialist film studio system.

Cultural authorship, institutionally reconfigured in Mao's China, also helped promote Chinese women's cultural participation and individual agency. The relationship between authorship and historical women has been a thorny issue in feminist film theory. The traditional author-centered interpretation and the sociological understanding of biographical materials in relation to creative works were seriously challenged during the rise of poststructuralism in the late 1960s and early 1970s. In poststructuralist-bent feminist theory, especially feminist film theory that emerged during the same period, the critique of traditional patriarchal author-centered studies went along with the repudiation of the female author's or director's sociohistorical constitution and political position. As Nancy Miller and other feminist scholars have critically reflected, "The removal of the Author has not so much made room for a revision of the concept of authorship as it has . . . repressed and inhibited discussion of any writing identity in favor of the (new) monolith of anonymous textuality."[6] Although Clare Johnston, Pam Cook, and others made attempts in the early formation of feminist film theory to revitalize debates about authorship and bring female directors into central discussions of film studies, Western feminist film theory has in general "fail[ed] to consider the problem of authorship as it interacts with issues of history, biography, and textuality."[7] During the last several decades, feminist critics have paid increasingly more attention to films directed by female directors, but these directors' lives and experiences, as well as their social positions in history, were not only rendered irrelevant but also barred from discussions of their films.[8]

In retrospect, socialist cultural practice has provided us an alternative concept of authorship that challenges both the traditional idea of (male) individual-author as the origin of meaning and the poststructuralist total dismissal of the role of historical authors in the process of signification. In the context of socialist public ownership and pedagogically oriented cultural production, while individual authors still functioned as the major anchor, a film's authorship was understood as contingent on the dynamic interplay of political, institutional, cultural, and individual factors. That is to say, socialist cultural authorship, particularly cinematic authorship, neither endorsed the individual author as the origin or owner of meaning, nor granted the text an autonomous role in meaning production. At the same time, contrary to the stereotypical Cold War perception of socialist cultural production, socialist authorship did not necessarily thwart individual agency, if we understand individual agency as historically constituted and sociopolitically enabled rather than essentially (pre)determined. Indeed, as socialist authorship highlights interactions among personal elements and different historical forces, including sociopolitical and institutional formations,[9] an individual author's agency becomes enacted, transformed, and recognized in the process. For example, in socialist filmmaking, the socialist public ownership and mass-oriented practice worked with state-sponsored socialist feminism, ushering Chinese women into the domain of film production and rigorously promoting and constructing women's cultural and individual agencies. Whereas it is crucial to discuss specific cinematic signification at the textual level by carefully examining the narrative structure, images, and sound of a film, the discussion must be grounded in the contemporary political-economic and institutional (re)configuration of culture's role and the author's function. For the study of women's cinema, the socialist model calls our attention to the historical constitutions of gender, filmmaking, and aesthetics as well as their interactions with other sociopolitical and personal forces.

In the 1950s and 1960s, different generations of Chinese filmmakers with different backgrounds worked together to produce a socialist cinema with diverse cinematic styles. In addition to contemporary sociopolitical and institutional forces, the director's experience, including both his or her life story and artistic practice, played a critical role in specifically negotiating socialist authorship and diversifying socialist mainstream cinema. A historical director's experience by no means forms the origin of cinematic authorship or determines the meaning of a film, but it is a crucial factor that forms and informs the director's sociopolitical position and cultural vision, thus contributing to the overall signification of a given film's authorship. A female director's life story and her changing roles in different historical periods or sociopolitical systems thus offers us important references for exploring the gendered and historical dimensions of cinematic authorship.

Wang Ping had an extraordinary life as both a woman and a cultural figure in modern China. A discussion of her life's transformations can help us understand how sociopolitical changes taking place in modern China influenced her personal position and cultural vision and affected the meaning of certain aspects of her film adaptations and film authorship. An examination of Wang's life trajectory also provides us an opportunity to review the history of a modern Chinese "new woman" (新女性) and female authorship—its transitions and stages from the May Fourth to the left-wing and then socialist periods—addressing the ahistorical charges post-Mao feminist film scholars lobbied against socialist female directors for adhering to a male standard under socialist gender equality and relinquishing the female difference and culture that had surfaced in the May Fourth era.[10]

A brief summary here of post-Mao feminist film criticism on socialist women's cinema can direct us to a set of important issues as we explore Wang Ping's life. Emerging in the late 1980s and early 1990s under the influence of post-second-wave Western feminism(s) and in line with the continued post-Mao reaction to the Cultural Revolution, as well as socialist culture in general, post-Mao feminist film scholars promoted sexual difference, marginalized and subversive cultures, and a critique of men and mainstream culture.[11] They particularly devalued the significance of women's liberation in political, social, and economic realms, arguing that Chinese women, because of their sociopolitical liberation in socialist China, had lost their female essence and cultural subjectivity, both of which emerged in China during the May Fourth Movement.[12] One of the influential post-Mao feminist cultural scholars, Dai Jinhua (戴锦华), once asserted, "Paradoxically, the arrival of women's de jure 'liberation' once again vitiated any chance Woman had to become a historical discursive subject."[13] Another scholar, Shuqin Cui, further elaborates: "The emergence of female directors does not signal the possibility of a woman's cinema. . . . They [socialist female directors] fail to realize . . . that by identifying with the male gender and submitting to the nation-state they acquire sociopolitical recognition but sacrifice gender identity and subject position."[14] Post-Mao feminist scholars thus consider

Wang Ping, despite or because of her success in socialist mainstream cinema, as a "Hua Mulan" (花木兰) figure,[15] who became recognized by following a male model and suppressing or concealing her female difference.[16] Further, Wang is criticized as a director who neither "experiment[ed] with radical, therefore marginal cinema," or "anti-cinema,"[17] nor manifested any independent female values in her films. Wang's popularity, consequently, came "not from any gender markers in her works but from her successful production of mainstream [sociopolitical] films,"[18] and as a result, her films reinforced male consciousness and gender hierarchy.[19] What does it mean to forge an opposition between women's/feminist cinema, and women's sociopolitical liberation and socialist mainstream film? How did socialist gender equality function to conceal female or gender difference and cause women to model themselves after men? How can Wang's life experience and film practice help us rethink these serious charges made in post-Mao feminist film studies?

Wang Ping: From Left-Wing Nora to the First Socialist Female Director

Born into a well-to-do but conservative Muslim family in Nanjing in 1916, Wang Guangzhen (王光珍, Wang Ping's original name) was the youngest and most beloved child of her parents.[20] Her father was a typical authoritarian patriarch who did not think women should be educated. After Wang graduated from primary school, paid for by one of her elder siblings, she fought to continue her education, against her father's wishes. With her siblings' support, Wang passed the public school exams and went to a top public middle school, where she became influenced by May Fourth literature and inspired by the May Fourth new woman archetype: a modern, educated female figure who embraced romantic love and possessed an "independent personality" (独立人格) especially in relation to the traditional family system.

In 1931, Wang Ping gained admittance to Nanjing's First High School, where she studied public school teaching. During her second year there, she exhibited extraordinary talents in sports and performance. She was soon recruited as the only female member of her school's drama society, organized by underground Communist Party members and tied to the Shanghai left-wing drama movement. She became acquainted with such left-wing dramatists and critics as Chen Liting (陈鲤庭), Qu Baiyin (瞿白音), Shu Qiang (舒强), and Shui Hua (水华). In 1934, the Mofeng Art Troupe (磨风剧社), a Nanjing division of the Chinese Left-wing Dramatists Association (中国左翼戏剧家联盟, 1931–1936), chose Wang to play the lead role in Huang Zuolin (黄佐临)'s spoken drama *My Elder Sister* (姐姐)—this marked the beginning of her stage career. In July of that year, she graduated as the top female student in her high school and began teaching elementary school in Nanjing.

The year 1935 proved to be a major turning point in Wang Ping's young adult life. The Mofeng Art Troupe stage director Zhang Min (章泯) had chosen her earlier to play Nora in Henrik Ibsen's *A Doll's House*. The play was first staged on January 1, 1935, at Taotao Grand Theater in the national capital, Nanjing, and played for three consecutive days. It was a huge success. Wang Ping instantly became famous nationwide and was later called Nanjing Nora. (In June 1935, Lan Ping [蓝苹, original name, Li Yunhe (李云鹤), who later became Mao Zedong's wife and changed her name to Jiang Qing (江青)] performed the role of Nora in Shanghai as part of the Shanghai left-wing drama movement and became the "Shanghai Nora.") Wang had taken the stage name Wang Ping when she agreed to play Nora, but the play's enormous popularity rendered her unable to hide her true identity. Her school fired her, and soon thereafter the Nanjing government prohibited all schools in its system from recruiting her. The aftershock of this nationally known "Nora incident" led to the arrest of several left-wing and underground communist drama activists in Nanjing. Qu Baiyin, Mao Dun (茅盾), and many left-wing and communist critics published newspaper articles in Nanjing and Shanghai in support of Wang, denouncing the Nanjing government's inhumane treatment of her and its conservative attitude toward women's independence. Wang herself also published a public letter in the *New People Newspaper* (新民报), expressing her unwavering love for the arts and her determination to continue performing on the stage.

The intense coverage of the "Nora incident" led Wang's father to discover his daughter's role. Furious, he beat Wang and locked her in the attic of the family home. Following pressure from relatives, he also tried to arrange a marriage for Wang. With help from her siblings, Shui Hua, and other left-wing artists, Wang received a job offer from a school in a mountainous area outside Nanjing and finally broke free from her father's hold. But the subsequently increased censorship and frequent arrests of left-wing and underground communist dramatists in Nanjing and the Jiangsu area forced the Mofeng Art Troupe to close and its artists to leave the region. At the age of eighteen, Wang Ping decided to leave her home region to pursue her left-wing performance career in Shanxi Province in the northwest region, where the censorship was less severe in the fall of 1935.

As Song Zhao (宋昭), Wang's daughter and biographer, points out, Wang's performance of Nora, a foreign female character self-awakened during her home imprisonment, entailed a real family revolution in Wang's own life.[21]

But Wang's revolution went beyond the domestic realm. A decade after the end of the May Fourth Movement,[22] Wang Ping reenacted one of the central May Fourth dramas—Nora leaving home—both on stage (her character's husband's home) and in reality (her father's house). The sociocultural and political situations, however, had radically changed by the mid-1930s, and *A Doll's House*, popular in the May Fourth era for promoting both individual liberation from the traditional patriarchal family and Chinese women's independent personalities, became politically provocative under Jiang Jieshi's (蒋介石) central government.

Generally speaking, Wang's left-wing Nora of 1935 departed from the May Fourth Nora in two significant ways. First, her leaving home no longer embodied an individualistic act tied purely to the rejection of arranged marriage and the pursuit of romantic love. For many May Fourth new women, leaving traditional homes meant committing themselves to the ideal of romantic love and freedom of marriage. The discrepancy between the newly introduced Western individualistic discourse and China's social and economic reality, however, often led to unfortunate endings for May Fourth Noras, who bravely stepped out of their fathers' houses only to find themselves years later either betrayed or abandoned by their lovers, or caged in their husbands' homes. As a matter of fact, in early March 1935 when Wang Ping fled her father's home for a rural area, Ruan Lingyu (阮玲玉), the iconic Chinese new woman on the silver screen, took her own life in Shanghai soon after the premier of a film she starred in, *The New Woman* (新女性, dir. Cai Chusheng [蔡楚生], 1934), which in turn was based on the true story of Ai Xia (艾霞), a May Fourth Nora who had committed suicide in 1934. The sobering question Lu Xun (鲁迅) had asked in December 1923 in his talk at the Beijing Women's Normal College, "What happens after Nora leaves home?," and the tragic ending of the heroine in his story "Regret for the Past" (伤逝, 1925), a May Fourth new woman who withered away in a broken romantic relationship and died after returning to her patriarchal uncle's house—became all the more relevant for many young women in 1930s China. Wang's left-wing feminist position effectively steered her away from the fate of many other modern new women, who remained trapped in an emotionally conflicted and politically isolated modern female selfhood, or else in a bourgeois family that deprived them of a sense of historical agency in a rapidly changing China. The left-wing Nora of 1935, therefore, moved beyond and turned critical of May Fourth middle-class individualistic idealism. She symbolized instead a politically awakened new woman, who confronted a socioeconomic reality sustained by not only Confucian ethics but also a semicolonized capitalist structure, both of which imprisoned Chinese women in the family (traditional or modern) and collaborated in commodifying and victimizing women in commercialist mass media.

Second, the Nora of 1935 signified the rise of a particular kind of historical and political consciousness among young people. After Jiang's Nationalist Party violently turned against CCP members and organizations in the Shanghai massacre (April 12, 1927) and subsequently brutally suppressed female activists nationwide, it adopted an extremely conservative, repressive policy in building the central government. In 1934, Jiang's government promoted traditional female virtues in its New Life Movement. When staged in the mid-1930s by left-wing dramatists, Ibsen's play directly targeted what the Nanjing government represented: cultural traditionalism, political repression, corrupting capitalism, and treasonous collaboration with Western imperialism. In Wang Ping's case, while the father figure still played a domineering role in China in the 1930s, Wang's flight from both home and hometown was forced by the government's harassment and imprisonment of left-wing and communist artists and critics. By 1935, Ibsen's Nora had acquired not only cultural but, more importantly, (geo)political significance in local contexts. The May Fourth version of an independent woman walking out of her traditional father's house for romantic love underwent serious revision, and in her place emerged the left-wing new woman who was socially engaged, politically committed, and culturally active.

The post-Mao feminist critique of socialist culture in general, and Wang Ping specifically, as departing from "true female culture" as first manifested in May Fourth women's literature reveals its own blindness to the serious historical and theoretical limitations of May Fourth individualist, cultural feminism. Borrowing Western Enlightenment discourse, liberal individualism, and bourgeois sentimentalism, May Fourth urban feminism was largely removed from the political-economic conditions of then semicolonized and semifeudal China as well as its large (about 85 percent) rural population—despite its contribution to cultural radicalism and antitraditionalism. The deterioration of May Fourth cultural feminism in the mid- and late 1920s demonstrated that an elite, marginal cultural practice does not necessarily subvert the symbolic system or lead to substantial social and political changes. Nor could such a practice sustain itself when confronting socioeconomic reality and the return of a centralized, conservative political force in the late 1920s. To a large extent, May Fourth cultural feminism's separation of the "woman question" from China's sociopolitical environment led to its own demise in the turbulent history of modern China.

Wang Ping's central role in the "Nanjing Nora" incident irreversibly affected her life trajectory. It made her a firm left-wing activist throughout the 1930s and 1940s with a deeply integrated understanding of women's issues. In the fall of 1935, Wang left Jiangsu Province and, on her way to Shanxi, met Song Zhidi (宋之的, 1914–1956), a talented young left-wing playwright and, later, important left-wing drama-movement organizer—as well as Wang's own future husband. Wang continued her left-wing political and cultural engagement in Shanxi by playing the proletarian lead role in her first film, the new Northwest Film Company's *Endless Years* (无限生涯, 1935), and the working-class female lead in Song's stage drama *The Criminal* (罪犯). Class, gender, and political struggle occupied the center of the left-wing cultural movement at the time, and Wang actively expressed those ideas through her performance. The political climate in Shanxi quickly changed, however, and the local warlord, Yan Xishan (阎锡山), banned left-wing and procommunist films and plays. As a result, Wang's first film was not released, and the play was also effectively shut down after only two shows.

Wang was terribly disappointed by this unexpected career halt in Shanxi, but her life took another major turn when she and Song Zhidi fell in love. They married in the early spring of 1936, moved back to the Shanghai-Nanjing area, and soon thereafter Wang found herself pregnant. The next one to two years proved extremely hard for the couple. Song, who had been imprisoned twice by the Nationalist government before he met Wang, could not find a job in Shanghai due to the increasing "white terror" Jiang's government enforced, persecuting underground CCP and left-wing citizens. Wang's father, enraged by his daughter's decision to marry a non-Muslim man, forbade her siblings from lending any financial support to her. Struggling with severe poverty, Wang had to find odd jobs—mostly unwanted, minor roles on the stage and in films—but they were not enough to make the family's ends meet. Wang decided to quit her performing career in order to support Song's left-wing writing and their family. From 1936 to 1939, Wang gave birth to three children (one died in 1938, during the Second Sino-Japanese War).

During the period from 1936 to 1948, Wang could not pursue a career of her own due to the brutal white terror, the devastated financial situation of her family, and her new role as a mother. But she did not confine herself to her home or lose her sense of agency. On the contrary, she devoted more time to left-wing and antiwar movements by taking on various roles. In 1938, Song became a central leader of the first division of the Shanghai Antiwar Drama Troupe. Wang traveled with the troupe to Nanjing, Wuhan, and Shanxi, then on with Song to Chongqing and Hong Kong, performing antiwar plays on both street and stage. Wang was also essential in managing the whole troupe's daily business. In the last two years of this period, as the government's political suppression intensified, the CCP quickly arranged for Song to leave for a communist base area. Wang demonstrated enormous self-reliance, discipline, and courage by staying in Shanghai and taking care of her two children, while also working for the underground CCP organization. In 1947 and 1948, she participated in Shanghai film activities, playing supporting roles in such well-known left-wing films as *A Spring River Flows East* (一江春水向东流, 1947), *An Eight-Thousand-Li Road of Clouds and Moon* (八千里路云和月, 1947), *Myriads of Lights* (万家灯火, 1948), *Spring Scenery Can't Be Shut Up* (关不住的春光, 1948), and *Three Girls* (丽人行, 1949). A devoted wife and mother, Wang also made herself known as a dedicated left-wing activist exhibiting extraordinary talents for public organization, teamwork, and theatrical and cinematic performance.

Wang's life entered another phase when her safety in Shanghai became threatened, and toward the end of 1948 she had to leave for Shijiazhang, a liberated area, where she reunited with her husband. From 1948 to 1956, situated in a new sociopolitical environment, Wang was able not only to reconsider her own career but also to transform herself into the first Chinese female film director. In 1948, she taught performance courses at a college in Shijiazhuang, and in 1949 she tried to resume her acting career with the Northeast Film Studio. In 1950, Wang was transferred from the Northeast Film Studio to the PLA cultural system in Beijing, appointed as a vice director of the film production team, a position in which she began to thrive. In March 1951, she was recruited into a new team to help establish a military education film studio in the PLA system. Soon after, she was entrusted with making the studio's first film: *Hechuan Offensive*, a military education documentary. In 1953, she became a CCP member. From 1954 to 1956 she directed her first feature film, *Darkness before Dawn*.

Wang's transformation into a socialist director was accompanied by two unexpected emotional crises: one over gender and self-agency and the other over love and companionship. Both produced complicated personal ramifications as well as historical implications. The first came soon after she arrived in Shijiazhuang in 1948. After twelve years of devoted matrimony, Song suddenly informed Wang that before they two had met, he had already had a wife—through an arranged marriage—who had stayed with his parents in his rural home. Although he and his first wife had spent only a few days together, the union had produced a daughter. Song's family sent his daughter to him in 1948, so she could have a better education. Devastated, hurt, and enraged, Wang fought for a divorce despite Song's explanation and pleas to save their marriage, as well as the interventions of many of their friends and colleagues.

Arranged marriage was a central target of the May Fourth Movement, and by the late 1920s it had become widely accepted for younger generations to escape from or leave behind marriages arranged by their parents against their will. Song's story was therefore not unusual. Indeed, when Cheng Fangwu (成仿吾), the CCP cultural official in charge of Wang's working unit, tried to dissuade Wang from getting a divorce, he used exactly the May Fourth rhetoric against traditionalism and arranged marriage.[23] In hindsight, Wang's strong desire to divorce revealed a crisis in her sense of agency. Wang felt she had been blindfolded and duped into a situation of which she had thought herself the driving force. At a social level, her reaction also showcased a gendered critique of the commonly accepted love discourse and anti–arranged marriage practice in modern China. Whereas the May Fourth discourses generated enormous liberating effects for educated youth, both men and women, in their search for a modern individual subjectivity, they contained a gendered double standard. After all, individual liberation from an arranged marriage was enacted amid the silent sacrifice of many rural women—who had also been forced into arranged marriage and who often remained stuck in the traditional family, spending their lives serving their in-laws while their husbands lived with their young, urban, educated wives. Wang's initial insistence on divorce indicated her strong disapproval of Chinese men's practice of maintaining two marriages in the name of progressive modernity. In her conversation with Cheng Fangwu, Wang firmly stated that if she had known that Song had a wife, she would not have married him.[24] Wang's request for a divorce was, however, complicated by the fact that she became pregnant again. After all, Wang and Song had loved, supported, and been devoted to each other since they had met. Song's ceaseless effort to regain her trust and Wang's senior colleagues' interventions eventually convinced Wang to drop the idea of divorce.

Wang's career advancement in early socialist China helped restore her marriage, and her last child, Song Zhao, was conceived in 1954. Just as Wang finally got her personal, political, and professional life back together, however, another unexpected blow hit. On April 10, 1956, Song, who had been overworked throughout his left-wing years, was diagnosed with late-stage liver cancer, and seven days later he passed away. Wang had been busy working on her first feature from 1954 to 1956, and Song's sudden death completely devastated her. She was overwhelmed by guilt and suffered severe depression. For quite some time, Wang refused to work or leave her apartment.

Wang's two intense emotional experiences during this period illustrate how manifold and complicated Chinese women's gendered negotiations could be and how personal life was intimately tied to sociopolitical forces in modern China. The experiences Wang had to negotiate also help us understand the director's feminist stance and her decision to make *The Story of Liubao Village*, a film that highlights love, revolution, and the female self. The year 1956 was hard for Wang, yet, in retrospect, it was also the year her directing career really took off. She completed her first film, *Darkness before Dawn* and, more importantly, was ready to work on *The Story of Liubao Village*, which would establish her as an important and popular director in socialist China.

Wang's surviving her emotional trauma and her subsequent triumph as a successful film director would have been unimaginable without socialist institutionalized support. Socialist gender equality, public day care centers and boarding schools, and the state studio system provided key structural resources for Wang during her most difficult time. According to Song Zhao, during her mother's most depressed period, the two heads of the August First Liberation Army Film Studio, Chen Bo (陈播) and Hu Jiemin (胡介民), visited Wang at her home to offer support and to revive her passion and feeling of responsibility for her work. They physically put Wang into their car and drove her to the studio. Four months after losing her husband, Wang completed *Darkness before Dawn*.

Post-Mao feminist scholars have argued that socialist women's liberation in economic, social, and political realms prohibited women from becoming cultural subjects and expressing their true female difference. Quite to the contrary, socialist gender equality (as in Wang's case) was fundamental to enabling and sustaining women's cultural participation and production. It also empowered women like Wang Ping to actively and directly battle traditional, capitalist essentialization and/or naturalization of gender/sexual difference, re-presenting gender difference as sociopolitically configured and historically negotiated.[25] After all, the May Fourth women's articulation of a modern Westernized romantic individual subjectivity itself was a geopolitical event anchored in history rather than a manifestation of some universal essential female difference. Before the founding of socialist China, this individual cultural subjectivity was already critically transformed in left-wing cultural and political movements. Post-Mao feminist film scholars' search for an absolute, universal female difference and subjectivity, therefore, has not only once again detached gender from its political and historical configurations but also ignored important transformations of gender in modern China.

If Wang Ping was a socialist Hua Mulan, this Hua Mulan did not model herself on traditional men or any transhistorical male figure, as post-Mao feminist scholars have suggested. As a matter of fact, in socialist China both men and women were transformed, and both men and women were called on to demolish gender- and class-based hierarchies to build an egalitarian society. The assertion or assumption that there is a universal, unchanging patriarchal male standard reveals another layer of the post-Mao feminist essentialist stance. Although certain gender issues and historical limitations of socialist feminism still existed, they did not result from the socialist institutionalization of gender equality or the socialist advancement of women's economic and social status.

Wang Ping's successful filmmaking career continued until the outbreak of the Cultural Revolution in 1966, when she was publicly denounced like many other filmmakers. Wang was detained for half a year from 1968 to 1969, then in October of 1969 was sent to rural Shanxi with other filmmakers from the August First Liberation Army Studio to work in the countryside. In 1972 socialist feature film production resumed,[26] and in 1973 Wang was asked to step in to direct *Sparkling Red Star* (闪闪的红星). The film "became a huge hit with Chinese of all ages."[27] In 1978, at the age of sixty-two, Wang was appointed vice director of the August First Liberation Army Film Studio, and she remained in this position until the early 1980s. She made three additional films in the 1980s. In 1990 Wang died of liver cancer, the disease that had taken her husband's life thirty-five years earlier.

From Chinese Nora in the spotlight to left-wing activist off stage, wife and mother to socialist film director, and then political victim to rehabilitated veteran filmmaker, Wang's life was full of individual and political negotiations. Wang's transformation into the first female director in early socialist China, and a successful one at that, involved three indispensable factors. First, Wang's life experiences, closely tied to the historical and political movements in modern Chinese history, operated as pivotal personal touchstones for her articulations of revolutionary ideals and aesthetics in socialist cinema. Her political vision, feminist commitment, and sense of self-agency, all developed during her left-wing years, played a fundamental role. Second, her extensive cultural experiences in left-wing, proletarian, and antiwar drama and film movements during the 1930s and 1940s greatly assisted her in addressing socialist demands for a mass-oriented mainstream cinema with a modern national and revolutionary aesthetic. Last and perhaps most significantly, the institutional implementation of gender equality in all areas, the collectivization of the film industry, and the formation of proletarian mainstream cinema offered key support and inspiration for women like Wang to transform themselves into new socialist filmmakers. Wang's gender, political-cultural engagement, and integrated sense of self were forged during the left-wing and Sino-Japanese War periods, then further strengthened and transformed in the early socialist period. These factors contributed to her authorial articulation of ideas in ways that ultimately diversified socialist mainstream cinema and contributed to the multilevel significance of her films.

The Story of Liubao Village: A Revolutionary Tale, an Intellectual Love Discourse, and the Emergence of the Proletarian Female Self

The first generation of female film directors, witnessing the radical changes in women's political, social, and cultural status, as well as their public representation, all enthusiastically embraced the new system and actively engaged in articulating, via mainstream cinema, a socialist feminist vision and a dynamic new relationship between the female self and the socialist environment. At the same time, as the first generation of socialist film directors, these women also seriously took up the charge of building a national cinema that would represent the new China, create new socialist subjects, and target a new mass audience with socialist ideals and a revolutionary aesthetic. Several of Wang Ping's films charted previously unexplored thematic and artistic territories. *The Story of Liubao Village*, for instance, was the first socialist film to center on romantic love during the revolutionary war period and created a Chinese poetic folk style; *The Everlasting Radio Signals* was the first to combine a communist spy film with a character- and hero-centered drama; *The Land Rich in Beauty* (江山多娇, 1959) was the first to portray "iron girl" (铁姑娘) characters (model young women in the socialist construction of rural China) on the silver screen; and *East Is Red* was the first epic film production of staged music-and-dance performances in modern China. Wang's reputation soared in the 1960s after she made *Locust Tree Village* and *Sentinels under the Neon Lights*, both of which focus on the theme of permanent revolution in rural and urban settings, respectively, in the era after 1949. *Locust Tree Village*, with its historic-epic style and unprecedented central characterization of a rural grandmother, won Wang the Hundred Flower Film Festival's Best Director award for 1962.

In this section, I focus on *The Story of Liubao Village*, one of the most popular films in China under Mao, to further explore the following topics: socialist collaborative cinematic authorship, the diverse nature and multilevel signification of socialist mainstream films, and integrated feminist cultural practice and embedded female agency. The film does not center on gender or feature a model female figure as some of Wang's other films do, but it best illustrates the pervasiveness of socialist feminist culture in the China of the 1950s. Indeed, the popularity and ubiquity of socialist feminist culture manifested in not only films with female heroes but also those like *The Story of Liubao Village*, where a young peasant woman's personal strength and individual agency, although minor themes, are unequivocally expressed.

Wang based *The Story of Liubao Village* on Hu Shiyan's (胡石言) story published in *Literature and Art* (文艺) in March 1950. Huang Zongjiang (黄宗江), a left-wing and antiwar drama activist, was asked by his superior to produce a screenplay of the story together with Hu. Although Huang and Hu produced several drafts, none were initially approved. Huang and Hu were especially preoccupied with how to represent romantic love—a deemphasized topic in the early socialist era—in a revolutionary war film. The tension and potential conflict between individual interest and the revolutionary cause, especially in the military, made for risky negotiations. Whereas the written story employs a subjective perspective, first-person narrator, and internal monologues to alleviate this tension, a big-screen adaptation, presented directly to a mass audience, would generate quite different effects.

Indeed, the experimental nature of socialist cinema involved dynamic interactions among political, cultural, and individual forces.[28] From 1949 to 1956, socialist film policy experienced alternating periods of tightening and relaxation. As the culmination of a series of changes in cultural policy, the Hundred Flowers Campaign of 1956 enabled greater artistic control, contributing to a new pinnacle in socialist filmmaking. The screenplay of *The Story of Liubao Village* finally won approval toward the end of 1956. In early 1957, the August First Liberation Army Film Studio decided to shoot the film and assigned Wang, upon her request, as the director. Wang endorsed the screenplay and, showing her support for the two writers, invited them to work with her on the shooting script. The film's success certainly resulted from collaboration between Wang, Huang, and Hu, whose similar backgrounds hint at why they worked with one another so successfully. All three came from the Jiangnan/Jiangbei area, where the story takes place. They all lived in Shanghai in the 1930s or 1940s and participated in left-wing and antiwar movements. All three joined the communist army later, working as writers and directors. Their shared left-wing intellectual backgrounds, related life experiences, and communist revolutionary credentials compelled them to emphasize both the importance of individual "emotions" or "feelings" (情感) and the proletarian class revolution. Rather than viewing love and revolution as incompatible or conflicting, they strove to represent individual love and class revolution as interconnected goals. The public discourse on romantic love had been marginalized in early socialist China, especially in cinema, because of romance's alleged ties to Western individualism and bourgeois sensibilities.[29] Hu, Huang, and Wang questioned this general dismissal of individual emotions and successfully reclaimed romantic love by reconfiguring its relationship to communist revolution and the working class in socialist cinema. The filmmakers' joint efforts made the film a popular hit and ultimately a socialist classic, but closer examination reveals that Wang, Huang, and Hu each contributed to the film in particular ways, sometimes complementary and other times contrary.

Hu's contributions to early socialist literature and art, in addition to the major theme of romantic love and revolution, centered on his articulation of the emotional bond between revolutionary soldiers. The original story germinated from his memory of Xu Jincheng (徐金成), a young deputy squad leader in the New Fourth Army, who died in battle against the Japanese after secretly confiding to Hu that he was in love with a girl from Baoying. During their conversation, Xu confessed he had considered leaving the army to work in Baoying but remained proud of himself for fighting the Japanese and felt he had made the right decision. Hu could not forget the young soldier, especially when he learned of Baoying's liberation in 1949, and also wondered about the girl left behind. Hu wrote: "People know that all revolutions demand life sacrifice, but not many know that revolution also demanded in the past the sacrifice of love. The latter could be more difficult to accomplish."[30] Originally, Hu considered having his protagonist, Li Jin, killed in battle just as Xu had been but admitted he could not accept such a sad ending. Instead, Hu's young lovers reunite in 1949 when the army passes by Liubao again, on the way to liberate the entire country.

The significance of Hu's story, however, goes beyond its central theme of heterosexual love and revolution. *The Story of Liubao Village* is told via first-person narrator Song Wei, whose status is historically identical to the author's. As the narrative unfolds, the strong emotional bond between the central character, Li Jin, and the narrator, Song Wei, who is Li's political superior in the story, strikes readers. The romantic relationship between Li

Jin and Er meizi (Second younger sister, 二妹子), which occupies the heart of Li and Song's communications, also enhances a mutual understanding and identification between Song and Li. In other words, despite the heterosexual love plot, *The Story of Liubao Village* hinges on an interpersonal and emotional attachment, a comradeship, between men. After all, the story is created by one man's unfading memory of another man as well as his bemoaning the loss of the other man's life. The narrative devices of first-person narrator and subjective flashbacks both enhance the sentimental effect of the story, pronouncing a distinctive homoemotional relationship.

Huang and Hu's screenplay,[31] a product of multilevel negotiations, alters the original story in several ways. Most significantly, the coauthors reconfigured the subjective first-person narrator and revised the emotional bond between Song Wei and Li Jin. Because the medium of film does not easily allow for internal monologues and exclusive first-person narration, and because socialist cinema's proletarian-masses demographic demanded a more direct style, the two writers toned down Song's intellectual tendency toward self-reflection and replaced it with more action in the screenplay. As the film script received several rounds of commentary from colleagues and cadres at the film studio, the screenwriters also modified their script based on those suggestions. In the case of Song Wei, they eliminated some ambivalent internal thoughts and sentimental remarks.

However, both Huang and Hu seemed deeply attached to the emotive nature of the original story and the intimate bond between Song Wei and Li Jin (fig. 2.1). Despite their significant modifications to Song Wei's role, they maintained him as the film's primary narrative anchor for cinematic flashbacks and voice-overs. As a result, many of the love story's central scenes take place outside Song's area of knowledge or in his physical absence. Song's anchoring role thus became technically flawed. This technical limitation and narrative incoherence reveal the screenwriters' insistence on certain styles, while also juggling a particular official demand.

In the screenplay, Huang and Hu also successfully transformed the romantic love plot into direct cinematic presentation. As the romance is foregrounded, Er meizi, who was mediated in the original story via Li Jin's and Song Wei's narratives, is ushered onto center stage. Like Li and Song, Er meizi presents herself directly to the camera and audience. However, compared to Song and Li, whose extensive dialogues illustrate Li's emotional and inner struggles, Er meizi's character lacks psychological depth in the screenplay. Her emotions and inner thoughts are merely hinted at and sometimes still only mediated through Li.

2.1 Song Wei closely listens to Li Jin's plan for the future. *The Story of Liubao Village* (柳堡的故事), directed by Wang Ping, 1957.

When Wang took over the film project in 1956, the screenplay had been officially approved, and the central theme, narrative structure, and major characters finalized. Wang's individual authorship, therefore, should be measured not by the story's overall plot but by her specific approach to socialist film, her deployment of cinematic expressions to enhance or revise the projected vision of the screenplay, and her visual (re)presentations of central characters. As a revolutionary female film director in early socialist China, a seasoned left-wing intellectual artist with a strong political consciousness and sense of agency, and a woman from the region highlighted in the film, Wang strove to accomplish multiple goals in her filmmaking. Gender, although an important focus of Wang's adaptation, is not set apart from other ideas expressed in the film. Wang's major contributions to *The Story of Liubao Village* are fourfold: her cinematic endorsement of an intellectual discourse on emotion and revolution, her creation of a new national cinematic style and form, her construction of a proletarian mass audience, and her gendered negotiations in re-presenting the female lead in the process of film adaptation.

Most Chinese discussions praise the "feminine" and poetic style of *The Story of Liubao Village*, attributing this aesthetic to Wang's being a woman.[32] While the characterization of the film's style is accurate, the direct connection of poetic style to the author's gender is highly problematic. Such generalizations elide Wang's specific choices in making this particular film while simultaneously overlooking her talent across a variety of film styles over her career. None of Wang's other films can be characterized as "feminine" in style. If we closely compare the story, the screenplay, and the film, it is not difficult to determine that this feminine style actually originates in *Hu's* story, which concentrates on an intellectual revolutionary's subjective views on emotional bonds, love, and revolution. Unlike other stories of the period, which stress masculine heroism on the battleground and matters of life and death, Hu's story leaves military battles in the background, highlighting instead emotional and intersubjective relationships. Furthermore, the first-person narrator, though a political superior in the army, expresses sentiment and uncertainty usually characterized as feminine in relation to the prevalent heroic revolutionary discourse of the time.

Wang generally followed the screenplay's plot but actively and creatively intervened when it came to cinematic style and expression. In her "Director's Notes," Wang describes her stylistic goal for the film as "a beautiful poem," endorsing the sentimental structure of the original story.[33] Wang's directorial choices also illustrate her confidence in using cinematic language to convey a visual and auditory mood best suited for the emotive nature of the original story. Yet Wang's poetic, "feminine," aesthetic ventures beyond the story's original intellectual sentiment. She creatively expanded the poetic scale to include visual compositions of Jiangnan rural scenery, folk music and culture, and the voices and facial expressions of proletarian figures. Many scenes, especially repeated shots of scenery from the first several images of the film, particularly accentuate the Jiangnan-Jiangbei area's poetic prospect: white clouds, clear rivers, weeping willows, wooden bridges, small boats, scattered cottages, and windmills in the water-filled rice fields (figs. 2.2 and 2.3). The cinematic configuration of this landscape pronounces a visual style reminiscent of classical Chinese painting and poetry. Music plays an equal, if not more important, role in articulating the film's poetic sentiment. Many have argued that this film's great popularity results partially from its folk love song, "Sunny Days of September" (九九艳阳天), which plays four times throughout the film, dividing the film narrative into stanzas and punctuating the development of Li Jin and Er meizi's relationship.

2.2 Poetic shot of scenery in the Jiangnan area (1). *The Story of Liubao Village* (柳堡的故事), directed by Wang Ping, 1957.

2.3 Poetic shot of scenery in the Jiangnan area (2). *The Story of Liubao Village* (柳堡的故事), directed by Wang Ping, 1957.

As they sing, the young lovers express their personal feelings and become important emotional narrative ballasts. Indeed, the film's aesthetic demonstrates Wang's unusual talent, as a devoted revolutionary artist, for incorporating national traditions that would reach a mass audience. She was unique in creating a Chinese cinematic style that combines classic poetic imagery with folk music and lyrics, integrating intellectual, individual sentiments with the emotions of the (soldier and peasant) masses.

Wang's other significant revision centers on Er meizi's character. In the film, the young woman's story stays true to the original work and the screenplay, but her (re)presentation and function show subtle yet important differences. As Hu's original story focuses on male revolutionary comradeship, Er meizi is entirely mediated through Li's, Song's, and even her younger brother's subjective perspectives and narratives. Readers come to know bits and pieces about her, but only through other characters. Two-thirds into the story, Li Jin reports to the whole squad that the local bully Liu huzi (Liu beard), who collaborates with the Japanese, has mistreated Er meizi, forcing Er meizi to marry him after the death of his wife (Er meizi's older sister). The report functions mostly to show Li's awakening about cruel social reality and thus helps discipline his personal emotions and desires. At the same time, the revelation of Er meizi's experience also incites the soldiers' determination to save her, granting the New Fourth Army the exclusive role of political agent and savior.

In the published screenplay, partially due to both the demands of the film medium and the public promotion of gender equality in the early 1950s, Er meizi becomes more visible and plays a more active role in her relationship with Li. She searches for solutions to her problems rather than simply responding to Li's questions. In the scene where Li and Er meizi are alone together, it is Er meizi who asks about the war and female soldiers. When she learns women and men are treated equally in the New Fourth Army, she quickly expresses her eagerness to join. Despite these revisions, Er meizi's psychological ground remains underdeveloped. She shows no particular interest in the army prior to this scene but soon afterward, when she (mistakenly) believes the army is leaving the village, she asks her younger brother to find out whether the army gives soldiers permission to marry. Does she want to join the army to escape her sad fate? Has she fallen in love with Li and wishes to marry him? Or does she simply want to leave the village by any available means? Compared to Li and Song, who still function as the main emotive anchors and narrators in the screenplay, Er meizi's thoughts and feelings are less apparent. Perhaps because Li's story constitutes the main line of the narrative, such inconsistencies in this secondary female character did not bother the two screenwriters.

In the film, Wang effectively recasts the role of Er meizi not through plot changes but by making palpable the internal logic of her actions and emotions, particularly through Tao Yuling's performance. Wang devoted an entire section of her "Director's Notes" to "analyses of characters and their mutual relationships."[34] She wrote a long paragraph on Er meizi, succinctly delineating her character, her background, her relationships to her father, younger brother, and Li Jin, and, most importantly, the logic behind her decision making. From Wang's sketches, Er meizi, a girl from a poor peasant family who had lost her mother when she was a child, grows into a capable, strong young woman who loves her family but has no intention of taking after her weak, submissive father. She is fully aware of Liu huzi's power yet would rather die than follow her elder sister's example by marrying him. Despite her desperation, Er meizi actively seeks ways to solve her problems. Consequently, when she witnesses what the New Fourth Army soldiers have done to help her family, including how they protect the village by fending off assaults by local Japanese-backed troops, she begins to hope for change. According to Hu Shiyan, Wang Ping added several episodes about Er meizi in the early part of the film to show her growing trust in the army and her attentive responses to their needs.[35] These additional scenes, correcting Er meizi's lack of psychological depth and inconsistent agency in the screenplay, build an important psychological and emotional foundation for Er meizi's actions as the film progresses to the central scene when Li and Er meizi engage in conversation for the first time. In previous versions, Li's motivation for meeting Er meizi is clear, but Er meizi's intentions remain ambiguous. One of Wang's crucial revisions is her illustration that even though the heroine's strong desire to approach Li matches his to approach her, the nature of their desires is different.

Wang, in her analysis of act 5, titled "Love with Admiration," first differentiates Er meizi's feelings of love from those of Li. While Li's love for Er meizi is oriented to Er meizi as an individual, her love for Li comes from her love for the army in general. In a discussion of the scene where Li and Er meizi converse, Wang particularly emphasizes the differences in their desires and motivations for meeting. Li Jin loves Er meizi and is attracted to her, but Er meizi approaches Li because she wants to know more about the New Fourth Army and the possibility of joining. She might have some embryonic feelings of love, but they are kept at an unconscious level. Thus, when Ma Xiaobao rushes suddenly into the room, Er meizi feels shy but not embarrassed, because she is, in Wang's words, "hugely burdened by her

2.4 Er meizi is concerned about her own fate as she first approaches Li Jin. *The Story of Liubao Village* (柳堡的故事), directed by Wang Ping, 1957.

own problems and has no intention of even considering love. Her thoughts completely center on how to save herself."[36] Er meizi's concern, "how to save herself," remains only vaguely implied in the first two versions of the narrative but becomes her primary psychological motivation and the central theme of her story in Wang's film (fig 2.4).

Of the eighteen acts Wang discusses in her director's notes, five center on Er meizi, highlighting her personal agency and her determination to seek help from Li Jin and the army. Wang's summaries for acts 7, 9, and 10 begin with Er meizi as active initiator: Er meizi asks Xiao niu (Little bull), her younger brother to seek information from Song Wei; Er meizi asks Xiao niu to meet with Li Jin; Er meizi confronts Li directly after he refuses her previous proposal. Whereas Li distances himself from Er meizi as he struggles to prioritize the revolutionary cause and army discipline over personal emotions, Er meizi bravely steps out of an ordinary young peasant girl's role to initiate meetings with Li. Wang's analysis of Er meizi's character underscores how the young woman understands the New Fourth Army as the only hope for herself and her family and therefore feels compelled to explain her situation to Li in person. Until obtaining her personal freedom, Er meizi does not reveal her feelings toward Li. To enhance the coherent character of Er meizi, Wang removed Er meizi's inquiry regarding the army's marriage policy from the screenplay version.

Adhering to the socialist demand of a new, national, mass-oriented cinema—and to the left-wing intellectual sentiment that valorizes individual emotions—Wang nevertheless articulates a nonsentimental and gendered discourse in the film, which stresses a young peasant woman's agency in self-salvation and self-fulfillment. Her detailed descriptions of Er meizi's character provided solid psychological ground from which Tao Yuling (陶玉玲) could craft her performance. The film succeeds in representing a new kind of young proletarian woman: down-to-earth, resilient, and self-reliant.

Wang's own experience as a young woman from the same region as the film's setting and her strong sense of self-agency and political consciousness mattered greatly in the adaptation process. Her revisions significantly strengthened the female character's self-consciousness, diversifying the representation of proletarian women in socialist cinema. In other canonical socialist films, such as *The White-Haired Girl* (白毛女, dir. Wang Bin [王滨] and Shui Hua [水华], 1950), set in a Shaanxi village, or *The Red Detachment of Women* (红色娘子军, dir. Xie Jin [谢晋], 1961), set on Hainan Island, peasant women's prerevolutionary selfhood is defined largely by their victimization, and their prerevolutionary agency is signified by the traditional discourse of "family revenge" (报仇). In *The Story of Liubao Village*, Wang Ping articulates a different female peasant figure in preliberation Jiangnan, whose self-saving initiative and conscious effort play an equal (if not more important) role as the revolutionary force in transforming her future. This important difference in the representation of a rural woman in socialist cinema has been (dis)missed by previous scholarly works, which tend to hold a monolithic view of socialist mainstream culture.[37]

Conclusion

The close reexamination of Wang's life, particularly her role in the filmmaking process for *The Story of Liubao Village*, reveals several critical insights concerning socialist feminism, feminist culture, and socialist cinematic authorship in the China of the 1950s. First, mainstream and institutionalized socialist feminism and the subsequent formation of a proletarian public space not only ushered in the first generation of female directors in mainland China but also gave rise to a popular and diverse socialist feminist culture that battled patriarchal traditions and ideas and helped construct new socialist female subjects. Proletarian women, including revolutionary intellectuals, dominated the silver screen, and more importantly, their routes to revolution, their psychological and emotional underpinnings, and their senses of agency were all represented differently.

Second, and more pertinent to transnational feminist cinema, this study of the first mainstream female director in socialist China also challenges the universalized and persistent assumption that feminist cinema occupies only a counter-, minor, marginalized, or independent position regardless of its specific geopolitical and sociopolitical contexts. Socialist mainstream cinema contained a distinctive feminist structure, dedicating itself to gender equality and socialist feminist causes—even though historical limitations and individual artists' blind spots are evident in some films. To dismiss socialist female directors' contributions to the production of feminist culture because they conformed to mainstream political and artistic ideologies betrays a dogmatic ignorance of different political and economic structures, as well as a hypocritical naïveté that willfully denies the intrinsic interconnection between all feminist practices and their particular political and economic systems. Indeed, conformity is a complex concept that underlies the very possibility of political and artistic actions.[38] As I argue in the next chapter, socialist female directors' conformities neither exhaust nor cement the meaning of their artistic practices, nor do they prevent critiques of the system's extant problems.

Finally, socialist cinematic authorship is a collaborative and contingent concept. The political and pedagogical demands of socialist cinema required team efforts, but the varied life experiences of early socialist filmmakers brought different ideas and recourses into the dynamic filmmaking process. Furthermore, the highly experimental nature of film production in the 1950s mobilized writers and filmmakers to explore different visions and versions of revolution, emotions, class, and gender. Thanks to Chinese socialist filmmaking's extensive records—including regular publications of director's notes; the availability of different versions of each story; biographies and autobiographies; interviews; and memoirs—individual artists' negotiations and experiments become palpable. The final version of *The Story of Liubao Village* bears its three filmmakers' strongly individual and shared negotiations; the film's authorship is clearly contingent on, as well as embedded in, their dynamic and experimental collaboration.

Zooming in on socialist women filmmakers, we find their gendered experience and negotiations exhibit another layer of embeddedness. As Wang Ping's life story illustrates, women in socialist China did not form a singular or essential identity; nor did they experience historical transformations exclusively through a unified, "standard" woman's perspective. As integrated socialist feminism championed and embodied multidimensional agency, Chinese women brought with them different historical resources in forging multiple political, social, and professional positions in history. As I have illustrated, by the time Wang was directing *The Story of Liubao Village*, she was all at once a socialist and revolutionary filmmaker in the August First Liberation Army Film Studio, a well-educated intellectual strongly affiliated with left-wing drama and film movements of the 1930s and 1940s, a socialist feminist who promoted women's self-reliance as an integrated part of socialist revolution and construction, and one of the first Chinese women to rely on socialist institutionalized gender equality through childcare and the public school system in order to pursue her career. These positions did not always coalesce into a harmonious whole; negotiations and adjustments were constant. Even with gender being a central concern for Wang, it remained a deeply embedded and complex factor in her life and work that demands examination at the intersections of multiple historical forces in modern China. The female agency and feminist articulations in *The Story of Liubao Village*, as a result, must be understood through Wang's contingent negotiations among multiple yet related practices—that is, her active response to the socialist state's call for a new revolutionary cinema with a Chinese aesthetic that would reach the masses; her endorsement and enrichment of a left-wing intellectual discourse on emotion, love, and intersubjective bonding; and her critical revisions of the female character, articulating an active, proletarian, female self.

3 Socialist Experimentalism, Critical Revision, and Gender Difference

Dong Kena's *Small Grass Grows on the Kunlun Mountains* (1962)

One of the main arguments made by 1980s American feminist scholars about Chinese socialism and women's liberation centers on the betrayal, postponement, or incompleteness of Chinese women's liberation in socialist revolution.[1] This argument not only assumes a universal—Western liberal and radical feminist—standard for women's liberation across geopolitical regions and political-economic systems but also insists on the separation or independence of gender from other sociopolitical issues. The demand that gender should always occupy the center and socialist revolution should ultimately resolve all women's issues as defined in liberal and radical feminist terms reveals Western feminisms' blindness to their own constrained positions in the Cold War–affected capitalist system and to their ignorant denial of the complex entanglement of gender, socioeconomic structures, and geopolitics in history.

It is true that women's issues did not always exclusively occupy the center in Mao's socialist period, but socialist gender equality was a central component of the sociocultural structure, present and implicated in all socialist practices. As Wang Ping's making of *The Story of Liubao Village* illustrated, socialist feminist cultural practice made gender equality an aesthetic convention so that even in a film where women's emancipation and gender issues are not central focuses, a young peasant woman's suffering, desire, and agency are substantially articulated as essential components of the socialist revolution. It is also true that socialist feminism encountered setbacks in socialist China, but so did socialist development. China's overall development in the 1950s and early 1960s did not proceed in a stable or linear manner due to the severe Cold War constraints on the country's economic development, the scarcity of domestic resources available for economic and social advancement after a century of Western economic colonialism, military threats and occupations, civil wars, and the deteriorating relationship between China and the Soviet Union that led to their formal split in 1961. In addition, newly emerging contradictions and issues in socialist construction, such as the relationship between economic advancement and egalitarian social relations, as well as internal divisions and mistakes manifested in the process of the CCP's policy making, also posed historic challenges to the smooth continuation of socialist revolution and modernization. Internationally conditioned and historically situated, Chinese socialist feminism could not transcend history, moving forward all by itself when other geopolitical and sociopolitical issues persisted.[2] Chinese socialist feminist practice once again demonstrated that women's liberation was a complicated process and could not be achieved alone or independently. To impose a universal liberal and radical feminist standard when discussing Chinese socialist women's liberation, therefore, significantly distorts the historical condition and political aim of socialist feminism. More critically, it erases the fundamental achievements and alternative vision of Chinese socialist feminism in history.

This logic of both applying a universal measurement and canceling out what socialist feminism accomplished also underpins Chinese feminist film studies in the late 1980s and 1990s. Influenced by post-second-wave Western feminist practices, including liberal, radical, and cine-feminisms, and implicated in the search for a universal and market modernity, post-Mao feminist film scholars studying Chinese women's cinema deliberately searched for a politically antagonistic (meaning independent), essentially female (separated), and artistically marginalized (antimainstream) practice. They became particularly critical of socialist women's cinema, charging socialist female directors with blind conformism to state policy and male standards and maligning their films as mainstream practice and political propaganda.[3] The Western Cold War ideology that pits socialist political culture against artistic merits has also been reinforced in post-Mao feminist research on socialist women's cinema. These critical charges have not simply endorsed certain Western feminist ideas outside their own contexts but also turned a blind eye to the diverse experimental aesthetics and alternative feminist imaginations articulated in socialist women's cinema.

This chapter turns to another socialist female director, Dong Kena (董克娜, 1930–2016), and her popular 1962 film, *Small Grass Grows on the Kunlun Mountains* (昆仑山上一棵草; *Small Grass* hereafter), particularly its reflective, aesthetic, and gendered dimensions, to further illustrate what Chinese socialist women's cinema has accomplished. To foreground these aspects of Dong's film is not, however, to prove the presence of certain universal features of women's cinema, which Chinese feminist scholars and international scholars of China since the late 1980s have claimed absent from Chinese socialist films. Rather, it is to interrogate the Cold War–conditioned political-versus-artistic paradigm underpinning most scholarly research on socialist culture, challenge the Western radical feminist reassertion of individualist and independent nature of women's liberation, and question the cine-feminist definition of women's or feminist cinema as counter-, marginalized, or minor film practice. The artistic features and formal styles of Dong's film bear close similarities to post-Mao and Western women's experimental cinema, but Dong deployed them in her socialist mainstream film practice to convey a revolutionary imaginary, address a proletarian mass audience, and produce a socialist aesthetic. Dong's film practice defies the extant Cold War and feminist frameworks universalized to measure women's cultural practices across geopolitical locations and socioeconomic systems and thus provides us a unique opportunity to critically reassess and rehistoricize a set of important concepts, such as conformity, individual creativity, gender or sexual difference, and experimental cinema, charting their alternative significations in a different geopolitical and socioeconomic context.

From Short Story to Film: Socialist Pedagogical Cultural Practice

Small Grass is based on Wang Zongyuan's (王宗元) short story "Hui Sao" (惠嫂, Brother Hui's wife), published in the *People's Daily* in 1961; its film adaptation was assigned to Dong by the head of the Beijing Film Studio, Wang Yang (汪洋), in August of the same year. Although Dong had obtained some experience by the early 1960s as an assistant director, this was the first film she directed independently. When released in 1962, the film (black-and-white, sixty-two minutes) received critical acclaim and became an instant hit among young audiences. The image and life of the Kunlun grass in the film articulated a new, hardworking spirit called for during a period in which China was undergoing huge economic setbacks, international isolation, and natural disasters. The film influenced many young people of the time, encouraging them to confront the difficult conditions of their nation and devote their lives and learning to build a strong socialist environment. The film also inspired audiences at the time to critically engage with emerging sociopolitical issues, consolidate the egalitarian social relationship and the proletarian community, and diversify sociocultural imaginations.

The film mostly follows the original short story's plot line. It tells of Li Wanli, a seventeen-year-old Shanghai woman who, upon graduation from a geological college, enthusiastically volunteers to go to the Qinghai-Tibet Plateau to work but on the way becomes disillusioned by the desolate reality of the mountainous areas. As she hesitates, deciding whether to return to Shanghai, she meets a peasant woman addressed by people as Hui sao (Brother Hui's wife) at the Kunlun mountain pass. Hui sao is a model figure who originally moved there to reunite with her husband and later built a homelike dormitory, Drivers' Home (司机之家), to house the long-distance drivers traversing the plateau day and night. After listening to Hui sao's narration of how she overcame her own disillusionment and found meaning in her life by serving those heroic drivers, Li is enlightened and decides to learn from Hui sao and devote herself to transforming the area.

The film reinscribes mainstream tropes developed in socialist literature and film on several levels. First, it is an educational film, in which an apprentice character learns from a model figure and grows to become a socialist or revolutionary subject.[4] In the Chinese context, the social roles of apprentice characters vary, and the degree of apprenticeship also depends on the political and cinematic position of the characters in the film. A general rule, however, is that when literature or film depicts intellectuals or those who are not party members in relation to the working class (workers, peasants, soldiers) or members of the CCP, they are often put in the position of apprentice and witness.[5] The relationships between Li and Hui sao, and between Hui sao (who is not a Communist Party member) and her husband (a committed Communist Party member), follow the typical apprenticeship structure.

Second, the director employs a common flashback device used in socialist films, in which either heroic or bitter stories of the past are told to educate and enlighten as well as to reveal information to characters in the film and to its audience. According to Chris Berry, "In this trope, memory is not just personal, but part of a collective process of learning from experience."[6] *Small Grass* contains more than one such flashback narratives: the second flashback, which is also the major one, is narrated and anchored by Hui sao and addressed to the targeted listener, Li; the third flashback, situated *within*

Hui sao's flashback, is narrated by her husband to his targeted listener, Hui sao. Both flashback narratives function to enlighten the targeted listeners in the film. Third, the film ends on a politically satisfactory and personally uplifting note: Li is significantly transformed, moving happily forward to her new job.

There is little dispute that Dong's *Small Grass*, like the original short story on which it is based, belongs to mainstream socialist culture and has a visible pedagogical goal embedded in its narrative. As I discussed in chapter 1, film production was reconfigured in socialist China as an important part of the pedagogical apparatus, and its primary function was to promote the socialist vision, construct new proletarian subject positions, and educate as well as entertain the masses. However, socialist cinema's pedagogical role does not preclude artistic creativity and critical reflections. On the contrary, as socialist film practice was often positioned at the forefront of various national, political, and aesthetic debates, it best manifested the experimental nature of socialist culture in its continued explorations of a socialist imaginary and artistic expression.[7]

Dong, in her film adaptation of "Hui Sao," creatively experiments with first-person voice-over, subjective camera, and multiple flashback narratives to articulate different individuals' critical reflections, gendered concerns, and personal transformations. These devices generate multiple critical discourses that, contrary to prevailing arguments in the study of socialist films,[8] are sustained throughout the film and do not really "subordinate" themselves to a singular or dominant topic. Nor do they form any antagonistic or "independent" consciousness in relation to socialist mainstream ideas. Instead, the critical and subjective engagements in Dong's film function to diversify and advance socialist sociocultural development rather than undermine it. Indeed, the logic and significance of cinematic experimentalism, critical intervention, and gender difference are differently configured in Chinese socialist cultural practice and thus require a different research framework to approach them.

Female Voice-Overs and Narrative Flashbacks: Cinematic Experiments and Critical Interventions

Jin Fenglan (靳凤兰), in her book on Dong Kena's life and films,[9] lists the cinematic devices Dong deploys in *Small Grass*: subjective camera, female voice-overs and voice-offs, flashbacks, and long takes. The sustained use of subjective camera throughout the film, as Jin indicates, was a rare case in socialist films. Although directors in socialist filmmaking employed subjective devices and techniques, such as flashbacks and a woman's voice-over to frame their film narratives,[10] rarely did they adhere to these subjective narrative devices throughout their films. In fact, not until the early 1980s were subjective camera and narrative structure heavily deployed in films by female directors. Wei Shiyu (魏时煜, S. Louisa Wei), in her article on historical changes in Chinese women's images in film and women's cinema, points out that Dong's *Small Grass*, rather than any films made by female directors in the 1980s, should be considered the first piece of Chinese women's cinema.[11] Although I do not endorse Wei's concept of women's cinema—which refers only to those women's films with subjective cinematic devices and female perspectives, excluding films with Chinese folk and popular styles and revolutionary realist aesthetics (such as those by Wang Ping)—Wei nonetheless reveals the aesthetic diversity in socialist film practice, making an important connection between Mao-era and post-Mao women's cinema. Indeed, as I illustrate in chapter 6, such post-Mao female directors as Zhang Nuanxin, who initiated subjective experimental cinema in 1980, were exposed to European experimental cinema in Mao's China during the late 1950s and early 1960s.

Small Grass is highly experimental in its temporal arrangement as well. Instead of moving in a linear fashion, it uniquely deploys several levels of flashback, generating many regressions, suspensions, and repetitions. Until its very end, the film produces the effect of moving backward, as flashbacks within flashbacks continuously defer the force that functions in the original story to push the story forward—the political and symbolic signifier of the small grass. Although the small grass finally comes into view in Lao Hui's (Hui sao's husband, who is addressed by people in the film as Old Hui) flashback—itself framed within Hui sao's flashback—the small grass has enormous difficulty reversing layers of regressive moves and thus becomes less determined in its designated political function. By modifying the role of the small grass, the film opens up space for other imaginaries to transform Hui sao and Li Wanli toward the end.

Socialist cinema in the first seventeen years of Mao's China was both politically and artistically experimental.[12] To elucidate the sociocultural significance of Dong's artistic experimentation, an in-depth and close analysis of the film is needed. In the rest of this section, I will illustrate how Dong revised the original story in adapting it into the film and how her cinematic experiments engendered a critical cinematic space, revealing extant issues such as dogmatism in socialist China on the one hand and articulating different identification processes and diverse sociocultural imaginations on the other.

The film begins with a lone truck bumping along in the great wilderness of China's northwest plateau with literally no road before or after it. As the days and nights pass, the landscape changes to snowy mountains and an endless, icy mountain path. The camera then cuts to the truck's cab to reveal a young male driver and a young woman sitting next to him. Simply by observing their facial expressions and body language, the audience can see that the two are not on good terms. When a truck passes by from the opposite direction, the girl turns around, her look following the truck until it disappears. After the girl turns back to her original position, with disappointment legible on her face, the audience is exposed to her inner thoughts through voice-over: "The plateau . . . Is this the plateau [I know through other representations]?"

The most salient narrative device in Dong's *Small Grass* is the female voice-over, which is anchored within the diegetic frame, synchronically communicating the inner thoughts and emotions of the main character, Li Wanli. The original story by Wang Zongyuan has a different narrative device. It begins with a primary first-person narrator (presumably a male reporter) who meets Li at a large celebratory meeting held for young model workers and socialist construction activists in the Qaidam Basin area. He becomes interested in Li, a model youth with a Shanghai background. When he asks her about her first impression on arriving on the Qinghai-Tibet Plateau, she answers by telling a story about Hui sao, a peasant woman who helped transform her life on the plateau. Although Li narrates the main story from then on, her first-person narration is enveloped by the male journalist's questions and narrative frame.

In their adaptation of the short story the two scriptwriters, Dong and Hua Ming (华明) remove both the authorial male narrator and Li's retrospective first-person narration and instead begin directly with Li's story as she experiences it. This rearrangement of the temporal and spatial frame in the film's opening transforms the entire story from a recounting of a past learning experience with a historically vindicated perspective (the character is now herself a model youth)—a narrative device used in some other revolutionary films—to a direct presentation of a moment Li is experiencing on her journey. This change in narrative structure fundamentally alters Li's experience from a teleologically vindicated trajectory to a historical reality in which multiple discourses, as well as their contradictions, are enunciated and sustained.

In addition, the voice-over, which speaks Li's inner thoughts and feelings as she is embarking on a new life journey, emphasizes her internal and psychological struggles. Indeed, the director prioritizes Li's psychological experience so much that she uses a full reel of her six-reel film to depict Li riding in the truck, highlighting her subjective reflections through voice-over. At one level, the film visually and metaphorically represents Li's experience on the mountain road as the beginning of a learning journey, evoking the pedagogical significance of socialist cinema. At another level, however, Li's voice-over tells the audience stories of her physical suffering, her past life, her psychological expectations for her new work, and her current struggles on the trip, effectively expressing her disillusionment and the important reason for her emotional hesitation.

If Li's revelation of her physical suffering—which includes severe headache, back pain, loss of appetite, and fatigue, all the symptoms of altitude sickness—indicates a required *tempering* process for young people to become socialist heroes and heroines, Dong's film goes beyond simply endorsing the pedagogical function. Li's voice-over also suggests that her "(female) body is terribly uncomfortable" (身上难受), possibly implying that she is menstruating as well. More importantly, Dong illustrates via her camera's sympathetic gaze that Li has to suppress what she is experiencing due to the silencing effect produced by Xiao Liu, a model driver and heroic figure, who, as the film later reveals, looks down on Li when he senses that this newcomer from Shanghai may be unable to endure the hardships of working on the plateau. To a certain extent, Dong's film shows that Xiao Liu's attitude literally intensifies Li's bodily suffering.

Physical pains, however, are only a small part of Li's problem. More troubling is her psychological disillusionment. It turns out, as revealed in her voice-over and a flashback, that one of Li's emotional motivations to volunteer to work on the Qinghai-Tibet Plateau came from a magazine cover photo of a young Tibetan woman dressed in colorful ethnic dress and standing happily on the vast green grassland, where the sun above her is bright, the sky behind her is blue, and the sheep surrounding her are white (fig. 3.1). In the first flashback of the film, we see Li as a young college student from a well-to-do urban family gazing at the photo in her cozy bed at home. Greatly inspired, Li desires to join the happy and high-spirited young woman and work in the high mountainous area in the far west. The subsequent montage shows that Li works hard in college and upon graduation volunteers to leave Shanghai for the Qinghai-Tibet Plateau. Reality, however, crushes her dream. Since entering the plateau area two weeks earlier, not only has she seen no one like the girl on the magazine cover, but she has seen no women at all. Furthermore, the ruthless natural environment fully exhibits its icy, stormy, and desolate lifelessness, departing entirely from the beautiful na-

3.1 The magazine cover photo of a young Tibetan woman. *Small Grass Grows on the Kunlun Mountains* (昆仑山上一棵草), directed by Dong Kena, 1962.

ture showcased on the magazine cover. Li feels strangled by the environment of the plateau, the same place where she had once dreamed of beginning a new life. Psychologically, Li feels suddenly in the dark: on the one hand, the subject with whom she so desired to identify—the young Tibetan woman on the magazine cover—never appears; on the other hand, the heroic male drivers she meets are far less relatable and cannot motivate her to identify with them. Li had a concrete vision of herself and her future when she volunteered to work on the Qinghai-Tibet Plateau; Li's voice-over illustrates how that vision has been totally shattered by the unbridgeable gap between the official representation of life and the reality on the plateau.

It is important to note that this crucial detail of the Tibetan girl on the magazine cover is not in the original story; Dong and Hua added it in their adaptation. As a woman and former left-wing actress, Dong understood that it was both simplistic and untruthful to interpret Li's early reaction to the plateau, as the original story did, as purely a sign of lack of courage or determination. Such a stereotypical and abstract judgment would obscure and dismiss many important issues, some of which are related to gender. Dong once stressed that her previous experience as an actress helped her direct films because an actress needs to emotionally identify with her character, not simply perform her character rationally or externally.[13] For Dong, the sudden change in Li's attitude toward the plateau at the beginning of the original short story lacked convincing psychological and emotional logic. In an article on the art of film directing, Dong writes, "I make much effort to explore and discover characters' internal worlds in order to move audiences with [appropriate] emotions."[14] She continues, "My films are full of emotions and artistic appeal because I rely on my own feelings when I direct."[15]

Relying on her own historically constituted emotions, feelings, and sense of reality, Dong questioned certain stereotypes associated with young intellectual women and bridged the emotional and psychological gaps in the original story by creating scenes to reveal Li's inner desires and her initial model figure. But when Li's original motivation and desire are illustrated, the film inadvertently uncovers certain ideological gaps: first, between the particular official public representation and the reality of the plateau and, second, between the assumption of what women should do when confronting misrepresented reality and women's historically informed psychological and emotional negotiations in the situation. These ideological discrepancies and historical gaps are no small matters, and Dong's film repeatedly foregrounds them through its experimental style.

Indeed, later in the film Dong elaborates on how Hui sao dwells on the total disillusionment caused by her husband's (mis)representation of reality. By employing Hui sao's first-person voice-off and subjective flashbacks, the film details how she had been misled by her husband's letter in which he described the area in favorable terms and how she had traveled all the way from Shanxi to the plateau, dreaming of building a prosperous new home there. Hui sao brought with her all the domestic necessities she could possibly carry, including small animals and a variety of vegetable seeds. But the reality that appeared before her eyes completely shocked her. The first sentence of Li's voice-over at the beginning of the film rings loud: "The plateau . . . Is this the plateau [I know through other representations]?"

Compared to Li, Hui sao was even more resolute in her desire to return home. Hui sao's determination to leave was not caused by the hardship and difficulty associated with the area. After all, Hui sao was very different from Li; she was a strong peasant woman and had endured enormous suffering in the past. When she first arrived in the area, Hui sao showed no sign of physical fatigue. Instead, she was full of energy and enthusiasm and eager to settle down in her imagined new home. What turned her completely around was the huge discrepancy between her husband's representation of the area and the situation before her eyes. Reality, bearing no trace of her husband's depictions, smashed her imagination of home and self. Although her husband used his own story as well as a story about the small grass to persuade Hui sao, Hui sao was not particularly moved by it. Having a full life in her village back in Shanxi, Hui sao had no intention of identifying with or following her husband, a Communist Party member specially appointed to work in the area.

In both Li's and Hui sao's cases, Dong's effort to make their transformations emotionally convincing leads to the critical revelation of issues existing in official and male characters' (mis)representations of reality. Furthermore, when Li and Hui sao, the only two women in the film, react to the (mis)representations, the heroic characters in the film (aligned with male positions represented by Xiao Liu and Lao Hui) not only associate their reactions with cowardice but also dogmatically demand that the women overcome their emotional difficulty to identify themselves with a one-dimensional ideal. Xiao Liu, the model male driver in the film, functions exactly as this silencing and demanding force. In socialist China, women were said to have held up half of the sky, so shouldn't they be capable of doing what men do? Li's and Hui sao's voice-overs and flashbacks place these arbitrary, uniform assumptions under scrutiny.

Indeed, Dong's emphasis on psychological negotiations and her experiments with subjective camera and narrative structure effectively constitute a cinematic space that provides a base for the film's critical intervention of certain official (mis)representations of reality and some categorical demands for a uniform model everyone must follow. At the same time, however, these critical interventions are not made for the sake of targeting men or subverting socialist mainstream culture, as some post-Mao feminist scholars have hoped. On the contrary, the film's critical engagements—which were enabled by the socialist vision and construction of a lively proletarian community, progressive modernization, and gender-class equality—aim to productively address both extant and emerging issues and open up space for different visions to thrive in the China of the early 1960s. That is to say, the critical negotiations manifested in *Small Grass* embodied the overall dynamic character of socialist endeavors at the time.

Negotiating a Diverse Socialist Feminist Imaginary: Individual Self, Intersubjectivity, and Socialist Community

In addition to exposing the gaps and contradictions in certain socialist representations and constructions of new subject positions for individual identification, Dong's subjective narrative devices diversify the socialist imaginary, foregrounding a historically gendered negotiation of self, inter-subjective relationship, and social community.

Wang Ban, in his study of pleasure, individual self, and collective spectacles in such socialist revolutionary films as *Song of Youth* (青春之歌, dir. Cui Wei [崔嵬], 1959) pays particular attention to the aesthetic dimension of politics.[16] Questioning the conventional belief that politics represses individual desires, he argues that individual libidinal forces are in fact maintained and reoriented by socialist politics and artistic practice through sublimation and other collective means. Regarding the process of individual identification with the collective or revolutionary subject, Wang points out that socialist revolutionary films often explicitly or implicitly adopt the Western narrative convention of bildungsroman to tie the narrative of individual growth to revolutionary history. He also quotes Dai Jinhua, to elucidate the relationship: "Giving up oneself to revolution means not only getting a glorious new life and obtaining the meaning of existence, but also taking a final departure from loneliness, weakness, and helplessness, and acquiring a new home, new affection, new concerns, and new power."[17] Wang's characterization focuses on revolutionary history films, and his argument on the process of individual identification in those films not only captures important aesthetic effects of revolutionary films but also provides insights for our general understanding of socialist films.

Dong's *Small Grass* furthers Wang's argument by representing Drivers' Home as a nurturing, dynamic, and purposeful socialist community for individual men and women. Following the opening scene in the truck, Dong employs extensive subjective-oriented camera shots with Li's voice-over to show Li's emotions when she first enters the public Drivers' Home at the Kunlun mountain pass. Drivers' Home signifies the socialist concept and practice of proletarian family in which people care about each other, based not on blood ties but on shared sociopolitical vision and commitments. Li witnesses the harmonious and happy atmosphere in this unique socialist space, and it is here that Li begins to feel at home and gradually revives her sense of belonging.

Dong's film also significantly complements Wang's argument by forging particularly gendered and intersubjective mechanisms for individual desire and identity formation. Indeed, at the center of Drivers' Home is neither a model party member nor one of the heroic male drivers but a Chinese peasant woman, Hui sao. Although the audience learns that Hui sao became a model figure by establishing this Drivers' Home and providing a much needed service to long-distance drivers in the desolate mountain area, Li's subjective perspective and her voice-over display a fascination with Hui sao that goes beyond the latter's model service. After witnessing the dynamic and life-filled Drivers' Home and learning of Hui sao's model status, Li wonders via her voice-over how Hui sao, the first and only woman in the area, has managed to survive in the environment: "Doesn't she feel lonely?"[18] Later, when Li sees how much Hui sao has transplanted her northwestern home to the desolate plateau, she becomes further fascinated and cannot help but ask herself how this is all possible and, more importantly: "What does she [Hui sao] *think* [as a woman]?" Obviously, the status of model figure does not address Li's problems as a woman in the almost all-male environment. Li desires to learn how Hui sao, a peasant woman, transforms the environment into a warm and inspiring collective community. Her questions particularly highlight gendered issues emerging in certain areas of postrevolutionary construction, where women's loneliness can arise after joining a collective force populated mostly by men. These questions further challenge a uniform way of representing female heroes or model figures in socialist cultural practice. For Li, the extraordinary achievement Hui sao has made lies not just in her successful effort to embody socialist heroic models but more importantly in her unusual ability to help build a proletarian community that exhibits liveliness, compassion, and mutual support, embraces different senses of self, and fosters different life imaginations.

Although Li is situated in an apprentice position in socialist cultural convention, her bold questions grant her critical agency to move the cinematic narrative forward and explore Hui sao's significance as a gendered being in the plateau area. These questions also initiate the formation of a special female intersubjective relationship that proves key to Li's own self-transformation and the women's mutual recognition. The second question about what Hui sao thinks is added by Dong in her adaption. This question also works to introduce Hui sao's self-narration and flashback, which reveal how she finally transforms herself and decides to stay in the area. Again Dong's revisions in this scene significantly diversify the original story.

In the original short story Hui sao's husband, Lao Hui, unsuccessfully tries to persuade her to stay. At last, he decides to tell a story about how, at a most dangerous and desperate moment in his career in the Kunlun Mountains, he came across a type of nameless small grass growing vigorously in the adverse climate of the plateau. Inspired by the grass, he thought that the will of a Communist Party member should be at least as strong as the small grass. He brought to his comrades a sample of the grass, which proved effective in encouraging the team to overcome the difficult situation.

Although this story does contain inspiring elements, especially the small grass standing for a vigorous form of life, Dong must have found it hard to convince herself and the audience that Hui sao's strong determination to leave the place could be so suddenly and utterly changed by her husband's story about the local grass. Furthermore, the crisis Lao Hui and his comrades confronted was related to their careers as party members and to their initial struggle to survive the area's brutal weather and climate. Even Mao Zedong's quotation that Lao Hui used to encourage his comrades had originally been addressed directly to party members and not to common people. So Lao Hui, by turning his story into an educational one intended for everyone, implicitly forged a uniform model. Hui sao has no wish to identify with her husband via his career, nor is she a Communist Party member. Unlike apprentice characters in other revolutionary films, who are often stuck in deadlocked situations and desire to join revolutionary forces in search of new homes and identities, Hui sao has, in socialist China, a home and life of her own to which she very much desires to return even though her husband must stay in a different place. Heterosexual romance, which indexes some other revolutionary films like *Song of Youth*, also loses its "magic" in this film because the central character is a middle-aged peasant woman with a strong character who knows what she wants. Although Hui sao is in the conventional apprentice position in relation to her husband, she is depicted as having her own vision of self, home, and life.

As a historical woman herself, Dong understands that Lao Hui's abstract and dogmatic lesson does not address Hui sao's real problem. So, she rearranges some material of the original story and creates an episode in which the driver Xiao Liu risks his own life to deliver food on a stormy night to a group of workers in another area of the plateau. As soon as the young driver, who has not slept or eaten fresh food for days, arrives at the drivers' station where Hui sao and her husband live (prior to the Driver's Home), he collapses from fatigue and falls into a deep sleep. Meanwhile, Hui sao accidentally finds a stone-hard steamed bun that falls onto the ground from Xiao Liu's coat pocket. Realizing this is the only food source the child (Hui sao's term) relies on for two days and two nights, Hui sao goes speechless. A silent close-up reveals Hui sao in total disbelief (fig. 3.2). The camera then cuts to the next close-up shot, which shows, from Hui sao's perspective, the sleeping driver's young, innocent, exhausted face (fig. 3.3). From these two shots as well as the following scene, audiences recognize that Hui sao's maternal instinct is aroused and that some real changes in Hui sao have begun to take place. This revised arrangement is significant in that it addresses the original logical gap in Hui sao's transformation. After all, Hui sao, a strong, down-to-earth peasant woman, does not wholly buy into the abstract logic of the heroic spirit; nor does she give in to her husband's pressure. She stays, in the end, because she feels emotionally compelled to help brave and dedicated young drivers—just as she was motivated in the past to support socialist revolutionary endeavors prior to 1949.

In a study of labor and labor utopias in socialist narratives, Cai Xiang (蔡翔) discusses how socialist literature resorts to revised traditional Chinese moral ideals, such as "moral politics" or "the folk ethical order" (德性政治), to help peasants or proletarian masses understand the socialist vision and thus better localize and legitimize modern socialist practices. At the same time, the revised folk ethical order is used to test the limits of socialist policy as well as its popularity among the masses.[19] Indeed, socialist culture has never been closed off from foreign or traditional cultural conventions. Socialist cultural practice, in its selected adaptations of foreign and traditional conventions, also aims to modernize, revolutionize, and popularize those conventions and values.

Dong, in revising the logic of Hui sao's self-transformation, questions the effect of the uniform model used in the original story. Instead, she taps into Chinese folk convention and socialist revolutionary history to re-create the image of a compassionate and prorevolutionary rural woman. The revised image Hui sao embodies not only bridges the psychological gap in the original story but also showcases how socialist culture both works with and effectively transforms various extant cultural and social conventions. Indeed, Hui sao's maternal instinct is by no means essentialized because it is resignified in the socialist, collective environment beyond blood relations. In China in the late 1950s and early 1960s, naturalized maternal love and traditional instincts were often questioned. Hui sao's working-class maternal instincts therefore articulated a reflective, renegotiated, and gendered approach to self-transformation as well as to the political demands of the era. This revision also grants Hui sao, a rural woman of the working class, much of her own historically constituted agency, which accounts for her subsequent motivation to bring her vision of life and home to the Kunlun Mountains through establishing the socialist Drivers' Home.

3.2 Hui sao is left speechless and deeply moved when she accidently finds a stone-hard steamed bun in Xiao Liu's pocket. *Small Grass Grows on the Kunlun Mountains* (昆仑山上一棵草), directed by Dong Kena, 1962.

3.3 A close-up shot of Xiao Liu's sleeping face. *Small Grass Grows on the Kunlun Mountains* (昆仑山上一棵草), directed by Dong Kena, 1962.

With this new episode, which reflects a socialist female director's understanding of historical women and their emotions, Dong critically revises the original story that implicitly upholds a dogmatic ideal and thus prevents Hui sao from being reduced to an abstract and ineffective symbol. In a unique and complex way, female individuals in *Small Grass* reach the socialist collective goal neither by "giving up oneself" to the cause as shown in revolutionary-history films Wang Ban has discussed, nor by erasing their gender differences, as many feminist scholars in their critique of socialist China have argued.[20] Rather, they achieve the goal by transforming their previous visions of self and life and creating new relationships in the socialist context. These gendered visions are more historically constructed than they are essentially determined because their ultimate meanings depend on their overall historical and sociopolitical context. As an active peasant woman carrying a historically specific vision of life and home, Hui sao's self-transformation offers great insight into both the inherently diverse identities of socialist women and the dynamic function of socialist culture. Aesthetically, unlike the socialist melodrama and revolutionary romanticism typical of revolutionary history films, Dong's film foregrounds psychological and emotional realism and experiments with subjective narrative devices, demonstrating the coexistence of a wide range of aesthetic styles in socialist cinema.

If Hui sao's transformation hinges on a revision of conventional maternal passion, Li Wanli's relies on a female intersubjective relationship resignified in the socialist context to address individual desire, self-identity, emotional bonding, and women's mutual recognition. During her initial journey, prior to arriving at Hui sao's Drivers' Home, Li's vision and sense of self are completely shattered. Struck with homesickness, she desperately desires to return home. As a recent college graduate, the seventeen-year-old Li is looking for a concrete model to whom she can relate. Abstract reasoning and uniform identity do not help her emotionally, and her failure to relate to young male drivers in the area deepens her sense of loneliness and alienation.

Li's spark of life is rekindled at the Drivers' Home when she is greeted by Hui sao, the first person to address her directly as a beautiful girl and ask her name. This detail is not in the original story. The warm, familial interactions between Hui sao and all the drivers at the home further help Li to recover from the exhaustion and isolation of the long journey. After most of the drivers have left, Hui sao takes Li to her bedroom, a scene that begins with a shot of Hui sao's cat lying on her cozy bed. Dong uses point-of-view shots and voice-over to illustrate Li's gradual revival as she attentively observes Hui sao and the details of her room. The film further stresses the liveliness of Hui

3.4 A shot of a basket full of little chicks in Hui sao's room. *Small Grass Grows on the Kunlun Mountains* (昆仑山上一棵草), directed by Dong Kena, 1962.

sao's space by showing a full basket of little chicks she has raised (fig. 3.4). As the Drivers' Home reanimates Li's sense of life, the tone of her voice-over expresses her awestruck admiration for Hui sao, who has, in Li's eyes, magically transplanted to the area the beauty of life and home for which everyone longs. It is in this lively space that Li's hopefulness and sense of belonging are restored. Consequently, a meaningful intersubjective relationship that foregrounds life, trust, and mutual recognition between the two women is forged. Clearly, Hui sao functions as a crucial maternal figure for Li's rebirth and transformation and Li via voice-over also explicitly articulates her admiration and love for Hui sao. More significantly, the intersubjective relationship awakens Li's sense of self-worth as a young female intellectual. In their conversations, Hui sao enthusiastically explains the local situation to Li, pointing out that the area's future development depends a great deal on educated young people like Li. Li's initial response is full of self-doubt: "Me? Am I good enough?" With no hesitation, Hui sao confirms, "Yes, of course!" Her recognition of Li's inner strength and her admiration for Li's higher education do not simply rekindle Li's determination to work in a most challenging and formidable environment; more important, they make Li realize with pride that she does not have to duplicate Hui sao's path but can contribute to socialist construction in her own way.

The intersubjective relationship in Dong's film highlights the need for psychological and emotional connections and motivations in socialist identity formation. It also showcases differences between socialist women (region, education, age, and urban and rural areas) and thus stresses the importance of their mutual recognition. Hui sao is the only person in the film who asks Li her name, formally introducing Li—the only young woman and college graduate there—to members of the Drivers' Home and to the mass audience outside the film. Later, in Hui sao's bedroom, the tables turn: Li finds Hui sao's own name on the framed award hung on the wall, and reads aloud to herself and the audience the name of Hui sao: "Comrade He Lianzhen." A peasant woman's individual status and her unique contribution are recognized, but not in an antagonistic relation to her husband's merits. Indeed, Hui sao's story confirms that individuals (should) form their own ways of relating to the socialist vision and contributing to socialist community building. Dong's film thus critically revives an important component of the socialist imaginary, showing that revolution and socialist construction, despite their demand for self-sacrifice and collective effort, should inspire and maintain various senses of self and life as individuals strive for a proletarian community for all.

Conclusion: Shot/Reverse-Shot and Gender Difference in Socialist Women's Cinema

In a comparative study of *Li Shuangshuang* (李双双, dir. Lu Ren [鲁韧], 1962), which came out the same year as *Small Grass*, and *The In-Laws* (喜盈门, dir. Zhao Huanzhang [赵焕章], 1981), Chris Berry reveals the significant transformation of cinematic portrayals of strong rural women in Mao's socialist era and Deng's reform era.[21] Berry argues that whereas the female lead Li Shuangshuang (who aligns her position with the Great Leap Forward and wins the support of the local party secretary) receives praise for her independence from her husband and traditional family structure as a socialist woman, the female lead in *The In-Laws*, Qiangying (who desires to separate her own family from her extended in-law family), gets targeted as selfish, uncaring, and aggressive, and eventually loses the support of the party. In the 1981 film the party not only backs up the extended family, a directorial choice Berry views as patriarchal, but also takes the place of the dead father-in-law to mediate the situation. Furthermore, based on Berry's personal experience, when *The In-Laws* zooms in for a close-up of Qiangying's punishment as her husband turns around to slap her in the face, Chinese audiences in the early 1980s often cheered in excitement. Traditional family values returned in the mass media of the post-Mao era, and strong women were represented as aggressive, unethical, and even villainous, an unknown situation in Mao's China, according to Berry.[22]

Berry continues to examine the cinematic significance of the two films, especially the shot/reverse-shot (point-of-view shot), seeking to discern whether this cinematic device often deployed in classic American cinema produces similar meanings in socialist Chinese films regarding sexual difference and the projected viewing subject. Berry conducts a close analysis of point-of-view shots and finds that unlike the Western cinematic paradigm, which often associates the camera/subject place with the lead male figure and relegates the female figure to the status of an object of gaze (where, as a result, "maleness, subjectivity, and centered ordering are all hooked up into each other to constitute one phallocentric viewing subject"[23]), the Chinese cinematic convention of the Maoist and early post-Mao periods does not consistently call on the close association of the viewing subject with any one figure in the male-female (husband-wife) pair.[24] Despite the different representations of women in *Li Shuangshuang* and *The In-Laws*, point-of-view shots in the two films, according to Berry, function in similar ways and are used only to signify "negative" moments of transgression, division, and/or the collapse of a harmonious relation. Whereas division and reunion play a major role in Chinese narrative convention, the shot/reverse-shot does not assign genders along the male-subject/female-object structure as classic American cinema does. Instead, the Chinese convention illustrates an anti-individualistic aesthetic that, Berry reasons, accounts for the absence of "a discourse of sexual difference concerned with the individual interests of one gender versus the other."[25]

My study of Dong's *Small Grass* supports Berry's argument regarding positive representations of strong, confident rural women in socialist cinema. Hui sao's case testifies even more to the creativity and initiative of a rural woman in socialist China. She directly challenges her husband, a Chinese Communist Party member and heroic socialist figure, and contributes to the construction of a socialist imaginary in her own way, revising the dogmatic and abstract model of identity formation. Berry also rightly points out that the phallocentric arrangement along male-female/subject-object lines in constructing the viewing subject in classic American cinema is absent in socialist cinema, and so is essentialized sexual difference on the men-women hierarchy. However, Berry's arguments that Chinese cinema of the Mao and early post-Mao periods does not positively associate the viewing subject with an individual, and that there lacks discussion of sexual or gender difference in socialist cinema, need to be revised.

In *Small Grass*, the camera is positively aligned with Li Wanli's and Hui sao's perspectives. Whereas Li's perspective reflects a situation in which a young educated woman transforms herself from apprentice to confident working intellectual, Hui sao's perspective manifests her initiation and agency. The point-of-view shots for both characters imply neither fixation and objectification (as in Hollywood cinema) nor pure transgression and division (as Berry sees in other socialist films). Although some of Li's point-of-view shots suggest difference (not necessarily the value divisions as shown in *Li Shuangshuang* and *The In-Laws*), most of those shots express a desire to forge a sense of relatedness and shared belonging. Particularly significant are those shot/reverse-shots between Li and Hui sao, which establish an intersubjective relationship that endorses emotional connection, identification, and mutual recognition among socialist women.

Early Western cine-feminists have forcefully argued that classic Hollywood cinema reproduced phallocentric values because it was part of the capitalist patriarchal ideological apparatus. In a socialist environment where gender and class equality were held as fundamental principles and mass media was used to promote new social and cultural values, cinematic devices like shot/reverse-shots could carry radically different meanings. As shown in Dong's film, shot/reverse-shots do not assume a heterosexual paradigm; nor do they exhibit a subject-object gazing mechanism. At the same time, although the sexual difference represented in Hollywood commercial cinema as biologically determined and subject-object configured is mostly absent as a narrative structure of socialist cinema, gender difference as historically articulated in different geopolitical and cultural contexts is by no means lacking in socialist Chinese films. Dong's *Small Grass* has vividly demonstrated that gender difference is not only *not* erased, as post-Mao and Western feminists have repeatedly claimed,[26] but can in fact function as a privileged site for critical interventions.

In socialist China of the 1950s and 1960s, gender and gender difference occupied a prominent position as they were considered an integrated part of the overall economic, social, cultural, and (geo)political structure. Their representations in socialist cultural practices were thus foregrounded to reflect and promote the general goal and value of socialist feminism. Typical Confucian and bourgeois gender hierarchies and their ramifications were still depicted in socialist literature and film, so continued and sustained interrogations against the capitalist biological essentialization of gender and the Chinese traditional cultural fixation on the gender relationship could be launched and substantial transformations could be made in a new society as a result. Emerging gender issues under new historical circumstances were also singled out in socialist mass culture for critical scrutiny and criticism. Most significantly, representations of socialist new gender relationship highlighted unprecedented socioeconomic and cultural roles for women, including their different yet privileged position in fighting male supremacy and questioning gendered blind spots in socialist practice. In addition, many historical, folk, earlier modern and Western gender configurations became incorporated into socialist culture with critical revisions and transformations. Whereas both physical and historical differences between men and women were well recognized in socialist culture, they were rearticulated to both challenge men's objectification of women or men's superiority over women in all realms and promote equity and equality among different groups of people.

The gender difference as shown in Dong's film does not fix on any essential determinants. Historically constituted gender conventions, such as maternal love, can be summoned to diversify the socialist imaginary; in the process, those conventions are transformed to embody socialist values. The gendered critique articulated in the film does not target men as naturally patriarchal, but it does suggest that new issues can emerge under new historical conditions along gender lines, such as the dogmatism about a uniform identity mostly represented via male characters in a virtually all-male community. Hui sao's ability as a peasant woman to question—and eventually revise—the dogmatic model best reveals how gender difference is conceived in the socialist culture as historically constituted, and how proletarian women in the socialist environment can occupy a different but privileged position to address emerging gender issues, diversify the socialist imagination, and bring positive changes. Furthermore, the film highlights the difference between

Hui sao and Li Wanli, stressing the sociocultural nature of gender formation and the dynamic situation even among women themselves when gender interacts with other historical and social differences. Gender and gender difference as represented in Dong's *Small Grass* thus showcase the historical constitution of self and collective community in a socialist environment, which holds up social equality as a fundamental principle and resignifies differences to enhance equity and diversity, questioning any naturalization or essentialization of women's subjection to men. Research on gender difference, as a result, requires a critical rethinking of gender as a historical and social (re)configuration tied to a particular political-economic structure in a specific geopolitical location. The specific meaning and function of gender difference are time- and space-sensitive, contingent on a constant interaction with other domestic and international forces.

As a female director empowered by the socioeconomic structure of socialist China, Dong Kena showed in making *Small Grass* how she embraced the socialist vision, endorsed gender equality, and dedicated to the pedagogical function of socialist cinema. However, Dong's conformity to general socialist values, policies, and cultural functions by no means reduced her artistic creativity or her critical stance toward problems appearing on the ground.[27] As her adaptation of *Small Grass* illustrated, Dong exhibited a strong individual (not individualistic), gendered (not essentialized), artistic (not depoliticized), and critical (not antagonistic or autonomous) agency in endorsing and revising the original story. The Cold War assertion that socialist art is merely political and collective and thus has no aesthetic merit or distinctive individual style, the Western liberal and radical feminist demand that the women's liberation movement embody individualistic and independent values, and post-Mao feminist charges about socialist female directors conforming to mainstream socialist ideology and male standards (repressive of aesthetic creativity and female difference) require continued interrogation and serious critique. In Dong's case, socialist ideals of community, modernization, and equality and the demand of the proletarian mass audience inspired and enabled rather than hampered her critical and artistic interventions. That is to say, socialist institutional feminism and collective forces were key in the formation of socialist individual (female) authorship and agency. In the context of socialist China in the 1950s and early 1960s, Dong's experience as a woman and a revolutionary cultural worker granted her a vanguard position, allowing her to play an active and visible role in diversifying the socialist feminist imaginary, making *Small Grass* a subjectively mediated, mass-audience-oriented, and critically and artistically engaged film.

Chinese socialist feminism and its cultural practice continued developing in the 1950s and 1960s, addressing remaining and emerging issues, revising the socialist vision and imagination, and charting new grounds for the future. Despite historical setbacks and limitations, socialist feminist practice made manifold, unprecedented accomplishments in the 1950s and 1960s. As a film director in socialist China, Dong's multidimensional contributions to socialist feminist cinema can thus be summarized as follows: she supported the pedagogical function of socialist cinema and promoted the socialist vision and relationship in China's economic development; she forged a productively critical and gendered space to tackle emerging problems in socialist representation and construction; she created a new aesthetic and psychological model that, instead of essentializing gender or suppressing historical and social differences,[28] encourages people to embrace and transform their personal/local/historical visions in their dedication to socialist and collective work; and finally her work manifested the experimental and diverse nature of socialist mainstream cinema with its subjective cinematic narrative devices and multiple discourses in the film's diegetic frame, exhibiting a mechanism of overdetermination in the meaning production of socialist mass culture.

4 Feminist Practice after Mao

Independence, Sexual Difference, and the Universal Model

In 1986, the bimonthly *Contemporary Cinema* (当代电影) and the China Film Art Research Center co-organized a symposium on Chinese women's films in the New Era (1978 to the present). Held in Beijing from May 5 to 7, this symposium used "women's cinema" (女性电影) to address and reconfigure female directors' works in contemporary China. However, the phrase ignited debates and met with considerable opposition, especially among participating female directors. One anonymous editor of *Contemporary Cinema* summarized three main objections in a published editorial, "Female Directors and Women's Cinema."[1] First, films by women did not yet display enough unity or degree of distinction from films directed by men to warrant their being grouped together. Second, the very use of the term indicated prejudice against women in its implication that cinema is normally male and required a special term for films deviating from this so-called norm. Third, the term *women's cinema* was inappropriate as it derived from the Western term *feminist cinema*, a product of Western capitalist society and a reflection of Western women's movements in filmmaking.[2] The majority of symposium participants—including cultural officials, critics, and female directors, according to this anonymous editor—demanded a theoretical definition of the term and believed that only films containing "female consciousness" (女性意识, editor's term) should qualify as *women's cinema*. The editor then offered a summary of possible definitions of *female consciousness*, showing an equally uncertain understanding of this alternative phrase. According to that writer, female consciousness is generally defined as "women's consciousness about themselves as women," but specifically it contains three dimensions: physical/ psychological, social, and historical. Using these three qualifications, female consciousness can denote either a negative (traditional) or positive (contemporary and self-reflective) meaning. Adding to the confusion, Mao's socialist China remained ostensibly absent from this binary configuration of female consciousness. Did women in Mao's China have self-consciousness? And what does it mean that by the mid- to late 1980s, women's cinema had to be defined through female consciousness?

Despite the ambiguity prevalent in the discussion, by the mid-1980s *female consciousness* had become a buzzword and crucial concept in setting a new direction for both feminist and women's cultural practices. In this chapter I trace the rise of post-Mao feminism, closely examining its personal, institutional, and transnational origins; I also analyze its initial promise for further improving socialist feminist practice during the thought liberation movement, followed by its subsequent development in the mid- to late 1980s into a universal cultural discourse implicated in contemporary capitalist globalization as China marched toward a market economy. Specifically, the chapter moves from discussing women's autobiographical literature of the late 1970s and early 1980s to examining the formation and central theoretical arguments of post-Mao feminism in the mid-1980s, and then to investigating the contradictory position occupied by post-Mao feminism and its complicated entanglements with the economic-reform state, the masculine mainstream intellectual discourse, and Western post-second-wave feminism.

The Emergence of the Gendered Personal:
Critique of Both Socialist Gender Discrepancies
and the New Era's Gender Discrimination

In December 1978, at the Eleventh Central Committee's Third Plenary Session, Chinese Communist Party leaders under Deng Xiaoping's representation marked the beginning of a new era by formally laying out the party's economic reform and open-door policy. Deng's new state policy reoriented China's priority to developing the economy through the Four Modernizations: agriculture, industry, science and technology, and national defense. Science and technology in particular represented the foundation of China's overall economic reform. In a speech to the National Science Conference in March 1978, then-vice-premier Deng Xiaoping declared: "The crux of the Four Modernizations is the mastery of modern science and technology. Without the high-speed development of science and technology, it is impossible to develop the national economy at a high speed."[3] In the cultural realm, the thought liberation policy inspired Chinese intellectuals, leading to a sustained cultural and intellectual movement. Both the liberal and Marxist humanisms (re)emerging in the early reform era became a linchpin for dynamic intellectual debates and cultural practice at the time. Humanism in general functioned as a critical outcry against the Cultural Revolution, particularly its irrational idealism (perceived as inhumane and utopian in the New Era), anti-intellectualism, and overpoliticized ideology (class struggle). Chinese intellectuals, many of whom had been persecuted or dismissed from their professions during the Cultural Revolution, were not simply rehabilitated in the New Era but also designated as the key group to advance China's Four Modernizations. Both male and female intellectuals thus wholeheartedly supported Deng's economic reform and modernization, which they believed would redirect China to a universally "right" path to modernity.

During the early post-Mao era—as the state was still experimenting and negotiating while Chinese intellectuals, encouraged by the thought liberation campaign and relaxed cultural policy, were also in a state of exploration—a cultural pluralism emerged, enunciating different voices and embracing a variety of ideas.[4] This cultural pluralism, different from market-oriented pluralism in a capitalist society, contained values and visions generated from different historical periods and sociopolitical structures. The first national debate on humanism and alienation in the early post-Mao period (1979–1984), for example, involved heated exchanges of ideas between those who promoted a transhistorical, universal human nature,[5] defying the class-based understanding of human history, and those who insisted on historical materialism and the political-economic specificity of the human condition.[6] Some scholars argued that socialist values and practice should be maintained despite their need of critical revisions.[7] The relationship between human nature and class, humanism and Marxism, with reference to alienation, occupied the center of the debate.[8] Although Chinese intellectuals from all sides embraced humanism, their theoretical and political interpretations were different. Not until the second national debate about humanism (1985–1986), when China's economic reform had further expanded and deepened, did a mainstream and dominant discourse appear that endorsed a vision of human nature across history and class, independent subjectivity (literary or individual), and Enlightenment consciousness (reason, scientism, and universalism).[9]

Despite the pluralistic character of the early New Era's mainstream cultural practice and intellectual debates, however, sexual and gender difference nonetheless became a distinctive marker of the post-Mao times. The topic of sexual and gender difference appeared neutral at first as it was part of the general discussion of humanism and human nature in reaction to the uniform androgynous model propagated by the Cultural Revolution. Soon, however, it began to designate a new and naturalized gender hierarchy in post-Mao society, challenging the long-held socialist ideology of gender equality. At the turn of the 1980s, after thirty years' practice of gender equality, male intellectuals after Mao appropriated an old term, "the prosperity of the feminine and the decline of the masculine" (or "stronger women and weaker men" [阴盛阳衰]), to link China's national problems with men's emasculation and women's defeminization (political liberation and gender equality) in the socialist era.[10] This phrase had been used in traditional Chinese history to indicate natural, social, and dynastic disorder. Male writers and artists, in subsequent cultural movements launched in the early and mid-1980s like root-seeking or the search for "real men" (寻找男子汉), continued their efforts to restore the "right" order of the nation by reestablishing the "normal" order between masculine "real men" and feminine "real women." Their conscious or unconscious negation of socialist gender configuration was manifested in literary and cinematic representations that promoted traditional femininity and female virtue in the name of human nature.[11] Meanwhile, the early-1980s state-promoted scientific discourse (biology, physiology, and psychology) was used to define female intellectual, physical, and emotional differences, producing spheres in which women were deemed inferior to men.[12] Biology became destiny and, more critically, women's destiny was measured in terms of men's biology. This process of differentiating women from men coincided with the reemergence of the gendered division of labor following the logic of economic development and the state's remapping of spaces; consequently, women became increasingly associated with the private sphere, perceived to require less intellectual, rational, and physical capability. In the areas of theory and philosophy, Li Zehou (李泽厚) and other male intellectuals in the 1980s began articulating a new, individual, autonomous, and reflective subject position to be occupied mostly or only by educated men. As Tani Barlow states, "What is utterly missing in all of this discussion is any admission of a sex continuum or a gender differential or any social or biological difference that might allow a request to be lodged for redress rooted in a claim that oppressions are gendered."[13] Undoubtedly the gender blindness of their Western counterparts directly influenced Chinese intellectuals in Enlightenment philosophy, but this "masculine humanism,"[14] as discussed above, also has roots in its own historical and political context—that is, the crisis of intellectual masculinity that surfaced in early post-Mao China.

Chinese women's post-Mao literary and academic practices emerged exactly in this relatively relaxing yet highly gendered cultural and social environment. A brief study of early post-Mao women's cultural practice can offer us critical insights into the personal, subjective, and socioeconomic underpinnings of the rise of the post-Mao independent feminist movement. Situated in the initial cultural pluralism that had developed in the early New Era and influenced by first-wave discussions of humanism and subjectivity, Chinese women writers of different generations rose at the turn of the 1980s, producing a large body of literary works with varied concerns and different narrative styles. Socially concerned realism continued in the texts of veteran writer Ru Zhijuan (茹志鹃); critical reflection of the Cultural Revolution from the humanistic perspective occupied works of middle-aged writers Dai Houying (戴厚英) and Chen Rong (谌容); and literary representations of contemporary economic reform won both critical acclaims and literary prizes for writers like Zhang Jie (张洁): her *Heavy Wings* (1981) earned the prestigious Mao Dun literary prize in 1985. But the most critically acclaimed and heatedly debated literary practice carried out by a group of female writers across generations— including Zhang Jie, Zhang Xinxin (张辛欣), Zhang Kangkang (张抗抗), and Yu Luojin (遇罗锦)—was women's autobiographical literature. This personally oriented and gendered literary practice significantly diversified the overall post-Mao mainstream cultural practice, articulating the important subjective experiences of urban female intellectuals.[15] More importantly, this autobiographical practice was double-edged: it reflected critically on the Cultural Revolution, revealing gender- and culture-related issues in socialist practice; at the same time it targeted the reemergence of male-centered values and the return of gender discrimination in the post-Mao era.

Zhang Jie was the most vocal writer to express educated women's critiques of conventional marriage and their frustration searching for true love during both the Mao and post-Mao eras. In her short story "Love Must Not Be Forgotten" (爱是不能忘的, 1979), Zhang reclaims the value and legitimacy of emotional and romantic love, which had virtually disappeared in cultural representation during the Cultural Revolution. The story illustrates, via a late widowed mother's diary, the conflict between love and revolutionary ethics in Mao's China, and expresses intellectual women's desire to pursue individual and ideal love. But at the same time, the mother's diary also reveals that her love for a married man, a high-ranking cultural cadre, is enhanced and sustained precisely by the man's moral integrity, including his commitment to revolutionary ethics, his self-sacrificing spirit, and his devotion to his working-class wife. Despite the unfulfilled love, in the end the mother indirectly endorses the revolutionary moral foundation that helps constitute her ideal love. "Love Must Not Be Forgotten" is not, however, simply about the mother's story and her times. The daughter narrates the mother's love, the role of which helps the daughter, Shanshan, make her own decision about love and marriage in the post-Mao setting. Here we find Zhang's story manifesting a critical stance against the emerging new conventions of love and marriage in the New Era, when young people were turning more materialist and superficial, paying attention only to the appearance and social status of their potential partners. The daughter's final decision to go against conventional expectations and turn down a marriage proposal from her boyfriend, who is incredibly handsome but has neither critical intelligence nor professional pursuit, showcases early post-Mao socialist women writers' active and critical engagement with the changing social ethics of their times.

Zhang Xinxin, in her critically acclaimed short story "Where Did I Miss You?" (我在哪儿错过了你, 1980), continues the Shanshan's story from "Love Must Not Be Forgotten." The heroine in this story—a bus ticket conductor and amateur playwright, who grew up in socialist China and became a physically strong, mentally independent, and professionally ambitious young woman—also refuses a marriage proposal from her boyfriend, a handsome and conventionally valued young man who, again, does not possess intellectual acumen or pursue a passionate life. But Zhang Xinxin's story centers on what happens when such a strong young woman meets and falls in love with a compatible man in the rapidly changing New Era. This man happens to be the director of her play, and the heroine is attracted to him because of his physical strength, his intellectual maturity, his deep understanding of her play, and his passionate pursuit of his own career. The heroine struggles to get close to the man only to find out that he prefers a gentle, feminine young woman in his life. Furthermore, the heroine accidently overhears the man telling others that she is too "manly" (男子气质过多), an attitude toward strong socialist women shared by Chinese male intellectuals in the early post-Mao period. The emotional blow forces the heroine to ponder the discrepancy between the androgynous model-for-all that Mao's socialist China promoted and the traditional standard for women that made a public return in the next era. If God made her a woman, the heroine reflects, the Cultural

Revolution and her family and life experiences have made her a self-reliant and manlike woman. More critically, the heroine realizes that in the past she was proud of herself as an androgynous and independent woman, but now, after knowing the man's preference, she begins to feel dispirited about her situation. Toward the end of the story, although the heroine longs for femininity that she seems to have missed and that might bring her love and happiness, she decides to continue her current path because she is no longer able to—and indeed, perhaps does not *intend*—to take off the "masculine mask," which has become the essence of her sense of self. Despite being strong and self-reliant, successful young women like the heroine often encountered enormous difficulty in fulfilling their emotional lives in the early post-Mao era. "Where Did I Miss You?" perceptively articulates the historical and gendered transformation taking place in contemporary China, which moved away from the socialist gender equality that had promoted strong women and toward a sexual difference that valued traditional femininity.

This public return of traditional feminine virtue and the increasing gender discrimination in the early post-Mao era became the target of Zhang Jie's popular and controversial novella *The Ark* (方舟), published in 1982. Set in the economic reform era, the story portrays the daily trials and patent harassment endured by three female roommates, all urban intellectuals, as they struggle to carry on their lives and professions after divorcing or separating from their husbands. Zhang Jie uses the "sex/gender gap" (性沟) to illustrate, first, society's different standards for men and women—that is, women's double burden of public and private duties—and, second, women's despair at the growing sex/gender gap that degraded women and prevented men and women from understanding each other in the early post-Mao era.[16] The novella calls for a women's self-strengthening movement that would go beyond traditional Marxist theory on women's emancipation and social production: "If women want to achieve the ultimate liberation, not merely political and economic liberation, they have to maintain sufficient self-confidence and strive for the realization of the value of self-existence." This statement articulates two critical points that post-Mao feminist and cultural practice would emphasize: the need to further women's liberation after political and economic liberation, and the self-focused direction for this future endeavor. Little did Zhang or her characters realize in 1982 that the return of prejudice and discrimination against women in early post-Mao China signaled a broader change to come in women's political and economic status and thus was by no means an isolated issue that could be addressed through sheer individual self-improvement. In the cultural realm, Zhang's attempt at self-realization and her promotion of strong women functioned to critique the emerging trend of advocating traditional femininity and female sexual appeal. Adhering to both socialist socioeconomic gender equality and the rise of individual self and subjectivity in the New Era, the story ends with an ambivalent view of the possibility of bridging the sex/gender gap between men and women.

This gendered personal space created by Chinese women writers did not stop at literary practice. Other female intellectuals, including filmmakers and scholars, shared the discontent expressed by these writers.[17] Li Xiao-jiang (李小江, b. 1951), a Western literature scholar at the time and later a representative post-Mao feminist figure, strongly identified with these writers' personal experience and perceptions.[18] She directly adopted Zhang Jie's term *sex/gender gap* as the title of her book published in 1989 to explore broader gendered issues in human history. An interviewer asked Li, after she had become a well-known feminist scholar, "Why do you go out of your way to pioneer women's studies in contemporary China?" Li's reply: the motivation *came from* her life experience as a woman in socialist China.[19] "What has driven me onto the career track of women's studies is not society, nor the ten-year disaster [the Cultural Revolution], nor my profession [Western literature], but my female life path; it [the cause] could be viewed as something quite personal."[20] Li turned to women's studies initially and primarily to find answers to questions arising in her own life. She grew up identifying with successful men and enjoying her independent way of life. But her experience as a wife and mother during the late Cultural Revolution shattered her previous understanding of women and caused painful struggles. On the one hand, she recognized women's difference in her reproductive role and realized the power of love, especially the maternal bond and sacrifice; on the other hand, she felt trapped in her familial roles as they encroached on her career and independent identity, since society did not recognize the value of those bonds. She strove to maintain both ways of life only to find herself on the verge of emotional and physical exhaustion, unable to maintain a sense of self. She could not help asking why it had to be women who carried the double burden.[21] "I wanted to know," she said, "why women's lives were so difficult and full of humiliation. Why did women still feel so worn out and repressed during the socialist era of gender equality?"[22] These questions led Li to study women, a subject about which she felt she knew little.

Chinese women's autobiographical writing in the early post-Mao era thus not only diversified the cultural practice of the time but also enunciated the need to advance socialist feminism to address a set of discrepancies female intellectuals had experienced in their lives as socialist women: the official discourse of gender equality versus the continued traditional demands on women at home, the revolutionary androgynous model held for both men and women under Mao versus the public return of traditional femininity and female virtue in Deng's reform era. Despite their personal orientation, Chinese women's autobiographical stories at the turn of the 1980s were sociopolitically engaged as they directly and critically negotiated with both socialist feminist practice and the New Era's gender (re)configuration, articulating a double critique of the remaining issues in the socialist system and the (re) emerging gender hierarchy in the era of economic reform. Indeed, the return of gender discrimination, conventional marriage, and the radical change of attitude toward women from their male peers spurred women writers and female intellectuals to explore options for feminism to advance beyond traditional Marxist theory. This shared sentiment and ambition among female intellectuals contributed to the formation of post-Mao independent feminism around the mid-1980s.

Theoretical Negotiation of Post-Mao Feminism: Marxist Theory, Women's Separate History, and Nonalienated Sexual Difference

The gendered personal, which Chinese women writers articulated in the early reform era, offered an important personal and subjectively mediated index to the rise of the Chinese independent feminist movement in the mid-1980s. This section turns to the most representative feminist figure of the 1980s, Li Xiaojiang, and some of her important works to illustrate the theoretical negotiation of post-Mao independent feminism, particularly its revision of Marxist theory and its proposed new direction for Chinese socialist feminism.

Li Xiaojiang is the quintessential figure of the women's studies movement of the 1980s, part of the general post-Mao feminist endeavor. She was the first to retheorize women's issues in a published article in 1983, the first to organize a nongovernmental women's studies association in 1985, the first to advocate developing women's studies as an independent academic discipline in 1986, the first to establish a center for women's studies in 1987, and the first to edit and publish a series of women's studies books in 1988. In the late 1980s, Li published several major books on women's studies: *Eve's Exploration* (夏娃的探索, 1988), *Women, a Distant and Beautiful Legend* (女人一个悠远美丽的传说, 1989), *Inquiry into the Female Aesthetic Consciousness* (女性审美意识探微, 1989), and *The Sex/Gender Gap* (性沟, 1989). Whereas these books explore a wide range of topics, their major arguments center on the necessity of separating gender from class as well as women from men, the importance of female self-consciousness in defining modern feminism, and the introduction of natural sexual difference as the new foundation for the ultimate women's liberation as well as for feminist research and practice. Li has often been perceived as an essentialist feminist.[23] In addition, due to Li's promotion of Enlightenment discourse, science, and individualism, which all contributed to China's development and transformation into a market economy in the 1990s, such scholars as Barlow have linked Li's works to market feminism.[24]

What do sexual and/or gender differences mean in women's literature and women's studies of the 1980s? How did Li Xiaojiang situate her feminist position in history, and what is her vision for Chinese women's liberation? What theoretical frameworks did she use, and what new theoretical ground has she broken for future studies of gender and women? Li is a prolific writer, and her writing traverses multiple genres—critical, scholarly, literary, and popular—and so reaches a wide audience. However, her first theoretical article, "The Progress of Humanity and Women's Liberation" (人类进步和妇女解放, 1983),[25] in which she critically revises Marxist theory and lays out her revised feminist framework, has been largely overlooked in later studies of post-Mao Chinese feminism—and of Li's works themselves. In all of her major publications of the late 1980s, Li repeatedly and continuously returns to the major points made in this article. This article not only offers critical insights into the questions raised above; it also opens up an illuminating dialogue with Western Marxist, radical, and socialist feminist theories of the 1970s and 1980s. Claiming to be both Marxist *and* feminist and negotiating between the historical materialist, transhistorical, and universal cultural approaches to gender, Li manifests in her writing an internal bifurcation similar to the Western radical and socialist feminist thought of the 1970s.

In "The Progress of Humanity and Women's Liberation," Li covers a set of issues, including the material and economic base of women's subjugation and liberation, the relationship between production and reproduction, sexual division of labor, class history, the history of women's liberation, women's relationship with society, family, men, and children, and the socialization of family responsibility. Together, her major revision of Marxist theory, which derived from the vantage point of the socialist stage, combined with her personal experience during the late Cultural Revolution and the early post-Mao era and with her study of Western feminist movements and theory, center on the following three areas. *First*, she constructs a separate, three-stage women's history, which is connected to but distinct from the Marxist five-stage history: primitive society, slave society, feudalism, capitalism, and socialism-communism. She states that "women's historical situation and the change of their social status are not directly linked to the progress of [Marxist] social stages, but are tied to the evolution of [all of] humanity"[26] (143). Women's history moves from the primitive stage to the slave stage, then on to the liberated stage (143–47), a trajectory that corresponds to three frameworks defining women in human history—nature, family, and society (153–57). Li argues that men and women have different evolutions in human history. Like the national independence movement and class struggle, the women's movement also emerged in capitalist society when women obtained self-consciousness, but, different from the previous two political endeavors, the women's movement targeted the entire male-dominant (patriarchal) society that had lasted for thousands of years (148). *Second*, Li argues that the Marxist five-stage history centers on economic development, changes in class structure, and male values, and thus alienates the histories of nature, labor, and women (158). Li states that women's liberation movements for gender equality started when women obtained their self-consciousness in capitalist society, but women's ultimate liberation goes beyond this stage. Gender equality is thus not the final criterion for women's liberation. More critically it imposes a male standard on women (165). Li suggests the need for another movement to destroy the male-centered value system and establish a new social and ethical order. *Third*, after women achieve equality in the liberated stage, the "family," which has inherited the psychological and cultural legacies of gender hierarchy from all the previous stages of human history, proves the ultimate obstacle to women's final liberation. To challenge the internal subordination of women within the family, the formation of a new value system must combine nonalienated natural difference with social regulation: on the one hand, family duties need to be socialized and shared with men so women are not doubly burdened (159, 165); on the other hand, women's maternal relationship with children, which stands as the base of all human emotions and embodies human beings' self-responsibility as well as the spirit of self-sacrifice for later generations, needs to be socially recognized and promoted as the ultimate value of humankind (165). Li's personal experience as a mother substantiated her emphasis on the role of reproduction in human history. The purpose, however, is not to strengthen race and nation or stress women's sexual desire and selection, as argued in early modern progressive feminism,[27] but to forge a nonalienated ethical and cultural system. Women's liberation cannot be separated from the liberation of humanity. Women can achieve final liberation only when humanity, on the basis of the public ownership of the means of production, achieves total liberation and society becomes a union of free people (165).

Li's article also articulates two different concepts of "sexual and gender difference" (性别差异). One is historically constituted, male-centered, and hierarchical, and the other is naturally signified and nonhierarchical. The gender/sex gap, a term Li adopted from Zhang Jie's writing, is formed through a long-term consolidation of historical and hierarchical sexual and gender difference. Li stresses that human civilization centers on economic development, takes man as the standard, and establishes itself on women's alienation (158). Women in this male-dominant history were first rendered as inferior to men (a claim based on natural difference) and then called on to become the same as men (gender equality that demands women overcome their natural difference). Li emphasizes that gender equality, which granted male rights to women without transforming the male-centered value system, was not the final goal of women's liberation but only one step forward in the process. Li was among the first few post-Mao female scholars to perceive the history and development of human civilization as a process of men's domination over nature and women.[28]

Natural or nonalienated sexual and gender difference entered Li's work most significantly as a base for a future reconfiguration of the abovementioned historical sexual and gender difference. Early post-Mao discussions of human nature and alienation, especially the humanistic argument that history should return from class struggle to human nature, directly influenced Li's formulation of a naturally based sexual and gender difference. In the 1980s, Li joined other women in addressing the largely overlooked issues of women's physical differences, their health, and their special psychological needs and desires. Li strongly argues, in her other writing as well, that society could not deliberately ignore the physiological differences between men and women. Ignorance had contributed to women's double burden, damaging their health and psychological well-being.[29] But Li's political and theoretical argument for the natural gender and sex difference contains a distinctively ethical and metaphorical dimension, expressing her feminist vision for the future. In a political move that is similar to Luce Irigaray's articulation of sexual difference,[30] Li resorted to natural difference to reconfigure sexual and gender difference as nonhierarchical (or mutually supportive and harmonious) and containing new ethical values (not male-centered). As post-Mao feminists were also keen on establishing an independent female subject, a nature-based identity seemed more promising than any extant concepts of women, which, according to Li, are already loaded with male values.[31] For Li, the development of male-centered human civilization has naturalized the hierarchical social relationship through perpetuating a double alienation (the objectification of labor and women). A feminist endeavor should return to the true natural difference to develop a new model that promotes nonhierarchical differences between men and women, forging a mutually dependent and harmonious relationship embodied, for example, in the mother-child relationship. Although it is not far-fetched to call Li an essentialist, given her insistence on natural sexual and gender differences and the natural mother-child relationship, Li's essentialism contains a profound understanding that natural differences can lead to radically different imaginings of society and ethics. Her natural essentialism interrogates the social determinism that has perpetuated male domination in history.

The Political, Intellectual, and Transnational Implications of Post-Mao Feminist Practice in the 1980s

The significance of post-Mao Chinese feminism and women's cultural practice is undeniable. It challenged the Marxist theory on setting the premise and criterion of women's liberation exclusively through women's participation in social production, and questioned the Marxist assumption that socioeconomic and material changes (class revolution) in history would automatically solve gender issues. It critically revealed existing issues in socialist feminist practice, pushing forward the need to revise Marxist theory, and articulated a new theory that could address gendered issues beyond socioeconomic equality or, in Li Xiaojiang's term, beyond social liberation. It also made a sustained critique of the return of traditional values and discrimination against women in the economic reform era and of the sexual difference predicated on women's alienation in history. In addition, post-Mao feminist practice forged for the first time in Chinese socialist history a public academic space where feminist theories could be developed and feminist knowledge (re)produced, challenging the gender blindness of the emerging mainstream discourse of liberal humanism, individual subjectivity, and cultural consciousness authorized by male intellectuals at the time.[32]

Despite these important achievements, post-Mao independent feminism was heavily implicated in and seriously conditioned by major contemporary political, intellectual, and transnational forces. These forces not only played a critical role in configuring the condition of post-Mao feminism's development but, eventually, also transformed its original inspirations and critical aims. It is thus crucial to probe the various entanglements between post-Mao feminism and other major discourses of the time to further contextualize post-Mao feminist practice and historicize its significance. What did the term *independence* mean, and what did a separate history of women signify in China in the early 1980s? How did women's studies become a scientific discipline disconnected from sociopolitical forces and movements? Where did the transhistorical antagonism between men and women come from? And why did the emergence and development of post-Mao independent feminism coincide with the overall decline of Chinese women's status in contemporary China? The following section explores the institutional, intellectual, and transnational underpinnings and conditions of post-Mao feminism, discussing particularly its contradictory engagements with various historical forces in the endeavor to forge an independent theoretical and cultural movement.

Institutional Formation of an "Independent Sphere": Separating Feminism from Party-State Policies in the Economic Reform Era

In the history of the Chinese socialist revolution and construction prior to the reform era, women's liberation had been much integrated into both Chinese socialist endeavors and the international socialist vision of human emancipation. The "woman question" was central to the imagination of socialist modernity, and socialist revolutionaries (male and female alike) shared the socialist ideal that all structural oppressions and exploitations should be eliminated. In fighting against Western and Japanese imperialism, Chinese men and women also fought together for the liberation of the proletarian class and of women. Feminism constituted an essential part of China's socialist movement, and the interdependence between feminism and socialism characterized the nature of CCP-led socialist undertakings before and after 1949, despite certain setbacks, compromises, and historical limitations.[33]

In the late 1950s some CCP leaders, basing their views on Marxist social production theory, believed that Chinese women were already liberated as they had been integrated into socialist social production and gender equality had been institutionalized. Consequently, some preliminary discussions arose regarding whether China still needed the official All-China Women's Federation (ACWF), which had been established in January 1949 under direct party leadership.[34] This discussion showed once again the limitation of Marxist theory in directing a continued women's liberation in a specific socialist setting and the influence of those in the party who emphasized more economic development in China's socialist practice at the time. But overall, the discussion never questioned the central ideology of gender equality, the continued structural support for women, and the belief that socialist women could play pioneering roles in all aspects of society. In the wake of the Cultural Revolution, the ACWF—together with the All-China Federation of Trade Unions (ACFTU) and the Communist Youth League—was criticized by more radical forces in the party for its increasingly bureaucratic problems and was in the beginning process of restructuring. The goal was to address the (re)emerging social (class and gender) issues in socialist China and to integrate women's work into the party-led mass movement more fully by replacing the ACWF with a mass-oriented women's organization. This important project, however, became derailed as the Cultural Revolution turned chaotic and political struggles took the central stage.[35] Consequently, this temporary paralysis of the ACWF and the absence of any women's organizations nationwide during the Cultural Revolution entailed additional problems that contributed to the return of certain traditional prejudices against women in the later period of the Cultural Revolution. In the early 1970s, discussions started about restoring the ACWF, ACFTU, and Communist Youth League, and in 1973 most local chapters of the ACWF were reestablished. The ACWF at the national level, however, did not resume work until 1978.[36]

The rebuilding of the national ACWF was consequently conducted in a quite different political-economic environment. As Barlow observed, "the restoration of a Maoist Women's Federation and the growing attack on its Mao-style concept of women's liberation unfolded at around the same time."[37] Despite the attempt made by some senior feminist figures from the Mao period to restore the Maoist Women's Federation altogether, the role of the ACWF became reconfigured in the post-Mao era, "when the political consensus that had bound women to the state was collapsing."[38] The party's leadership in the ACWF and the connection between the ACWF and the central party committees at various levels were significantly weakened compared to the pre–Cultural Revolution period.[39] "The women's movements on the whole are no longer directed by the Party," the claim went.[40] Many party committees stopped taking the work of the ACWF seriously, and the organization's overall status and resources declined.[41] More critically, the state policy that prioritized market development gradually revalidated the privatization of the socialist economy and private property rights, leading to the (re)emergence of various structural inequalities in contemporary China. The market-oriented environment thus "not only directly affected women, but also posed a challenge to the established ideology of gender equality."[42] The state eventually turned the ACWF into a nongovernmental organization in 1995.

This political-economic and institutional context is critical for us to understand the rise of post-Mao independent feminism. During the early reform era, the party-state launched a broad reconfiguration of the relationship between the political-economic, social, and cultural realms, disintegrating these areas from one another and paving the way for the appearance of semiautonomous sociocultural spheres more or less detached from state authority.[43] As Lin Chun has rightly pointed out, the rise of an autonomous, independent women's movement was "enabled by two parallel processes: a significant retreat of the state and a rapid expansion of the market."[44] The state not only designated economic and market development as China's priorities but also gradually separated some sociocultural realms from the central practice of the party-state and central administrative system. The first National Conference on Women's Issues of the New Era (1984) was thus already a joint event convened by the ACWF and several universities and research institutes, and the next meeting, in 1985, involved "even more organizers and participants from nongovernment institutions or as independent individuals/collectives."[45]

As the ACWF turned "independent," it fell out from the central party's decision-making process, losing institutional endorsement and recourses for its previously defined role and function. Struggling with its uncertain and sometimes contradictory role in China's economic transformation, the ACWF in the early 1980s promoted a self-improvement policy, dropping its previous insistence on the principle of equality.[46] At its fifth congress, held in 1983, the ACWF adopted the slogan "Four Selves"—namely, self-respect, self-love, self-possession, and self-improvement. In 1989, the ACWF slightly revised the Four Selves—self-respect, self-reliance, self-confidence, and self-improvement—with a strong reiteration of the need for "independence": "Instead of relying on the protection of society and government, in a market economy women had to become more independent and rely only on themselves."[47] Some Chinese feminist scholars have rightly argued that this self-focused movement reflected a direct and strong influence from Western liberal feminist ideas,[48] which were (re)introduced to China in the 1980s. This line of thinking, however, has neglected another major factor, namely, the role of the state in initiating various independent spheres when China began to implement a liberal-bent policy toward the end of the 1970s. Intriguingly, despite its independent status, the ACWF continued to commit itself to the official state policy of economic development, helping to alleviate the empirical and social justice issues resulting from market development, such as abuses of women and children, poverty, social disparities, job insecurity, women's health care issues, and environmental problems. In an ironic way, the overly positive rhetoric of independence not only legitimated the state's decision to renounce one of its previous central responsibilities concerning gender equality but also granted the ACWF a sense of self-agency despite their wholehearted service to the state's market development.

In a similar fashion, post-Mao feminist practices outside the ACWF, especially the women's studies movement launched by scholars like Li Xiaojiang, also highlighted the value of independence and attributed the historical significance of post-Mao feminism to its fully developed self-consciousness. Li Xiaojiang once evaluated the women's studies movement of the mid-1980s in the following way: "In the history of Chinese women, it marked a new starting point. Chinese women for the first time shed their entanglement with the nation-state, looked beyond the protection of home and the guidance of men, and relied on themselves and their own full self-consciousness to organize a women's movement. In the 1980s New Enlightenment Movement, women were not only not absent, but they also independently made their voices heard. This was a historical moment."[49]

The overall enthusiasm and embrace of independence revealed post-Mao feminists' significant blindness to their own historical formation; furthermore, such unconditional endorsement of independence inadvertently led post-Mao feminists to participate in the state-initiated dissolution of previous integrated socialist feminist practices. They thus indirectly assisted the state in removing feminist principles and practice from its central operation and its core responsibilities. As a reaction to the culturally uniform ideology of the Cultural Revolution, Chinese female intellectuals, like their male counterparts, were understandably eager to espouse the concepts of autonomy and independence in the post–Cultural Revolution times. But their immediate, uncritical occupation of the independent position exposed their inadequate assessment of the importance of integrated and centralized feminist practice in Mao's socialist China. In addition, this positioning rendered post-Mao feminists unable to challenge the state as it withdrew from its previous social and political commitment. That is to say, post-Mao female intellectuals' critical response to the party's rigid ideological campaign during the Cultural Revolution ultimately led to their dismissal of the party-state's fundamental obligation to commit itself to the feminist cause and to the structural support for feminist endeavors, both of which are indispensable for advancing socialist feminism.

In their promotion of self and independence, post-Mao feminists turned to science's infallible objectivity for a new foundation. One of Li Xiaojiang's ambitions in the 1980s was to revise Marxist theory and separate gender from class, establishing gender as a scientific category.[50] This logic of resorting to science when launching a new direction for future development, however, was hardly an independent feminist methodology. Deng Xiaoping famously stated, at the Opening Ceremony of the National Science Conference held in Beijing on March 18, 1978, "Science and technology are productive forces."[51] The subsequent, officially sponsored national debates among Chinese intellectuals on "Criteria for Measuring the Truth" (检验真理的标准) and "Seeking Truth from Facts" (实事求是) in May 1978 played the most critical role in forging an opposition between science and objectivity on one side and Maoist thought and Marxist political theory on the other.[52] The latter became reviewed as mere ideology or political deception. Indeed, the early New Era exercised economic rationality and scientific objectivity to reconfigure China's future orientation and repudiate sociopolitical theories (Maoist *and* Marxist) as the guiding principle for China's future development. Soon, science and knowledge became mainstreamed in intellectual discourses in the early 1980s. Marxist theory became reconsidered as a scientific discipline and research inquiry,[53] and male Marxist theorists began advocating for demobilization and cultural reflexivity rather than mobilization and cultural revolution.[54] Li Zehou's liberal revision of Marxist theory through Enlightenment modernization thought (Kant) in the 1980s further "sought to jettison the political . . . and return the economic field to ontological priority,"[55] establishing economic rationality, self-autonomy and individual agency, and scientific modernization as the keys to China's development. Chinese intellectuals' effort to reconnect with the liberal and scientific branch of humanism in the May Fourth Movement (1919) also indicated their intended negation of class revolution as pivotal to modern Chinese history.

Indeed, this official and intellectual promotion of science and rationality went hand in hand with the emerging trend of depoliticization at the time. This depoliticization was by no means apolitical: it represented "a strategy demanded by the dominant ideology of the new period."[56] It paved the way for the state's departure from certain important socialist commitments, reorienting its central agenda toward economic development instead. At the same time, as some scholars have already argued, this liberal-bent intellectual discourse of the 1980s was also highly gendered, forging an individual self-conscious subject that could be occupied only by an educated male.[57] The depoliticization embodied in the scientific, humanistic, autonomous Enlightenment discourse consequently also contributed to the rise of sexual and gender difference in the early post-Mao era as a powerful means to re-configure gender and the division of labor.

Post-Mao feminism was thus deeply entangled with the emerging main-stream intellectual discourses of scientific truth, depoliticization, human na-ture or ontology, and sexual difference.[58] In *The Sex/Gender Gap*, Li argues that the issue of women is ontological (nonpolitical) and the issue of class is sociohistorical (political): "Women and class are two different categories: the former is human ontological and the latter, social historical. The making and evolution of the female sex was prior to the formation of classes and intrinsi-cally transcends class relations. Under certain historical circumstances, women acquire class identities through [their relationship with] men and are indirectly dictated to by the commands of class struggle. However, the issue of class an-tagonism and its resolution by no means embraces the issues of women."[59]

Li, in her influential *Eve's Exploration*, calls for a reorientation of femi-nist theory and women's studies in contemporary China away from political practice. She challenges the long-accepted assumption that feminist theory provides a means to achieve women's political liberation. Women's political liberation, according to Li, belongs to an early stage of the women's move-ment, an argument post-Mao film feminists like Yuan Ying (远婴) would repeatedly proffer in their study of Chinese women's cinema in the early 1990s.[60] Feminist theory as part of women's studies, Li argues, should be viewed as a scientific discipline; its major task is to test the limits and prob-lems of political movements. In the book's preface, Li emphasizes that she launched her campaign for feminist theory and women's studies in the mid-1980s from the position of a female being, not from that of a politicized and manlike woman.[61] Socialist women and their integrated, political conscious-ness are thus positioned as antithetical to the rising independent conscious-ness predicated on sexual difference.

Feminists targeted contemporary male intellectuals' chauvinism and the rising discrimination against women in post-Mao society and culture, carving out an important feminist space in public. They turned a blind eye, however, to the political and economic forces underpinning the liberal and science-oriented mainstream discourse, which had led to the accelerating rise of male superiority and prejudice against women in post-Mao China. More critically, many core post-Mao feminist ideas—independence, the essential female subject, autonomous self-consciousness, natural sexual difference, the scientific nature of women's studies and feminist theory, and gender as a separate scientific category—were not only *not* independently born, but also closely linked to China's economic and political transformation as well as the newly mainstreamed discourse.

By participating in and endorsing major ideas of the mainstream discourse of the 1980s, post-Mao feminists began departing from their initial attempt to consolidate and improve socialist feminism. They gradually became dismissive of socialist feminist practice in general. Post-Mao feminists in the 1980s reviewed socialist women's liberation and gender equality as (1) imposed or bestowed from above by the party-state and men, not originating from women's independent consciousness or their own volition; (2) based on the male standard promoting equality and sameness; (3) politically and class-oriented (rather than gender and scientifically based); and accordingly (4) repressive toward female natural difference and dispossessing the female sex of its separate status. Toward the end of the 1980s, post-Mao feminist scholars like Meng Yue and Dai Jinhua even argued that the "'equality of men and women' was once a mythical trap, and equal pay for equal work was all but forced upon her. Gender difference is not a concept to be discarded or abandoned, but a necessary path through which she must pass."[62]

In an indirect but significant way, post-Mao feminists reinforced, from a different angle, most male intellectuals' negation of the importance of class revolution in modern Chinese history, their resentment of the socialist state in empowering women, and their promotion of natural sexual and gender difference as a tactic for reclaiming male virility and power. As China entered the market era in the early 1990s, some male intellectuals also relied directly on major post-Mao feminist arguments to further their idea that socialist gender equality had contributed to many of the problems China was facing. Zheng Yefu (郑也夫), for example, in his influential book *On Paying a Price* (代价论, 1995), not only openly argues for a necessary gendered division of labor but also categorically designates women as the weaker sex/gender. In addition to Western anthropological and free-market perspectives, Zheng particularly draws from post-Mao feminist points about socialist gender equality as a purely political endeavor (nonscientific), bestowed from above, and based on a male standard (unnatural, making women manlike) in his arguments.[63] He states, "Through adding the weak [women] and suppressing the strong [men], a huge administrative force has interfered with and damaged the normal division of labor between the strong and the weak, and made the weak mistake themselves as strong (non-weak), and strong lose their rightful self-confidence."[64] According to Zheng, this disorder in the socialist position accounts for the lack of "real men" (男子汉) and real women (*nonmenlike*) in China, as well as China's low economic productivity. He claims that equal pay for equal work is simply absurd and that Chinese women should return home.

On the surface, various parties used sexual difference differently in the New Era: the state for the market and gendered division of labor, male intellectuals for reasserting male superiority and returning women to the home, and feminists for an essential female self and consciousness; but in effect, their practices have directly and indirectly worked together, contributing to the repudiation of socialist egalitarianism and gender equality and causing the rapid and massive decline of Chinese women's socioeconomic and cultural status in China in the 1980s and 1990s. Even though Li Xiaojiang painstakingly retheorized sexual difference as nonalienated difference in order to claim a universal maternal ethics, the path to that idealized, ahistorical, and naturalized state remained far from clear. Furthermore, given the emerging mainstream reconfiguration of women in relation to the private sphere, especially the roles of wives and mothers, Li's argument could be easily appropriated to expedite women's return to the home.

The History and Theory of the Western Feminist Movement: The Universal Model

Chinese post-Mao feminist scholars and theorists started their feminist careers mostly by reworking Marxist theory on women's liberation, but many of them also looked to Western feminist history and theory for ideas and inspiration during an era when the path of Western Enlightenment modernity was deemed the universal model. Although formal Chinese translations of contemporary Western feminist theories remained limited in the early and mid-1980s, scholars were able to access Western books through foreign friends and other informal communication channels.[65] Post-Mao feminist scholars trained in Western literature and culture had more direct access to Western feminist works. For example, Li Xiaojiang first studied Western literature when she entered graduate school in 1979 and then switched to women's studies in 1980 after reading some materials about Western feminist theory and the feminist movement. She wrote, "Western feminism was an ally and support, offering the first gleam of enlightening female insight into my study of Marxism. I found rich spiritual resources in early European and American women writers. It was after I compared the Western and Chinese feminist movements that I began to question the assumption that Chinese women were liberated. Following the Western forerunners of women's liberation, I called for the awakening of Chinese women's female consciousness [in contemporary China]."[66]

Indeed, Li has attributed her theoretical works in the 1980s to the influences of both Marxist theory and Western feminism. She counts among the first group of scholars who translated Western feminist theories into Chinese, and her translated articles were published in *Selected Works of the Foreign Feminist Movement* (1987).[67] In addition to the Enlightenment discourse and liberal feminist ideas that informed the post-Mao feminist search for autonomy, individual subjectivity and freedom, and female self-consciousness,[68] post-Mao feminists like Li also actively sought other Western feminisms, especially those that could offer critical reflections on Marxist and socialist feminism. Among the three Western feminist articles Li translated and published in *Selected Works of the Foreign Feminist Movement*, for example, two can be considered important works by Western radical feminists: Heidi I. Hartmann and Ann R. Markusen's "Contemporary Marxist Theory and Practice: A Feminist Critique" (1980) and James Lin and Anna Paczuska's "Socialism Needs Feminism" (1981).[69] Some of Li's important arguments in "The Progress of Humanity and Women's Liberation" and her later works bear strong similarities to Western radical feminism, particularly those ideas emerging during the debate between the then-rising radical feminism and Marxist feminism at the turn of the 1980s.[70]

Historically, Western radical feminism and Chinese post-Mao feminism shared certain comparable sociopolitical conditions. Western radical feminism developed as a critical reaction to the male chauvinism and gender hierarchy that continued in Western left-wing and socialist movements, while post-Mao independent feminism responded to lingering issues in Chinese socialist feminism and the reemerging gender discrimination of the post-Mao reform era. As radical feminism became influential in the United States in the 1970s and 1980s, its central ideas became widely adopted by Western scholars researching socialist revolution and feminism practiced in other parts of the world, including China.[71]

Both post-Mao and radical feminist theories critically challenged the economic determinism and gender blindness of Marxist theory. In addition, Li's article and her later writings articulate several radical feminist arguments—that patriarchy is transhistorical and universal; that sexual oppression is different from class oppression and is the primary cause for all oppressions; and that Marxist theory centers on *production* (economic development) and dismisses the value inherent in the "women's work" of *re*production. More importantly, radical feminist proposals for forging an independent sex and gender system and for making changes through raising individual women's consciousness and promoting a female culture also echo through Li's works of the 1980s. Li's construction of a women's history separate from Marxist production- and class-oriented history, her critique of the whole history of human civilization as male-centered (patriarchal) and thus a history of women's alienation, her insistence on the difference between gender (ontological) and class (sociohistorical), and her proposed resolution for the ultimate women's liberation—namely, to return to natural (nonalienated) sexual difference and build a new ethics based on female experience in reproduction and a maternal culture—illustrate a theoretical logic and trajectory identical to Western radical feminism.

We cannot deny the importance of radical feminism's initial rise in the 1970s; it challenged Marxist theory on its inadequate theorization of gender issues and fought against continued male chauvinism in the Western left-wing movement. But when radical feminism evolved into cultural feminism while at the same time consolidating liberal feminist ideas after 1975, the movement not only failed to deliver what it had first appeared to promise but also turned, itself, into a conservative practice.[72] Rather than offering any original revisions of Marxist theory in the class-gender relationship, radical feminism gradually dismissed the Marxist theory of class altogether. Originating in left-wing sociopolitical movements of the 1960s, radical feminism eventually repudiated its initial goal of assaulting and critiquing capitalism and laid aside its previous approach of historical materialism, metamorphosing into an ahistorical and cultural practice within capitalist society. The radical feminist perception of patriarchy as transhistorical, permeating all sociopolitical institutions, rendered its proposal to change women's status by raising people's consciousness utterly inadequate and lacking in any persuasion. The radical feminist conservative and cultural turn, as I discussed in chapter 1, was far from a singular event at the time: it corresponded closely to the rise of the Second Cold War in the mid- to late 1970s and the renewal of an overall conservative trend in the United States reasserting the universality of Western capitalist values.[73]

Post-Mao feminist endeavors were thus also implicated in this confluence of global conservative forces which, in retrospect, were also tied to the emergence of a global neoliberal approach to governance and the market. China in the post-Mao economic reform era, from the late 1970s to the early 1980s, inadvertently but directly participated in this new global trend.[74] The intensified Second Cold War also produced a new wave of scholarship attacking the socialist system. Western feminist scholarship began to refute Chinese socialist women's liberation and, consolidating liberal feminism with the radical feminist perspective, (re)defined feminism as an individualistic and independent endeavor, claimed socialism failed to liberate women, and concluded that capitalism was a more suitable system for feminist endeavors.[75] Feminism's repudiation of socioeconomic and political movements and its subsequent settlement in academia and the cultural realm became the new global norm. The separations of gender from class, feminism from central policy making, and the question of women from men in China's context also, for the first time in the history of the socialist revolution, not only rendered feminism an elitist practice but also designated it as women's business alone.[76] The subsequent wholesale downturn of Chinese women's collective status in society, family, and culture has thus raised serious questions about the disintegration of feminism from central political-economic practices, a move initiated by the Chinese state and blindly embraced by post-Mao feminists in the New Era.

Indisputably, Western feminist practices and theories provide important references and critical insights for women's liberation movements taking place in other areas. But when they become a universal norm and model, as shown in the China of the 1980s, they begin to suppress important geopolitical differences, erase their own historical constitution and political limitation, and obliterate the historical and political significance of other feminist endeavors. Li's article "The Progress of Humanity and Women's Liberation" (1983) testifies to this suppressing effect. In it, Li traces a universal history of women's liberation movements entirely based on Western feminist movements, from the French Revolution to the suffrage movement in the United States and then to women's fights and work in World Wars I and II. Li does give passing mention to women's suffrage organizations after 1911 in China, but situates the allusion in the framework of Western and thus universal feminist movements.[77] Whereas the original goal of Li's essay was to address the topic of continued feminist practice in the socialist period, the histories of socialist revolution and socialist women's liberation are notably absent from the article. Chinese socialist experiences seemed incompatible with the standardized, universal model and thus had to be excluded. Given the argument Li made elsewhere, that socialist gender equality was bestowed from above rather than fought for by women themselves with their awakened female consciousness (and thus could not bring real liberation),[78] the absence of socialist feminism in the article also seems to suggest that Chinese women should move back to an earlier stage to make up what they missed in order to move forward on the right track. In any case, the erasure of the socialist revolution and socialist feminism in the article not only derailed the initial goal of Li's theoretical intervention but also precluded an important comparative study of feminist practices in different socioeconomic systems. Although Li does, toward the end of her article, insist on a Marxist view that the abolition of private property ownership is the precondition for women's final liberation, this point is by no means integrated into the overall argument, especially with the absence of any discussion of socialist feminist practice.

When female intellectuals voiced their personal gendered experiences in the early post-Mao era, their ideas were rooted in China's changing history, and their primary aim was to address the remaining gaps in both socialist feminist practice and new emerging issues during the period of reform after Mao. They had no intention to question the critical importance of public ownership, institutionalized gender equality, and structural support for women in the socialist system. With the advancement of independent post-Mao feminism around the mid- and late 1980s, especially its intimate interactions with the state's policy, mainstream-intellectual discourses, and post-second-wave radical and cultural feminisms, the original goal became seriously compromised and reoriented. Where Western radical feminism abandoned its original left-wing, anticapitalist objective after separating gender from class, the post-Mao feminism, in its search for independent status and a universal position, abandoned the very socialist foundation—institutionalized gender equality and the integration of feminism into socialist political-economic and sociocultural structure—upon which it had initially attempted to further feminist endeavors. Implicated in the global sea change and complicit with national market development, post-Mao feminism renounced socialist integrated feminism, forging during the mid- to late 1980s an independent feminism and female culture that emphasized a separate gender and sex system, transhistorical patriarchy, sexual difference, a critique of men, and a universal female consciousness. This emanant female consciousness, as I discussed at the beginning of this chapter, was only possible through eclipsing socialist history, including socialist women and their sociopolitically oriented consciousness. Post-Mao feminist ideas gained momentum and became popularized in the late 1980s, significantly affecting Chinese women's cultural practice. As my chapter 7 shows, post-Mao feminism, together with male-centered mainstream discourse, transformed Chinese women's cinema toward the end of the 1980s and further developed into a universal cultural feminist discourse in the early 1990s.

5 Film Theory, Avant-Gardism, and the Rise of Masculine Aesthetics

Chinese Mainstream Cinema in the 1980s

As part of the general post-Mao cultural production, the cinema of the New Era (roughly 1978–1987) initially manifested two tendencies. On the one hand, it was a cultural practice carried out by Chinese intellectuals as a critical reaction to the Cultural Revolution, especially its class-struggle ideology and politicized cultural practice. The new regime under Deng Xiaoping lost no time offering the final "verdict" on the Cultural Revolution in 1981 and restructuring the state's priorities: it shifted the nation's focus from the political-cultural campaign of the Cultural Revolution to the urgency of economic reform; rehabilitated almost all of those who had been "wronged" or victimized during that time (mostly senior party officials and intellectuals); and reconstructed the party's image by attributing most problems to the Gang of Four while relaxing political control of cultural production.[1] Effectively, the Cultural Revolution—described as a period of economic disaster, political turmoil, social trauma, and cultural destruction—became a negative yet powerful force for uniting and mobilizing the nation to move in a different direction. On the other hand, within a more relaxed environment, Chinese cultural practice in the early post-Mao era also generated various creative bursts, testing previously taboo subjects and exploring new styles and genres.[2] As scholars have rightly observed, the early New Era was another period of a "hundred flowers blooming,"[3] with the emergence of cultural pluralism.

In early New Era film production, several generations of filmmakers from vastly different historical and artistic backgrounds resumed film practices with varied ideas and artistic visions. They not only looked to Chinese film history, from both the golden era of left-wing cinema (the 1930s and 1940s) and socialist mainstream films (the 1950s and 1960s), but also explored foreign, especially European, film theory and experimental styles. Initiated by the Fourth Generation Chinese filmmakers, most of whom were born in the 1940s and educated in socialist film academies or theater schools in the late 1950s and early 1960s, another period of cinematic experimentation began. A diverse body of mainstream films appeared in the New Era, ranging from social realism to experimentalism, political melodrama to documentary aesthetics and avant-gardism, and the return of pre–Cultural Revolution socialist film genres (like rural films, socialist comedies, traditional opera films, children's films, spy films, and literary adaptations) to the return of commercial genres (martial arts, romances, and thrillers).

In retrospect, scholarship on Chinese cinema has inadequately studied the significance of this early post-Mao pluralism. The cause of the dismissal has much to do with the subsequent rise and dominance of the mid-1980s' new mainstream discourse that rationalized and endorsed a depoliticized and universalized direction for China's economic and cultural development. This mainstream discourse neutralized the sociopolitical heterogeneity of the New Era's cinematic pluralism and reoriented post-Mao experimental cinema toward an avant-gardism spearheaded primarily by the fledgling Fifth Generation Chinese filmmakers, most of whom, born in the 1950s, had graduated from the Beijing Film Academy in 1982. In the hands of this new generation, New Era experimental cinema reached its pinnacle: abstract cultural reflection, stylistic renovation, and a masculine reimagination of China's past and future. Indeed, the most influential film criticism and scholarship produced in China at the turn of the 1980s and beyond worked mainly to advance a total break from socialist era filmmaking, canonize European film theory, rationalize universal aesthetic values, and promote an independent experimentalism. This chapter explores major contributing factors in the development of New Era film discourse and practice, which helped mainstream a universal path to modernity, whether cinematic or historical, in 1980s China. In addition, it compares the conventionally perceived New Era experimental cinema with its European inspiration—namely, the French New Wave—critically probing their shared political motivations, sociocultural stances, and gendered underpinnings.

Film Theory, Film Studies, and the Depoliticization of Film Production

According to scholar Xia Hong, one of the salient features of Chinese film development in the New Era was its focus on film theory: "Never in the history of Chinese film has film theory been explored so enthusiastically and extensively."[4] Whereas early New Era film practice manifested different traditions and diverse significations, film theory and criticism tended to reflect on problems in the socialist Chinese film aesthetic and techniques, and to promote film styles and languages from other (mainly European) cinematic traditions since the 1950s. Hong elaborates on four areas of theoretical debate at the time: (1) realism, (2) the cognition and exploration of film, (3) film studies, and (4) nationalization.[5] Although film critics discussed all these topics, a general consensus held that Chinese film practice was outdated, lagging behind world film practice, and thus needed to catch up.

One of the most critical and controversial topics appearing in this period concerns the ontology of film—namely, film as a medium of its own, independent from drama and literature. Bai Jingsheng (白景晟) first voiced the necessity for film to "throw away the drama crutch" in early 1979, but it was Zhang Nuanxin (张暖忻) and Li Tuo (李陀)'s coauthored 1979 article, "On the Modernization of Film Language,"[6] that paved the way for not simply "recognizing" film as an art of its own but also, more importantly, establishing a link between film language's evolution and China's overall modernization. Although the article, read through a twenty-first-century optic, contains certain contradictions and tensions (which may reflect differences between the two authors),[7] its framing and overall rhetoric both anticipated and *contributed to* the liberal turn of Chinese cinema and culture in the mid-1980s.

Zhang and Li, in their article, sketch a "progressive" history of world (predominantly Western) cinema and Western film theory. Using this history as the norm and standard for film development, the authors argue that Chinese film production had fallen far behind due to the Gang of Four's fascist political control of cultural production, which exclusively emphasized politics, content, and filmmakers' world views at the expense of art, form, aesthetics, and techniques. The outdated film language and mode of production reflected China's political and cultural backwardness. Zhang and Li also point out that this politically oriented cultural practice did not begin with the Gang of Four, suggesting that the same problems had existed in socialist or even left-wing cultural productions of the 1930s.[8] By drawing readers' attention to the film aesthetic of Italian neorealism, the style of the French New

Wave, and André Bazin's theory of the long take—all of which promote everyday life, ordinary details, and the "natural" state of being, turning critical of drama, political conflicts, and montage—Zhang and Li call on Chinese filmmakers to embrace these "progressive" ideas and forms. Only by following this progressive norm would Chinese film production be liberated from both the constraints of melodramatic or literary scripts and the dominance of general and ultraleftist politics in socialist Chinese history. With their depoliticized remapping of world film history in terms of film ontology, form, and style, the authors conclude that the most efficient way to modernize Chinese film language is to learn from world (again, mostly Western) film art and adapt Western practice for Chinese use. The two authors also quote Mao Zedong (毛泽东) and Lu Xun (鲁迅) to legitimize their claim that Westernization represented the first step toward building a modern Chinese film language.[9]

Published when China was in the midst of its initial transformation after the Cultural Revolution, the article helped break new ground in diversifying Chinese film theory and practice. But the historical implication of the article goes beyond both its immediate context and the realm of Chinese filmmaking. Considered later by Chinese film scholars and critics as "the artistic manifesto of the Fourth Generation [film directors]" and "the outline of experimental cinema" for the New Era,[10] the article corresponded closely to official New Era discourses, including modernization, thought liberation, seeking truth from facts, humanism, and scientism. More importantly, the article's binary dichotomies—content/form, drama/film, fabrication/truth (or nature), Chinese film/world cinema, backwardness/modernization, (leftist) politics/universal art, nationalization/Westernization—played a critical role in championing the idea that only depoliticizing China's culture and redirecting it to a universal, normal path as exemplified in the Western model could save China from its chaotic or irrational past. This idea became mainstreamed in the mid-1980s, and contributed to neutralizing and eventually repudiating the heterogeneity and diversity manifested in early post-Mao film practice.

Subsequent public debates about the role of (melo)drama and literature in film production among Chinese film critics and directors occurred on two different levels. At the more technical and stylistic level, directors and critics across several generations expressed their different understandings of film as an art form. Some stressed modernist film as just one cinematic type, while others upheld film as a comprehensive art that should get "married" to rather than "divorced" from other arts.[11] One critic argued that neither the dramatic nor the filmic should be taken as the sole criterion for judging a film's quality,[12] arguing that good and bad films exist in both categories.

On the more abstract level, however, the discussion of film's independence from other art forms carried far-reaching implications. First, as the dramatic mode and dramatization were, at the time of the article's publication, closely associated with the art of the Cultural Revolution with implications of falsity and political control, the call for film autonomy functioned to challenge the socialist utilitarian approach to cultural production, specifically the rule requiring the arts to serve politics.[13] Zhang and Li's article clearly equates the modernization of film language with the depoliticization of film production. That is to say, promoting film theory and film's independent status meant departing from politics in Chinese cinematic practice in general. Second, echoing other groups of Chinese intellectuals and scholars of the time, this call for autonomy expressed Chinese intellectuals' desire to achieve a sense of freedom in cultural production and an independent status in the New Era.

In this context, the rise of film studies as an academic discipline in the New Era further endorsed film as an independent and depoliticized medium.[14] In her essay "The Mainstream Trend of 1980s–1990s Chinese Film Theory Development" Yuan Ying states, "The dominant discourse concerning 1980s literary and art theory centers on the expression and exploration of disciplinary autonomy and independence, the transcendence of the utilitarian function of art and literature, and the critique of the idea that viewed artistic thought as a political tool." Yuan concludes, "Film studies returning to its own ontological entity is therefore the manifestation [of the general discourse] in this particular discipline."[15] The development of film theory and film studies in early New Era China therefore had close ties to the general transformation of Chinese economic and cultural landscapes, a shift that highlighted rationality, modernization, depoliticization, and disengagements from social (particularly class and gender) and regional issues.

It is indisputable that after nearly a decade of tight control of cultural production, Chinese intellectuals' desire for pluralist cultural practice was not only legitimate but also critical for resuming a basic level of cultural productivity and creativity. In retrospect, the problem lay not in this historical desire itself but in several hasty assumptions and untested conclusions, which led inadvertently to the rise of an elitist, masculine-focused cultural modernism oblivious to the ongoing socioeconomic structural metamorphosis. First, denouncing the ideology of the Cultural Revolution and its politicization of cultural production was often equated with totally repudiating politics in cultural practices. This equation not only distorts the historical nature of art and cultural production, which is always politically informed and conditioned, but also obscures the ideological underpinning of reform-era cultural practices. As others have argued, the process of depoliticization and thought liberation after Mao was by no means apolitical. Rather, this process itself was "a strategy demanded by the dominant ideology of the new period."[16] Indeed, "scar literature" (伤痕文学), which accentuated the destruction of familial and humanistic values during the Cultural Revolution and rendered those values natural and universal, played an important role in legitimizing the new regime and its politico-economic role in China's post-Mao transformation. The issue was not about politicization versus depoliticization, or politics versus art, but what *kind* of politicization or politics. The belief that art must exist separately from politics prevented reform-era Chinese intellectuals from reflecting critically on their own political stances as well as on the political effects of their cultural practice.

Second, the belief in artistic autonomy, which set the aesthetic *against* the political in the post–Cultural Revolution context, also negated artistic achievements made during the Cultural Revolution and earlier socialist periods. Indeed, the socialist experimental cinema that had creatively engaged with social and political ideals during the Cold War was virtually erased in the post-Mao promotion of film theory, artistic autonomy, and experimental cinema. That is to say, when art was perceived as something antithetical to politics during the New Era, condemning the politicization of cultural practice automatically denied the artistic accomplishments of the socialist period.[17]

Third, and most critically, though the critique of the Cultural Revolution's dogmatism and tendency to reduce art to politics has a legitimate place in history, its total rejection of socialist literary theory—particularly the part concerning the integrated and interlocking relationship between cultural practice and sociopolitical change—led to the premature demise of a mainstream culture that could potentially develop into a socially rooted, politically engaged, and artistically pluralistic practice. This repudiation also discouraged Chinese intellectuals from critically (re)addressing relationships between the aesthetic and the political, intellectuals and the masses, and cultural and economic practices as China augmented economic reform in the mid-1980s. As a matter of fact, the emergence of the cultural practice that was detached from the growing sociopolitical concerns caused by the contemporary economic transformation was part of the process the new regime had initiated in its prioritizing the market development. Contrary to what most intellectuals believed they were doing at the time—that is, forging a cultural space independent from politics—their cultural practice often implicitly complied with the state's new policy direction, gradually disintegrating culture from the sociopolitical and economic restructuring and, consequently, diminishing culture's role in affecting and questioning the trajectory of social and economic development.

The Political and Gendered Underpinnings
of French New Wave and New Chinese Cinema

Prioritizing the aesthetic over the political (especially the socialist political commitment) was hardly a phenomenon of post–Cultural Revolution China alone. This valorization had had already a long history in the development of capitalist modernity[18] and was further trumpeted in Western Cold War ideology, which widely promulgated the notion that "socialist political commitment is incompatible with the production of genuine art."[19] By associating aesthetics exclusively with capitalist society's individualistic creativity and middle-class freedom, the Western Cold War ideology worked to deny artistic achievements of socialist culture as well as to champion socially disengaged and apolitical cultural practices in the West. A brief detour through the rise and canonization of French New Wave cinema, which inspired Chinese filmmakers and film critics to advocate film-language modernization in the New Era, can help us reassess both the local and global significance of post-Mao Chinese experimental cinema.

Geneviève Sellier, in her *Masculinity Singular: French New Wave Cinema* (2008), departs from the prevailing aesthetic or "auteurist" approach, foregrounding instead a sociocultural perspective that helps situate the New Wave's formative years (1957 to 1962) in postwar and Cold War political contexts.[20] She traces a sociocultural and historical research model established by a minority of scholars studying the New Wave to critically reveal complex political underpinnings of the cinema. In postwar France (after 1945), when the conservative bourgeoisie represented by business, the church, and the military reasserted its power, not only had all Nazi collaborators received official pardons by 1950, but Resistance heroes were maligned and prosecuted as communists. Pressured by the United States to participate in the Cold War, France initiated its own brand of McCarthyism. French politics moved steadily to the right from 1945 to 1950 until all the representatives of the working class were finally removed from governmental participation. Given the prominent economic hardship, political uncertainty, and fear of nuclear war in this period, many French intellectuals desired to withdraw from the chaotic situation and thus rejected the idea that art should be socially committed. This rejection, according to John Hess, turned against Jean-Paul Sartre's advocacy of engaged literature and promoted art for art's sake instead, illustrating a resolute return "to the standard bourgeois conception of art as autonomous and out of time."[21]

French film criticism of the 1950s, according to Sellier, actually drew extensively from Cold War divisions. While French communist critics fell back on a local version of socialist realism due to the political situation's increasing rigidity, the critics of *Cahiers du cinema*, who became key figures of the New Wave movement toward the end of the decade, "championed an American cinema seen afresh through a cultivated optic."[22] The significance of French New Wave lies exactly in the fact that it was often perceived as a new cinema that "transcended politics and that would, in the end, make an aesthetic and apolitical vision of the value of these films prevail in France."[23] It established a value system "whereby artistic genius, and not morality or politics, becomes the measure of everything."[24] Although French New Wave as a movement lasted only a few years, its toxic influence, at once formalist and chauvinist, has continued—as has its dominance over film discourse in France and the world in the dismissal of politics, society, class, and gender (content, in a word) in favor of experimenting with form and style. Indeed, as Sellier insightfully points out, "the New Wave has become synonymous with modernity— modernity as it is generally understood in France, in the aesthetic rather than historical sense of the term."[25] When cinema obtained its autonomous status, distinguishing itself from literature (scripts as well) and "accede[d] to the dignity of modern art,"[26] it became a turning point of the postwar period.

The sociocultural approach to the New Wave as outlined in Sellier's book offers critical insights into such acclaimed concepts as universal aesthetics and individual genius. It illustrates a significant mutual implication between the auteur theory and France's social and economic modernization in the 1950s. The emergence of a young generation eager to acquire sexual and economic freedom coincided with the emergence of a cultural turn in France (and the West in general) that tended to disassociate the spiritual and cultural realms from the sociopolitical and economic ones,[27] endorse individual subjectivity and capitalist freedom over collective interests, stress the autonomy of the text (work) at the expense of the social, and redefine cultural elitism itself as a sort of political radicality.[28]

Jean-Pierre Esquenzre's study of the New Wave particularly demonstrates that the movement arose at the very moment "when French society begins to valorize a form of modernity, characterized as subversive, that is practiced only within the cultural field."[29] This detached or distanced cultural practice in the name of auteur theory, however, was by no means apolitical. Rather, it functioned as, in Hess's word, "a justification, couched in aesthetic terms, of a culturally conservative and politically reactionary attempt to remove film from the realm of social and political concern, in which the progressive forces of the Resistance had placed all the arts in the years immediately after the war."[30] As Sellier's book also notes, the New Wave represented a general cultural trend that not only rejected the Zhdanovism[31] incarnated by the French Communist Party in the Cold War's anticommunist context but also expressed hostility to Jean-Paul Sartre, who advocated for a socially engaged literature.[32]

The claim to the universal value of aesthetic and artistic genius is not only conservative and elitist but also, as current scholarship has forcefully uncovered, masculine in nature. Sellier's feminist investigation of the New Wave brings to light additional traditional and conservative underpinnings of the movement: "Of the 150 filmmakers who made their first full-length fictional film between 1957 and 1962, there isn't a single woman."[33] The backbone of the auteur theory includes traditional Romanticism, the guiding paradigm of the lone male creator,[34] and male fetishism and voyeurism.[35] The social condition in France of the late 1950s also witnessed the return of conservatism in young French men with regard to gender relations. "In general, the fear is expressed by the whole New Wave generation that women would become more masculine because they are working and becoming interested in men's professions, that they would cease to be 'real women.'"[36] (Chinese male intellectuals in the post-Mao New Era also strongly expressed a similar anxiety in reaction to socialist China via the term "stronger women and weaker men."[37]) Through a close analysis of women's representations in two New Wave films from the early 1960s, Sellier reaches the following conclusion: "Contrary to received opinion that New Wave cinema expressed both artistic modernity and a throwing off of moral constraint, the films were crisscrossed by contradictory currents linked both to the elitist and masculine nature of this cinema and specific French cultural traditions. . . . For want of a better term, I shall call this phenomenon 'male libertinage.'"[38] In the absence of any substantial female participation in the creative process, the modern vision provided by the New Wave films "offers glaring contradiction on the question of equality."[39] New Wave directors, in choosing narcissistic formalism, pronounced at the heart of the movement a masculine first-person singular "I" that considered itself universal.[40]

Although the historical and political situations of postwar France in the 1950s and post–Cultural Revolution China in the 1980s were not identical, they generated similar political, economic, and cultural concerns and desires, especially among intellectuals, which led to an enthusiastic reception of both French New Wave ideology and its aesthetic in the early and mid-1980s in China. Both countries were in the process of revising and making sense of an immediate political past (antifascist war or the Cultural Revolution), while simultaneously implementing a rigorous, liberal, and state-sponsored economic modernization. Although left-wing and socialist legacies continued in both countries, the rejection of politically engaged and utilitarian cultural practices—socialist, left-wing, or revolutionary realism, characteristic of the previous era in both countries' histories—emerged as a dominant trend among intellectuals, together with the rise of cultural elitism, the call for capitalist freedom of expression and artistic autonomy, and the articulation of a universal aesthetic or culturalist modernity. Realism, or the "truthful state of the real" (真实性), became resignified through the highlighted practice of an apolitical documentary style in both French and Chinese contexts[41]—whether to reveal a spiritual or religious presence (Bazin's long-take theory); to express a personal or subjective interiority, destiny, and salvation (the New Wave);[42] or to manifest a brand of universal, cultural, and Enlightenment humanism (Chinese experimental cinema)—and retreated from any critical engagements with contemporary social and political-economic transformations.

To return to Zhang and Li, their 1979 article argues the need to prioritize their writing on the form, style, and techniques of film art because China particularly lagged in those areas due to the severe constraints of Cultural Revolution policy. Consequently, the authors had to omit discussions of film content and the political and economic forces that enabled various film developments in history. This statement functioned at the time to defend their choice of discussion topics; in retrospect, it also revealed the emerging trend of sociopolitical disengagement in the cultural practice of the 1980s. No major or effective attempt was made in either film theory or film studies to connect cinematic practice with the period's growing social concerns. The prevalence of Chinese critics' and filmmakers' fascination with European film experimentalism, particularly French New Wave and Italian neorealism, thus indicated a similar desire for a cultural practice that would bring a sense of eternity and stability stripped of sociopolitical uncertainties as well as historical contingencies and in the form of an aesthetic universalism. The overall Chinese reception of French New Wave and Italian neorealism in the early New Era, therefore, echoed and reinforced the New Wave's vision of aesthetic modernity and artistic genius.[43]

This vision of aesthetic universalism and artistic individuality began to dominate cultural practice in China in the mid-1980s as the state pushed forward its economic reform in urban areas and reoriented its cultural policy. From December 29, 1984, to January 5, 1985, the Fourth National Congress of the Chinese Writers Association (中国作家协会第四次全国代表大会) was held in Beijing and a new slogan, "creative freedom" (创作自由), was promoted, indicating the beginning of a new stage in literary and cultural development.[44] During this congress, the party spokesman Hu Qili (胡启立) approved literary and cultural production with the primary function of entertainment, rather than education, of the masses. Furthermore, "in pointed contrast to the Maoist dictum that writers should identify with the masses of workers, Hu asserted that literary works do and should reveal the individuality of the writer; literature should express the writer's own views and artistic skills."[45] Thus, Hu proclaimed, "Creative writing must be free!" As some scholars have already pointed out, to Hu and the party leadership, "this means freedom for the writer in choice of subject matter and theme and artistic method, and in expressing their own thoughts and emotions."[46] Although Hu also called for Chinese writers to recognize their own social responsibility to oppose both bourgeois values and the negative remnants of China's traditional ideologies, he implicitly yet effectively predicated "creative freedom" on the separation of literary and artistic practice from the socioeconomic and political realms, attaching it instead to individual expression, artistic talent, and entertainment.

Writers and artists across generations embraced Hu's speech, including esteemed veteran author Ba Jin (巴金), known both for his promotion of creative freedom in post–Cultural Revolution China and his literary dedication to social progress. It was, however, the younger generation of male writers and artists—most of them had been sent down to rural areas as young educated youth (知青) to get reeducated by peasants during the Cultural Revolution—who played the most important role in reorienting Chinese literary and artistic creations on this new stage. This young generation stormed the cultural scene and, while exploring the causes for China's lagging behind the modern world, launched the Root-Seeking Movement— turning to cultural reflection, marginalized cultural traditions, universal humanism, and aesthetic experiments to reimagine alternative national and individual identities.

In an active response to the new cultural policy, male members of this generation, mostly root-seeking writers and Fifth Generation filmmakers, finally made, through their literary and cinematic creations, a recognizable break from the socialist mainstream cultural practice. As some scholars have insightfully pointed out, it was during the rise of the Root-Seeking Move-

ment that Sartre's existentialism, as well as his concept of engaged literature, which enjoyed tremendous popularity in the early post-Mao era, was
replaced by Freudian psychoanalysis, Jung's collective unconsciousness and
archetypes, Arnold J. Toynbee's philosophy of civilization, and Li Zehou's
revival of ancient Chinese thought and culture, all of which stressed, in the
Chinese context, an abstract, determining, and universal structure indifferent to concrete sociopolitical changes.[47] This break received high recognition by global intellectuals on the international stage as it conformed to the
concept of literature and art as autonomous and universal, transcending
sociopolitical context. In "Culture against Politics: Roots-Seeking Literature," Mark Leenhouts concludes that root-seeking "moved literature away
from its *narrow* sociopolitical engagement by stressing much *broader* cultural aspects of literature. By drawing attention to aesthetic dimensions of
literature and delving into questions of identity and subjectivity, moreover, it
paved the way for the 'avant-garde' literature of the later 1980s and 1990s."[48]

The underpinning logic of the cinematic break enacted by Fifth Generation male filmmakers, together with China's development of avant-gardism
in the mid- and late 1980s, is not dissimilar to that of the French New Wave.
Esther C. M. Yau, in her well-received article on a Fifth Generation signature
film, "*Yellow Earth*: Western Analysis and a Non-Western Text," insightfully
and succinctly exposes what is behind such an avant-gardist practice:

> The China that partakes in the world's market economy no longer oper-
> ates in an "ideological context" that is uniquely Chinese (as it had dur-
> ing the Cultural Revolution). Inevitably (and maybe unfortunately), this
> changing, modernizing "ideological context" in China also informs the
> "avant-gardist" project of *Yellow Earth*, which has focused its criticism
> *only* on the patriarchal and feudal ideologies of that culture. Arguably,
> then, *Yellow Earth*'s modernistic power of critique of Chinese culture and
> history comes from its sub-textual, noncritical promotion of capitalist-
> democracy as an alternative; it is (also arguably) this grain in the text that
> attracts the global intellectuals as well.[49]

This subtextual, noncritical promotion of capitalist democracy in avant-
gardist films like *Yellow Earth* coincided with an increasingly noticeable repudiation of socialist filmmaking in the cultural production of the late 1980s and
1990s. In their *One Hundred Years of Chinese Cinema* (中国电影百年) volumes,
Sun Xiantao (孙献韬) and Li Duoyu (李多钰) call for a critical reflection on
the diminishing of the socialist legacy in post-Mao film production.[50] Indeed,
the early New Era's denouncement of the Cultural Revolution soon developed

into an overarching dismissal of socialist history and cultural production as a whole.[51] Sun and Li earnestly remind readers that a planned economy, contrary to popular opinion, proved in the early-1980s Chinese context to be a necessary base for a truly diverse development of film genres. They illustrate how socialist genre films, established in the 1950s and early 1960s, reemerged in the New Era with great success—not only attracting audiences and making profits but also, together with newly developed film trends, forging a true pluralism in terms of both production and reception.[52] Starting from the mid-1980s, two growing trends curbed the development of pluralism in early post-Mao cinema: the gradual privatization of the film industry and the rise of the avant-gardism epitomized in Fifth Generation filmmaking.[53] As the state retreated from its previous support for film production, film varieties shrank immediately. At the same time, Sun and Li argue, the Fifth Generation directors, by emphasizing avant-gardism and the auteur theory so heavily, began losing touch with their audience and ultimately failed to elevate the general quality of film production as a whole. As this cultural avant-gardism became the new intellectual trend and won international acclaim, socialist genre films were perceived as outdated among most Chinese directors.

Chinese film theory, criticism, and scholarship also played a critical role in accelerating the separation of aesthetics from politics by canonizing Fifth Generation filmmakers. The disproportionately extensive focus film critics and scholars placed on Fifth Generation male directors, for example, came at the expense of serious discussions of many socialist genre films. The overlooked films included box office hits like the traditional opera film *Legend of the White Snake* (白蛇传, dir. Fu Chaowu [傅超武], 1980), the socialist rural film *Our Niu Baisui* (咱们的牛百岁, dir. Zhao Huanzhang [赵焕章],1983), and the socially engaged realist film *Enchanting Band* (迷人的乐队, dir. Wang Haowei [王好为], 1985).[54] Although the number of avant-gardist films by male directors is very small, the group has received the lion's share of criticism and scholarship. Consequently, many other types of films, including those by New Era *female* directors, became marginalized and their historical and artistic significance dismissed. Socialist film genres gradually became, in Sun and Li's term, "wiped out" (灭绝) as the New Cinema no longer concerned itself with "grassroots folk" audiences or social issues.[55] In the late 1980s and early 1990s when the market began shaping dominant film genres in terms of consumption, profit, and reproducibility,[56] Chinese film production moved further away from the socially embedded pluralism of the early post-Mao New Era.

The rise of avant-gardism and increasing market demand corresponded to a major transformation of gender in both film production and representation. Humanism in the early post-Mao era already reconfigured the cinematic representation of gender and sexuality by highlighting human nature and women's feminine, as well as domestic, roles in films like *Oh Cradle!* (啊摇篮, dir. Xie Jin [谢晋], 1979),[57] but it did not objectify women in a dominant fashion. Similarly, although the initial sign of a male-centered masculine cinema can be traced back to male directors' experimental cinema of the early 1980s, like Yang Yanjin's [杨延晋] 1981 *Narrow Street* (小街),[58] it was not until the middle of the decade that the masculine character became the norm. Women directors like Zhang Nuanxin, who pioneered experimental cinema in both theory and practice in the early post-Mao New Era, soon found themselves dismissed and marginalized in the late 1980s and early 1990s. As the state retreated from social interventions and granted more space to market-conditioned free expression, the experimental film movement followed other male-centered cultural movements, increasingly detaching itself from contemporary sociopolitical and economic issues and affording priority instead to cultural and aesthetic reflections on socialist China's "abnormality," especially the loss of male masculinity. As mentioned in the last chapter, post-Mao male intellectuals used the term "the prosperity of the feminine and the decline of the masculine" (stronger women and weaker men) to imply that the cause of China's problems lay in socialist gender equality.[59] Chinese male writers and artists, in the Searching for Real Men and Root-Seeking Movements, revealed a strong desire to reinstate the "right" order of the nation by restoring the "normal" and "natural" order between "real men" and "real women"—echoing a similar sentiment French New Wave male directors had articulated about thirty years previous.

As Fourth and Fifth Generation male directors turned to cultural reflections and masculine restoration in their experimental films in the mid- and late 1980s, their female characters became socially objectified, culturally emptied,[60] symbolically invisible,[61] and sexually repressed or exhibited.[62] Traditional virtuous women and naturalized femininity returned, and the female sexualized body filled the screen. The mid-1980s cultural transformation thus not only endorsed the ongoing economic reform—characterized as a return to a universal/normal/market modernity—but also facilitated the reassertion of male superiority in terms of both naturalized male virility and critical reflectivity.

Conclusion: From the Avant-Garde to the Commercial

Film criticism and experimental cinema once played an essential role in creating a political and popular cinema in Shanghai's left-wing movement in the 1930s and socialist China in the 1950s and early 1960s.[63] In the mid-1980s, however, due to the joint effect produced by state-initiated economic reform, Chinese (male) intellectuals' pursuit of a universal aesthetic, and the international trend of culturalism and market globalization, Chinese New Cinema broke from both the left-wing and socialist cultural legacies, advancing a sociopolitically disengaged, formally experimentalist, and culturally masculine (male-centered) and reflective style.[64] As part of the general cultural trend that began to sever itself from everyday socioeconomic practices and struggles, the new experimental cinema also, in a seemingly ironic way, contributed to the overall transformation of Chinese filmmaking to commercial production in the late 1980s and early 1990s.

The year 1987 marked the Fifth Generation male directors' intriguing transition from avant-gardism to commercialism, with the releases of both Chen Kaige's (陈凯歌) *King of the Children* (孩子王) and Zhang Yimou's (张艺谋) *Red Sorghum* (红高粱). *King of the Children* was one of Chen's last attempts to continue the avant-gardist practice of cultural reflection in which the female character becomes symbolically invisible or irrelevant compared with a highly reflective male subjectivity. By contrast, *Red Sorghum*, which won the Golden Bear Award at the Thirty-Eighth Berlin International Film Festival in 1988, marked Fifth Generation filmmakers' successful exit from avant-gardism by returning to dramatic and commercial cinematic conventions, in which the female figure is sexually configured and objectified in relation to male masculinity, nationalism, and male lineage.[65] Whereas Chen's film was a box office bomb, Zhang's became a success. Together, both signaled the coming end of Fifth Generation experimentalism. The year 1987 also saw the appearance of Fifth Generation male director Zhou Xiaowen's (周晓文) *The Last Frenzy* (最后的疯狂), a film recognized as the Fifth Generation's first successful commercial film and a critical indicator of the general transition of Chinese filmmaking toward commercial production as a whole.[66]

Cultural avant-gardism and commercialism have often been perceived in the Western context as representing opposite values and antagonistic positions: innovative versus conventional in terms of aesthetic style, radical and subversive versus conservative and confirmative in terms of politics, elitist (minor) versus popular (mainstream) in terms of production and reception. The Fifth Generation male filmmakers' quick transition from avant-gardism to commercialism in 1980s China has thus simply raised serious questions about these widely accepted dichotomies between the avant-garde and the commercial. More importantly, it has exposed an inner connection and shared logic between the two. As I discussed earlier in this chapter, when China's economic reform deepened in the mid-1980s, the mainstream discourse turned from a heterogeneous, socially engaged practice toward an abstract promotion of universal human nature (including sexual difference), transhistorical cultural (un)consciousness, and global, and masculine avant-gardist aesthetic reflection and expression. This abstract cultural practice aimed to critically reflect on socialist politics, but as it turned its central attention away from contemporary socioeconomic issues, it also indirectly endorsed, in Esther Yau's term, "capitalist democracy,"[67] or capitalist modernity in general. On the surface, avant-gardist art as an elite minor practice differs from mainstream commercial culture in capitalist society, but they share a sociopolitically detached approach to art and literature, a male-centered masculine value, and a self-generating or reproductive mode of representation. Western feminist studies have long demonstrated that male-centered avant-gardist and commercial cinemas represent two sides of the capitalist and misogynist system.[68] In the Chinese context, the similarities between the two cinemas were also reinforced by their shared negation of both a socialist past and a sociopolitically integrated approach to cultural practice. It was thus not surprising that when the market finally gained the upper hand, the avant-gardists simply flipped their experimental cinema into commercial cinema and even played a leading role in commercializing Chinese film production.

As Yingjin Zhang has contended, "by the end of the 1980s, the critical thrust of New Chinese Cinema had largely been spent."[69] More critically, the potential for developing a socially engaged, artistically diverse, and mass-oriented cinema dwindled. Chinese cinema thereafter fell into three broad categories all dominated by male directors: leitmotif films, art films, and commercial films. As China furthered its market development and became implicated in global neoliberalism, art films became a shrinking minority[70] and both socialist integrated cultural practice and critical individualism got repudiated.[71] The leitmotif films heavily subsidized by the state do not really engage with the reality of contemporary China. Their original focus on Chinese revolutionary history has ironically raised serious questions about the relationship between the past socialist revolution and present political-economic orientation. Furthermore, the leitmotif films' subsequent development into a highly commercial genre has significantly invalidated its existence as a separate film category.

Socially informed films have continuously come out, mostly by female directors and Sixth Generation filmmakers, but they have become significantly reduced in number and categorically marginalized in production, distribution, and reception, especially since China's film industry became formally and increasingly privatized beginning in the early 1990s. Furthermore, due to the absence of any significant sociopolitical vision and lack of a large audience, these films have no longer been able to seriously engage with, not to mention play a role in transforming, China's social reality. International recognition of Sixth Generation male filmmakers has once again highlighted individual talents, cinematic aesthetics, or an assumed subversive hypothesis, continuously undermining the need for and importance of a socially engaged and popular cinema.

In my next chapter, I turn to the most representative female film director in the New Era, Zhang Nuanxin, and her struggle to maintain a socially engaged and aesthetically innovative mainstream film practice in China in the 1980s and 1990s. From her enthusiastic embrace of thought liberation at the turn of the 1980s and her pioneering role in post-Mao experimental cinema, to her increasingly critical stance toward China's economic reform in the early 1990s and her subsequent return to political melodrama, the chapter explores alternative and socioculturally engaged visions articulated in Zhang's films. The chapter also probes Zhang's repudiation in the scholarly discourse from the 1990s and her public reception as her films turned critical of the rising new mainstream discourse of universal modernity, post-Mao independent and culturalist feminism, and the socioeconomic effects of China's market economy.

6 Alternative Experimental Cinema

Zhang Nuanxin's Socially Committed
Mainstream Film Practice of the 1980s

Early post-Mao China witnessed the arrival and development of cultural pluralism. Situated in a unique moment of historical transformations and motivated by a shared desire to revise and advance socialist vision and modernizations, Chinese culture of the late 1970s and early 1980s embraced ideas and practices originating from different historical periods and diverse sociopolitical contexts. In the mid- and late 1980s, however, as a new mainstream trend of thought and culture rose to dominate, the early post-Mao cultural experiments were recast as transitional and dismissed as insignificant.[1] More than two and half decades later, following China's rapid transformation into a world economic power—a process that also produced various social and environmental issues—Chinese scholars began to call for a return to the 1980s to trace and reexamine the initial articulations of plural post-Mao sociocultural and intellectual discourses, which were more heterogeneous than we think of them today.[2] For the study of Chinese women's cinema and literature, it is also important to revisit women artists' practices in the early post-Mao era, especially their different reflections on history and diverse imaginations for the future. Critical attention should be paid particularly to those ideas and aspirations that became derailed, compromised, or marginalized in China's process of developing a market economy and a mainstream discourse of universal modernity.

In the 1980s, Chinese women's filmmaking reached its climax, producing a large and varied body of films. Over thirty female directors from at least three different generations became active in the early post-Mao era, and over the course of approximately a decade, they made more than one hundred films, a world record that endures today in *any* national film history. The first-generation veteran female directors from the 1950s to the 1960s, such as Wang Ping, Dong Kena, Wang Shaoyan, and Yan Bili, returned to filmmaking even before the Cultural Revolution formally ended in 1976. Those who, like Jiang Shusen (姜树森), worked as assistant directors in the 1960s and early 1970s began their independent productive filmmaking careers at the turn of the 1980s. The second generation (also known as Fourth Generation filmmakers in Chinese film history since the 1920s), who were mostly born in the late 1930s and 1940s and grew up in Mao's socialist China, constituted the most significant portion of 1980s female directors. A large majority of this group graduated from Beijing or Shanghai film and drama academies and schools. Owing to institutionalized gender equality and the public promotion of proletarian and feminist mainstream culture, the top two film academies of socialist China—the Beijing Film Academy (北京电影学院) and the Central Academy of Drama in Beijing (中央戏剧学院)—admitted about 20 percent female directors to every directing class in the late 1950s and the 1960s. Consequently, in the early post-Mao era, more than fifty Chinese women graduated from the two academies, half becoming active in their assigned studios.[3] Zhang Nuanxin (张暖忻), Huang Shuqin (黄蜀芹), Wang Haowei (王好为), Shi Shujun (史蜀君), Ji Wenyan (季文彦), Guang Chunlan (广春兰), Xiao Guiyun (肖桂云), Ling Zi (凌子), Wang Junzheng (王君正), and Qiqin Gaowa (琪琴高娃) are among the best known of the group. Institutional support and the professional training of female directors in Mao's socialist China proved key to the blossoming of Chinese women's mainstream cinema in the 1980s. According to recent research, the training and education of filmmakers in socialist China were more diverse than we used to assume. Take Beijing Film Academy, for example. Although the Soviet Union's model of film theory and practice constituted the initial backbone of the curriculum, the academy introduced other traditions of world cinema and popular cultures for study as well, such as Italian neorealism, French New Wave, and Chinese left-wing cinema along with traditional opera and drama.[4] In addition, other Eastern European and Asian cinemas became available not only to filmmaking professionals and students but also to the mass audience in Mao's China. Wang Haowei and Zhang Nuanxin both studied at the Beijing Film Academy during the period 1958–1962.

Whereas the Soviet Union's film theories and the general practice of social-ist realism attracted Wang, French New Wave and Italian neorealism, espe-cially their subjective camera and documentary style, inspired Zhang. The link between the socialist reception of different world cinemas in the Mao era and China's own new experimental cinema in the early post-Mao period should be seriously recognized and carefully studied. Other female directors of this second generation include graduates from the Shanghai Professional Film School (上海电影专科学校), such as Shi Xiaohua (石晓华), Bao Zhifang (鲍芝芳), and Wu Zhennian (武珍年) in the 1960s, and actresses from the 1960s and 1970s, such as Zhang Yuan (张圆), Qin Zhiyu (秦志钰), and Lu Xiaoya (陆小雅). The third and youngest generation of Chinese female di-rectors mostly came from the first class of the Beijing Film Academy after the Cultural Revolution (1978–1982), including Hu Mei (胡玫), Li Shaohong (李少红), Peng Xiaolian (彭小莲), Liu Miaomiao (刘苗苗), and Ning Ying (宁瀛). Most were born in the 1950s and directly or indirectly participated in the Cultural Revolution; additionally, these female counterparts of the well-known Fifth Generation Chinese filmmakers were most innovative and diverse in their cinematic styles when they started their filmmaking careers in the 1980s.

This chapter responds to the call for a return to the cultural practices of the 1980s by exploring post-Mao Chinese women's mainstream experi-mental cinema with a focus on Zhang Nuanxin (1940–1995). Zhang was a pioneering figure in both the theory and practice of post-Mao New Cinema. In 1979 she coauthored with Li Tuo a highly influential article titled, "On the Modernization of Film Language,"[5] introducing French New Wave and Italian neorealism; and in 1981, she spearheaded a subjective-documentary experimental film practice with her first film, *Drive to Win* (沙鸥). In 1990, she made *Good Morning, Beijing* (北京你早), a precursor to the aesthetic and critical trend of Chinese Sixth Generation filmmaking. Despite Zhang's various pioneering roles and achievements, film scholars and critics since the 1990s have seldom credited her with significantly influencing post-Mao experimental cinema. Furthermore, feminist scholars both inside and out-side China have exhibited great uncertainty toward her films, particularly *Sacrificed Youth* (青春祭, 1985), which best represents Zhang's documentary style, gendered voice, and subjective narrative structure. My penultimate chapter probes the causes for Zhang's marginalization and dismissal in the 1990s. More importantly, in this chapter I reexamine Zhang's cinematic en-gagement with both socialist history and emerging mainstream discourses in the 1980s and offer an alternative analysis of her film practice.

Subjective-Documentary Experimental Cinema: Historical Reality, Film Practice, and Cultural Pluralism

Film theory played an unprecedented role in transforming Chinese film practice in the early post-Mao era.[6] In their article "On the Modernization of Film Language" Zhang Nuanxin and Li Tuo call for the dedramatization and depoliticalization of Chinese filmmaking, instead promoting Italian neorealism and French New Wave. Though regarded by Chinese film scholars and critics as "the artistic manifesto of the Fourth Generation [film directors]" and "the outline of experimental cinema" for the New Era,[7] the article also puts forth some irreconcilable ideas and arguments. Composed when both official (state) and intellectual discourses undertook a reevaluation of not simply the Cultural Revolution but also socialist ideology and culture as a whole, the article critiques the political control of filmmaking and challenges the tradition of socialist melodrama, projecting the following new goals for early post-Mao filmmaking: to (re)connect with the universal path of (cultural) modernity, catch up with the progressive world history of film art, and achieve artistic and individual creative autonomy.

Within the article, however, where many film examples are analyzed, more complex and sometimes contrary views are articulated. For instance, when discussing specific Italian neorealism and French New Wave films of the 1950s and 1960s, the article ties the significance of these films to their ability to "document" social history and everyday life and express the individual filmmaker's psychic state and subjective feelings. These social, historical, and subjective significations contradict the universal, linear, progressive model as outlined by the authors. Indeed, despite the overall critique of Chinese melodrama's backwardness and political content, many examples elaborated in the article highlight how film editing (both long take and montage), camera work, and shooting techniques are used mostly to dramatize (rather than *de*dramatize) the emotional effect on the audience in order to enhance a film's political (antifascist) and reflective purposes.[8]

The tension and sometimes contradiction between the authors' general theoretical argument and their concrete analyses of film scenes partially reflect the transitional character of the early post-Mao era, when different ideas competed with one another for primacy in a potential new mainstream direction. A closer examination also shows that the divergent views expressed in the article may well result from the two authors' nonidentical positions. Li Tuo is known for his leading liberal position in the post-Mao New Era and his major role in the 1980s effort to mold mainstream literary and cultural practice into a socially detached, universal discourse with an emphatic aesthetic orientation.[9] He wrote an in-depth introduction on Bazin's long-take theory in an article published in 1980, focusing exclusively on film aesthetics, the truthful state of the real, and the duration of the individual shot.[10] In his article with Zhang Nuanxin, Li's position seems to dominate the article's theoretical framework, as the concrete film analyses are subdued while such major themes as the importance of film form and aesthetics, the universal norm (or truth) of film development as an art, and the necessity of film practice's dedramatization/depoliticization are trumpeted.

Later, in their separate discussions of Zhang's first film, *Drive to Win*, for which Zhang and Li cowrote the screenplay, the authors once again demonstrated different emphases. Whereas Li's article "The Cinematic Aesthetic of Screenplay" centers the discussion on the "aesthetic" (美感), style, and visual pleasure and thereby makes them the very goal of both screenplay and filmmaking,[11] Zhang highlights, in her "Director's Notes on *Drive to Win*," the importance and necessity of new film styles to convey ideas more effectively and enhance the didactic function of film practice.[12] In an interview conducted in the late 1980s, Zhang reflects on her filmmaking, stressing the difference between film theory and filmmaking: "After all, filmmaking and writing articles are two different things. In the film, I still need to rely on my own senses and need to search for a self rather than just imitate [Western theory]."[13] According to Zhang, film practice requires historical and subjective mediation and thus should not be done by copying an abstract theory. More fundamentally, this statement reveals Zhang's conscious self-distancing from the theory she had been associated with—which, as I will discuss later, does not completely convey her worldview or her approach to film practice. By (somewhat defensively) resorting to the "natural" difference between theory and practice, Zhang clarifies her position and offers an explanation for her departure, in her film practice, from certain theoretical arguments made in her article with Li.

To verify Zhang's historical position as a socialist female director in the early post-Mao era, the rest of this section analyzes Zhang's other published essays and director's notes, her first film (*Drive to Win*), and her scattered interviews to critically trace her important ideas about filmmaking, particularly those related to the "truthful state of the real" (真实性), subjective expression, the gendered personal, and cultural pluralism. These ideas are crucial for understanding Zhang's unique negotiations with (then) recent Chinese history, contemporary economic reform, and the film aesthetic of the French New Wave. Her unique stance also reveals the implicit causes for critics' dismissal of her as a seminal figure in Chinese experimental cinema in the late 1980s and 1990s.

As China at the end of the 1970s made a radical shift from its immediate past, literature and art began to reorient themselves, seeking to represent the truthful state of the real. In 1978, Zhang Nuanxin published "Let Historical Reality Return to the Silver Screen" (让历史真实回到银幕), which has attracted little attention from scholars in Chinese film studies. In her essay, which came out earlier than her coauthored article with Li Tuo, Zhang tries to address the question about how Chinese films can represent social and historical reality experienced especially by common people, articulating both a critique of the cultural politics of the Cultural Revolution and a demand for a concrete historical engagement in the filmmaking of the New Era. More specifically, she targets films made during the Cultural Revolution and the period immediately after as divorcing themselves from historical reality as well as the life and thought of people, thus violating the basic principle of historical materialism. She argues that one of the central features of cinema is its "closeness to reality" (逼真).[14] At the same time, she also points out, film art should also work as a cultural means to advance China's modernization and to serve the people by especially representing their voices and fulfill their cultural needs.[15] In a 1987 interview, Zhang insists that the truthful state of the real is useful to correct the Cultural Revolution's overly melodramatic film-production style. But as discussions above show, Zhang's critical stance against some radical politics of the Cultural Revolution and her promotion of film language reform did not translate into a desire to accept wholesale a new theory detached from the Chinese social context and historical reality and deprived of concrete historical and personal negotiations. Indeed, Zhang's emphasis on the truthful state of historical reality, which also manifests in her film practice, demonstrates, directly and indirectly, her objection to cultural abstraction, political fabrication, or the uniform perspective of idealism (唯心主义) when it comes to filmmaking.[16] Inspired by early post-Mao debates on truth and facts, however, Zhang seems to move away from the newly inscribed objective, rational, and universal status of truth in the early post-Mao era. *Her* truthful state of reality is mediated through historical people. Consequently, Zhang promotes subjective perspectives and expressions that are historically constituted and socially engaged. In a later interview, Zhang stresses that "narrative is not objective, so I have never told my stories objectively. Instead, I always do my stories subjectively to express my feelings."[17]

In his essay on Zhang Nuanxin's films, the critic Zhen Xin (震钦) perceptively observes that Zhang's interpretation of the New Wave centers on how to represent reality subjectively. In addition to her overall concern about historical and social realities in filmmaking, Zhang also wants to produce films that can "manifest the author's temperament and express her emotions."[18] This idea of film as the expression of the director's temperament and feelings reveals the New Wave's most significant influence, which valorizes the individual auteur and his (or her) "personal vision of the world."[19] But Zhang's reception of the New Wave was much affected by the socialist environment of the 1950s and early 1960s within which she was first exposed to French New Wave films. As my following analysis of Zhang's films reveals, her interest in the subjective mediation of cinematic narrative contained a distinctive historical and social dimension that departs from the canonical French New Wave practice. At the same time, Zhang's notion of subjective expression also resulted from an ongoing autobiographical cultural practice Chinese women writers had initiated at the end of the 1970s, which,[20] although personally oriented, contained an important sociopolitical engagement rooted in contemporary Chinese history.[21] The autobiographical practice centered on the gendered personal, attempting to address both the gendered gap existing in earlier socialist feminist practice and the return of traditional gender values in the New Era. Protagonists of women's autobiographical literature and films are almost always strong, confident, socially concerned, self-reflective women, an outcome of both the Mao era's institutionalized gender equality and the New Era's thought liberation policy: the former empowered Chinese women as equal socialist subjects while the latter granted Chinese intellectuals a cultural space to express their ideas after the Cultural Revolution. Thus, Zhang's cinematic focus on subjective mediation and expression, although inspired by French New Wave, is distinct from the New Wave's ideal of detached or autonomous individual genius.[22] Her films enacted a subjective and reflective engagement with the changing social and historical situations in contemporary China.

Zhang's first film *Drive to Win*, set in the decade 1969–1979, is about the Chinese national women's basketball team struggling to win the international championship in the early post-Mao era. Stimulated by French New Wave's emphasis on everyday life, individual style, and the long take,[23] Zhang develops a subjective documentary style: a female voice-over and subjective camerawork accompanying on-location shooting, amateur actors, natural lighting, and direct sound recordings. This new style, however, does not achieve a personal destiny separate from society or foreground cinematic aesthetics at the expense of the film's didactic function. According to Zhang, the film's documentary style, a counterbalance to the overdramatized and artificial convention of filmmaking at the time, more effectively moves the audience, encouraging them to continue pursuing social ideals despite historical and political setbacks and obstacles.[24] At the level of film narrative, Zhang's experimental style accentuates an individual woman's agency, illustrating her subjective responses to the call of nation and society, her self-determination in pursuing her life ideal after confronting various setbacks, and her strong will to participate in public affairs. In her written reflections on this film, Zhang describes Sha Ou, the central female character, as the hope for China's future: she embodies the spirit of a generation "educated with communist ideals prior to the 1960s," "who often cited as their motto the quotes from *How the Steel Is Tempered* [Nikolai Ostrovsky]: 'Man's dearest possession is life. It is given to him but once, and he must live it so as to feel no torturing regrets for wasted years, never know the burning shame of a mean and petty past; so live that, dying, he might say: all my life, all my strength were given to the finest cause in all the world——the fight for the Liberation of Mankind.'"[25] At the same time, Sha Ou is also an ordinary person, someone who represents "the common experience of several generations of Chinese people during the last thirty years. They have ambitions and ideals, and [although] the ten-year turmoil [of the Cultural Revolution] ruined many of their beautiful things, they have strived, despite their physical and emotional wounds, for a bright future through China's four modernizations."[26] As the critic Han Xiaolei (韩小磊) points out, "the zeitgeist the film *Drive to Win* expresses" is embodied in Sha Ou's dedication to "personal growth, social progress, and national rejuvenation."[27]

Zhang's discussions of her first film are key to understanding the social and collective dimension of Chinese women's personal cultural practice in the early 1980s, wherein individual subjectivity is represented as a critical agent for advancing social interest and cultural pluralism along with individuality. Zhang's comments also help us understand other women characters in *Drive to Win*, particularly Sha Ou's mother, basketball teammates, and coach. They are all strong individual women and active social subjects, passionate about their careers and playing important roles in national and international settings. Zhang represents romantic love and personal emotions in the film, indicating the film's significant departure from Cultural Revolution cinematic representation but, far from echoing the rising demand for the return of traditional family values, Zhang's film refuses to represent love or marriage as women's destiny. Sha Ou remains single through the end of the film, devoting herself to the advancement of the team. A woman achieves self-fulfillment, as Zhang's subjective documentary style portrays, primarily through her subjectively mediated commitment to collective causes and social interests. As I will discuss in the next section, Zhang's repeated references to the collective—or, in Chris Berry's term, "consensus ideology"[28]—seriously frustrated scholars of the late 1980s and early 1990s, who sought instead an individualistic and antagonistic feminist consciousness in post-Mao women's cinema.

Zhang conveyed an integrated sense of the personal and social, the subjective and collective, in her making of *Drive to Win*; she also demonstrated an unsegregated approach to cinematic form and content. Despite her repeated emphasis on expanding the camera's expressions in early post-Mao China, Zhang was against any attempts to either separate film form from content or to set modern film style as the "goal" of filmmaking.[29] While shooting *Drive to Win*, Zhang stressed to her crew members that "[we should] explore new film language, but this is not done for the sake of form. . . . Form should be in service of content . . . and its goal is to express the content."[30] Han Xiaolei, in his study of Zhang's first film, remarks that Zhang pioneered an experimental cinema in which film style is inseparable from film content.[31] Once again, Zhang significantly revised the theory according to which film is an autonomous and progressive art form, and questioned the set of dichotomies laid out in the article coauthored with Li.

Individual reflection, subjective perception, and female voice-overs, combined with a documentary style, define *Drive to Win* as an experimental film in the early post-Mao era, but these experimental features do not project a path toward a universal truth, propose an individual destination for personal salvation or autonomy, or suggest a separation of form from content (or the aesthetic from the political). Rather, Zhang envisioned a historically grounded and socially committed cultural pluralism in her promotion of subjective filmmaking and experimentalism. In a 1987 interview, she maintained that film practice should not be limited to any single style or form: "Film can manifest vastly different styles in different hands and have inexhaustible functions and thus cannot be defined solely by one singular character, [whether in the] documentary style or expression of emotion."[32] She further argues that "Chinese film [production] needs to be aware of this [the importance of plurality] and should not place more constraint on filmmakers. [Filmmakers] . . . can make political films, [or] epic films, [as well as] realist or fictional films. Every director should make films according to his/her own character and style [气质]."[33] Significantly, Zhang links her idea of filmmakers' individual characters and subjective styles to cultural pluralism, an important feature of early post-Mao cultural practice. This pluralism, when charged with social concerns and commitments in the hands of women film directors like Zhang, worked to both critique the Cultural Revolution's uniform control of cultural production and question the post-Mao era's theoretical claims about a singular, universal truth—whether objectively, aesthetically, or individualistically oriented.[34]

Western (Feminist) Theories, Binary Logic, and the Ambiguity of Chinese Women's Experimental Cinema

Among Chinese female directors of the 1980s, Zhang Nuanxin and Hu Mei are generally recognized as pioneers of a modernist women's cinema. Zhang's *Sacrificed Youth* and Hu's *Army Nurse* (女儿楼, 1984; also translated as *The Chamber of Maidens*) best represent this new practice. Some critics focus on the two films' subjective and introspective perspectives, first-person female voice-overs, and female subjectivity;[35] some focus on sexual desire and difference, modernist feminism, and individual bourgeois subjectivity;[36] still others highlight their landmark "female style" and promise for making visible the "true" female identity.[37] An indisputable consensus remains, especially among film and post-Mao feminist scholars, on the pathbreaking visions, expressions, and innovative features of these two films. Despite their enthusiasm for the films, however, these scholars have also reached another, more intriguing consensus: both films manifest a strikingly ambiguous, mystical (vague), unsettling or uncertain, and even contradictory quality.[38] This blurriness eventually disqualified the two directors as key facilitators of a significant break from socialist filmmaking and past collective values. Indeed, the most important discovery made by (feminist) film scholars around 1990 concerns the ambiguity of Zhang's and Hu's films and their deeper-than-expected attachment to the past. In this section, I turn to the analytic frameworks and specific theoretical and historical arguments some influential scholars have put forth regarding the ambiguity of Chinese women's experimental cinema in order to explore the critical reasoning behind this thesis, as well as its direct or indirect contribution to Zhang's dismissal in the early 1990s when China moved steadily toward a market economy.

In his pioneering study of Chinese female directors of the 1980s, "China's New 'Women's Cinema'" published in 1988,[39] Chris Berry provides a contextualized analysis for his English-speaking readers. Several of his observations shed light on both the importance and difficulty of researching Chinese women's cinema. He first notes the lack of English-language studies on Chinese women's culture: the extant English scholarship on Chinese women was almost exclusively conducted in the empirical social sciences.[40] His research also finds that what concerned Chinese women's cinema and women filmmakers in the post-Mao era "[was] not issues of equality in the broad social sphere but the reassertion of difference and the validation of the personal."[41] Aware of the important role that broad sociopolitical history has played in shaping Chinese culture, Berry promotes a contextual approach to the subject.[42] Toward the end of his short introduction, Berry asks: "How are we to assess the new advocacy of the personal among China's educated urban women? Is it regressive or positive, and by what standards? Are these often *ambiguous* films breaking with an old order or reforming it?"[43]

Berry deploys a consensus-versus-difference framework for his study, arguing that the dominant Chinese ideology has insisted, from 1949 forward, on consensus, resisting difference and contradictions.[44] He sketches a political, social (gendered), and cinematic context wherein consensus is uniformly upheld, including (1) China's democratic centralism since 1949; (2) Chinese socialist women's liberation which, according to Western feminist scholars like Judith Stacey,[45] consistently subordinates itself (difference) to broader projects (consensus); and (3) the narrative structure of classical socialist cinema in which the third-person perspective (consensus) exceeds that of any single character, individual subjectivity is resisted, and techniques like shot/reverse-shot (individual difference) represent a collapse of order.[46] Furthermore, the critical discussion published in the bimonthly *Contemporary Cinema* on women's cinema and female consciousness adopts the speaking position of "we," the collective plural, thus stressing consensus. To study Chinese women's highly subjective cinema against this constructed context is, for Berry, to examine whether any significant difference or opposition has emerged, and in what way.

Discussing Zhang's *Sacrificed Youth*, Hu's *Army Nurse*, and Wuer Shana's (乌尔莎娜) *The Season for Love* (恋爱的季节, 1986), all of which are known for their reflective individual female characters, Berry points out: "Although these films seem to me to be doing something very significant and innovative in their construction of individual female subjectivity, it must be noted that this subjectivity itself has also a distinct form and an ambiguous relation to consensus ideology."[47] He argues that instead of a clear-cut oppositional stance to the collective consensus, these films exhibit simultaneous attachments to two seemingly opposite poles, particularly through the heroines' ambiguous choices during crucial moments of their lives. Noting that Chinese women's cinematic narrative of subjectivity displays significant differences from the Western oedipal narrative, wherein subjectivity is a positive goal to be attained through mastery over an object, Berry posits that "this particular form of [Chinese women's] subjectivity seems best understood as born of the dominant consensus ideology,"[48] because it evokes something "negative," a loss or a separation that cannot be repaired. In addition, all central characters demonstrate a desire or longing for a return to the presubjective (consensus) state. At the same time, however, although subjective drives are attached to consensus ideology, they no longer fit the ideology neatly. "It is here," Berry claims, that these films' "full ambiguity may be understood."[49] Berry concludes: "These films . . . construct a major contradiction within consensus ideology, but not necessarily in opposition to it."[50] He also suggests that intense, individual subjectivity is merely another technique women filmmakers use to move toward difference without expressing opposition to consensus.[51]

It is certainly debatable whether the Western oedipal narrative generates a positive goal that successfully eliminates the desire to return to the presubjective state or the symbiotic relationship with the mother; it is also highly questionable whether the Western oedipal complex contributes in any way toward a positive goal or position for women in the cultural or symbolic order.[52] More critically, it demands a rigorous argument if one intends to equate the pre-oedipal state in Western discourse with the sociopolitical history of socialist China. Whereas Berry has carefully and rightly denoted certain ambiguities in Chinese women's cinema of the 1980s, we should scrutinize his value-laden suggestion—to wit, because it could not make real breakthroughs or oppose itself to the consensus ideology, women's cinema at the time (much like socialist women's liberation) remained nonindependent, subordinating its difference to the consensus. To clarify his position, Berry directly quotes Judith Stacey's conclusion about Chinese socialist feminism: "Socialism has not liberated women. . . . Many capitalist societies have been able to provide richer soil for the growth of feminist consciousness and an independent feminist movement."[53] As my discussion of Stacey's research in chapter 1 illustrates, the so-called empirical social-science research on socialist women is severely delimited by the binary Cold War ideology that promotes individualistic independence in capitalist society.

Furthermore, Berry's consensus-difference binary logic inadvertently projects a monolithic socialist entity, dismissing many other kinds of political, social (gendered or individual), and cultural differences that are not conceptualized through the oppositional/antagonistic relationship characteristic of the capitalist system.[54] Rather than exploring what Chinese women's subjective cinema has signified through its *nonbinary* difference in its own sociopolitical structure and cultural context, the binary framework narrowly sets its own research goal at simply examining the possibility of opposition, conceived in binary terms. Berry does draw readers' attention to changes in Chinese political and economic realms in order to account for emerging differences in Chinese film production, but the framework of (collective) consensus versus (individual) difference indirectly evokes a Western cultural ideology, which holds that meaningful differences can prevail only in a Western-style democratic political system, independent-oriented feminist endeavors, or individual(istic)-driven artistic practice.

Sexual difference is the central analytic framework by which Ann E. Kaplan discusses Hu Mei's *Army Nurse* in her 1988 essay, "Problematizing Cross-Cultural Analysis." Although Kaplan mentions Zhang Nuanxin in passing, she places *Sacrificed Youth* in the same category as *Army Nurse*, asserting that this group of newer films by women "manifest[s] a new self-conscious split between an evident, but socially forbidden eroticism and romantic love, and the subject's interpellation by the State."[55] According to Kaplan, standard Western feminism assumes that human subjectivity is con-stituted through sexual difference, as "one cannot be no sex" and thus "a na-tion that does not evidence preoccupation with sexual difference must then be 'repressing' this difference." As a result, "the underlying issue for women in China . . . would seem not to be entry into the public sphere—the right to work, to equal pay, to equal participation in the work force (issues that preoccupied Western feminists in the sixties and seventies), but a new, as yet not fully articulated, realization about subjectivity."[56] Like Berry, Kaplan also relies on Stacey's research on socialist China, projecting a monolithic picture in which sexual difference and individual subjectivity are repressed by the state.[57] Based on the Western feminist framework and a naturalized concept of sexual difference, Kaplan argues that *Army Nurse* focuses entirely on the heroine's conflict between love and duty, aligning audience empathy with the heroine's erotic desire, and thus exposes "the constraints that con-temporary Chinese culture imposes on sexual expression and fulfillment."[58]

Fully aware of the potential risk associated with cultural imperialism, the-ory's cross-cultural translatability, and different audiences, Kaplan offers two possible conclusions to her study of Chinese women's cinema of the 1980s, one with Western and the other with non-Western connotations. First, Ka-plan posits: "One could see Chinese women as working their way through a modernist phase in their assertion of subjectivity."[59] She then concedes that this process is problematic because "we [Western feminists] worked hard in the sixties and seventies to rid ourselves of bourgeois subjectivities. . . . In the eighties, however, Chinese women . . . want a subjectivity we had identified as linked to bourgeois capitalism and to a modernism that we were attempting to move beyond."[60] Kaplan continues: "Meanwhile, those of us in America who went through the sixties confront a paradigm shift variously called postmodernism, postindustrialism, or New Age Consciousness. Having long ago abandoned the utopian ideal of submersion of self in the collective, we now seem on the brink of a postmodern crisis presaging the impossibility of subjectivity in the old senses. Here then we find a big distance between women in China and in America today."[61] Keeping with this linear model, Kaplan presumes that modern subjectivity should result exclusively from bourgeois individuality and sexual difference in a capitalist system, and thereby suggests that post-Mao China and Chinese women remain in the transition from premodern to modern, a stage that U.S. feminists had already passed.

What is neglected or denied in this linear model is the concept of socialist China as a *different* modern system, one established as anticapitalist, as well as against bourgeois individual subjectivity. The equation of China's socialist system with a short period of collectively inspired social movements in the Western capitalist society of the 1960s and the dismissal of socialism as a utopian ideal that history has to overcome reveal exactly the problem of cross-cultural studies Kaplan seeks to avoid.[62] Clearly, cross-cultural studies cannot be conducted exclusively at the discursive level, given geopolitical power dynamics, different political-economic systems, and divergent social values and visions.

In response to Hu Mei's own insistence that her film is not really about sexual difference or female erotic desire but rather portrays a common experience among both men and women in China,[63] Kaplan offers her second conclusion. She argues that instead of centering on individual subjectivity and sexual difference, Hu "resorted to an analysis that would apply to *all* the Chinese, that would reassert the collective,"[64] as well as the framework of "national allegory."[65] Hu's film thus embodies everyone's frustrations—the impossibility for both men and women to function as individuals. "Given the prior phallic order, and given classical Oedipal rivalry with the father," Kaplan further argues, "[Chinese men] may be harmed even more than women [by the State]."[66] In a move similar to Berry's, which equates the Western presubjective/pre-oedipal state with Mao's socialist China, Kaplan replaces the collective in a socialist system (the model Hu insists on) with the Western, middle-class, nuclear-family structure, in which the oedipal complex supplies the primary social entrance into sexually differentiated subjectivity. Even this so-called non-Western analysis, therefore, remains thoroughly Western. Kaplan's subsequent hesitation significantly reveals the inadequacy of feminist cross-cultural research, which has placed its focus on the binary opposition, linear progressiveness, and the cultural-psychic domain: "It is . . . hard to be certain about such readings that rely on a perhaps culturally specific concept of the psyche. . . . The uncertainty exposes the need for more research."[67]

By the early 1990s, as China further embraced the market economy and a universal model for economic and cultural production, Western post-second-wave feminist thought had been enthusiastically accepted by Chinese scholars as the most advanced theoretical basis for research on Chinese women and culture. In film studies specifically, Western poststructuralist and cine-feminist theory was introduced to China around 1988,[68] producing influential scholarship on Chinese women's cinema. In one of the most representative articles from this period, "Feminism and Chinese Women's Cinema" (女权主义与中国女性电影, 1990), Yuan Ying introduces Western post-second-wave feminist theories, constructing a universal frame of reference for the contemporary study of Chinese women's cinema. She differentiates Western feminism of the post-1960s from earlier, sociopolitical-rights feminism, emphasizing how this newer feminism moved away from concrete political movements and into a general *cultural* critique.[69] This cultural turn in Western intellectual discourses, as I argue in chapters 4 and 5, coincided with Chinese intellectuals' general retreat from socioeconomic and political engagement in the mid- and late 1980s.

Cultural critique, combined with a focus on individual(istic) subjectivity, underpins Yuan's analysis of the difference between Western feminism and socialist Chinese women's liberation. She argues that the logic and trajectory of Western feminist movements progressed from social revolution to the critique of men and then on to reflections on the female self, whereas Chinese women's liberation remains stuck in the stage of social revolution. "This profound difference makes the Western feminist movement possess great self-reflectivity and self-sufficiency," whereas "Chinese women's liberation has manifested passivity and dependency."[70] This difference, Yuan further argues, also explains why China has never really had a feminist movement or a social revolution in the truly feminist sense,[71] because the Chinese women's movement, burying itself in social and political movements throughout modern Chinese history, has never (1) become independent, (2) addressed women's own existence, or (3) developed a female consciousness to vie with male consciousness. Any women's movement that ties itself to sociopolitical movements, Yuan reasons, would become a trap for "true feminists" as it automatically endorses collective values, which are always already male-centered. The term *feminism* is used in Yuan's article in such a way that it refers exclusively to the Western model of women's movements, especially their last two stages (cultural critique of men and female self-reflection). The requisite criteria for a feminist movement, according to Yuan, include the destruction of male-centered culture, the expression of women's special physical and spiritual difference, and the development of female consciousness to create a (separate) space for women's existence and growth[72]—all points that echo and reinforce Li Xiaojiang's arguments made in the 1980s.[73]

Yuan's article challenges socialist feminism, which, she argues, has failed to address and express women's particular experiences, emotions, and consciousness.[74] Consequently, Chinese socialist women's films produced in the 1950s and 1960s embodied contemporary collective, male values, positioning man as the standard and excluding female consciousness. In Yuan's writing, concepts like "female consciousness," "women's essential experience" (本体体验),[75] and "women's independent values" all appear self-evident and immune to historical changes, social transformations, and the influence of economic and political institutions. Although sexual difference via the oedipal complex is not emphasized, an ontological difference between man and woman appears to underpin Yuan's post-Mao feminist endeavor. The content of this "essential" or ontological difference, however, remains unspecified; sexual difference is simply assumed as something natural and inherent.

Although the Western-based, linear trajectory of feminist movements Yuan and other feminist scholars outline actually reduces the complexity of Western feminisms in history and distorts the condition and context of Chinese women's liberation, it was upheld as the universal measurement in the feminist study of Chinese women's cinema during the late 1980s and 1990s. Whereas Kaplan believes Western feminism has already moved from modern, individual bourgeois female consciousness to postmodernism's split identity, Yuan lingers on Western radical and cultural feminisms of the 1970s and 1980s, demonstrating an individualistic and transhistorical take on patriarchy and male dominance.[76] Despite the differences between postmodern feminism and radical feminism, both movements repudiated socialist women's liberation as well as the sociopolitically oriented movements of the 1960s and 1970s in the West, moving to a difference-based cultural critique. This dismissal of political, economic, and social factors also precluded any productive discussion of socialist versus capitalist systems and their different configurations of and for women's liberation.[77]

Moving on to post-Mao Chinese women's cinema of the 1980s, Yuan acknowledges that great changes took place as female directors began "establishing a direct relationship with female culture."[78] But she also expresses strong reservations. In her brief discussion of *Sacrificed Youth*, Yuan praises the film as the first to directly narrate women's spiritual or psychic world, coming close to the (fully) "self-conscious female entity" (自觉的女性体). "However," Yuan points out with disappointment, "the scriptwriter and director [Zhang Nuanxin] deserted her original plan in order to pursue broader [social] impacts."[79] Yuan laments that the film does not sustain its topic on the social repression of female consciousness, and consequently the sentiment evoked applies to both young men and women at the time. For Yuan, *Sacrificed Youth*'s director became too involved in larger issues, like "civilized versus savage," making the woman question lose its centrality and depriving the heroine's self-reflection of gendered specificity. By "[juxtaposing] different types of contradictions in its structure," the film attempts to "maximize [the number of] its thematic concerns, [which damages] its purity." According to Yuan, this impurity—that is, the mixture of social, historical, and cultural themes—reflects Zhang's lack of a definite vision of female consciousness.[80]

The demand to disintegrate gender and female consciousness from all other sociopolitical issues was high in post-Mao feminist discourse in the 1990s. This trend reflected both a continuing reaction to the socialist gender policy and an eager embrace of Western feminist theory and its universal truth value among Chinese feminist scholars. Dai Jinhua, in her 1994 article "Invisible Women: Contemporary Chinese Cinema and Women's Cinema" (不可见的女性：当代中国电影中的女性与女性电影), builds on Yuan's ideas to further argue that gender equality brought about through political and social revolution essentially repressed female difference and women's cultural voice. She states that although Chinese women obtained social, political, and economic equality with men in socialist China, they remained barred from becoming discursive subjects, their true female voices prohibited.[81] "Paradoxically," Dai points out, "the arrival of women's de jure 'liberation' once again vitiated any chance Woman had to become a historical discursive subject."[82] Her point echoes Kaplan's argument: "The underlying issue for women in China . . . would seem not to be entry into the public sphere—the right to work, to equal pay, to equal participation in the work force, but a new, as yet not fully articulated, realization about subjectivity."[83] Whereas Kaplan and Yuan place women's social revolution as an early stage of feminist endeavor, Dai places women's sociopolitical liberation as nearly antithetical to their discursive or cultural agency and to true female identity.

Although Dai does not explicitly discuss or cite Western theory in her article, certain influences are palpable.[84] Dai's insistence on a fixed, monolithic patriarchal structure that represses female difference at the discursive, symbolic, and cultural levels fundamentally reiterates the Lacanian (post) structuralist position in two important ways. First, in Lacanian theory the symbolic, which functions as the universal law for the formation of male and female subjects via the Oedipus complex, is phallocentric (male-centered) and ahistorical, defined more through its intimate ties to language (discursive) and the unconscious than through its relationship to changing historical and social reality. Second, in the Lacanian model, women (in the conventional sense) exist in historical and social reality by following the phallocentric rule, but the Woman with true female difference is forever repressed by the symbolic order as the Other or unconsciousness. That is to say, Woman stands for the negativity of the symbolic order, sustaining the phallic order while never appearing in it. Similarly, Dai argues that although Chinese women became social and political subjects in socialist China, their true female essence was largely repressed by the male-centered symbolic and discursive order. Women simply performed male roles in social and political realms. As a result, Dai views socialist cinema as necessarily masculine and categorizes all female directors in socialist China in the 1950s and 1960s as Hua Mulan figures, who model themselves on the Chinese legendary heroine Hua Mulan, concealing their *femaleness* and measure themselves via male standards and language in order to become sociopolitical subjects.[85]

Inconsistencies arise in Dai's designation of two historical moments— one, the May Fourth Movement; the other, the early post-Mao era—when (she claims) women's dissenting voices (implying true differences) emerged and reentered the historical order.[86] Given that Western liberal individualism and Enlightenment modernity transformed China's elite cultural landscape and women's cultural practice during those two periods,[87] it is tempting to ask whether true (Chinese) female difference can be expressed only through Western individualist and Enlightenment discourse or whether Western liberal and individual discourse remains the only force that gives rise to universal female difference and female cultural practice. More critically, Dai's theoretical and historical arguments expose an unbridgeable discrepancy between two positions she upholds simultaneously: (1) the liberal individualist position associated with Enlightenment modernity, on which she relies to advance her historical analysis of women's cultural practice during the May Fourth Movement and the 1980s, and (2) the poststructuralist Lacanian position, via which she develops her sweeping conclusion about Woman's invisibility in the socialist era. Because Lacanian poststructuralism both critiques Enlightenment individualism and humanism and transforms the human subject-centered framework to a linguistic and unconscious structure, Dai's two positions seem to contradict each other and are hard to reconcile. Indeed, Lacanian feminists argue that true sexual difference has never appeared in (Western) history and culture. Whereas Dai emphasizes Western cultural critique and poststructuralist discourse, she is simultaneously pulled "back" (in Kaplan's linear model) by her fixation on the liberal, radical feminist values of individual subjectivity, essential female difference, and women's independence from the ahistorical patriarchal order. Similar to Kaplan and Yuan but from a different point of departure, Dai (dis)misses the modern socialist system and its integrated practice, rendering them problematic to the feminist cause.

Dai is clearly influenced by cine-feminist theory as well,[88] especially on avant-garde or marginalized cinema. She divides Chinese women's cinema into three categories. The first refers to the mainstream socialist film production of the Mao era, in which, according to her analysis, women performed male roles and women's films focused on broad sociopolitical issues without expressing their true female difference. Dai further argues that women's cinema, which expresses female difference, cannot grow from *mainstream* film production, echoing Laura Mulvey in a vastly different era and context. "Almost without exception," Dai writes, "contemporary women directors are the makers of mainstream films. They do not experiment with radical, therefore marginal, cinema, nor did they attempt to create works that can be categorized as 'anti-cinema.'"[89] Her second category pertains to films produced in the mid- and late 1980s, when many female directors became aware of sexual difference and focused their filmmaking on women's representations. But because this large group of female directors collaborated with men and were confused by various contemporary constructions of sexual difference, Dai argues that their films tended to conform to mainstream (male) reconfigurations of women's difference without disruption or subversion. Her third category centers on the women's experimental cinema I discuss in this chapter. The formation of this cinema in the early 1980s, according to Dai, evidences a critical and difficult step toward the cinematic emergence of a true female subjectivity. Unlike Chinese women authors' personal writing, which was traceable to the May Fourth era of the early 1920s, Chinese women filmmakers of the 1980s started with a blank slate.[90] Their task to make female individual subjectivity visible in cinema was thus significantly more challenging.

Despite the historical importance of this third category, Dai writes only two short paragraphs (less than her discussion of the other two categories) about women's experimental cinema. More intriguingly, Dai's analysis of Zhang Nuanxin's and Hu Mei's films centers on their ambiguity and inconsequentiality in advancing a true female subjectivity and consciousness. Regarding *Sacrificed Youth*, Dai writes: "A woman comes to a recognition of her own gender in the historical context of the Cultural Revolution, through the inspiration gained from her contact with an ethnic minority culture. But what this recognition brings to her is nothing more than humiliation and embarrassment."[91] On *Army Nurse*, she writes: "The atmosphere is mystical, and things have the quality of flowing out of the mists. For the female protagonist, there is a sense of lament and of the ending of life. What women experienced in this age of historical disaster cannot form a story, or even a photograph."[92] Dai claims that although Zhang's and Hu's films show "the figure of woman beginning to emerge from the mists and vagueness and beginning to express herself, the sentiment and style of their films are still not sufficiently consistent and self-conscious."[93] In Dai's assessment, the two films are neither radical nor marginal enough to be considered feminist anticinema (or avant-garde countercinema). From a different angle, Dai's statement also suggests that the two films are still attached to mainstream film practice as well as the sociopolitical order which, as discussed previously, either represses female difference or traps women at a stage that makes pure and independent self-reflection impossible.

The four essays discussed here became highly influential in the late 1980s and early 1990s, establishing a new analytic framework for the study of Chinese women's cinema. This intellectual trend in Chinese women's film studies was shaped by both Western and Chinese researchers at a historical moment when China was about to enter the global market fully, "integrating" (接轨) itself into the world economy and endorsing a universal value system. These scholarly pieces are not, however, completely identical; some espouse a reference to (liberal) individualist difference with a deliberate consideration of the Chinese context, some evince a postmodern feminist stance with a strong awareness of cultural imperialism, while others blend liberalism, cultural or radical feminism, and Lacanian poststructuralism, critically reviewing Chinese feminist experience in history. But overall, the four essays have all concurred that collective consensus, the socialist state, and mainstream social and cultural movements automatically suppress true female and individual differences. They have all in their own ways denied historical dynamics within the Chinese socialist system and repudiated sociopolitically oriented feminist practice, contributing to the continuous rise and development of universal and cultural feminism in China in the late 1980s and 1990s.

My critical assessment of this new feminist trend of scholarship does not, however, suggest that it lacks any critical insights. On the contrary, the uncertainty and ambiguity these scholars have detected regarding Chinese women's experimental cinema of the 1980s are important discoveries. Unlike other researchers who willfully view Zhang's films as an exemplary practice following China's market development and promotion of a universal modernity,[94] these scholars have perceptively revealed that women's experimental cinema of the 1980s does not conform to a uniform, linear, or universal direction. They further observe that there is no clear-cut break between Zhang and socialist mainstream female directors in the Mao era. The questions I raise in this section thus concern their expressed disappointment and value-laden judgments of such discoveries. Their conclusions suggest that the experimental film practice of the 1980s by Zhang and other women was not individualistic, independent, self-conscious, or antagonistic *enough* to qualify as women's or feminist cinema. Indeed, this new wave of scholarship assesses these female directors' films as ambiguously incomplete and inadequate as a new cinema because of their continued attachment to the "consensus," the State (socialist political system), and mainstream socialist culture, all negatively connoted in the four scholarly essays. These scholarly endeavors strongly suggest, if they do not explicitly endorse, the temporal-spatial configuration of "Western" as advanced and "Chinese" as behind. In its search for a definite and antagonistic break from the past, the new feminist intellectual trend forged during the late 1980s and early 1990s inadvertently cancels out the major achievements and historical significance of socialist feminism and mainstream film practice.

One of the most critical issues to emerge in the discussion of 1980s Chinese women's cinema, therefore, concerns how to make sense of the ambiguity and uncertainty that characterize female directors' films. Are these characteristics caused by China's conflicting ideologies in the 1980s? Or do they indicate an emerging new vision and cinema, still in an embryonic stage? Is such uncertainty symptomatic of all cross-cultural analysis, as Kaplan suggests? Or, by contrast, is it a problem embedded in the teleological and binary research framework itself, which configures some kinds of ambiguity as the lack of a resolute break from the past or insufficiency for the expected new position? What, then, has possibly been precluded and barred from this binary, universal structure? In the next section, I provide an alternative reading and analysis of Zhang's *Sacrificed Youth*, exploring the meaning of the film's ambiguity in its historical context and probing into the film's critical approach to both socialist history and China in the 1980s.

Sacrificed Youth: Experimental Cinema as a Double Critique of the Cultural Revolution and Mainstream Discourses of the Mid-1980s

In the mid-1980s, Zhang Nuanxin was directly or indirectly engaged with two emerging and overlapping mainstream intellectual movements. One concerned gender and the personal, part of the post-Mao feminist movement and women's autobiographical cultural practice,[95] and the other regarded experimental filmmaking, part of the early cultural fever phenomenon of the 1980s, which developed later into the Root-Seeking Movement and avant-garde cinema.[96] Whereas both intellectual movements critiqued the Cultural Revolution and endorsed thought liberation, they parted ways in their reconceptualizations of gender and projections for the future. Although institutionalized socialist feminism served as a critical foundation for early post-Mao feminism and women's cultural production, participants' perceptions varied. Some disavowed or took for granted socialist feminism in their critique of the Cultural Revolution or in their promotion of individual and independent feminism; others reclaimed the necessity of institutionalized feminism in their critical reflection on the Cultural Revolution, advocating a feminism that was both socially engaged and personally reflective. Zhang, in making *Sacrificed Youth*, articulated a critical revisionist stance that targeted the uniform control of cultural production during the Cultural Revolution while adhering to some fundamental socialist values, thereby challenging not only the masculine discourses of mid-1980s experimental cinema and the Root-Seeking Movement but also post-Mao feminist endeavors to break away from an integrated and institutionalized feminist practice. This section closely studies Zhang's *Sacrificed Youth*, illustrating her complex negotiations with different and competing cultural forces around the middle of the decade and reexamining the historical significance of Chinese women's subjectively oriented cultural practice in the early post-Mao era, when socialist feminism still held sway while the thought liberation movement enabled women to articulate their concerns about and reimaginations of gender, community, and self.

Chinese Women's Autobiographical Practice in the Post-Mao Era: From Zhang Manling's "A Beautiful Place" to Zhang Nuanxin's *Sacrificed Youth*

Sacrificed Youth was adapted from Zhang Manling's (张曼菱, b. 1948) autobiographical novella "A Beautiful Place" (有一个美丽的地方), published in *Contemporary Time* (当代) in 1982.[97] Women's autobiographical literature re-emerged as a critical practice toward the end of the 1970s, becoming popular in the 1980s and continuing into the 1990s and beyond. If we examine what constitutes the autobiographical and the personal, however, the distinction between women's autobiographical literature practiced in the early post-Mao era (that is, roughly from the late 1970s to the mid-1980s), and that produced afterward is hard to miss. Whereas the personal is strongly signified by the social and political as well as the subjective in the first period, women's autobiography toward the end of the 1980s and 1990s turned inward and somatic, increasingly tied to individual desire and public consumption.[98]

Zhang Manling's "A Beautiful Place" is part of the autobiographical trend within women's literature in the early 1980s. The novella centers on the personal subjective experiences of a young educated woman, Li Chun, one of the urban youths "sent down" to minority and rural villages during the Cultural Revolution. The novella directly participated in the general ongoing historical reflection on the Cultural Revolution, especially regarding the problematic consequences of an entire generation's loss of youth and education.[99] "A Beautiful Place" also indirectly touches on the emerging critique of the Han (majority, 汉族) civilization as a weak, submissive, yet autocratic culture. However, Zhang's novella is by no means a one-dimensional representation of the Cultural Revolution's Up to the Mountain and Down to the Countryside Movement (上山下乡运动). While questioning the policy's rationale, the novella also describes, as the title indicates, the heroine's time spent with Dai minority people as one of the most transformative and rewarding experiences of her life. The heroine not only finds a new home in the rural Dai family and village but also becomes reflective as her understanding of community, family, gender, and beauty expands and deepens. She even submits a counterintuitive refusal to leave the place when her boyfriend, her first love, whom she met in the Dai village, makes such a proposal. Of particular note, when Li Chun leaves her urban home for a remote location in Yunnan Province at the age of nineteen, she already possesses an active and confident sense of self. Growing up in an intellectual family in socialist China, she was an excellent student (before the Cultural Revolution) and took as her model such successful international female figures as Zoya Kosmodemyanskaya (a heroine of the Soviet Union) and the Polish-French scientist Marie Curie. Li's strong sense of self and her understanding of gender equality are mostly conveyed in the novella through internal monologues.

Upon arriving, Li Chun feels both disoriented by and attracted to the Dai people's unfamiliar culture, which celebrates female (feminine) beauty and openly displays heterosexual attraction among young people. After she follows local custom by wearing Dai-style feminine dress, Li's sense of herself is expanded and enriched. Comparing her own experience as a young girl, wearing a unisex blue uniform in urban China, to young Dai women's attire, full of life and color, she reflects: "I have wished to become Zoya Kosmodemyanskaya and Marie Skłodowska Curie, but I have never dreamed of myself so eager to become Bilang" (a local Dai beauty).[100] At the same time, however, Li shows perceptivity and understanding toward Dai youth culture, especially the Dai women's social position. She is aware of the much less promising future young Dai women have in comparison to men. Indeed, the expressive and colorful lifestyle of young Dai women exists to attract and secure a husband. After Dai women marry, Li reflects, "Nobody will care much about their feelings or will subject himself to their wills. Instead, everyone will order them around. Betel nuts will blacken their teeth and they will finally become middle-aged women. In the early evening, they can no longer go out freely singing under the local dragon trees."[101] Women's domestication after marriage in Dai minority culture is also represented through female characters in the story, particularly Ya, the old grandma of the family with whom Li stays.[102] Li's desire to identify with Bilang, therefore, does not translate into a total endorsement of the gender norm in Dai society and culture.

In the context of China in the early 1980s, when an emerging mainstream discourse practiced predominantly by male intellectuals deployed minority cultures and customs as "natural" and "instinctual/primitive" forces to critique the "abnormal" Cultural Revolution and the submissive majority of Han Chinese, Zhang's novella stands out by refusing to romanticize minority culture. Her autobiographical writing about a woman's self-negotiation in the Dai community does not fall into a simple, binary framework. Critically, the heroine's earlier education and experience in socialist urban China, where gender equality is institutionally implemented and ideologically upheld, provide her an important foundation to discern gender issues in Dai society. Rather than representing Dai culture as something natural and ideal in opposition to the socialist Han culture, Zhang Manling identifies problems in both societies while adhering to fundamental socialist values of gender equality.

Li's sense of self is enriched as she embraces the local female culture, but her sense of self-worth with a social purpose is never shaken. Her self-reliance is particularly highlighted when she refuses to accept the love of Big Brother, the son of the Dai family Li stays with, whose attention to Li originates partially in her donning of Dai dress. Li understands that a Dai woman's expression of female beauty is tied to her future marriage, so in rebuffing Big Brother she makes a statement, reorienting her self-exploration of beauty away from the predetermined local trajectory. Li's sense of self-reliance is further illustrated in her relationship with Ren Jia, a young man sent down from the same city, with whom she develops a mutual trust and embryonic love. In the novella, Ren is from a family of musicians; his father lives in the United States. After years of staying in the Dai area, and once China's political situation began to change in the mid- and late 1970s, Ren proposes to bring Li to the United States, where they can both go to school to study. To his (as well as the readers') surprise, Li does not feel joyful about the proposal. Instead, she is torn between her choices, sensing a strong pressure and even threat from Ren's love proposal, which indirectly but effectively renders her a dependent. Li's final refusal of Ren is grounded in her sense of female self-reliance, which has been cultivated in her since her socialist childhood. In addition, the novella's concrete depiction of how well Li integrates into this Dai community suggests that her turning down Ren's proposal also stems from an attachment and commitment to the social fabric of the local community.

Women's (auto)biographical literature served as a most important source for women's experimental cinema in the 1980s.[103] For Zhang Nuanxin, who aspired to pioneer a subjective experimental cinema in China, Zhang Manling's "A Beautiful Place" provided both a compelling, reflexive story and a fitting experimental style and structure for the film. According to Zhang Nuanxin, the story is highly (auto)biographical for her as well and thus contains collective values as it "explores our generation's feelings and reflections."[104] Set in a rural, minority village and with a subjective, fragmented narrative structure that frequently has recourse to stream of consciousness, the novella fulfilled Zhang's desire to make a unique film to counter the Cultural Revolution's dogmatic literary policy and the dominant cinematic mode of melodrama, foregrounding instead personal memory, subjective enunciation, and documentary imagery.[105] In her published director's notes on this film, Zhang recounts her excitement when, after reading the novella, she realized the story would enable her to "make a brand-new film that would depart from all other films."[106] The historical background of the story—namely, the Cultural Revolution, and particularly the Up to the Mountain and Down to the Countryside Movement—also offered Zhang an entry point to participate in the mainstream discourse of the mid-1980s on the Cultural Revolution.

Sacrificed Youth was especially applauded on its release as the most modern experimental film up to that point. In the film, Zhang expanded the experimentalism that first developed in *Drive to Win*, which included first-person voice-over, subjective flashbacks, on-location shooting, amateur actors, natural lighting, and direct sound recordings. The film's narrative takes the form of the heroine's flashback and is thus subjectively mediated rather than event- or plot-driven. In "Director's Notes on *Sacrificed Youth*," Zhang defines the narrative style of her film as "fragmented, emotive prose poetry" (抒情散文诗) and suggests the entire film be filtered through a warm red color to highlight the lens of subjective memory.[107] Whereas natural light and sound are used extensively, they are anchored through the heroine's subjective senses. In addition, Zhang recommends wide-angle and telephoto lenses be used to accentuate subjective mediations. For the camerawork, Zhang insists on the combined usage of long takes and montage, long shots and close-ups, and motion and still shots. The soundtrack of the film reflects the local and ethnic music tradition, but the theme song, a tune Li learned in her childhood, holds distinctively modern and popular appeal. Despite the film's experimental style, Zhang firmly envisions *Sacrificed Youth* as a mainstream film with mass appeal.

Although *Sacrificed Youth* was celebrated as a successful film with a truly modern style at the time, Zhang did not perceive the modern style as inherently more meaningful or valuable than other styles. Zhang states in interviews that she experiments with film styles in order to find a cinematic language to express her thoughts and reflections.[108] Style is merely a part and a means of artistic expression and should not be separated from what is expressed. How, then, did Zhang Nuanxin convey her own thoughts and ideas through a newly developed "modern" style? What did subjective experimental filmmaking enable women to do in China in the 1980s in general, and what did Zhang Nuanxin accomplish by making *Sacrificed Youth* in particular?

Adaptive Revisions: Critiquing Uniformity, Essentialized Sexual Difference, and Detached Individualism

Zhang Manling's autobiographical novella was itself part of the complex historical and cultural negotiations taking place in early post-Mao China. Her work articulates a subjective, gendered experience and historical reflection in an experimental form. Zhang Nuanxin adhered to central elements of the original story in her cinematic adaptation, yet her revisions reflect different negotiations within the cultural movement of the mid-1980s, thus providing critical insights into the historical significance of the film's perceived ambiguity.

Among the major revisions Zhang Nuanxin made in adapting Zhang Manling's novella, two deserve special attention and discussion. First, Zhang Nuanxin critiques the radicalism of the Cultural Revolution, especially in the first half hour when she contrasts Dai ethnic youth culture to urban (Han) Chinese culture of the late 1960s and early 1970s. One of the central themes of cultural reflection and post-Mao feminism in the 1980s concerns the repression

6.1 Li Chun contemplates different beauty concepts after Da-die's comments. *Sacrificed Youth* (青春祭), directed by Zhang Nuanxin, 1985.

of human nature and gender or sexual difference in the Cultural Revolution. By the time Zhang was making her film, this repression theme had developed into a negative assessment of Han civilization as a whole, often against a contrasting representation of minority or "primitive" cultures. Although critical reflections on the Cultural Revolution also constitute an important part of the original novella, they are balanced by the heroine's simultaneous critique of Dai culture via her internal monologue. In her revisions, however, Zhang Nuanxin took out most of Zhang Manling's critical comments on Dai minority culture in order to foreground her own critique of the Cultural Revolution's radicalism. One scene that has attracted much critical attention centers on the topic of feminine beauty. Zhang re-created this scene from the novella but with a concentrated individual reflection via subjective camera and the heroine's voice-over.

The film shows that after staying in the Dai village for some time and witnessing young Dai people's open expressions of beauty and love, Li Chun grows frustrated with how the local village's young women remain distant from her. When she complains to Da-die (Big Uncle), the head of her host family, who is also a community leader, he replies that the reason is her plain gray clothing. Da-die then asks, with a puzzled expression, "You are a young girl. Why don't you dress yourself up a bit?" He further explains: "Young Dai ethnic women are most passionate about being pretty." The silence that follows and the close-up shots of Li Chun's slow body movement and contemplative expression show how shaken she is by Da-die's comments and question (fig. 6.1). The

6.2 A dragonfly on the tip of a lotus flower bud. *Sacrificed Youth* (青春祭), directed by Zhang Nuanxin, 1985.

6.3 Li Chun in a Dai dress. *Sacrificed Youth* (青春祭), directed by Zhang Nuanxin, 1985.

accompanying first-person voice-over tells the audience exactly what is going through her mind: "[I had never realized that] being pretty is so important." She further reflects, "I have been taught since childhood that not making yourself attractive is beautiful. I used to wash my new clothes repeatedly only to make them appear worn out. It has never occurred to me that a girl should make herself pretty ['dress herself up']." The camera then cuts to a close-up shot from Li's perspective, in which a beautiful pink lotus flower is attracting a dragonfly to land on the tip of its bud (fig. 6.2). The cinematic signification is clearly conveyed: like a budding flower, a young girl should exhibit her beauty and display her attractiveness. At the end of the scene, Li rushes home to make herself a pretty Dai dress (fig. 6.3).

For a cultural critic of China in the 1980s, the scene unambiguously drives home the idea that Han culture and the Cultural Revolution have repressed human nature and desires.[109] The literal wording of Li's memory about the beauty standard in socialist China, "being not-pretty is beautiful" (不美就是美), seems also to echo the general intellectual critique of the Cultural Revolution as an unnatural, abnormal period. The minority culture functions in Zhang's film as a corrective or liberating force against the overall practice of the Cultural Revolution.[110] Post-Mao feminist scholars concerned with female consciousness and sexual difference often recall this scene to argue that *Sacrificed Youth* reveals the Cultural Revolution's social repression of female consciousness and that the film is mostly about a girl's awakening to gender or sexual difference.[111] This scene could also be read through the post-Mao feminist criticism of gender erasure, a critique of socialist Chinese gender policy in general.[112]

However, as I mentioned earlier, most scholars have also expressed great uncertainty about this scene, as well as the overall message of the film. Some argue that the director became distracted in making the rest of the film and subsequently discontinued this thread on gender or sexual difference and female consciousness; some state that this realization of difference does not lead anywhere; still others reason that Li's dressing herself up in Dai costume does not (re)solve her issues as a Han woman. Despite the initial thirty-minute introduction to colorful Dai youth culture and this concentrated scene on feminine beauty, the film, according to some scholars, failed to articulate a fundamental difference that counters the Cultural Revolution or socialism as a totality. Such unsatisfactory scholarly conclusions obligate us to examine Zhang Nuanxin's film practice further. What does her critique of the Cultural Revolution as represented in *Sacrificed Youth* really mean, and where does this critique lead?

Han Chen (韩琛), in his article "Three Theoretical Resources for Chinese Female Film Discourse," argues that, similar to the effect of sexual cross-dressing in other social contexts, the ethnic "cross-dressing" emphasized in *Sacrificed Youth* during the Cultural Revolution also cracks open an antipatriarchal space by showing that female identity is not natural but a masquerade, a social construct.[113] It is certainly questionable whether the illustration of gender as a performance alone would automatically generate an antipatriarchal space in a given society, but this line of argument, which ties gendered identity to social and cultural codes, offers important insights for my discussion of the feminine beauty scene in *Sacrificed Youth*, as well as the scene's relationship to the entire film. This observation suggests that the target of critique and the significance of the scene may lie elsewhere. In foregrounding this scene, Zhang Nuanxin makes an emphatic point about the radicalism of the Cultural Revolution. However, the content of her critique is perhaps less about its unnatural disposition or abnormality than about its uniformity. Indeed, linking female beauty standards to dress code, this scene illustrates the constructive rather than natural character of gender identities. The heroine suddenly realizes that "beauty" or "being pretty" can be understood and practiced differently depending on culture and location. The scene's, and the film's as a whole, critique of the Cultural Revolution, especially its gender configuration in the late 1960s and early 1970s when men and women wore similar working uniforms and embodied androgynous identities, focuses more on uniformity and the constraint placed on self-expression than on abnormality.

This critical discovery was, in a significant and ironic way, much enabled by Chinese socialist feminist practice, which had effectively denaturalized both Chinese traditional femininity and capitalist sexual difference. Socialist feminism was premised on challenging previous gender essentialisms, and this legacy was in fact continued rather than discontinued in both Zhang Manling's and Zhang Nuanxin's works in the 1980s. This continuation explains why Zhang's critique of the Cultural Revolution does not, to the disappointment of some scholars, lead to an oppositional stance rejecting socialist gender equality altogether, promoting an essential female difference or feminine beauty. Zhang's critical engagement also suggests that the practice of extreme uniformity during the Cultural Revolution paradoxically contradicted fundamental socialist feminist values, as uniformity leads to cultural essentialism with a potentially naturalized effect.

Zhang's challenge to uniformity and essentialism is further upheld later in the film when the heroine not only turns away from the love of Big

Brother but also changes her clothes back to the plain style worn by sent-down youth. Li Chun's refusal to affix herself to the Dai feminine position may indeed have frustrated some critics in the late 1980s, who eagerly antici-pated a resolute pursuit of the liberation of human nature (cultural critique) or essential female difference (feminism) in the form of a conclusive and unrestrained heterosexual relationship (sexual difference). The heroine's re-sistance to becoming a love interest of the martial and masculine young man illustrates a nonbinary approach to women's difference and consciousness. In other words, while Zhang Nuanxin foregrounds her critique of Cultural Revolution beauty norms, she does not introduce an oppositional code as more truthful, natural, or ideal. The film questions any uniform model of beauty, gender, or sexual difference. When the heroine wears Dai women's clothing, she feels a more dynamic and expanded sense of self. To a large extent, Li's "cross-dressing" is practiced mostly to integrate herself into the local female community. Later, when such feminine clothes become Cinderella's shoes (Li Chun's wording in the film version only)—subjecting Li to local customs that tie a woman's beauty and its expression exclusively to (hetero)sexual desire, domestic femininity, and marriage—Li rejects the at-tendant expectations and returns to her previous clothing. This unsettling of a fixed form of sexual and gender (non)difference, which accounts for much of the film's ambiguity, marks one of the most significant contributions of *Sacrificed Youth*. Zhang is critical not only of the rigid, political control of people's identities during the Cultural Revolution but also of the naturaliza-tion of sexual difference and women's domesticity that emerged in the 1980s.

The second important revision in Zhang's film adaptation that demands our critical attention concerns the reconfiguration of the male character Ren Jia and his relationship with Li Chun. This change involves several scenes that express Zhang's serious concerns about the rising, elitist individualism of China in the 1980s. After the tightening of the Anti-Spiritual-Pollution Campaign of 1983, the Chinese government relaxed its cultural policy to grant more freedom and space for liberal cultural reflections.[114] As discussed in the previous chapter, this official discourse on "creative freedom," how-ever, significantly redirected cultural practice away from socioeconomic and political engagements. In terms of film production, the year 1985 is regarded as the height of individualization, especially in experimental cinema. This individualization was not simply expressed in cinematic style but also "man-ifested in the ideology [of the new cinema], which further enhanced the separation of central characters from society, intensifying their loneliness."[115] Exemplary films include such titles (by Fifth Generation directors) as Chen

Kaige's *Yellow Earth* (黄土地), Tian Zhuangzuang's (田壮壮) *On the Hunting Ground* (猎场扎撒), and Huang Jianxin's (黄建新) *The Black Cannon Incident* (黑炮事件). *Sacrificed Youth* also came out in 1985 but has been mostly excluded from this high-profile list of experimental films, despite its experimental nature and unique cinematic style. While the director's gender may be an important reason for such exclusion, Zhang's film also questions the trademark of those experimental films—namely, heightened avant-gardism and individuality detached from the social.

In the original story, Ren Jia is a sent-down youth who, like Li Chun, originates from an intellectual family in Beijing. He becomes acquainted with Li in the local post office on the first day she wears Dai-style clothes. Ren's mother is a music teacher in Beijing, and his father lives in the United States. He is depicted as a unique young man, one who plays violin, ponders matters deeply, worries about losing his original goal (to become a successful musician), and has won the trust and respect of the local Dai people. He reminds Li of her family background and former dreams; he also urges the heroine not simply to subject herself to her surroundings. Toward the end of the story, Ren sacrifices his own life to save the lives of local people and livestock during an unexpected, large-scale mudslide.

In her cinematic adaptation, Zhang Nuanxin significantly revises Ren Jia's character, creating an individualist type of educated youth. Whereas the original story underscores the similarities between Ren and Li, the film highlights their fundamental differences. Ren appears more cynical and self-centered; he frequently criticizes the current political situation, ridicules the heroine's adoption of the local dress and her attachment to the Dai community, and sees nothing worthy in his new surroundings. His heart and mind always seem somewhere else; he remains removed from the local people and constantly dreams of returning to the city.

The most telling detail Zhang inserted in the film concerns the different books Li and Ren wish to read as sent-down youth. While Li fights to purchase the last copy of *A Rural Doctor's Manual* (农村医生手册) in a local market (a tremendously popular book among sent-down youth at the time), intending to serve the Dai community as a barefoot doctor, Ren secretly obtains a copy of Jean-Jacques Rousseau's *Confessions*, marking his significant distance from the people around him (fig. 6.4). The sheer mention of the name Rousseau in such a remote village during the Cultural Revolution period is extraordinary, as Rousseau's *Confessions* did not become popular among Chinese intellectuals until the early 1980s when the nation began engaging in critical reflection on the Cultural Revolution, truth telling, and

6.4 Li Chun grabs the last copy of *A Rural Doctor's Manual*. *Sacrificed Youth*
(青春祭), directed by Zhang Nuanxin, 1985.

freedom of individual expression.[116] The contrast between the two youths'
reading materials and interests is stark, to say the least. Li's immediate response to Rousseau's *Confessions* and the subsequent dialogues between Li
and Ren are equally telling, foreshadowing the pair's future separation. After
glancing at the first page, Li quickly returns the book to Ren's bag, comment-
ing: "I cannot understand this book. I am not interested in this thing [这玩意
儿]" (fig. 6.5). Li's rejection comes as an unpleasant surprise and disappointment to Ren, as he immediately senses Li does not embrace the sort of individualism with which he identifies. He retorts, ridiculing her: "Then what are
you interested in [exactly]? What you are obsessed with all day long are just
colorful clothes and floral skirts." With Ren's sarcastic remarks on Li's cross-
dressing, Zhang Nuanxin circles back to the feminine beauty scene, making
it clear that Ren does not even attempt to understand the significance of
Li's "cross-dressing," not to mention her resistance to uniformity. While Ren
does support Li in an earlier scene, when she shares how her urban school-
mates mock her Dai dress, even then Ren's response is less about Li's ethnic

6.5 "I cannot understand this book. I am not interested in this thing." *Sacrificed Youth* (青春祭), directed by Zhang Nuanxin, 1985.

cross-dressing than individuality. Quoting Dante Alighieri's adage "Go your own way, let others talk," Ren's response evokes, especially among the audience of the 1980s, a strong sense of individualistic heroism, conveying at the same time a contempt for social conventions and average or common folks, who are implicated as blind followers.[117] Now, when Li dismisses Rousseau, Ren reveals his contempt for her behavior as well.

This added detail of Rousseau's *Confessions* emblematizes Ren Jia's individualism in the film, a position that separates Ren from his social environment, highlighting his elitist disdain for others. Indeed, the film does not show Ren interacting with anyone besides Li. His individualism is further marked by his desire for a new self-worth based on social hierarchy, his pursuit of a Western-style freedom of expression, and his physical detachment from the local community. Although *Sacrificed Youth* takes place during the Cultural Revolution, the film carves a critical space to reflect on individualist subjectivity as articulated in the early and mid-1980s, raising questions about future sociocultural directions.

6.6 Li Chun disagrees with Ren Jia about their lives in the Dai village. *Sacrificed Youth* (青春祭), directed by Zhang Nuanxin, 1985.

To further emphasize Li's and Ren's different visions, as well as the pressure Ren increasingly imposes on Li, Zhang Nuanxin creates a confrontational scene in the film. After years of staying in the Dai village, Li and Ren's hope for a quick return to the city has dwindled. One sunny day, they encounter an abandoned temple, where their conversation conveys how far apart they have drifted (fig. 6.6).

REN JIA In the past, it was really foolish of us to believe so many [political] lies. I really do not know when these dreadful days will come to an end.

LI CHUN But I feel we are pretty good here. In any case, my experience here has brought me a new understanding of life.

REN JIA [Are you saying] you want to live like this forever?

LI CHUN [*Silence*]

REN JIA Are you contented with life like this? Have you noticed that the Dai girls are charming in their prime years, but it doesn't last long. After they get married, they soon become old women, teeth blackened from chewing betel nut. Do you really want to become one of them?

LI CHUN [*Silence*]

It is important to note that in this added scene, Zhang Nuanxin has Ren comment on the unpromising future for young local women after marriage. In the novella, Li herself offers this critical reflection. Whereas the wording of their comments is similar, the focus and significance part ways completely. As I discussed above, when Li utters her reflection, especially on women's status after marriage in Dai culture, she illustrates her earlier education and upbringing in socialist urban China, including her adherence to such socialist feminist principles as gender equality, women's self-reliance, and women's public or social contributions. But Ren's comments target women themselves, especially women's concern for their appearance and their apparent lack of individual(istic) ambitions or agency, functioning, in the context of their conversation, more to undermine Li's sense of self-worth and her commitment to the local community than as a critique of gender inequity. Rather than targeting the gendered hierarchies of Dai culture, Ren voices a distinct prejudice against local women as naturally inferior individuals.

Zhang Manling, through her heroine's critical reflection on local gendered cultural practice, reveals a strong socialist feminist legacy in her autobiographical novella. Zhang Nuanxin, on the other hand, by changing the subject of reflection from Li to Ren, turns her critical lens on the emerging force of individualism and socially detached rationality during the late Cultural Revolution. Ren's perception and ideas in the film correspond to the intellectual movement of the mid-1980s wherein individualistic subjectivity, Enlightenment rationality, and cultural essentialization or naturalization coproduced a new, mainstream discourse of universal modernity. Zhang Nuanxin's changing of the speaker, therefore, does not necessarily suggest a departure from the novella's fundamental position. On the contrary, this shift reinforces, from a different angle and with a different focus, the values and beliefs Zhang Manling articulated in her story.

Moreover, this additional, confrontational scene is strategically sandwiched between two scenes that highlight Li's integration into her Dai host family and village. The first scene shows an ordinary evening she spends with Da-die's whole family. The oil lamp's warm light, the family members' expressing peaceful joy and love, and the beautiful melody and lyrics of the (theme) song she sings for Da-die's family—the only time she sings in the film—all strongly suggest Li's sense of feeling at home. Indeed, Li has found a new home in Da-die's rural, Dai-minority family. Her own happiness and peace are highlighted through subjectively mediated shots, warm colors, and her singing voice. The second scene shows Li's direct participation in the Dai peasants' annual fall harvest celebration. The carnival-like dancing scene permeated with the warm orange glow from bonfires reiterates how she has become a happy, active member of the local community. These two scenes, together with the film's subjective portrayal of Li's inner growth and expanded sense of self since her arrival in the rural Dai community, significantly represent the ideal of a social community that thrives on an egalitarian socioeconomic and ethical system, transcends biological (blood) relationship and ethnic bonds, and endorses cultural pluralism and individual differences. In this sense of the social, the film reveals later, Li recognizes the real source of her life and thus refuses to give up at the juncture of impending changes in national and personal lives.

Two different kinds of self-reconfiguration among educated youth, in the context of the Up to the Mountain and Down to the Countryside Movement, are thus foregrounded in Zhang's film: one is community-oriented and the other individual-centered. Although both Li and Ren are critical of the Cultural Revolution, their experiences in a rural minority community, their commitments to an egalitarian society, and their visions for China's future differ greatly. Li makes clear, in her dialogue with Ren and engagement with the Dai community, that although things are not all satisfactory, her life experience has been expanded and enriched, and her sense of personal agency enhanced. Ren, on the contrary, feels cheated, suffocated, and totally out of place. His vision for his own and China's future entails a total break from the present.

Ren also plays a key role in the subsequent, important change in Li's life immediately after the harvest celebration. He shows up at the fall festival where Li is dancing and celebrating with the Dai peasants. Instead of joining the community, Ren signals Li to meet him, alone, away from the crowd. His presence at the festival thus immediately produces a separation effect. His ensuing stay at Da-die's place, albeit at Li's suggestion due to his leg injury, leads to an (un)expected fight between him and Big Brother, eventually causing Li to run away from the very place she has embraced as home. The image of Li on a raft alone, going down a long river in the pitch-dark night and accompanied by an eerie, unsettling melody, expressively reveals her second loss of "home."

Li leaves her Dai home partially because of Big Brother's love, which seems to grow stronger and could potentially subject her to a sexualized, domestic existence. However, Ren's presence ultimately pulls her out of the social environment to which she has become attached. The film thus powerfully suggests that neither the masculine (Big Brother) nor the individualistic (Ren Jia)—two configurations of manhood promoted in the Chinese cultural movement of the 1980s—offers women a sense of freedom or belonging. Li's departure from her second home certainly does not draw her closer to Ren; she returns to her original attire after leaving Da-die's village and teaches at an elementary school in another rural village for several years.

In this new setting Zhang Nuanxin creates another important scene, foregrounding Li and Ren's final separation. The scene begins with Ren driving a tractor, bringing Li her mother's letter from the local post office on a late spring day. Shot on a narrow village road, Ren's tractor occupies two-thirds of the screen whereas Li is positioned at the right edge. Ren asks Li if she has registered for the college entrance exam, a practice that resumed immediately after the Cultural Revolution ended in 1977. Li replies no and invites Ren to talk more inside. Ren becomes frustrated instantly upon hearing Li's answer. "Why didn't you?" He lights a cigarette without even looking at Li, who is taken aback by Ren's response. She hesitates and then offers her problematic family background as a reason. But Ren interrupts, in an interrogating tone: "Why can't you see that for people like us college is the only way out?" Indeed, the political situation has changed by that time. As Li's mother's letter indicates, many intellectuals have already returned to the cities and taken up their previous positions again. Ren can no longer control his anger: "We are already over twenty years old, and we have to think about our future. We are not going to end up dying here, right?" Li, positioned at the right edge of the screen, appears to be pushed off the frame by Ren's angry interrogation. Quickly gathering herself, Li firmly replies, "You go and register yourself. No need to care about me!" Startled by her answer, Ren jumps onto his tractor and takes off. Li then walks toward the center of the road/screen to watch Ren drive away. And so the relationship ends.

Zhang Nuanxin's revisions of Ren and Li's relationship significantly altered the structure of the original story, creating a narrative dimension in which to ponder issues particularly resonant with the Enlightenment-driven cultural movement of 1980s China. The heroine's subtle yet staunch refusal to embrace the values Ren embodies, despite her personal attachment to him, reveals Zhang's reservations about socially detached rationality and self-inflated, abstract individualism (predominantly promoted by male intellectuals of the time). In the novella, Ren dies heroically during a sudden mudslide. In the film, Li, back in the present time frame, only mentions in retrospective voice-over that Ren had died in a catastrophic mudslide. This revision shows how Zhang intentionally changed Ren's self-sacrificing spirit represented in the original story. Far from community-driven altruism, *her* Ren Jia instead embodies a self-centered individualism.

Zhang's cinematic adaptation resolutely avoids endorsing oppositional individualism or essentialist female consciousness, both of which became widely accepted in the late 1980s, accounting for scholars' disappointment with the film in the late 1980s and early 1990s. While critical of the uniform control of cultural and social practices during the Cultural Revolution, Zhang does not turn to universal human nature, essentialized sexual difference, independent female consciousness, or elitist detached individualism as potential alternatives. Furthermore, despite her embrace of the New Era's experimental cinema and subjective expression, Zhang does not separate aesthetic pursuit from sociopolitical commitment. The film's double critique, of the Cultural Revolution and of the emerging mainstream discourses of the mid-1980s, combined with its experimental style and gendered perspective, seriously unsettles the dominant binary cultural and research frameworks, advancing an alternative experimental cinematic practice in post-Mao China.

Conclusion: From Subjective-Documentary Cinema to Sociopolitical Melodrama

Chinese economic reform continued and expanded throughout the 1980s, across rural and urban areas. In the late 1980s and early 1990s, as the market became an increasingly dominant force in reconfiguring social relationships and cultural production, Chinese women's subjective, experimental, and socially engaged cinema, pioneered by Zhang Nuanxin and practiced by a small group of female directors, came to a stop. Chinese women's autobiographical writing, which was both personally and socially engaged, also came to a historic halt. Compelled by the changing socioeconomic and cultural reality, some second- and third-generation Chinese female directors began responding to market demand in the late 1980s, making commercial genre films or films that represented new sexual roles in contemporary China.

Zhang Nuanxin and a few others exploring social issues soon found themselves irreversibly marginalized. Compelled by what she was witnessing—namely, the social consequences of economic reform—Zhang moved away from her significant trademark, subjective cinema, and turned her camera toward the broader social issues of China in the 1990s. Especially worthy of note in Zhang's two later representative films is the absence of any social subjectivity or personal agency for women. Her films' cinematic authorship, characterized previously by her subjective style and strong authorial identification with her heroines, became resignified in her 1990s work as she exercised a distanced (nonsubjective) documentary approach in filming *Good Morning, Beijing* and resorted to sociopolitical melodrama in making her last film, *South China, 1994* (南中国, 1994, 1994).

We should recall how Zhang had repeatedly stressed in interviews that cinematic form should not separate from film content. Her aesthetic departures, therefore, also reveal a significant change in what she wanted to represent. In the early 1990s, answering a question about her changing relationship to her female characters at a Harvard University screening of *Good Morning, Beijing*, Zhang stated that she remained as true to life as always and "that it was life itself that had changed."[118] Zhang's filmmaking certainly shifted, from articulating socially integrated and subjectively mediated female subjectivity; to observing the massive process of social, political, and economic disintegration, including its particular effects on women's agency, via China's economic reforms (*Good Morning, Beijing*); and eventually to critiquing the victimization and subjugation of women in a special economic zone of southern China, where transnational market capital recoded gender and class relationships (*South China, 1994*). In Zhang's films of the 1990s, women become increasingly deprived of social and political agency, violently torn between ethical, emotional, and economic pursuits in a market-oriented China.

For *Good Morning, Beijing*, a film retrospectively regarded as the aesthetic precursor to Chinese Sixth Generation films, Zhang deploys documentary realism to show how young people working in the state-run public transportation department confront ground-shaking transformations in the capital city. Increasing desire for material wealth is coupled with deep anxiety and fear of falling behind in the face of unprecedented, massive competition. Ai Hong, the young female bus ticket conductor in the film, best represents this pervasive desire and anxiety. She leaves her boyfriend, an honest, hardworking young bus driver, for a self-styled poseur who frequents expensive stores designed for Westerners and pretends to be a foreign student studying at a Chinese university. Whereas some scholars argue that Ai Hong represents courage and change by aligning her personal pursuits with the nation's new market direction,[119] Zhang, in an interview on the film, shares her serious reservations about such tumultuous social and economic change. She uses the term "symptomatic crux" (症结) to describe the society her film depicts. The intensity and scale of the commodification wave's effect on ordinary Chinese people, according to Zhang, is no less than that of (previous) political movements: "The unjustified new social division of labor has become a more and more serious problem in everyday life . . . but no perfect solution has been found."[120] In Zhang's view, the original film script by Tang Danian (唐大年), written while he was still a student at the Beijing Film Academy, best represents the confusion and struggle Chinese young people experienced in suddenly confronting a shockingly abrasive commodity market.[121]

The potential problem Zhang Nuanxin articulated in *Sacrificed Youth*—socially detached, self-absorbed individualism—is further developed in *Good Morning, Beijing* into *commercialized* individualism. In the later film, Western-style consumerism and private entrepreneurship trumpet a type of individualism that manifests as mere "lifestyle," radically divorced from ethical or social concerns, emotional bonds like love, and even a minimal sense of authentic identity. Indeed, Ai Hong's endless struggle is caused not only by a forced divorce from the social environment she is emotionally attached to but also by the fact that this ruthless estrangement does not lead to any new ethical or constructive interpersonal relationships. Material lifestyle becomes the singular concern and measurement of success. While Zhang voices no direct criticism, due to her profound understanding of Chinese youths' confused struggle, her distanced and restrained camera lens nonetheless conveys a strong sense of fatalism, an uncontrollable deterioration of the egalitarian society, and a serious lack of agency among her characters.

When making her last film, *South China, 1994*, Zhang cast aside both subjective cinema and documentary realism. To the surprise of many filmmakers and scholars, she turned to sociopolitical melodrama, the very style from which she had purposefully departed in the early post-Mao era. *South China, 1994* was originally classified as an officially sponsored, "main melody film" (主旋律) project, but Zhang remained determined to imbue the genre with a new, critical edge. In her last interview "Experiencing Life," conducted on March 14, 1995, Zhang redefines "main melody film" by expanding its coverage to social tensions rather than simply conveying the party's message: "I want to reflect reality . . . and raise questions related to some social issues."[122] Through this redefinition, *Good Morning, Beijing*, according to Zhang, "is also a main melody film, as it reflects Chinese people's living situations."[123] Despite her intention to continue experimenting in this last film, by alternating melodrama with short, real-life documentary episodes, Zhang was unable to resolve certain technical and stylistic issues. As a result, sociopolitical melodrama defines her last film project.[124]

This resurrection of melodrama at the end of Zhang's filmmaking career appears ironic, given that she started her independent directing career in

1979 by veering away from the socialist melodramatic tradition of the time. But, as I have argued throughout this chapter, Zhang's cinematic style was never fixed. Her stylistic transformations throughout the 1980s and 1990s prove critical to understanding her authorship, aesthetic pursuit, and overall achievements. First, her dynamic approach demonstrates once again that her film style adheres to content and that, for her, the aesthetic does not "transcend" the social or historical. In her last interview, she particularly stresses this socially and historically embedded aesthetic, remarking that different stories demand different representational styles.[125] Second, all styles have their respective strengths and limitations. In the early post-Mao era, it was uniformity and its associated stereotypes and stagnation that Zhang resisted rather than revolutionary realism or melodrama per se. Cultural pluralism was promoted not for the sake of pure stylistic differences but for achieving the best filming effect which, according to Zhang, results from a combined concern for individual expressions, social content, and cinematic aesthetic. Third, and most importantly, it appeared to Zhang as the 1990s began that subjective and documentary experimentalism had clearly reached their limit when a cinematic and critical engagement with contemporary socioeconomic transformations must be foregrounded. That is to say, sociopolitical melodrama returned in Zhang's career because this form not only best captured the rising gender and class conflicts in the everyday life of contemporary China but also enabled both filmmaker and audience to reflect on broader issues concerning current economic, political, and social structures.

South China, 1994 tells the story of how social and working relations were radically restructured with the development of the transnational capitalist market in the early 1990s. Specifically, it zooms in on relationships between overseas Chinese (Taiwan-based) capitalists and mainland Chinese laborers, in a joint capitalist enterprise established in a southern Chinese city. In addition to the disturbing return of class exploitation and a company's ill treatment of (female) migrant laborers, the film focuses on how gender roles in general have been radically resignified. Liang Yifan is a capable and highly educated young woman, but in order to maintain her position in a company, she must become the mistress of Xu Jingfeng, the company's "foreign" chairman of the board, who is usually absent and shows little care for her. She struggles for independence, but her personal endeavors seem futile in the context of such major structural transformations. One new model made available for Chinese women during the transnational market's rise in the 1990s was, unsurprisingly, self-commodification. Trapped in her lifestyle and precarious economic status, Liang eventually finds herself unable to renounce this model. Jin Cuihua, a hardworking migrant female worker and section chief when the film begins, is forced to leave the company after fighting for (female) laborers' basic rights. Unable to land another job in this highly competitive city, she becomes a street prostitute. When, in front of a luxury hotel, Liang accidently discovers Jin's situation and hands her some money, Jin confronts Liang by pointing out that they are both prostitutes, simply serving different customers. Women from all walks of life and economic class are treated as and reduced to sexual commodities or victims. The film conjures no hope for these women, raising serious questions about the new transnational socioeconomic structure of China's special economic zones. *South China, 1994* reveals the structural commodification and victimization of women, and the triumph of market individualism, which either seduces migrant women into a false promise (which often collapses during their struggles, as happens in Jin's case), or compels educated women like Liang into self-commodification.

This last film of Zhang's also touches on the fraught position of special economic zones, precariously poised between transnational capitalism and domestic political power. Xu Jingfeng, the board chair, appoints Yuan Fang, a CCP member and high-level engineer, as acting head of the labor union just as workers are preparing for a strike. Sympathetic to the workers' demands, Yuan feels inclined to help them instead of enforcing punishment as the company has insisted. Then the CCP committee within the company, after receiving instruction from the central government to protect foreign investments in the area, opts for compromise rather than conflict. Although Yuan does not necessarily agree with the committee's view, he must follow its decision. In the process, he also develops a love interest in Liang and discovers her relationship with Xu. Toward the end of the film, the current overseas Chinese CEO, Yu Jie (who is "blamed" for all the problematic policies of the company) steps down, and at his recommendation Yuan becomes the first CCP CEO. Whereas this managerial replacement is indicative of compromises made on both sides, the film makes clear that (migrant women) laborers' interests are sacrificed in the negotiations.

The last shot—which freezes on Xu Jingfeng (transnational capitalist board chair), Yuan Fang (CCP member and new CEO), and Liang Yifan (secretary-mistress of Xu and love interest of Yuan) as they meet at the company entrance on the first day of Yuan's promotion—is highly ambiguous. First, this shot is identical to the beginning shot of the film, depicting Xu and Yu (then CEO) greeting employees at the entrance on a regular morning, as Liang (already

Xu's secretary and mistress) walks into the building and greets them in return. With this unchanging ritual and visual layout, the last shot exposes the structural power and stability of transnational capitalism. Second, sandwiched between Xu, the transnational capitalist, and Yuan, the CCP CEO representing China's need for further market development, Liang's attachments to both men represent a deeply troubling reality for Chinese women, who are mere measures of political and male power negotiations, unable to pursue or imagine an independent socioeconomic status. Individualism, championed as a universal form of agency in the 1980s, has not only trapped women in the context of transnational capitalism but also deprived them of social agency to make any possible structural changes to better their lives.

By 1994, when Zhang was making her last film, her own life as a female filmmaker had begun to disintegrate. As the socialist state film studios formally started to privatize in 1993, female directors, especially those who committed themselves to both experimental and socially engaged cinema, began encountering enormous difficulties in continuing their pursuits. Second-generation female directors including Zhang Nuanxin, Wang Haowei, and Huang Shuqin, who received their training in the socialist film academies of the 1950s and 1960s and became productive, award-winning directors in the 1980s, all publicly stated that they preferred to work in the state studio system. Having to search for private patrons in order to make films that primarily satisfied the market was devastating for this group of female directors.[126] Zhang's own failed attempt to negotiate between her ideas and investors' demands, when making her *The Story of Yunnan* (云南故事, 1993), testifies to both the repressive nature of commercial filmmaking and Zhang's individual resistance to the commercial market. As Zhang reflected, she was fundamentally against commercial film—its values, aesthetic, and representations of women—and thus her effort to bring widely divergent intentions to cohere with each other for *The Story of Yunnan* was doomed from the beginning.[127] When asked by Wu Guanping (吴冠平) during her last interview if she was still passionate about experimental filmmaking, Zhang replied: "I [still] have passion . . . but nobody is willing to invest [in experimental films]. If I had the money to do what I like, I would still be making experimental films."[128] The commodity market directly affected cultural production in the 1990s, seriously threatening Chinese women's experimental and socially concerned cinema in particular.

The enormous pressures of marketization took an irreversible toll on female directors' careers. On May 28, 1995, Zhang Nuanxin died of cancer at the age of fifty-five. Ironically, *South China, 1994*, Zhang's only film that bears a close affinity to socialist melodrama and also main melody films, was dismissed in public in 1990s China and unknown to Chinese audiences. Apparently the film's investigation of the systematic disintegration of the individual, economic, and social realms under transnational capitalism, including especially the degradation of women, led to its multilevel marginalization in China in the 1990s, a decade when the Chinese state needed to further develop the market, mainstream intellectuals desired to integrate China more thoroughly into the world system and maintain an autonomous space for elitist expression, the market demanded commercialized cultural production, and the audience anticipated more consumable films. These factors worked together to suppress the significance of films like *South China, 1994*.

From *Drive to Win* to *South China, 1994*, Zhang continued her dedication to a historically informed and socially engaged mainstream cinema with an experimental spirit and pluralist aesthetic styles. The trajectory of Zhang's films corresponded to women's changing roles in Chinese society, as well as to the changing orientations of mainstream intellectual discourse. If *Drive to Win* reveals Zhang's hopeful vision of socialist women rising to the historical occasion to address the issues that surfaced during the Cultural Revolution and participate in the sociocultural transformation of the New Era with individual commitment and agency, *Sacrificed Youth* conveys both Zhang's support of the relaxed and diversified sociocultural environment initiated by official thought liberation and her serious reservations about the mid-1980s mainstreaming of ideas of sexual difference and socially detached individualism linked to universal modernity. Zhang's critical attitude toward elitist individualism and essentialized female consciousness points to the ways in which integrated socialist feminism continued to influence her cinematic practice—an influence that, in turn, provides a crucial link to her subsequent film projects directly exploring the social consequences of market individualism and capitalist modernity. As her camera turned toward the social effects of market commercialism and women's self-commodification, Zhang moved from her early, subjective cinema in *Drive to Win* and *Sacrificed Youth* to a distanced, documentary style in *Good Morning, Beijing* and, finally, to a charged sociopolitical melodrama in *South China, 1994*.

Zhang's stylistic changes demonstrate how she questioned binaries—content and form, mainstream and experimentalism, and (socialist) politics and universal art—while insisting on cinematic engagement with sociohistorical reality. The filmmaker's cultural pluralist position, unwavering social stance, and integrated feminist approach largely explain why *Sacrificed*

Youth was viewed as problematically ambiguous and why she was disavowed as a seminal figure in post-Mao experimental cinema in the late 1980s and 1990s—when the masculine and avant-gardist break from socialist proletarian cinema was complete, post-Mao feminist discourse turned "independent" and essentialist, a market-oriented depoliticization of cultural production became the norm, and socially detached and market-oriented individualism thrived.

7 The Black Velvet Aesthetic

Universal Cultural Feminism and Chinese
Neotraditionalism in Huang Shuqin's
Woman Demon Human (1987)

Chinese women's experimental mainstream cinema practiced by Zhang Nuanxin and others in the early to mid-1980s was credited with unprecedented female subjectivity and innovative cinematic style. At the same time, however, it generated significant uncertainty among international film critics and feminist scholars due to its ambiguous relationship to the Maoist socialist mainstream culture. This ambiguity was finally cleared up by *Woman Demon Human* (人鬼情), a film released in 1987 and directed by Huang Shuqin (黄蜀芹, b. 1939), another second-generation female director, who also studied at the Beijing Film Academy (1959–1964). The film quickly garnered critical acclaim and is hailed by many as "the highest achievement of Chinese feminist cinema,"[1] full of female consciousness,[2] the only self-conscious female (feminist) film in Chinese film history,[3] and "the symbol that represents the maturity of the Fourth Generation filmmaking as a whole."[4] In other words, less than a year after "female consciousness" appeared as a hotly debated concept at the 1986 *Contemporary Cinema* symposium,[5] Huang's *Woman Demon Human* crystallized the concept, and thus marked a major transition in Chinese women's cinema.

This chapter focuses on *Woman Demon Human*, reexamining its aesthetic and historical significance in relation to the development of Chinese cinema, post-Mao feminist theory, and the newly mainstreamed cultural discourse on sexual difference and Chinese (traditional) cultural psychology in the late 1980s. What does it mean to designate *Woman Demon Human* as the first or only female/feminist film in Chinese history? What kind of female consciousness does it articulate, and what kind of connection does it forge with the rise of the masculine mode of filmmaking and the return of traditional values in China in the 1980s? How does *Woman Demon Human* stand in relation to the post-Mao search for cultural roots and gender reconfiguration, and to the notion of ideal/real men? And how does the film indicate the state of Chinese women's cinema in the late 1980s?

1987: A Transition in Post-Mao Chinese Women's Cinema

The year 1987 saw some important transformations in Chinese cinema. Most significantly, the new Chinese cinema that began with diverse experimentalism in the early 1980s and made a discernible break from mainstream socialist cultural practice around the mid-1980s through the achievements of the Fifth Generation male filmmakers underwent another change around 1987. Both Chen Kaige's *King of the Children* and Zhang Yimou's *Red Sorghum* came out in 1987, producing contrasting receptions among audiences with their different aesthetic styles. *King of the Children* showed an ultimate push but also a doomed attempt by Chen to continue the experimental and elitist practice of cultural reflection; *Red Sorghum*, on the other hand, won the 1988 Golden Bear Award at the Thirty-Eighth Berlin International Film Festival, and successfully marked Fifth Generation filmmakers' endeavor to exit the intellectual experimental mode of film production through a partial return to commercial cinematic conventions.[6] Despite their differences, however, both films indirectly announced the coming end of the signature Fifth Generation cinematic experimentalism. Also in 1987, *The Last Frenzy* by Zhou Xiaowen was released and immediately became recognized as the Fifth Generation's first successful commercial film.[7]

The year 1987 also witnessed some new developments in Chinese women's cinema. Out of the 140 films produced that year, 15 were by female directors across three generations.[8] Although most of the women's films, such as Dong Kena's *Third Party* (谁是第三者), Hu Mei's *Far Removed from War* (远离战争的年代), and Lu Xiaoya's *Red and White* (红与白), tackled emerging social issues in contemporary China—extramarital affairs, the long-ignored psychological struggles of war veterans, and the moral and legal responsibilities of contemporary Chinese medical doctors—they were mostly received as outdated and lacking innovation in the reconfigured cultural landscape and consequently did not generate much influence. Indeed, some critics have expressed great disappointment with Hu Mei and Lu Xiaoya, who were known for their 1985 films, *Army Nurse* and *The Girl in Red* (红衣少女), respectively, both of which highlight individual subjectivity and female self-reflection. For the general intellectual public, particularly feminist film critics, Hu's and Lu's return to contemporary social issues with a focus on neither individuality nor female subjectivity showed a backward movement in their filmmaking careers.[9] By the late 1980s, the major intellectual trend and mainstream cultural criticism had both shifted away from socially engaged and historically embedded cultural practice.

Another group of female directors actively responded to the shift in the mainstream intellectual and cultural trend, producing several women-centered films in 1987 that won critical recognition and scholarly attention. Set in different historical periods of modern China, these films highlight essentialized sexual or gender differences, transhistorical patriarchy, and individual female consciousness little affected by their particular and specific social contexts. *Women's Stories* (女人的故事) by Peng Xiaolian (1953–2019), a Fifth Generation female filmmaker, centers on the struggles and triumphs of rural peasant women in the era of post-Mao economic reform. The film portrays certain patriarchal values (male lineage and dominance) and cultural and social prejudices against women *not* as practices having vigorously returned and become resignified in the economic-reform era, but rather as an ever-present reality. Women are positioned essentially both against men *as* men, and against a changeless patriarchal sociocultural structure. Chris Berry rightly points out that Peng's *Women's Stories* especially appeals to Western feminists because it enunciates a female independent difference "not by subjective style, but by the fact that most of the scenes involve no male characters."[10] This particular kind of difference testifies to the palpable influence of Western feminism, post-Mao independent feminism, and the gradual establishment of sexual or gender difference in the China of the late 1980s.[11] The film portrays how improvement in women's status hinges on women's individual will and determination, their ability to make money (individual entrepreneurship), and exclusive female bonding or sisterhood. Indeed, the film highlights individual entrepreneurship and its broad market background as plausible means to change rural women's victimization and sufferings. Peng's film stands as an example of how, by the late 1980s, Chinese women's film practice had begun to rationalize and endorse universal sexual difference, female individual entrepreneurial agency, and the market as a progressive force for enacting desired changes in contemporary China.

Another 1987 film that highlights sexual difference and female nature is *Hoofbeats* (马蹄声碎) by Liu Miaomiao (b. 1962), the youngest female director of the Fifth Generation filmmakers. The film is set during the Long March (1934–1935) led by the Chinese Communist Party. Historically, the Long March followed the Red Army's suffering heavy losses in the fifth military encirclement campaign launched by the Nationalist government in 1934. The surviving 86,000 Red Army troops, including about 30 female soldiers, fled from their southeastern communist base for relocation in northwestern China. The Red Army troops crossed eighteen mountain ranges, twenty-four rivers, and other life-threatening areas while fighting Nationalist forces. By the time they reached the northwestern province of Shaanxi in October 1935, only 8,000 soldiers, less than one-tenth of the original number, had survived. *Hoofbeats* tells the story of a group of eight female Red Army soldiers who, after finding out that the party has arranged for them to stay in one area for a better chance of survival, fought to catch up with the central troops of the Red Army. Departing from the mainstream film practice during Mao's socialist China, which usually emphasized the female soldiers' heroism and self-sacrificing spirit, Liu's film instead follows the 1980s cultural trend of depoliticization. It humanizes the Long March by foregrounding female desires, emotions, inner feelings, and heterosexual attractions. Liu devotes much of the narrative time and space to "typical" female behaviors, such as crying, singing, dancing, laughing, and even catfighting, along with "natural" feminine traits like naivety, jealousy, and lack of discipline. As S. Louisa Wei has observed, "each of the eight women cries at a different point in the story," and the film's narrative tension and rhythm "correspond to the emotional ups and downs of female characters," including repressed romance, and the dispute and reconciliation between girls.[12] In its attempt to demonstrate that even the most brutal circumstances cannot erase female nature and sexual difference, *Hoofbeats* turns a blind eye to history, to the utterly unnatural and life-and-death situation of the Long March. More critically, the film turns to transhistorical concepts of female nature and difference to portray female soldiers, reinforcing a set of stereotypes that perceive women as naturally irrational, childish, and undisciplined. Against the violent background of war and survival, these naturalized features function not only to erase background and regional differences among the female Red Army soldiers but also to demonstrate the inferiority of women to their male counterparts. Liu deploys both melodrama and experimental techniques to accentuate the female soldiers' emotional expressions, sexual desires, and psychic activities.

This trend—eclipsing social and political history and foregrounding naturalized female or sexual difference and women's emotional struggles with an abstract patriarchal culture—culminates in Huang's *Woman Demon Human*. Set across time from the 1950s to the 1980s, the film tells the story of a young rural girl, Qiu Yun, who perseveres through emotional hardship to become a national opera star by performing ideal male figures from Chinese tradition, particularly the character of a male ghost, Zhong Kui (钟馗). With a successful combination of performative, subjective, and realistic modes of filmmaking, the film expresses female emotional suffering, critiques everlasting cultural prejudices, and depicts a woman's everyday life in the absence of any noticeable sociopolitical events or transformations in socialist China. Even for the film's contemporary Chinese viewers, not many had a clear sense of the changing historical backgrounds against which Qiu Yun's story unfolds.

Parallel to the changing trend of male avant-garde films around 1987, *Woman Demon Human*, together with Peng's, Liu's, and several other women directors' films, signaled the approaching end of women's sociohistorically engaged cinema (with realistic or experimental style) in China's mainstream film production. The year 1987 likewise witnessed the emergence of commercial genre films in women's film practice. Bao Zhifang produced one of the first Chinese horror films, *Two A.M.* (午夜两点, 1987), and the commercial trend was further developed in 1988 by a group of female directors across generations: Wang Haowei's *In Pursuit of the Monster* (寻找魔鬼), Li Shaohong's *Silver Snake Murder Case* (银蛇谋杀案), and Hu Mei's *Hit without Gun* (无枪枪手). Chinese women's cinema appeared to diversify in the late 1980s, but as some scholars have perceptively argued, the gradual domination of commercial genre films starting in the early 1990s has curtailed the development of true cultural pluralism; these new genre films have quickly reoriented the Chinese film industry toward the Hollywood and Hong Kong models, global reproducibility, and transnational market consumption,[13] diminishing the significance of socialist genre films and sociopolitically engaged mainstream film practice.

Woman Demon Human: A Cinematic Correspondence to Mainstream Intellectual Discourses of the 1980s

The excitement *Woman Demon Human* generated among Chinese critics and general audiences soon after its public release attested to its dynamic interactions with major ongoing intellectual and cultural discourses of the late

1980s: the promulgation of scientific knowledge and universal values among the general public; the obsession with cultural unconsciousness (positive or negative) as a determinist factor of history; the resurrection of Chinese folk culture for pure and essential aesthetic pursuit; and the rise of combined liberal, radical, and cultural feminism replacing socialist feminism in the public domain and individual practice. Criticism and scholarship on Chinese culture in the 1980s has demonstrated that as the Root-Seeking Movement pushed the previous cultural fever to the level of speculation around the mid-1980s, more socially engaged philosophies popular in the early post-Mao era were subsequently replaced by Freudian psychoanalysis, Jungian theories of collective unconsciousness and archetypes, Arnold J. Toynbee's philosophy of history and civilization, and Li Zehou's revival of ancient Chinese thought[14]—all of which, despite their different historical origins and trajectories, converged in China in the mid-to-late 1980s to forge an abstract, universal, and ever-present cultural structure indifferent to sociopolitical and economic changes. Although most Chinese female directors were still preoccupied with social issues in the New Era, social issues themselves had become, as shown in Peng Xiaolian's film, more culturalized, dehistoricized, and individualized toward the late 1980s as China's process of economic development began to erode the previous socialist structure.

To a large extent, *Woman Demon Human* epitomizes the newly mainstreamed intellectual and cultural movements in its contemporary time. An in-depth review of major scholarship on *Woman Demon Human* can help us to understand how and on what specific terms *Woman Demon Human* was hailed in the late 1980s and 1990s as one of the most successful films in the post-Mao era, and why its widespread recognition speaks volumes about the changing sociopolitical structure and cultural context within which the film was made and received. More importantly, a close analysis of major scholarship also illustrates how by the late 1980s various international discourses in history, despite their initial contradictions or conflicts, had worked together to coproduce in contemporary China a mutually sustaining cultural environment, where gender, culture, and feminism became reconfigured.

Culture against Politics: Aestheticism, Emotional Relationships, and Universal Humanism

Woman Demon Human has been praised since its release for its achievements in artistic experimentation, humanistic values, and cultural probing, all of which reflected the late 1980s Chinse cultural trend best represented by the Root-Seeking Movement.[15] In January 1988, the journal *New Films* and Shanghai Film Studio, where *Woman Demon Human* was produced, co-organized a symposium specifically to examine the artistic achievements and historical significance of this film. The published coverage of the event, the *New Films* article "Ardent Pursuit of Art," includes presentations by eight eminent and important male film critics, directors, and former and current Shanghai Film Studio heads, including Zhang Junxiang (张俊祥), Ye Ming (叶明), Xu Sangchu (徐桑楚), and Ren Zhonglun (任仲伦).[16] The participants discuss the film from a variety of perspectives, but they reach a consensus on three major topics. First, they emphasize that the film exemplifies a much needed aesthetic and artistic practice in contemporary China that balances or integrates many elements: realism and experimentalism (54–55), "Western modernism and Chinese traditional drama and opera" (戏曲; 57, 58, 60), objective depiction and subjective expression (54, 57, 61), critical reflection and emotional persuasion (58, 59), and a "stylistic"/"abstract"/"distancing" (风格化／虚／间离) aesthetic and a "realist"/"concrete" effect (写实／具象; 55, 56, 57, 59, 60, 61). Indeed, the abstract and essentialist (*xieyi*, 写意) aesthetic as well as the distancing effect strategy are highlighted by many critics as the film's great achievements (54, 58, 59, 60). Several speakers compare *Woman Demon Human* with experimental films made by the Fourth and Fifth Generation male directors, such as *Yellow Earth* or *Black Cannon Incident* (黑炮事件, 1985), arguing that Huang's film alone successfully brings modern experimental film to the Chinese audience with an emotionally effective narrative story and a renewed Chinese cultural signification (58, 59, 60).

Second, coming to the content of the film, all participants attribute the success of the film to its balanced, nonmelodramatic treatment of the relationship between "emotion" (情; 56, 57, 58, 61) and "reason" (理). One participant argues that Huang's film centers on the emotional relationship between the nonbiological father and daughter, but does not instigate "excessive emotions" (煽情) and thus leaves space for reflections (60). Another critic points out that although the film centers on Qiu Yun's predicament, loneliness, and defective life, the profundity of the film lies in its gentle or peaceful rather than outrageous manner of presenting Qiu Yun's hardship and helplessness (60). More importantly, some critics note that the film achieves its succinct and harmonious style by excluding all modern Chinese political movements. This exclusion allows the director to focus on the characters, their psychic conditions and life environments (58, 60). The appeal of the film is thus closely tied to its focus on representing "ordinary" (meaning depoliticized in post-Mao vocabulary) human relationships, individual feelings, and internal worlds, pruning back both political (melo)drama and the excessive emotions associated with Cultural Revolution propaganda.

Third, all symposium participants endorse a universal value expressed in the film: the heroine Qiu Yun's predicament is understood as a quintessentially human experience (59, 61). Indeed, many critics stress that the film evokes an eternal human struggle between the flesh and the spirit, reality and ideal, internal and external elements (59)—or ego and superego, to use Freud's terms (60). For this group of critics and artists, the film's significance should be determined first and foremost by its broad and universal appeal to human nature and to the essential, transhistorical human condition. It is also through this humanistic perspective that the film's critique of negative traits in Chinese tradition, like apathy, is endorsed at the symposium.

Gender, however, is mostly missing in the symposium discussion, although the term *female consciousness* appears once in passing. The absence of gender topics mirrors the absence of any serious discussion of socialist history at the symposium. This omission of any discussion of the sociocultural and gender transformations of socialist China further reinforces the film's approach that eclipses the relevance of sociopolitical forces in constituting the life and story of a socialist woman and artist.

Quintessential Female Struggle and Longing:
A Universal Cultural Feminist Practice

Although the scholarly consensus is that nobody discussed gender issues in Huang's *Woman Demon Human* until the early 1990s,[17] gender-focused criticisms in fact appeared as early as 1988. Most of those gender-related discussions, however, did not bring back Chinese socialist history either. Instead, they center on transhistorical, naturalized, and universalized concepts such as sexual difference, female desire, and female consciousness. In "Life Perceived through Female Consciousness,"[18] Shi Faming (石发明), a college student in the late 1980s, declares that no other film by a Chinese woman director has had such a great effect on audiences as Huang's *Woman Demon Human*. Shi attributes the film's success to the fact that it "is a pure 'female film'" (or women's cinema) (女性电影)—it examines a woman's life situation through a purely female perspective and then truthfully exhibits the [female] situation on the silver screen." Aware of diverging opinions on how to understand female film in China, Shi offers a working definition in his essay: "A female film should at least perceive life with a distinctively female consciousness and illustrate a woman's sense of life through female emotions (happiness, anger, sorrows, and joy)." By 1988, the concept of female consciousness, which had caused controversy in 1986 at a symposium on Chinese female film directors,[19] had become standardized, at least among the educated population. Critics and audiences adopted a biological and psychological approach to gender difference. Although the overall logic of Shi's essay about women's cinema appears incoherent at times, its central message that *Woman Demon Human* best represents "the female consciousness" in Chinese cinema heralded feminist scholars' endorsement in years to come.

Another 1988 article, "The Agony of Suppressing Female Id: A Reading of *Woman Demon Human*" by Shao Mujun (邵牧君),[20] went further by linking the film directly to not only female consciousness but also Western feminism. "*Woman Demon Human* is a film by a woman and about a woman, so the female consciousness and the female psyche revealed in the film deserve special attention." Here, the author validates female consciousness by automatically tying it to the biological producer of the film. Shao continues, "If this film had appeared in a Western country, it would definitely become a central object of [Western] feminist criticism [女权主义评论]" (40). Although Shao uses feminist criticism in a general manner, he actually refers to the "Western cine-feminism" (影评流派; 40) developed in relation to semiotics and psychoanalysis in the 1970s. Shao maintains that the cine-feminist analytic perspective is not necessarily applicable to all films, but insists that it can offer a satisfactory reading of *Woman Demon Human*, especially of its central contradiction, a source of confusion among (Chinese) critics (40). That central contradiction, according to Shao, is the question of why Qiu Yun, a successful woman artist, feels such unhappiness about her life that she resorts to Zhong Kui, the legendary demon/ghost, to communicate her problem (40). This question, according to Shao's reading of the film, cannot be addressed through social or political analyses of Qiu Yun's external environment, because her unhappiness has nothing to do with social evils or even political turmoil in modern Chinese history (40–42). Instead, Qiu Yun's unhappiness arises from the suppression of the "female id" (本我), a Freudian psychoanalytic concept, which Shao's essay further defines as the desire for male love (39, 42). Despite her beauty, the young Qiu Yun suffered from her inability to get a man's admiration and love. Furthermore, her suffering cannot be alleviated by her career success (39), because "it is a uniquely female psychic and emotional state [of being] to desire love and respect [from men]" (42). And this female desire "can only be fully expressed in a woman's work." "If we approach *Woman Demon Human* from this angle," Shao concludes, "the film is no doubt an important female film ['women's cinema,' 女性电影]" (42).

Shao makes three important points about Huang's film and China in the late 1980s. First, naturalized sexual difference, not social liberation or professional success, had become central in constituting a woman's identity by the time *Woman Demon Human* reached audiences. Second and consequently, a woman's happiness or suffering had been redefined through whether she could fulfill her natural desire which, according to Shao, is linked exclusively to male attraction. And third, psychoanalysis and Western feminist film theory, introduced in China in the late 1980s, could best "reveal" essential universal female problems associated with desire, emotional state, and heterosexual relationships.

Shao's essay emphasizes Qiu Yun's individual responsibility for suppressing her own desire, while subsequent post-Mao feminist publications link the suppression to socialist women's liberation and to a transhistorical phallocentric structure represented by men. In "Feminism and Chinese Women's Cinema" (1990), Yuan Ying uses Western feminist history as a model trajectory, arguing that social revolution should occur only at the early stage of any feminist movement.[21] Chinese women's liberation has unfortunately remained stuck in this early stage, unable to develop into the next two phases—critiquing men (patriarchy) and advancing (female) self-reflection in the cultural and theoretical realms (48–49, 50). The emphasis on the social realm, on socialization and social consciousness in the Chinese context, according to Yuan, has (naturally or automatically) endorsed the male standard, causing the loss of female self (49–51). Following this male-centered demand, Chinese women cannot recognize their own spiritual existence and thus have to suppress or repress their individual life force (49). Echoing Shao Mujun's point about the central contradiction confronted by Qiu Yun—namely, career pursuit versus female consciousness and personal happiness—Yuan argues that Chinese female directors' engagement with social symbolism in Mao's China failed to address their female emotional experiences or express their individual artistic consciousness (51). Yuan believes it was not until the 1980s that Chinese female directors began to engage female culture, reveal the loss of self, and expose the (split) female psyche (51, 52). Whereas Zhang Nuanxin's *Sacrificed Youth* and Hu Mei's *Army Nurse* should be commended for their pioneering roles in exploring new areas, Huang's *Woman Demon Human* completes the exploration (52).

More specifically, Yuan argues that Huang's film moves closer to the next two phases of Western feminism: the critique of men and the advancement of female difference and self-reflection. When Shao Mujun uses Western-influenced feminist film theory to argue that a woman's happiness relies on fulfilling her heterosexually oriented drive or id, he (re)articulates the critical role a man plays in a woman's life. But Qiu Yun's suffering, Shao maintains, results from her compromise with her fate, especially her suppression of her female desire and difference (39). Yuan endorses the logic that a woman can only *be* a woman if positioned against a man (52), but unlike Shao, she targets men rather than Qiu Yun herself, as the cause of the heroine's unhappiness. Yuan argues, Qiu Yun's biological father, her male coach Teacher Zhang, and her husband, who all have repeatedly displayed irresponsible and cowardly natures, are the cause of Qiu Yun's depression and her ultimate marriage to the stage (53). According to Yuan, the film is structured through contractual relationships, and all the men in Qiu Yun's life have broken their contracts—father-daughter, teacher-pupil, and husband-wife. Zhong Kui, therefore, stands for the ideal man in Chinese women's lives, and Qiu Yun's own embodiment of this imagined ideal man on stage further signifies the "cultural predicament" contemporary Chinese women confront (53). For Yuan, the significance of Huang's film lies exactly in its moving *away* from the gender equality promoted in socialist women's emancipation and *toward* sexual difference, where both female consciousness and a critique of men become possible.

Other post-Mao feminist film scholars endorse Yuan's position, although their theoretical frameworks may appear to vary. In "'Human, Woman, Demon': A Woman's Predicament"[22] (《人 · 鬼 · 情》: 一个女人的困境), for example, Dai Jinhua turns to poststructuralist psychoanalysis and cine-feminism to reframe the study of Chinese women's cinema.[23] Referencing stories about women in both Western novels and Chinese popular narratives, Dai evokes a universal theme of female exclusion or the silence of women, echoing the Lacanian poststructuralist stipulation that "a woman's reality [or subject] does not exist" because it is forever repressed by "the male, phallocentric, and logocentric discourse" (153). Distorted by layers of representations, historical women are mere images in a mirror: their real bodies and discourses are forever "absent in their presence" (152). Coincidentally, Huang's film opens with multiple mirrors in which Qiu Yun's image confuses both herself and the audience. "The predicament of women" thus "originates in the prison of language" (in man's language and mirrors) and in "the difficulty of self-recognition" (153). It is from this perspective that Dai states that Huang's *Woman Demon Human* is "to date the first and only 'feminist film' ['female film,' 女性电影] in China" (153).[24]

Dai's poststructuralist approach, as she herself is aware, has led to some serious gaps in her discussion of both *Woman Demon Human* and China in the late 1980s and early 1990s. First, whereas in the Western context poststructuralist cultural theory critiques the modern individual subject and positivist values concerning identity, knowledge, and a given system, China at the turn of the 1990s witnessed an ardent search for and urgent validation of universal values rooted in scientific, essentialist, and positivist thinking. Similarly, in feminist studies and culture, whereas poststructuralist feminism aims to challenge patriarchal ideology and culture, the heterosexual norm, and a naturalized understanding of women, Huang Shuqin's film, as Dai admits, "accepted an essentialist, irrefutable, 'common-sense' view of gender that [stipulates] a woman's happiness comes exclusively from marriage, the 'natural product' of heterosexual love" (153).[25] Second, in targeting commercial cinema and the male-centered pleasure principle embodied by the Hollywood commercial film industry, cine-feminist theory and film practice in the 1970s and 1980s either promoted avant-gardism in film practice to destroy Hollywood-coded film language and pleasure or endorsed women's mainstream film practice that potentially disrupts and subverts Hollywood's phallocentric and patriarchal ideology.[26] Huang's film, however, as Dai points out, is "by no means a radical feminist film that destructs viewers' pleasure" (167).[27] Nor does it resist or subvert a rooted commercial and phallocentric film industry, because China at the time had just begun commercializing its film production. As a matter of fact, Huang's film was produced at a moment when a major transition to the domination of commercial film production was taking place. That is to say, Huang's film was by no means made as a critical reaction to a dominant commercial and male-pleasure-oriented mainstream film industry.

Structuring the essay around the poststructuralist psychoanalytic feminist framework, Dai has difficulty addressing the discrepancy or contradiction between such a framework and Huang's film, although she occasionally resorts to the concept of "Chinese style" (167) to suggest possible local variations. She admits that the film is not centrally about repressed female (sexual) desire (usually perceived as potentially disruptive in poststructuralist feminist discussions of Western women's cinema) but about the "salvation of women" (161) or women's self-salvation (154, 168). Dai nonetheless concludes her essay with a poststructuralist feminist gesture: "Perhaps the true female self-redemption lies in ripping apart historical discourse, to allow the real process of her memory to take shape" (168). No trace of any potentially disruptive female/feminist memory, however, is located or even suggested by Dai in Huang's film.

The effect of Dai's poststructural framework, therefore, lies neither in its concrete analysis of Huang's film nor in issues related to the commercial film industry, male pleasure, or female desire. Rather, the essay's macro effect rests on its endorsement of a transhistorical, universal, and changeless patriarchal structure and language, and the subsequent application of this structure to Chinese culture throughout history including the socialist period. Indeed, despite its overall poststructuralist stance, which appears to differ from Yuan's position, Dai shares Yuan's dismissal of socialist women's liberation and gender equality. As my analysis of another essay by Dai illustrates,[28] she considers Chinese women's sociopolitical liberation nearly antithetical both to women's discursive and cultural agency and to their true female identity: "The arrival of women's de jure 'liberation' once again vitiated any chance Woman had to become a historical discursive subject."[29] Both Dai and Yuan regard social(ist) revolution and the quest for gender equality as either a prolonged trap or a totally incompatible move in relation to developing true feminist and female subjectivity because they use Man as the standard, prohibiting Woman from recognizing herself or expressing a distinctively female consciousness.[30] Feminism in both Yuan's and Dai's writing is thus delinked from sociopolitical transformations in human history and redefined through sexual difference and an essential female self and culture, a radical and cultural position characteristic of both post-second-wave Western and post-Mao Chinese feminisms in general.[31] In her specific discussion of Huang's film, Dai also shows a great similarity between her and Yang's approaches. She not only focuses on identical topics such as the heterosexual relationship, male abandonments, and a female self torn between career and personal happiness but also analyzes them to highlight eternal sexual difference and a universal female predicament.

Whereas Zhang Nuanxin's *Sacrificed Youth* still posed resistance to this universalized and culturally oriented feminist reading, Huang's *Woman Demon Human* finally allows and enables such a feminist interpretation. Huang's film represents female essence or fate in such a way that either an eternal (ahistorical) conflict and difference between men and women (Yuan Ying) or the lack of female language or culture in socialist women's emancipation (Dai) could be argued. In many aspects, Huang's *Woman Demon Human* emerged as a much-anticipated cinematic text that both confirmed and further developed the mainstream discourses of the late 1980s on aestheticism, humanism, female consciousness, and universal and cultural feminism.

The Effacement of Sociopolitical History and the Reinvention of Chinese Neotraditional Ritual for Female Self-Representation

Woman Demon Human is based on the life story of Pei Yanling (裴艳玲, b. 1947), a female opera artist, who became successful in Mao's socialist period by playing traditional male figures. Pei reclaimed her reputation with her remarkable performance of male martial heroes after the Cultural Revolution. Her re-creation of Zhong Kui, a legendary male demon in Chinese history, made her a national treasure in the mid-1980s. Huang learned about Pei's life initially through Jiang Zilong's (蒋子龙) reportage-style short story "A Boy with Long Hair" (长发男儿), but, after spending time with Pei and accompanying her on performance tours, eventually wrote her own working script. How did *Woman Demon Human*, a film about a socialist female opera artist playing traditional heroic and rebellious male figures onstage, become a critical turning point of Chinese women's cinema, breaking away from socialist mainstream cultural practice?

The Black Velvet Effect: Cultural Revision and the Xieyi Aesthetic in *Woman Demon Human*

In an interview conducted by Xu Feng (徐峰), Huang Shuqin discusses the aesthetic style of *Woman Demon Human*, particularly highlighting the use of "black velvet" (黑丝绒). The filmmaker devised black velvet to wrap the studio setting, creating a pitch-dark, dreamy world in which unfolds the colorful "Zhong Kui Marries Off His Sister," performed by Pei Yanling herself (fig. 7.1).[32] According to Huang, the special cinematic effect created by black velvet was first discussed by Tong Daoming (童道明) in his essay on cinema and theater (including both Chinese opera and Western drama) from 1991.[33] Tong uses the term "black velvet effect" (黑丝绒效果) in his discussion of *Woman Demon Human*, especially with regard to the operatic Zhong Kui scenes. The term stems from Konstantin Sergeyevich Stanislavsky's (1863–1938) remarks on the setting and costumes created for Maurice Maeterlinck's *The Blue Bird* when it was performed at the Moscow Art Theatre in 1908. However, Tong reconceptualizes the term according to the Chinese operatic aesthetic of xieyi (写意, essentialist), praising Huang for finally breaking from the realist convention adopted in set designs for modern revolutionary operas during the Cultural Revolution as well as for other, traditional, opera films made in modern China.[34] Huang finds this linkage between the black velvet effect and the xieyi aesthetic particularly helpful in understanding the

7.1 The first appearance of "Zhong Kui Marries Off His Sister" in Qiu Yun's imagination. *Woman Demon Human* (人鬼情), directed by Huang Shuqin, 1987.

overall style of her film. Huang had technically used the black velvet device in two of her earlier films, but not until *Woman Demon Human* did the device transcend its technical effects to manifest an aesthetic style.[35]

In the same interview, Huang Shuqin herself also draws a connection between her film and the aesthetic of "essentialist theater" (写意戏剧),[36] a concept her own father, Huang Zuolin (黄佐临), articulated and developed in 1962.[37] As my summary of mainstream criticism of *Woman Demon Human* in the last section shows, many critics in 1988 particularly praised the film's abstract and essentialist aesthetic, regarding that element as the greatest achievement of Huang's film. Indeed, most critics credit *Woman Demon Human*'s success to the overall xieyi aesthetic of the film.

Xieyi, originally referring to the aesthetic effect of Chinese literati's ink-wash painting, literally means "describing the inner essential, [or] the inner spirit."[38] The term was first used in 1914 by Feng Shuluan to highlight the nonmimetic character of Chinese opera and contrast it with Western *xieshi* (写实, describing the real, realist) spoken drama.[39] The term was also used in a similar fashion in the National Drama Movement (国剧运动) of the late 1920s, but not until 1962 did Huang Zuolin seriously reconceptualize it in relation to theories of Western drama. Among several potential English translations, Huang decided to use "essentialism" or "intrinsicalism" to express the aesthetic principle that reaches a higher or more typical level of the real beyond pure imitation.[40] The Cold War conditions and the Sino-Soviet split provided the immediate geopolitical context for the concept's reemergence. Huang Zuolin's xieyi emerged thus in reaction to the "realism theater" of Stanislavsky, who enjoyed a quasi-monopoly as a "revolutionary" theatrical icon in the Cold War context,[41] particularly in 1950s China. Huang Zuolin, in his essay from 1962, introduces Bertolt Brecht's (1898–1956) "distancing effect theater" and its intended sociopolitical and reflective engagement. He then reveals the initial connection between Brecht's didactic drama theory and the Chinese opera of Mei Lanfang (1894–1961), promoting in socialist China a political theater rooted in Chinese opera and aesthetics. Importantly, although Huang formulated his xieyi as a contrast to realism, Huang did not oppose the revolutionary engagement associated with Stanislavsky's theater. He questioned the realist illusion and challenged its aesthetic and political effectiveness.[42] In 1991, Huang published his account of the formation of his essentialist theater, in which he stresses the importance of integrating all three theatrical modes at a higher level. Quoting both Marx and Mao Zedong, he continuously challenges the concept and practice of art for art's sake, reiterating that art should engage life and society through certain typifications. According to him, Brecht's central contribution to world theater lies not merely in his theory of the distancing effect but more fundamentally in his Marxist dialectic reasoning.[43]

When Huang Zuolin's essentialist theater returned after the Cultural Revolution, especially in the 1980s, it incited a huge debate.[44] Critics who understood the political function of the 1960s xieyi aesthetic took a stance against using the concept, arguing that essentialist theater had served as a political tool during the Mao era and should therefore be repudiated. Others wanted to dismiss the concept's political implications and redeploy it exclusively for its cultural and aesthetic value. Some of the latter group went so far as to argue that the concept was created in the 1960s to counterbalance the political control exercised over theater at that time.[45] In any case, both sides rejected the political signification and intended sociopolitical engagement embedded in Huang's original concept, demonstrating that most Chinese intellectuals in the mid- and late 1980s are overwhelmingly in agreement to separate the cultural and aesthetic from the sociopolitical.

It is within this context of simultaneous depoliticization, aestheticization, and culturalization that we must situate the discussion of Huang Shuqin's *Woman Demon Human* and the film's *xieyi* aesthetic. Indeed, Huang Shuqin herself has disassociated her father's theory of essentialist theater from any sociopolitical engagements and dismissed his politically oriented art practice in Mao's China by attributing her father's achievements to his "ceaseless pursuit of art" even in adverse political environments.[46] How then did Huang (re)articulate this post-Mao *xieyi* aesthetic in her making of *Woman Demon Human*? More specifically, how did she adapt Pei Yanling's life story for the silver screen? And how did this *xieyi* approach work with the mainstream intellectual discourses of the 1980s to re-present socialist China and reconfigure gender and female selfhood?

In the essay "Director's Reflections on *Woman Demon Human*,"[47] Huang reveals the aesthetic principles she adhered to when representing Pei's life story on the big screen. She first expresses her admiration for the sublime sense of loneliness Pei feels toward life (91). She then links Pei's loneliness to the independent character highly valued in the post-Mao era. "In a modern society where humans' independent character carries more and more weight," Huang states, Pei's sense of loneliness "will be greatly understood and resonate among people" (92). Huang proceeds to argue that films should directly present life by focusing on people's inner spirit and psychological trajectory "rather than [centering on] the influence of political events on the character's fate." Indeed, she stresses, "This time I am determined not to represent human beings through social turmoil; [I] won't even prioritize historical backgrounds." Her argument continues, "As a matter of fact, when speaking of a character's psychological state [or changes], there is little difference whether the time is around the Liberation [period, 1949], the present, or years later. [Films] need to go deep into the human psychic world to explore the particular kind of national cultural mentality" (92). The sociopolitical history of socialist China, where Pei grew up to become a successful female artist, is thus viewed as a distraction or even a potential trap in Huang's film project and should be excluded from the film's adaptation.

To illustrate the Chinese cultural mentality, Huang reveals, "[we] have selected those events that would cause most pain and agony for a woman in the male dominant society."[48] These events, according to Huang, include Qiu Yun's mother's running away from home, Qiu Yun's nonbiological father's acquiescence to the situation, and Qiu Yun's first doomed love relationship (92–93). Huang's selection implies that the cause of a woman's pain and agony lies in the psychocultural realm, particularly linked to her nuclear family and her relationships with men. The painful personal and cultural experiences Chinese women endure, Huang argues, have pushed Qiu Yun to move closer to her alter ego—Zhong Kui (92). Although Huang stresses that the film represents two worlds—one abstract, centered on Zhong Kui, and the other realistic, centered on Qiu Yun's life as a woman—she makes two supplementary points. First, the narration of Qiu Yun's life should be condensed, in order to leave space for the narrative on Zhong Kui; and second, Qiu Yun's story itself should also be told in a culturalized and "decorative" (aestheticized) manner so it can be better connected and intermingled with Zhong Kui's world (94). Huang did not choose the style of "documentary" (纪实性) realism for this film, despite its popularity in the 1980s, as it would contradict the cultural expressiveness of Zhong Kui's world (97).

Huang makes it clear that the film will downplay and even omit sociopolitical and historical events, foregrounding instead the Chinese cultural mentality and Qiu Yun's inner world. This psychocultural focus loudly echoed the general cultural trend of the mid-to-late 1980s, which on the one hand emphasized the "sedimented" (积淀) or crystallized[49] Chinese cultural mentality or (un)consciousness, and on the other hand foregrounded universal human nature and transhistorical sexual difference and psychology. In Chinese film production, whereas Fifth Generation male directors had already showcased this cultural trend in their avant-garde experimentalism, Fifth Generation female directors (Peng Xiaolian and Liu Miaomiao) did so in their combination of emotional melodrama and psychological realism. Huang's *Woman Demon Human* furthered the psychocultural approach with its xieyi style, or the black velvet device.

From Pei Yanling's Life to *Woman Demon Human*: The Xieyi Adaptation

A closer examination of the film adaptation of Pei Yanling's life will further illuminate how Huang's xieyi style actively participated in the mainstream re-presentations of socialist China, female psychology, and Chinese cultural mentality in the late 1980s. *Woman Demon Human* is based on the life story of Pei Yanling and is viewed by some scholars as a special biographical film.[50] Huang has stated that the film's threads and content come from Pei's life.[51] A brief biographical sketch of Pei's life and times can help us understand how Huang selects and constructs the film's central plot and ideas.[52] By introducing Pei's life story into the discussion of the film, however, I do not suggest that Huang's film should mirror or capture the totality of Pei's life. After all, *Woman Demon Human* is an artistic re-creation, containing its own cultural and historical significations. But a brief comparison can give us a concrete sense of Huang's cinematic approach, specifically her xieyi adaption of Pei's life story.

Pei Yanling was born in 1947 in a Hebei village. The father figure in her family, Pei Yuan, was not her biological father. After her parents' divorce, Pei was with her mother initially but later chose to stay with her (nonbiological) father, a performer in local itinerant opera troupes. She herself received solid training from a local opera performer and became a child opera star in nearby villages and counties when she was only five years old. But Pei owed her success as a national young female artist to the social and cultural transformations in socialist China. Socialist gender equality placed Chinese women in an unprecedented vanguard position in social, economic, and cultural production, and the socialist endeavor to develop a new national and popular mass culture contributed to socialist reforms alongside the further development of Chinese traditional and regional cultures. To revitalize and reform China's traditional operas, the socialist government established official opera troupes and schools at both national and provincial levels. From 1953 to 1966, opera film production set a historical record: about 115 Chinese opera films were released, "an extraordinarily high number by any measure."[53] Pei was recruited to the Hebei Great Leap Forward Youth Opera Troupe (河北青年跃进剧团) in 1959 in Tianjin, and this recruitment marked the turning point of her life. With the socialist institutional endorsement of gender equality and popular cultural reform, Pei and other female artists thrived, benefiting from historically unparalleled resources and a strong sense of mission and pride. Pei was given the great opportunity to learn from and work with legendary opera masters from different schools, like Mei Lanfang (梅兰芳), Ma Lianliang (马连良), Li Shaochun (李少春), Xi Xiaobo (奚啸伯), and Zhang Junqiu (张君秋). In a TV interview from 2016, Pei repeatedly emphasizes how her experience of watching those masters' performances at the age of twelve had totally transformed her understanding of the opera art and her own performance.[54] Furthermore, the Hebei Great Leap Forward Youth Opera Troupe also invited Mei Lanfang, Xun Huisheng (荀慧生), Gao Shenglin (高盛麟), and Qiu Shengrong (裘盛戎) to coach its young artists and supervise their performances.

Although Pei was still a teenager when she was recruited to the provincial opera troupe to play Hebei opera (河北梆子, also known as clapper opera), she was entrusted with the task of reforming Hebei opera. That was how she established herself and became one of the most distinguished modern opera artists. She was received by Mao Zedong twice in Beijing for her successful performance of lead roles in *The Monkey King* (闹天宫, 1960) and *Lotus Lantern* (宝莲灯, 1962). Mao was an ardent lover and knowledgeable appreciator of Chinese operas, and he especially praised Pei's rebellious roles in both operas. When he learned that Pei would perform *Lin Chong Flees at Night* (林冲夜奔), he recommended she study with Hou Yongkui (侯永奎), an artist acclaimed for his northern-*kun*-style performance of *Lin Chong Flees at Night*. In the early post-Mao era, Pei's *Lin Chong Flees at Night* not only restored her reputation as a Hebei opera superstar after the Cultural Revolution in 1979 but also won her the Plum Performance Award in 1986, a nationally prestigious achievement. To this day, Pei still ranks *Lin Chong Flees at Night* the best of all her performances.[55]

Wang Zhongde (王仲德) emphatically states, in his biographical essay on Pei Yanling, "If Pei Yanling's [nonbiological] father, her private opera teachers Li Congshuai and Cui Shengbin, and her early training [all together] laid a foundation for her art performance before she was twelve years old, the artistic and cultural environment after she went to Tianjin [to join the provincial troupe in 1959], the intimate and in-depth teachings she received from all the opera masters, and the hands-on guidance provided particularly by Guo Jingchun 郭景春 [in the provincial troupe] essentially enabled Pei to soar high with a pair of sturdy wings later in her life."[56] Indeed, as a young woman Pei received unprecedented institutional endorsement, professional guidance, individualized trainings, and official and popular support in socialist China, all of which were key to establishing herself as a top national opera artist in modern Chinese history.

These sociocultural aspects of Pei's life in socialist China prior to the Cultural Revolution, however, are excluded from Huang's film, causing much confusion even among the Chinese audience of the late 1980s about the specific historical periods in which the film is set. As discussed previously, Huang makes two major statements about her exclusion of sociopolitical events. First, her film focuses on the heroine and her inner world rather than the sociopolitical events of the time. Second, following the intellectual trend of cultural reflection in the mid- and late 1980s, Huang adopts a cultural and aesthetic approach to socialist history. In her annotated film script, for example, Huang comments on several scenes where Qiu Yun is betrayed, humiliated, or bullied, stating that these evil behaviors are not products of political movements but manifestations of the deeply rooted Chinese national cultural character.[57] Huang then reasons that she should depict human evils in the everyday setting (meaning depoliticized) instead of linking them exclusively to political and historical events, which could potentially lead the film away from exploring Chinese cultural essence or the female inner world.

On the surface, Chinese intellectuals of the late 1980s intended to go deeper into the Chinese collective (un)consciousness to reflect on the problems appearing in socialist China. But by perceiving socialist movements as automatic and mostly negative manifestations of Chinese culture, and categorically dismissing the sociopolitical dimension in their exploration of culture, Chinese intellectuals at the time effectively—however inadvertently—negated any positive sociopolitical transformations and new cultural achievements made in socialist China. Indeed, socialist history is viewed in Huang's film mostly as a site that exhibits a negative Chinese cultural mentality. As a result, major sociopolitical and cultural transformations, particularly those in gender, class, and mass and popular cultural practice, all of which significantly contributed to Pei's success as a young female opera artist and to her sense of self, are completely effaced.

Huang's film thus deploys the xieyi aesthetic both to blot out the sociopolitical and cultural transformations of the socialist period and to stage an essential condition for the appearance of heroine's inner world. The female self thus comes into being exclusively through her individual negotiations with the rooted cultural mentality—manifested in both the changes of her nuclear family and her personal relationships with different men in her life. As such, the film reinforces mainstream cultural and feminist discourses of the late 1980s by eclipsing the role of socialist gender, class, and cultural transformations in constituting individual women's public ambition and personal happiness. The bifocal emphasis on individual female psychology and national cultural mentality significantly renders socialist history irrelevant as it severs the personal life from the sociopolitical realm. More critically it denies the possibility that sociopolitical forces can make changes in culture and gender relationship. The idea that a woman's emotional and psychic state can be insulated from sociopolitical history especially of the socialist period, when large-scale economic, sociopolitical, and cultural transformations were occurring, illustrates a radical change in Chinese women's cinema of the late 1980s.

In addition to applying the xieyi aesthetic to the overall film adaptation, Huang also deploys the black velvet device to shoot seminal scenes in the narrative structure. There are three major units of xieyi scenes in the film: (1) the opening and closing scenes, when black velvet is used to create a psychocultural space for Qiu Yun's self-quest, her search for self-representation and self-recognition; (2) the three haystack scenes, all set in the dark, which function to punctuate the filmic narrative from beginning to end with repeated emphases on female desire, sexual difference, and mythical mother-daughter bonding or identification; and (3) the segment "Zhongkui Marries Off His Sister," for which the black velvet device was initially designed. All three units of xieyi scenes play crucial roles in signifying central meanings of the film as well as interacting with mainstream discourses and thus demand a close analysis.

The Mother's Story Retold: Female Desire, Sexual Difference, and Mother-Daughter (Dis)Identification

In her published director's reflection, Huang highlights the importance of the role of Qiu Yun's mother, listing her leaving home as the first critical incident that conditions Qiu Yun's life.[58] But the mother's story is not that simple. A quick comparison of the film and Pei's life story shows that Huang's xieyi adaptation entails a significant retelling of Pei's mother's story. Why does the foundation of Pei's mother's story have to change? How does the mother's reconfiguration in the film reveal to us the sociocultural transformation occurring in late 1980s China?

Based on Wang Zhongde's biography of Pei Yanling, Pei's mother had been arranged to marry her nonbiological father, Pei Yuan, a local opera performer with a violent temper. Pei's mother was unhappy staying with Pei Yuan, and they divorced when Pei Yanling was two years old. Pei's mother, a strong woman, fought to keep her daughter but eventually lost her custody battle. Only later did Pei Yanling learn Pei Yuan was not her biological father.[59] Pei's mother's story was neither unique in modern Chinese history nor unusual in modern Chinese cultural representation. In fact, the popular and influential modern narrative developed in the May Fourth literature targeted arranged marriage and championed educated women's rights to free love, marriage of one's own choice, and divorce. Socialist women's liberation embraced and institutionalized these modern aspirations by promulgating and implementing a law in the early 1950s that grants all women legal and equal rights to marriage and divorce. In the early post-Mao era, female desire and rights to divorce were also advocated in the name of humanism and female independent consciousness.

Woman Demon Human, however, introduces a different position through its significant revision of the mother's story. The film leaves out the information of Pei's mother's arranged marriage and her unhappy relationship with her husband, recasting the mother as the lead actress in the local opera troupe, who has an extramarital relationship with another man (later revealed to be Qiu Yun's biological father). Pei's biological mother was not an actress; her first stepmother was. In the film, this locally known actress-mother hardly conceals her affair and eventually elopes with her lover in a most public way—during an opera performance. Worse still, she shows no concern about abandoning her daughter, inflicting traumatic pain and public humiliation on Qiu Yun over the course of her life. The film thus evokes the traditional stereotype of actresses (women in public) being morally problematic and unredeemable. Although the film deplores various inhumane prejudices and violence that childhood friends and later colleagues in the opera troupe inflict on Qiu Yun, it does not question the general condemnation of the mother. Qiu Yun's nonbiological father prohibits Qiu Yun from pursuing an acting career on the grounds that actresses, like her mother, are promiscuous. The film portrays the mother as a cultural stereotype, unaffected by history or socioeconomic changes. She is neither a victim of the traditional local practice of arranged marriage nor a new woman who bravely pursues her own happiness in socialist China. Rather, she embodies an essential female desire and typifies an immoral woman who violates Chinese cultural codes, especially for the roles of wife and mother.

This re-created mother figure sets in motion Qiu Yun's search for a different self-representation. Indeed, Qiu Yun's life struggle starts with confronting the negative consequences of her mother's actions, involving conscious compromises or choices made at different stages of her life—playing male roles on stage, escaping from her male mentor's approach, and staying in her unhappy marriage—to *dis*identify with the mother. The complicated effect of the mother, however, goes beyond the daughter's disidentification. This reconfigured mother in the film adaptation apparently also functions to represent something that deeply connects mother and daughter and that is worth redeeming. Indeed, the film repeatedly suggests an enigmatic psychological bonding or unconscious identification between Qiu Yun and her mother through the three mysterious haystack scenes, all set in the dark night with a unique, nightmarish xieyi mise-en-scène. In the film, the haystacks located on the outskirts of the village are closely associated with illicit and forbidden emotions and conduct (fig. 7.2).

The first haystack scene takes place before the mother runs away and when Qiu Yun is still a little girl with a "happy family." The scene depicts little Qiu Yun suddenly leaving a group of boy playmates on an early summer evening, making an unconventional statement: "I won't be a bride for any of you!" She then runs alone into the wild haystacks area located far away from the center of the village. Qiu Yun "intuitively" traces her mother's footsteps, and as a result, she bumps into the "primal scene," where her mother is making love

7.2 Haystacks on the outskirts of the village at night. *Woman Demon Human* (人鬼情), directed by Huang Shuqin, 1987.

to a strange man. Not sure how to make sense of what she witnesses, Qiu Yun, however, feels the imminent danger associated with the eerie, dark, and deserted setting. When she sees the haystack collapsing on her mother and the man, Qiu Yun screams uncontrollably and madly flees the scene as if escaping from the dark fate of her mother. She runs all the way back to the brightly lit local temple where her nonbiological father stays. When she is finally in this man's arms, Qiu Yun cries out loudly that she wants her mother back, indicating her sense that her mother has emotionally left her. The first haystack scene ends with Qiu Yun's terribly conflicted feelings about both her mother and herself: she is saddened by the loss of her mother (the unconventional self as well), but her feeling for her mother seems to become stronger.

The second haystack scene occurs when adolescent Qiu Yun confronts her own "illicit" desire. Qiu Yun becomes the top young artist in the provincial opera troupe, but she falls in love with her coach, Teacher Zhang, a married man with three children, a situation similar to her mother's but in a different way. The second haystack scene stages the mutual desire between Qiu Yun and Zhang, producing an uncannily familiar feel in relation to the first haystack scene. Once again, Qiu Yun senses the dangerous consequences of the situation and flees, but their relationship has already entered the forbidden zone and thus leads to some sort of inevitable public condemnation: Teacher Zhang is officially dismissed from the provincial opera troupe to his rural home, and people openly accuse Qiu Yun of behaving just like her mother. Qiu Yun even receives physical punishment, as someone places a long, sharp nail on the table where Qiu Yun needs to place her hand when she flips her body over in the air onstage.

The third haystack scene appears toward the end of the film when adult Qiu Yun returns to her village as a nationally known opera artist. The scene consists of a series of haystack montages when Qiu Yun attentively listens to her nanny's narration about how she was born as a little girl with a loud singing voice (suggesting a strong and unconventional personality and a successful career in the opera world just as her mother had had), whereas her nonbiological father was wholeheartedly wishing that the newborn was a son. The nanny's narrative voice and a newborn's crying accompany the dark visual images of haystacks, suggesting that the haystacks are indeed the place of Qiu Yun's conception, and thus linking female desire (mother) to the formation of a new life (daughter). In retrospect, Qiu Yun's determination to become an opera singer against the strong objection of her nonbiological father, who perceives all actresses like her mother as morally corrupt, significantly reveals Qiu Yun's unspeakable and unbroken identification with her mother, although she decides to perform only male roles in order to publicly distance herself from her mother.

Female desire, first expressed by the "immoral" mother, is thus not repudiated in the film. Indeed, female desire based on heterosexual difference is not only retained but also occupies a central position the film. In addition to the haystack scenes, the film devotes several other major scenes to emphasizing the importance of biologically determined sexual difference and heterosexual desire. The public toilet scene where young adolescent Qiu Yun is accused of being a boy sneaking into a women's public toilet near a rural marketplace is meant to highlight that although Qiu Yun looks like a boy (or performs male roles), she is in fact "female" (女的). Teacher Zhang from the provincial opera troupe rescues Qiu Yun from the agitated crowd. He does not even hide his contempt for the ignorance of the local villagers when he asks, "Mr. Mei Lanfang is performing female roles on stage. Is he a female?" In the context of

7.3 "You are a good-looking girl." *Woman Demon Human* (人鬼情), directed by Huang Shuqin, 1987.

the late 1980s, this question also worked to make an important comment on Maoist socialist women. It stresses the "truth" about women: no matter what types of masculine roles women perform in society or onstage, they are essentially female. Indeed, a major dimension of Qiu Yun's desire is to be recognized as an attractive young woman after she becomes known for her male roles onstage. One scene focuses on how all the young female performers in the provincial opera troupe compete for the attention and favor of Teacher Zhang. But when one girl jokingly calls Qiu Yun a tomboy in public, Qiu Yun instantly confronts the girl in anger, retorting, "Who is a tomboy?" She then formally declares, "I am a real girl!" (真闺女). The subsequent mutual desire expressed between Qiu Yun and Teacher Zhang also drives home the point that although they both perform male roles onstage, it is their natural sexes, male and female, that make them attractive to each other. Teacher Zhang not only desires Qiu Yun, he also confirms Qiu Yun's desire to be recognized as female: "You are a good-looking girl, very feminine" (fig. 7.3). "I feel as though I will never tire of watching you." Female desire and sexual difference are thus highlighted in the film as the natural foundation for the formation of female self and consciousness.

Qiu Yun's struggle with the mother's legacy thus entails a double movement: a conscious disidentification with the mother's actions and an unconscious identification with the mother's desire. How to redeem female desire initially embodied by the "immoral" mother thus becomes the central task underpinning Qiu Yun's life journey. The ideas of an unbreakable mother-daughter bond and unconscious identification might suggest a potential female subversion of the male-centered world in psychoanalytic and feminist terms, however Huang's film articulates a late-1980s Chinese negotiation with those concepts, a negotiation that aims to meet the demands of newly mainstreamed cultural values.

Female Self-Representation: Rescuing Female Desire through the Chinese Neotraditional Marriage Ritual

By the late 1980s, Mao-era socialism was considered a political disruption of Chinese culture due to its sociopolitical commitment to gender, class, and perpetual revolution and was thus generally excluded from the feverish discussion of culture. At the same time, Western-influenced radical liberalism and individualism, which played a significant role in both challenging socialist collectivism and critiquing traditional Chinese culture,[60] were also on retreat. In their places, rational/market liberalism,[61] international neo-Confucianism and national modern Confucianism,[62] and the Root-Seeking Movement rose to collaborate with the national demand for rapid modernization, creating an ideology that transformed previously antagonistic ideas and practices into a new relationship in the market era.[63] In the name of both universality (human nature, sexual difference, and market development) and essentiality (sedimented Chinese tradition, cultural and national archetypes, and Confucian values), the cultural practice and intellectual discourse of the late 1980s made modern Western universal values and market rationality compatible with traditional Chinese culture by repudiating sociopolitical interventions in economic and cultural developments. Traditional Chinese cultural values as a result returned in the 1980s, not only becoming instrumental to China's pursuit of a stronger national economy but also reconfiguring social relationships.

Dai Jinhua makes an important point when she argues that *Woman Demon Human* is a film more concerned with female self-salvation or self-representation than with female (sexual) desire.[64] But female desire, as discussed above, is by no means downplayed in the film; rather, it is rendered as an underlining essence constitutive of the female self. The representation of a sexually unconventional and publicly outcast mother sets the stage for Qiu Yun's female self-salvation by laying a natural and thus redeemable foundation for female desire, and spurs a search for an acceptable cultural form of female (re)presentation. The mother's behavior is deemed unacceptable not for her heterosexual desire but for her public defiance of traditional values concerning marriage and family, values that vigorously reappeared in late-1980s China. Another historical factor, the post-Mao lament over the "stronger women and weaker men" phenomenon, also indirectly contributes to the mother's ostracizing in the film. Deeming stronger women an unnatural product of the socialist era, male intellectuals and artists in the 1980s made a special effort to "normalize" the gender relationship in the 1980s by promoting male masculinity and female domesticity and by evoking the yin-yang and *nei-wai* (private domain vs. public domain) configurations as the foundation for a strong nation-state.[65] Huang was much influenced by such discourse. In one of her interviews, she emphasizes, "My thought is clear. I will not create that kind of strong woman (女强人) who is thorny and cannot get along with anyone."[66] Female self-salvation in China in the late 1980s thus entailed a critical reflection on Chinese women's open departure from domestic values and their renunciation of the long-upheld legitimate form of the Chinese family during Mao's socialist period.

Soon after her mother leaves home, the young Qiu Yun intuitively understands that in order to save herself, she needs to redeem her mother by separating her mother's natural desire from her open rebellion against cultural conventions. When little Qiu Yun initially summons the legendary Tang dynasty underground demon queller Zhong Kui, as she is bullied by her male playmates for her mother's behavior, in her imagination Zhong Kui does two things: expels evil spirits and marries his sister to a good man. This dual role of Zhong Kui strongly suggests that Qiu Yun wants to have both her young self protected (Zhong Kui as the exterminator of evil spirits) and her mother—by extension part of her future self—redeemed (Zhong Kui as the ideal patriarch fulfilling his sister's desire via a culturally acceptable method). It is by no means accidental that Zhong Kui emerges in Huang's film as the key figure in female self-salvation and self-representation. As an exemplary, albeit mistreated, Confucian figure Zhong Kui has the capacity for sympathizing with women, including their desire and predicament, as well as arranging a good destiny for them through a legitimate cultural ritual.

According to legend, Zhong took care of his younger sister after their parents passed away, while he himself became a promising Confucian scholar. His best friend, Du Ping, appreciated his unusual talent and sponsored his trip to the imperial capital to take the civil service examination. He achieved the highest rank at the palace examination, but the emperor did not grant him his title due to his hideous appearance. Heartbroken, Zhong killed himself on the spot. The emperor marveled at Zhong's upright character and courage and appointed him the demon king in charge of the order of the underworld. An exemplary Confucian gentleman, Zhong could not forget his unfulfilled duties in the human world as elder brother and friend. He thus returned to the human world to marry his sister to his best friend, Du Ping.

"Zhong Kui Marries Off His Sister" as opera performance can be traced back to a kun opera segment from 1891.[67] This performance continued and developed in many other regional operas, including those of Peking and Sichuan, through the late 1950s.[68] In 1984, when Pei Yanling was seeking to expand her own performing repertoire during a successful return to the opera stage after the Cultural Revolution, she saw "Zhong Kui Marries Off His Sister" performed by the Shanghai Kun Opera Troupe and became inspired by it.[69] Pei's ambition at the time, however, was not to bring this segment to Hebei opera but to create a full-length play of Zhong Kui. After studying other Zhong Kui plays in various regional operas, Pei staged her full-length Zhong Kui in Beijing in October 1985—a resounding success. Unlike the film's central message, Pei's full-length post-Mao Zhong Kui had little to do with her personal and emotional struggle as a young woman in Mao's socialist China. Rather, it showcased Pei's ambition to develop Hebei opera and resume a successful career established under the socialist regime.

Huang Shuqin became fascinated with Pei's Zhong Kui when she read Jiang Zilong's "A Boy with Long Hair," a short story about Pei Yanling. She was particularly intrigued by the transgressive gesture embodied in Pei's performance of not only male roles but also a ghost onstage.[70] Rather than linking Pei's breakthrough in playing a male ghost to any of the sociocultural changes taking place in modern history or to innovations made in the Chinese performing arts, Huang tied Pei's cross-dressing and human-ghost exchange exclusively to a personal pursuit and an essential female quest: Why does she (Pei) want to play a male ghost role? To address this question, Huang centers her film on "a conversation a woman conducts with herself."[71] Whereas this focus on the female inner world and consciousness confirmed the general post-Mao feminist endeavor, her insistence on reclaiming the female self and essence particularly through the segment of "Zhong Kui Marries Off His Sister" revealed Huang's special understanding of the possible solution to female self-salvation in late-1980s China. Indeed, as Huang points out in an interview, she is interested only in the segment rather than the full-length Zhong Kui story, because the segment both touches on the desire and fate of a woman and reiterates the essential Chinese gender ritual and values.[72]

The Zhong Kui in Huang's film is, of course, no longer a simple copy of the traditional patriarchal figure. Huang revises him: he embraces certain female concerns and understands female desire and emotional needs. After all, the Zhong Kui in *Woman Demon Human* is reimagined and embodied by three women: Huang as the scriptwriter and director of the film, Qiu Yun as the character who re-creates Zhong Kui in the diegetic narrative, and Pei Yanling as the real performer of Zhong Kui in the film. Cinematically, Zhong Kui's world directly represents Qiu Yun's internal world and her subjective imaginations. Xu Feng, in his interview with Huang, states that "when Zhong Kui appears from the darkness, an interior space emerges in Chinese cinema for the first time. This is what an individual's psychological space signifies, an interior, completely internalized world."[73] Initially called forth by the child Qiu Yun, cornered by a group of boys, as a lifesaver, the cinematic Zhong Kui witnesses a woman's struggle and sympathizes with her predicament; he eventually helps her express her concerns and desires. To a large extent, this Zhong Kui, as Huang indicates in her interview, is the alter ego of Qiu Yun.

At the same time, the Zhong Kui in Huang's film, no matter how reimagined, carries with him fundamental Confucian gender values. Qiu Yun's Zhong Kui knows how critical a proper marriage and family are for a woman in contemporary Chinese society, and his deep understanding of modern women's suffering seems only to reinforce his duty to marry a woman to a socially well-regarded husband. In this sense, the Zhong Kui in Huang's film is a *neotraditional* figure who, emerging from a modern woman's internal world, functions to mediate between female desire and acceptable (restored traditional) forms of female self-representation. Huang's film explicitly shows that only through Zhong Kui's mediation, which is also the mediation of a proper marriage and family, can certain post-Mao feminist ideas about female difference and desire be contained and accepted in China in the late 1980s.

Toward the end of the film, when Qiu Yun revisits her village as an internationally known opera artist in the 1980s, she reveals, in conversation with her nonbiological father, the significance of her interpretation of the Zhong Kui play:

QIU YUN My whole play of Zhong Kui accomplishes only one task.

FATHER What task?

QIU YUN The matchmaker's task.

FATHER What matchmaker's task?

QIU YUN Although Zhong Kui has a hideous appearance, he cares most about women's fate, and he is determined to marry his sister off to a good man.

FATHER So you have made a unique contribution?

QIU YUN Actually, I have always thought that a woman should [be guaranteed to] marry a good man.

With this dialogue Qiu Yun ties female desire, destiny, and happiness to—not freedom of love, social and familial gender equality, women's public ambition and success, or unconventional ways of expressing individual emotions and feelings, but—a proper marriage to a good man. In an interview, Huang Shuqin stresses that the segment "Zhong Kui Marries Off His Sister" reveals a central truth about women: namely, all women want to marry a good man. Huang admits that this truth is "very traditional and essential."[74] In her annotated script, she makes a special comment on the last scene: "Zhong Kui Marries Off His Sister" is about the pursuit of happiness.[75] The truth about a woman's happiness was thus not simply redefined in China in the late 1980s as related to a good man; more importantly, it needed to be signified through the cultural ritual of a proper (arranged) marriage. Qiu Yun's final move to marry herself off to the stage to continue performing Zhong Kui conveys, on the one hand, the lack of good and proper men in her life (implicitly a critique of Chinese men) and on the other hand her determination to redeem female desire and self through reinscribing the legitimized ritual process of Confucian marriage.

Conclusion: Chinese Female Consciousness as an Articulation of Neotraditional Values and Universal Cultural Feminism in the Market Era

Having illustrated that the making of *Woman Demon Human* with its black velvet aesthetic actively interacts with mainstream discourses of the 1980s, effacing socialist sociopolitical history and articulating a neotraditional model for female difference and self-representation, I do not mean to reject Chinese tradition as a whole. As we understand well today, Chinese tradition has diverse origins, heterogeneous components, and changing histories, and can never be reduced to a monolithic model. Furthermore, various Chinese traditions have not only continued but also played important roles throughout modern China even during the socialist period. Pei Yanling became known as a teenager in socialist China in the 1950s and 1960s by playing unconventional or rebellious (yet traditional) roles in the local opera. But at the same time, officially promoted traditions in modern China signify new sociocultural meanings and require close examination. The return of Confucian gender values in the mid-1980s, for example, has raised questions about the sociopolitical vision of contemporary China's economic development, and thus demands serious reflection.

By highlighting the central position of neotraditionalism in Huang's film, I want to draw particular critical attention to the following several points that have been largely overlooked in scholarly discussions of the film concerning Chinese gender, culture, and the market of the late 1980s. First, the appearance of Woman Demon Human signaled that by 1987 it had become widely accepted that a female director could explicitly endorse China's traditional gender values while exploring female self and consciousness. The overwhelmingly positive reception of the film by critics from diverse gender perspectives further indicates that many ideas expressed in the film had already been established and naturalized by the late 1980s and early 1990s. Indeed, feminist scholars raised no serious questions regarding Qiu Yun's having recourse to Zhong Kui, a benevolent patriarchal figure, or to the traditional marriage ritual associated with him, to reimagine Chinese women's happiness and self-redemption.

Second, the overall praise the film won from feminist and nonfeminist scholars alike were also indicative of the rise of cultural relativism in the late 1980s. Different cultural values, even if previously opposed (such as feminism and traditional gender values), had the capacity not only to coexist but to forge a sympathetic mutual understanding in Chinese women's cultural practice as well. This cultural relativism, however, should not be celebrated as a consequence of sociopolitical equal access to late-1980s self-expression and symbolic power in China. Rather, it shows that the parameters of cultural practice had radically changed as post-Mao China's priority was resolutely set on market development by downplaying the social equality promoted in socialist China. On the surface, this cultural relativism allows different discourses to coexist, but in actuality, this relativism is built upon the exclusion and marginalization of other fundamentally different discourses, like socialist feminism and sociopolitically oriented cultural practices. In other words, the concept of cultural difference was redefined. In China of the late 1980s, cultural differences were upheld with an implicit yet shared reference to market development and the rejection of sociopolitical engagements at the same time.

Needless to say, the coexistence of different discourses does not suggest that each discourse carries the same weight or maintains the same influence over time. Post-Mao feminism, for example, garnered momentum around the early and mid-1980s as it endorsed and helped articulate then-mainstream discourses of economic reform, cultural enlightenment and scientific modernity, sexual difference, female consciousness, and individual subjectivity. As China continued its economic transformation, however, the influence of post-Mao feminism gradually faded. Feminist scholars continued their practice, but their ideas became compromised as the market reshaped the cultural realm in the late 1980s and 1990s. As traditional Chinese culture (re)emerged as an important ideology, post-Mao cultural feminism was neutralized and disarmed. Huang's *Woman Demon Human* illustrates exactly how some feminist ideas, despite their subversive potentials in the imaginary, cultural, and psychological domains, can lead only to compromises when confronting the return of Confucian values as China expanded its economic development. The absence of concrete social and historical visions, as well as any specific means to link the psychological or cultural to possible sociohistorical changes, made post-Mao cultural feminism increasingly vulnerable in the context of market globalization.

Third, critics, especially post-Mao feminist scholars, have praised *Woman Demon Human* (in contrast to Zhang Nuanxin's *Sacrificed Youth*) for its representation of a fully developed female consciousness. Given the central position of female consciousness in articulating post-Mao feminist cultural practice, the rest of this section will be devoted to a brief but closer examination of what exactly constituted female consciousness at the beginning of the 1990s and the forces contributing to this concept's articulation in contemporary China.

Huang Shuqin, in "Women's Cinema: A Unique Perspective," uses the cultural feminist view established by such feminist scholars as Li Xiaojiang and Yuan Ying in the late 1980s and 1990s to discuss the difference between Chinese women's emancipation and the Western feminist movement.[76] The former, according to Huang, is a sociopolitical revolution, emphasizing gender equality and bestowing women's rights from above (meaning not fought for by women themselves), whereas the latter is a marginalized cultural critique of mainstream society, emphasizing female consciousness and self-reflection. Gender equality demands that women act like men, whereas "the establishment of female self-consciousness," Huang states, "reflects the existence and awakening of the other half of mankind." She believes that "as the economy and culture of the human world further develop, female culture will receive more adequate respect and recognition."[77]

Even if Huang was not familiar with post-Mao feminist terms when she made *Woman Demon Human*, the influence of popularized post-Mao feminist ideas as well as the general cultural trend is palpable in the film. *Woman Demon Human* generally moves along post-Mao cultural feminist reasoning, emphasizing sexual difference rather than gender equality as the basis of female consciousness or reflection. More significantly, the film directly participated in the development of post-Mao feminism in the late 1980s, negotiating cultural feminist ideas and the newly mainstreamed neo-Confucianism and traditional Chinese values. Biologically defined sexual difference and female desire, the film shows, remained meaningful in the late 1980s but had to be resignified through traditional gender values. The scene in the opening credits where Qiu Yun sits in front of multiple mirror frames seeing herself both as a modern woman and a traditional ideal patriarch, Zhong Kui, best illustrates how the film deploys different discursive frameworks, like post-Mao cultural feminism and revised traditional cultural values, in its exploration of female consciousness. In one long flashback, *Woman Demon Human* shows how Qiu Yun struggles to redeem the female (her mother's) desire and reaches a level of self-consciousness by resorting to a traditional patriarchal figure and the Confucian ritual of arranged marriage. In the last scene of the film (fig. 7.4), Qiu Yun finally confronts her own imagined Zhong Kui, also her alter ego:

QIU YUN Who is there?

ZHONG KUI I am you and you are me. You are unable to leave me; and I am unable to leave you. However, you are a woman. . . . I am a ghost, an ugly ghost. It is hard for men to play me. But you are a woman; it must be even harder.

[*Zhong Kui turns away, quietly leaving Qiu Yun*]

QIU YUN No, I do not mind working hard. I thoroughly enjoyed performing the role. Don't leave! Come back! I have waited for you since my childhood to exterminate evil ghosts and save me. Please do not leave. Come back!

ZHONG KUI There are too many evil ghosts in the human world. How much can a Zhong Kui do? I [actually] have come here to marry you off.

QIU YUN I am already married. You have married me to the stage.

7.4 Qiu Yun finally faces her imagined Zhong Kui. *Woman Demon Human* (人鬼情), directed by Huang Shuqin, 1987.

Shot in the dark and immediately following the last haystack scene where Qiu Yun's conception is suggested, this dialogue scene ties the natural site of the birth of female life to the ultimate psychocultural space where female self-consciousness is achieved. Furthermore, the smooth transition between the last two scenes via the black velvet device also displays the accomplished redemption of the mother's desire, a universal feminist theme, and the successful re-creation of self-representation via Zhong Kui. Huang Shuqin, in her annotated film script, specifies that this last dialogue scene also circles back to the first scene of the film, where Qiu Yun gazes at two different self-images in the mirror. According to Huang, the whole film shows how Qiu Yun moves from a "self-divided mirror image" or "two mirror images" (一分为二) to a "coherent self-identity" (合二为一), merging the two into one, and from a "self-gazing" (自视) state to a "self-articulating/expressing" (自语) psychological structure.[78]

To a certain extent, the film enunciates a female language in the form of an internal dialogue between the female self and the imagined Zhong Kui. In contrast to what Dai Jinhua has argued, that is, that a female language should simultaneously subvert the (transhistorical) patriarchal structure and articulate female self-consciousness, Qiu Yun's interlocutor, Zhong Kui, even in the film's revised form, embodies essential Chinese Confucian patriarchal values. The subversive female language envisioned or imagined by Western poststructuralist and psychoanalytic feminists as well as some post-Mao Chinese feminists does not seem able to materialize and deliver itself in a concrete sociohistorical context—not in the China of the late 1980s for sure. The merging of Zhong Kui and Qiu Yun at the end of the film thus strongly indicates that female language and consciousness in late-1980s China could be articulated only through the neotraditional psychocultural structure with the assistance of a black velvet device. Qiu's final claim to marry herself to the stage while staying passively in her loveless and unhappy marriage and making peace with her fate in a market society, significantly reveals the predicament of universal cultural feminism in the context of contemporary China.

The female consciousness resignified as such is actually compatible with a range of film genres in China in the 1990s. I want to end this chapter with a brief discussion of Huang Shuqin's next film, *A Soul Haunted by Painting* (画魂, 1993), in which Huang continues this logic of female consciousness in a commercial film. Starting from 1992 and 1993, China began formally marketing the socialist state-run studio system, reconfiguring film production, distribution, and exhibition primarily with market mechanisms. The new official documents "acknowledged film's economic function, endorsing a cinematic practice not necessarily in alignment with film's pedagogical function."[79] Such institutional transformation showcases how socioeconomic and institutional structures condition artistic practices. Huang's decision to go commercial with her next film was, therefore, by no means a purely personal choice.

A Soul Haunted by Painting, the story of Zhang Yuliang (张玉良, 1899–1977), is adapted from Shi Nan's (石楠) 1982 biographical novel of the same name.[80] Zhang Yuliang's sensational life trajectory, from young prostitute in a small provincial town to concubine of a known republican official, Pan Zanhua (潘赞化), and ultimately to internationally recognized artist, occupies the center of Huang's film. Adopting a commercial approach, with the most famous actress in China then, Gong Li (巩俐), playing the lead role in melodramatic style, the film was an instant box office hit upon its 1993 release. Critics and scholars, however, felt disappointed by the film. Some even argue that the film does not have a soul of its own and significantly departs from Huang's *Woman Demon Human*.[81]

Despite differences in genre, style, emphasis (inner world vs. outside world), and critical reception, *A Soul Haunted by Painting* is, according to the director, the logical continuation of *Woman Demon Human*. Huang has repeatedly defended *A Soul Haunted by Painting* in published essays and interviews, illustrating its multilevel connections with *Woman Demon Human*. She argues that the two heroines were created from the same mold. Indeed, *A Soul Haunted by Painting* follows *Woman Demon Human* in portraying Zhang Yuliang as the embodiment of traditional values and essential female consciousness: "Neither of my two heroines is born a rebel. They both grew up in traditional society and embraced a traditional sense of dependency, especially the traditional [female] longing for marrying a good man and having a happy ending. They are only lucky in the sense that when confronting life and death, they choose life—women's dignity and independence."[82] Although the turn from traditional dependency to independence in Huang's argument appears abrupt, the juxtaposition of two seemingly opposite terms exposes two sides of the same coin. Women's independence is understood here as an individual woman's brave acceptance of her unfortunate fate when there is no good man to rely on. It means that when facing ill fate, as Qiu Yun and Pan Yuliang (Zhang Yuliang used her husband's last name after marriage) do, an independent woman does not rebel, fight, or even complain. As we recall, among the praises *Woman Demon Human* received from the *New Films* 1988 article "Ardent Pursuit of Art," there was one that particularly highlighted the film's gentle and peaceful rather than outrageous manner of presenting Qiu Yun's hardship and helplessness. This sense of independence has little to do with modern women's struggle for independent status on economic, social, and political terms. Rather, it signifies a woman's "courageous" acceptance of her lot. Female consciousness articulated as such refers to an awareness of female essence as constituted by both a desire for a good man in marriage (dependence) and a nonconfrontational and quiet acceptance of her fate and suffering (independence) when her desire cannot be fulfilled in her lifetime. It is true that Huang does not activate as much space in *A Soul Haunted by Painting* to illustrate Pan Yuliang's inner world as in *Woman Demon Human*, but Pan Yuliang's art pursuits, especially her self-portraits, effectively manifest her self-reflection and female consciousness.

Traditional Chinese values returned in the 1980s to reconfigure gender and female consciousness and resignify universal humanism with Chinese characteristics. "As a film director," Huang states, "I seek female perspective from the traditional angle and then move to concerns for the whole human(kind)."[83] Neotraditionalism, female/sexual difference, and universal humanism, while not identical, worked together to forge a new ideology as China continued its market development. This unique combination, as Huang herself has argued, is clearly manifested in both of her films despite their different plots and styles.

Huang's persistent defense of *A Soul Haunted by Painting* exposes the blind spot in most published criticism of the film, which has overlooked its fundamental affinity to *Woman Demon Human* as well as the internal linkage between the high culturalism of the 1980s and the commercialism of the 1990s.[84] Furthermore, like her earlier film, *A Soul Haunted by Painting* also uses a filming mechanism that blots out the complex national and international histories during Pan Yuliang's lifetime (1889–1977), a period when major sociopolitical transformations occurred in both China and the world as a whole. This continual withdrawal from history functions to deny the relevance of sociopolitical forces in transforming gender and culture. The idea that a modern Chinese woman's story could be told without including the major sociopolitical contexts and historical changes in twentieth-century China adheres to the black velvet aesthetic first deployed in *Woman Demon Human*.

Huang was, however, both aware and critical of the masculine values expressed in commercial cinema. In several interviews, she discusses the negative effects of the commercial film industry on women and female directors. According to Huang, the nature of commercial culture in a capitalist society is totally male-centered, granting no space to women.[85] She laments the gradual loss of creative space for directors like herself, a feeling and perception shared by Zhang Nuanxin and other female directors growing up in the Mao era. But rather than evoking a critical reflection on the systematic issue or forging an alternative practice as Zhang did, Huang concedes, "China has just entered the commodity society and the commodity economy is accelerating in a lively and positive way. It is impossible to fight against male dominance or male-centered culture at this point. No way!" When asked what female directors should fight against and how she envisions the future of Chinese women's cinema, Huang replies, "What is the target of female directors' rebellion? [It is] the male-centered society. But this rebellion [can] only occur at the *unconscious* level and is thus very difficult to be understood. Perhaps only after the market economy reaches its peak as it does in the United States and France can female consciousness be noticed by more people and be understood and accepted by more people [in China]."[86]

In addition to demonstrating an independent—here rendered unconscious—way of negotiating women's fate in contemporary China, which echoes her two heroines' choice, Huang also inadvertently reveals that female consciousness, which had been both naturalized (biology and psychology) and culturalized (traditional and depoliticized) in Chinese mainstream discourses in the late 1980s, is linked on a deep level to the (capitalist) market economy. The more advanced the market, the better developed and understood the female consciousness. In 1986, when *Contemporary Cinema* and the China Film Art Research Center co-organized the Chinese Women's Films in the New Era, 1978–Present symposium, one of the most debated topics was how to define female consciousness.[87] What was ostensibly missing in the debate then was women's situation during Mao's socialist China. Huang's comments thus help clarify, in retrospect, the mutual exclusion of the socialist system and the individual female consciousness promoted in the 1980s.

In conclusion, Huang's film practice in the late 1980s and early 1990s, together with her interviews and essays, has offered us a multidimensional lens through which to understand the concept of female consciousness developed in China at the turn of the 1990s. Sexual difference laid a natural/biological/psychological foundation for the concept; and post-Mao universal cultural feminism, a depoliticized intellectual discourse, and modernized Confucian ideas, although in tension sometimes, cosignified its layered meanings and values. Further, the market economy, global and domestic, provided the very political and economic condition for the emergence and rise of female consciousness. As such, the acclaimed female or feminist *cultural* practice in China at the turn of the 1990s, as in Huang's *Woman Demon Human*, was attached to broader *socioeconomic* transformations that had discredited the sociopolitical role of cultural practice and (re)produced social stratifications in the name of natural or sexual difference and the progressive development of the market.

NOTES

Introduction

1. For a discussion of the overall cultural and aesthetic turn in both Western and Chinese contexts since the 1970s, see Jameson, *Cultural Turn*; Baumbach, Young, and Yue, *Cultural Logic*; and Leenhouts, "Culture against Politics." For a discussion of the ahistorical, cultural, and identity turn in feminist practice, see Hennessy and Ingraham, "Introduction: Reclaiming Anticapitalist Feminism," 1–3; and Fraser, "Feminism Tamed: From Redistribution to Recognition in the Age of Identity" and "Feminism, Capitalism, and the Cunning of History," in her *Fortunes of Feminism*, 139–88, 209–28.

2. Hennessy and Ingraham, "Introduction: Reclaiming Anticapitalist Feminism."

3. The question was first raised in English scholarship of the early 1970s on women's liberation in Eastern Europe. See Scott, *Does Socialism Liberate Women?*

4. Stacey, *Patriarchy and Socialist Revolution*, 1–5. See also my detailed discussion of the topic in chapter 1.

5. For a concrete discussion of the cultural movement in China in the mid- and late 1980s, see chapter 5. See also Zhong, *Masculinity Besieged?*

6. Yao, "Chinese New Cinema," 215.

7. Li Xiaojiang, *Eve's Exploration*; Yuan, "Feminism," 1–3. See chapter 4 of this volume for a detailed discussion of Western post-second-wave feminisms and their influence on the formation of post-Mao feminism.

8. These critiques or charges were vocally pronounced in the popular and influential documentary TV series *Deadsong of the River* (河殇), first aired in 1988.

9. See chapter 6 of this volume for a detailed discussion of the topic.

10. Yuan, "Feminism"; Dai, "Invisible Women"; Dai, "Gender and Narration," 134; and Cui, *Women through the Lens*, 171–99.

11. Berry, "China's New 'Women's Cinema'"; Kaplan, "Problematizing Cross-Cultural Analysis"; and Dai, "Invisible Women," 277.

12. See Eisenstein, "A Dangerous Liaison?"; Fraser, *Fortunes of Feminism*, 209–26; and Hennessy and Ingraham, "Introduction: Reclaiming Anticapitalist Feminism," 1–3.

13. Fraser, *Fortunes of Feminism*, 9.

14. On shared context, see Mohanty, "Cartographies of Struggle," 4; on destabilization, see Grewal and Kaplan, "Postcolonial Studies and Transnational Feminist Practice." For a critical discussion of the significance as well as limitation of transnational feminist theory and its further development in the Chinese context, see Lingzhen Wang, "Transnational Feminist Reconfiguration," 11–22. For a critical reassessment of historical materialism in feminist studies, see Hennessy and Ingraham, *Materialist Feminism*.

15. Meisner, "Chinese Revolution."

16. Rofel, *Other Modernities*, 21. As I discuss in chapter 4, the first post-Mao feminist theoretical article published in 1983 by Li Xiaojiang concerns "women's liberation."

17. Stacey, *Patriarchy and Socialist Revolution*, 5, 10 (emphasis mine).

18. Li Xiaojiang, "Responding to Tani Barlow," 176.

19. See my detailed discussion of post-Mao feminism in chapters 4, 6, and 7.

20. *State feminism* is also deployed by some scholars in their research on gender and women in socialist China. Initially used by social scientists to refer to the political style of feminist practice in Scandinavia, the term, when applied to the Chinese context, also encountered a Cold War distortion, evoking the monolithic and all-controlling image of a state patriarch. See Zheng Wang, *Finding Women*, 7.

21. See Dong Xuewen, "Issue of Mainstream"; Dai, "Invisible Women"; Xu and Shi, "Path Selection."

22. There are numerous examples. For one related to the study of Chinese socialist women's cinema, see Cui, *Women through the Lens*, 171–99.

23. Lu, "On the Construction."

24. Korte and Sternberg, *Bidding for the Mainstream?*, 7.

25. Korte and Sternberg, 8.

26. See Johnston, "Women's Cinema as Counter-Cinema"; Williams, *Television*.

27. Korte and Sternberg, *Bidding for the Mainstream?*, 10–11.

28. See, for example, Sellier, *Masculinity Singular*. See also chapter 5 for a gendered critique of the French New Wave and Chinese masculine avant-gardism.

29. For a discussion of the relationship among feminist avant-garde cinema, capitalist institution, and mainstream discourse, see chapter 1.

30. Khan, "Shared Space," 7.

31. The origin of this cultural configuration can be traced to the 1930s left-wing mass culture practiced in China's urban centers and to Mao Zedong's 1942 talk at the Yan'an forum.

32. Wu Di, "Exploration of 'People's Films.'"

33. Cheek, "Chinese Socialism"; Volland, *Socialist Cosmopolitanism*, 191.

34. Ying Zhu, *Chinese Cinema*, 19 (emphasis in the original).

35. Ying Zhu, 20.

36. Ying Zhu, 21.

1. A few of the scholarly works that have helped to diversify research on socialist culture, cinema, and gender include Clark, *Chinese Cinema* and "Artists, Cadres, and Audiences"; Marchetti, *Two Stage Sisters*; Tang Xiaobing, *Rereading*; Gilmartin, *Engendering the Chinese Revolution*; Ban Wang, "Desire and Pleasure"; Rofel, *Other Modernities*; Diamant, "Re-Examining the Impact" and *Revolutionizing the Family*; Berry, *Postsocialist Cinema*; Tina Mai Chen, "Female Icons, Feminist Iconography?" and "Socialism, Aestheticized Bodies"; Zhong, "Women Can Hold"; Lingzhen Wang, *Chinese Women's Cinema*; Barlow, *Question of Chinese Women*; Lin, *Transformation of Chinese Socialism*; and Zheng Wang, *Finding Women*.

2. Despite the outpouring of scholarly books on Chinese cinema during the last several decades, only a handful of publications focus on socialist cinema. See Juraga and Booker, *Socialist Cultures*, 6.

3. Chang, "Mechanics of State Propaganda," 89–90.

4. Chang, 5.

5. Chang, 9.

6. Chris Berry and E. Ann Kaplan pioneered the study of Chinese women's cinema in English-language academia. See Berry, "China's New 'Women's Cinema'"; and Kaplan, "Problematizing Cross-Cultural Analysis."

7. Only a few chapters and articles published in English discuss socialist Chinese women directors. See Cui, *Women through the Lens*; and Lingzhen Wang, "Socialist Cinema and Female Authorship," and "Wang Ping."

8. There are exceptions, but many influential works published in the 1980s were both implicated in and contributed to the intensified Cold War ideology of the time.

9. See Andors, *Unfinished Liberation*; Johnson, *Women, the Family*; and Wolf, *Revolution Postponed*.

10. See Stacey, *Patriarchy and Socialist Revolution*.

11. Diamant, "Re-Examining the Impact," 172.

12. Diamant, 173.

13. Berry, "China's New 'Women's Cinema'"; Kaplan, "Problematizing Cross-Cultural Analysis."

14. Cui, *Women through the Lens*, 178–80.

15. Modern Chinese women's individual agency, particularly their active roles in political, social, and cultural movements, became a major topic for a group of scholarly works published in the last two decades. See, for example, Gilmartin, *Engendering the Chinese Revolution*; Zheng Wang, *Chinese Enlightenment*; Dooling, *Women's Literary Feminism*; and Hershatter, *Gender of Memory*.

16. Saich, "Introduction"; Diamant, *Revolutionizing the Family*.

17. Diamant, "Re-Examining the Impact," 172.

18. Harding, "From China, with Disdain," 257.

19. Harding, 258.

20. In Stacey's own discussion, however, she attributes the radical change in her scholarly conclusions about socialist revolution to China's opening up in the late 1970s, which enabled Western scholars to access the "real China," although

she does note it was also the time when radicalism declined in the United States. Her explanation treats China as an object that can be objectively "decoded" with better access to information. See Stacey, *Patriarchy and Socialist Revolution*, 2–3.

21. Honig, "Socialist Revolution," 333; see also the blurbs on the back flap of the book's dust jacket.

22. For example, this social scientific book was written by a scholar who did not specialize in China, had not conducted any firsthand research in China, and demonstrated little sense of either the complexity of Chinese history or the dynamics of Chinese regional differences. In her highly selective synthesis of earlier second- and thirdhand materials, she displayed an inability to evaluate her selections. Most of her secondary social science–oriented sources were locally situated and time-specific, produced by scholars who had conducted research in a particular location—generally a village or a county—during a short period. Stacey's treatment of these sources and data erroneously rendered them as "facts" applicable everywhere in rural China.

23. Honig, "Socialist Revolution," 333.

24. Kay Ann Johnson draws a more nuanced picture of modern China and the socialist revolution in her book, yet she ultimately concludes that the Chinese socialist revolution was patriarchal and that the CCP failed to deliver its early May Fourth urban feminist promise. She offers no critical reflections regarding the global, national, economic, and social factors that contributed to the demise of May Fourth individualist feminism. Nor does she discuss the subsequent transformation of May Fourth liberal feminism into Chinese socialist feminism. Johnson claims to have avoided using her own field data from a long-term joint project in north China, partially because her interviews did not follow the "dominant trend" constructed in the book (Diamond, "Review"). Johnson's book's contradictions, between the historical materials she presents (or suppresses) and the monolithic conclusion she draws, reveal the heavy influence of the Cold War paradigm. See Johnson, *Women, the Family*; and Diamond, "Review."

25. Willis, "Radical Feminism"; and Hartmann, "Unhappy Marriage."

26. See the central arguments in Rubin, "Traffic in Women"; and Alexander and Taylor, "In Defence of 'Patriarchy.'"

27. See Ellen Willis's in-depth discussion of radical feminism in "Radical Feminism."

28. Stacey, *Patriarchy and Socialist Revolution*, 8–10.

29. Stacey, 10, 264–65.

30. Western socialist feminism emerged as a response to both left-wing male-centered practices and the rise of radical feminism. Theoretically, it attempted to incorporate radical feminist ahistorical and cultural ideas into the Marxist, or historical-materialist, approach, but the incompatible dualism rendered socialist feminism vulnerable and caused its further marginalization in the conservative Cold War environment of the 1970s and 1980s. For an in-depth discussion of the debate, see Sargent, *Women and Revolution*. For a critique of feminist dualism, see Young, "Beyond the Unhappy Marriage."

31. Stacey, *Patriarchy and Socialist Revolution*, 264.

32. Deng Yingchao's words translated and quoted in Davin, "Women in the Countryside," 263.

33. Meisner, "Significance of the Chinese Revolution," 6.

34. Davin, "Women in the Countryside," 264.

35. Rofel, *Other Modernities*, 14.

36. Davin, "Women in the Countryside," 262–64; Walker, "Party and Peasant Women," 75; Croll, *Feminism and Socialism*, 215.

37. Walker, "Party and Peasant Women," 75.

38. Croll, *Feminism and Socialism*, 215.

39. Stacey, *Patriarchy and Socialist Revolution*, 135.

40. Stacey, 262.

41. Stacey, 266.

42. Evans, "Language of Liberation." For the influence of radical feminism on post-Mao Chinese independent feminism, see my discussion in chapter 4.

43. This Cold War and liberal feminist approach, combined with the cine-feminist idea of "women's cinema," has seriously affected contemporary research on Chinese women directors. See my related discussion in the next section as well as chapters 2 and 3.

44. Johnston, "Women's Cinema as Counter-Cinema"; and "Dorothy Arzner: Critical Strategies," 7.

45. Mulvey, "Film, Feminism," 6.

46. Butler, *Women's Cinema*, 6.

47. Butler, 1–24, 119–23.

48. Butler, 119.

49. Butler, 20–21. For a detailed critique of Anglophone cine-feminism and a more elaborate discussion of Butler's revision, see "Introduction: Transnational Feminist Reconfiguration of Film Discourse and Women's Cinema," in Lingzhen Wang, *Chinese Women's Cinema*, 1–46.

50. See Dai, "Gender and Narration," 134. See also Cui, *Women through the Lens*, 177–80.

51. For a detailed discussion of socialist mainstream culture, see my introduction.

52. In the Republican era (1912–1949), the Nationalist government partially institutionalized liberal feminism, but its practice was heavily restrained by the limited development of capitalism and the middle class in modern China, by the right-wing conservative forces in the Nationalist Party, and by liberal feminist alienation from China's major rural and working-class population.

53. Li Dazhao, Chen Duxiu, Chen Wangdao, and others began introducing Marxist views on women's liberation during the May Fourth era. See Li Jingzhi, *Essays*, 156–58.

54. Tong and Kang, *Historical Development*, 66–67.

55. Li Jingzhi, *Essays*, 159.

56. Walker, "Party and Peasant Women," 58.

57. Li Jingzhi, *Essays*, 161–62.

58. Li Jingzhi, 240–44. Xiang was executed by the Nationalist government in 1928.

59. Mao, "Report on an Investigation," 44–46.

22222222

60. Li Jingzhi, *Essays*, 163. See also Croll, *Feminism and Socialism*, 185–86.

61. Walker, "Party and Peasant Women," 60. See also Barlow, "Theorizing Woman."

62. "Constitution," 21.

63. Cheng, "Women and Class Analysis," 65.

64. Cheng, 65.

65. Croll, *Feminism and Socialism*, 191.

66. Croll, 191–92.

67. Walker, "Party and Peasant Women," 60.

68. According to Kathy LeMons Walker, three main factors produced the women's movement's significant results: increased party support, newly developed methods and organizational forms to activate women, and war mobilization ("Party and Peasant Women," 61).

69. Croll, *Feminism and Socialism*, 199; Cheng, "Women and Class Analysis," 64.

70. Much of the published English-language scholarship focuses on the CCP's failure to accomplish its May Fourth feminist commitment. See Johnson, *Women, the Family*.

71. For the difficulty of launching a sustained and successful modern, proletarian revolution among Chinese peasants, see Saich, "Introduction," l–liv.

72. Tang Shuiqing, "Different Choices."

73. The practice of centering women's emancipation on marriage and divorce alone led to strong resistance from both male and female rural peasants during the Jiangxi Soviet period. See Tang Shuiqing, "Different Choices."

74. Walker, "Party and Peasant Women," 60.

75. "Circular 85."

76. Indeed, the CCP also "compromised" on class policy, including its relationship with rural elites, due to its focus on promoting economic growth during the Jiangxi Soviet period or in response to the need for a united front in the Sino-Japanese War. See Moise, *Modern China*, 80–82; Saich, "Introduction," xlvi–liv; Croll, *Feminism and Socialism*, 199.

77. Moise, *Modern China*, 82–84.

78. Walker, "Party and Peasant Women," 58–59.

79. Croll, *Feminism and Socialism*, 196–97.

80. Jackal, "Changes in Policy," 85–89.

81. Croll, *Feminism and Socialism*, 207–8.

82. Jackal, "Changes in Policy," 93–94.

83. Jackal, 83.

84. Croll, *Feminism and Socialism*, 216.

85. Jackal, "Changes in Policy," 110.

86. Croll, *Feminism and Socialism*, 203–4.

87. Dong Limin, "Getting Organized."

88. For detailed discussion of the limitations of Marxist theory on women's issues, see Sargent, *Women and Revolution*.

89. Lingzhen Wang, "Chinese Gender Morality Tale."

90. Stacey, *Patriarchy and Socialist Revolution*, 5, 10.

91. Sudo, "Concepts of Women's Rights," 475.

92. Tong and Kang, *Historical Development*, 133.

93. Moise, *Modern China*, 138–44; Lin, *Transformation of Chinese Socialism*, 60–83.

94. Tang Shuiqing, "Different Choices."

95. Lingzhen Wang, "Chinese Gender Morality Tale."

96. As Chinese socialist feminism interacted with other major political, economic, and social movements, it shifted trajectory in response to different mainstream priorities in different periods. See Tina Mai Chen, "They Love Battle Array," 263–82.

97. Volland, *Socialist Cosmopolitanism*.

98. Volland, 191.

99. Volland, 191.

100. Tina Mai Chen, "Internationalism and Cultural Experience."

101. Volland, *Socialist Cosmopolitanism*, 153–86.

102. Tina Mai Chen, "Female Icons, Feminist Iconography?," 284–89; and "Socialism, Aestheticized Bodies," 53–80.

103. For left-wing feminist figures turned socialist film directors, see chapters 1 and 2.

104. Zheng Wang, "Socialist Feminist Cultural Front," 827–49.

105. Tina Mai Chen, "Female Icons, Feminist Iconography?," 278.

106. Tina Mai Chen, 270.

107. Tina Mai Chen, 282.

108. Tina Mai Chen, 270.

109. Tina Mai Chen, 268, 292.

110. Glosser, *Li Fengjin*.

111. Zheng Wang, "Socialist Feminist Cultural Front," 836; Hershatter, *Gender of Memory*, 324.

112. Zheng Wang, *Finding Women*, 203.

113. Volland, *Socialist Cosmopolitanism*, 91.

114. Yingjin Zhang, *Chinese National Cinema*, 190–202.

115. Chen Bo'er, "Screenwriting and Film Directing," 65.

116. For a study of Chen Bo'er and her feminist endeavor, see Zheng Wang, "Chen Bo'er."

117. Chen Bo'er, "Screenwriting and Film Directing."

118. Zhong and Shu, "Films."

119. This argument is made by a Chinese film scholar, Zhang Jianyong. See Greg Lewis's discussion of Zhang's ideas in his article "History, Myth, and Memory," 165–66.

120. Lewis, 165.

121. Among the top CCP officials, Zhou Enlai, Deng Xiaoping, and Chen Yi are often singled out for their important roles in creating a more relaxed environment for socialist film production. See Zhong and Shu, "Films," 93–96.

122. For the specific roles Xia Yan and Chen Bo'er played in helping establish Chinese socialist New Cinema and policy, see Zheng Wang, *Finding Women*, 143–98.

123. Zhang Junxiang, *Special Ways*; Xia, "Several Issues."

124. Chen Huangmei, "Striving."

125. Hu Ke, *Critical History*, 200–204.

126. Farquhar and Berry, "Shadow Opera," 29, 33–37.

127. Both Mao Dun and Xia Yan, as cultural leaders of the 1950s, called for a new cinema with Chinese national forms. Xia Yan also articulated his ideas about national forms of Chinese cinema in his creative film scripts, such as *New Year's Sacrifice* (1956), *The Lin's Shop* (1959), and *The Revolutionary Family* (1961). See Chen Shan, "Socialist Classical Cinema," 230–32.

128. Chen Shan, "Formation of Socialist Classical Cinema," 231–32; Huang and Wang, "Exploration of the Cinematic."

129. Huang and Wang, "Exploration of the Cinematic," 211–12.

130. Zeitlin, "Operatic Ghosts on Screen," 220.

131. Lü, "Study of Shanghai Film," 280.

132. Marchetti, "Two Stage Sisters."

133. Tina Mai Chen, "Internationalism and Cultural Experience."

134. Lü, "Study of Shanghai Film."

135. Hong Hong, *Soviet Union's Influence*; Tina Mai Chen, "Internationalism and Cultural Experience."

136. Zhang Nuanxin, a pioneer of early post-Mao experimental cinema, was influenced by the French New Wave in the late 1950s when she was a student at the Beijing Film Academy. See chapter 6 for more on Zhang.

137. Huang and Wang, "Exploration of the Cinematic," 207; Meng, *Film Art*, 171.

138. Marchetti, "Two Stage Sisters."

139. Chen Bo'er is an earlier example. She received institutional endorsement for her filmmaking experience in Yan'an in the 1940s and later played an important role in helping to establish the first film studio in socialist China, the Northeast Film Studio.

140. In the history of Chinese film production up to the early 1950s, only one woman, Xie Caizhen (谢采真), had received credit as a film director, for only one film: *An Orphan's Cry* (1925). Little is known about Xie's filmmaking experience or her life in general; her involvement in the film appears to have been accidental. For a detailed discussion of Chinese women directors across different regions and eras, see Lingzhen Wang, "Chinese Women's Cinema."

Two. Articulating Embedded Feminist Agency in Socialist Mainstream Cinema

1. For a focused discussion of socialist mainstream culture, see the introduction and chapter 1.

2. See chapter 1 for a detailed discussion of the practice of socialist integrated and institutionalized feminism in modern China.

3. Song, *Life of My Mother*, 71–80.

4. Song, 86.

5. Xu and Song's "Collective Mutual Support" provides a detailed study of the Beijing public day care system in the 1950s.

6. Miller, "Changing the Subject," 104.

7. Petro, *Aftershocks of the New*, 40.

8. "Introduction: Transnational Feminist Reconfiguration of Film Discourse and Women's Cinema" (Lingzhen Wang, *Chinese Women's Cinema*, 1–46) offers a comprehensive discussion of female cinematic authorship.

9. Michel Foucault's "What Is an Author?" contains a useful discussion on authors' function and its institutional formation.

10. The idea that a modern female culture emerged during the May Fourth period and gradually disappeared as modern Chinese culture turned political was first articulated in the English-language scholarship of the 1980s on the Chinese socialist revolution and women's liberation. This idea was later embraced or echoed by post-Mao feminist scholars like Meng Yue and Dai Jinhua. See my discussion of the English-language scholarship of the 1980s in the introduction; see also Meng and Dai, *Emerging from the Historical*.

11. For scholarly discussions on Wang Ping, see Yuan, "History and Memory" and *Their Voices*, 30–32; Dai, *Cinema and Desire*, 134–35; Cui, *Women through the Lens*, 178–79; and Yang, "Revolution and Resonance." For an in-depth discussion of post-Mao feminist film criticism and its theoretical origins, see chapters 1, 6, and 7 in this book.

12. Dai, "Invisible Women," 276; see also Meng and Dai, *Emerging from the Historical*.

13. Dai, *Cinema and Desire*, 100.

14. Cui, *Women through the Lens*, 180.

15. Hua Mulan (花木兰) is a legendary female warrior from the Northern and Southern dynasties period of Chinese history. In the legend, Hua Mulan, disguised as a man, takes her aged father's place in the army and bravely fights foreign intruders. She was promoted to a general during the war and was later recognized by the emperor for her great achievements. But Mulan refuses any reward after the war. She resumes her female identity and returns to the domestic space. Hua Mulan became an inspiration for many Chinese women in both premodern and modern China. In the Chinese socialist revolution, Hua Mulan was evoked to encourage modern women to step outside the traditional family, devoting themselves to national independence and the liberation of women and the masses.

16. Dai, "Gender and Narration," 134; Cui, *Women through the Lens*, 179.

17. Dai, "Gender and Narration," 134.

18. Cui, *Women through the Lens*, 178.

19. Yuan, "History and Memory."

20. Unless otherwise noted, most information regarding Wang Ping's life is from Song, *Life of My Mother*.

21. Song, *Life of My Mother*, 12.

22. Scholars generally agree that the May Thirtieth Incident in Shanghai, which led to nationwide anti-imperialist demonstrations, marked the turn of Chinese intellectuals to the left and the end of the May Fourth Cultural Movement.

23. Song, *Life of My Mother*, 69.

24. Song, 69.

25. Chapter 3 gives a more intensive discussion on socialist gender difference.

26. Clark, *Chinese Cultural Revolution*, 134.

27. Clark, 155. For further discussion of the film and its popular status, see Clark, 142–43.

28. For an in-depth discussion of socialist experimental cinema, see also chapter 3.

29. For a genealogy of the relationship between revolution and love in Chinese literature, see Jianmei Liu, *Revolution Plus Love*.

30. Shi Yan, "Party, the Collective," 69.

31. Shi and Huang, *Story of Liubao Village*. According to Shi Yan, some of Wang's suggestions and revisions had already been incorporated into this screenplay version. See Shi Yan, "Party, the Collective."

32. Yuan, "History and Memory."

33. Wang Ping, "Director's Notes," 151.

34. Wang Ping, 160–61.

35. Shi Yan, "Party, the Collective," 69.

36. Wang Ping, "Director's Notes," 160.

37. Cui Shuqin compares Wang's *The Story of Liubao Village* with *The White-Haired Girl* and *The Red Detachment of Women* in her *Women through the Lens*, 179.

38. Louis Althusser first theorized this idea via his concept of interpellation. See Althusser, "Ideology."

Three. Socialist Experimentalism, Critical Revision, and Gender Difference

1. Andors, *Unfinished Liberation*; and Wolf, *Revolution Postponed*. See also the first section of chapter 1 for a detailed discussion of the West's conventional wisdom about socialist revolution and Chinese women's liberation.

2. See chapter 1 for a more detailed discussion.

3. For detailed arguments, see Dai, "Invisible Women"; Yuan, "Feminism"; and Cui, *Women through the Lens*. Also see chapter 2 for a discussion of additional issues raised by post-Mao Chinese feminist film scholars.

4. For a discussion of the apprenticeship structure in Western authoritarian fiction, see Suleiman, *Authoritarian Fictions*, 64–100; on the apprenticeship structure in early Soviet films, see Bordwell, *Narration*, 235–36; and on Chinese socialist film and its apprenticeship structure, see Berry, "Writing on Blank Paper."

5. During the Cultural Revolution, when Jiang Qing took control of artistic production, women leaders appeared often in Chinese literature and film.

6. Berry, *Postsocialist Cinema*, 49.

7. See my discussion of socialist experimental cinema in chapter 1.

8. Berry, *Postsocialist Cinema*, 22–65.

9. Jin, *Career Life*, 73–84.

10. For examples, see Tao Jin's (淘金) *A Nurse's Diary* (护士日记, 1957), Lin Nong's (林农) *Daughter of the Party* (党的女儿, 1958), and Shui Hua's (水华) *Revolutionary Family* (革命家庭, 1960).

11. Wei, "Transformations," 468.

12. See my discussion in chapter 1 on socialist mainstream experimental cinema.

13. Jin, *Career Life*, 79.

14. Dong Kena, "Film Art and Me," 14.

15. Dong Kena, 16.

16. Ban Wang, "Desire and Pleasure."

17. Ban Wang, 136.

18. This question about loneliness is in the original story, showing the sensitivity of the original author. But the overall treatment of the question is different in the story than in the film. First, the question is rather isolated and functions to highlight Hui sao's courage in staying. Consequently, in the original story, Li answers her own question, stating that Hui sao does not appear to be lonely at all. Second, the question is not tied to Hui sao's sense of self and belonging as a peasant woman and thus is cut off from any further exploration of her contribution to diversifying the socialist imaginary.

19. See chapter 5 of Cai, *Revolution and Its Narratives*, 251–306.

20. See, for example, Mayfair Mei-hui Yang, "From Gender Erasure."

21. Berry, "Sexual Difference."

22. Berry, 34.

23. Berry, 36.

24. Berry, 37.

25. Berry, 42.

26. Mayfair Mei-hui Yang, "From Gender Erasure."

27. For additional discussion of conformity in socialist cultural practice, see the last section of chapter 2.

28. In the late 1980s, some Chinese female directors chose a psychological approach to women's representation to essentialize female difference and consciousness, eclipsing sociohistorical contexts for gender constructions. See chapter 7 for a detailed discussion.

Four. Feminist Practice after Mao

1. Anonymous, "Female Directors."

2. See also Berry, "China's New 'Women's Cinema,'" 10.

3. Deng, "Speech at Opening Ceremony," 10.

4. Kang Liu, "Subjectivity, Marxism"; Xudong Zhang, "On Some Motifs."

5. Zhu Guangqian, "On Human Nature"; Zhou Yang, "Exploration of Several Issues."

6. Xing, "How to Discern Humanism."

7. Xing, "How to Discern Humanism."

8. Tuo, "Summary of Discussions."

9. Liu Zaifu, "On the Subjectivity"; Tuo, "Summary of Discussions."

10. Zhong, *Masculinity Besieged?*, 155.

11. Chapter 5 of this book further discusses the topic.

12. Honig and Hershatter, *Personal Voices*.

13. Barlow, "Socialist Modernization," 271.

14. Barlow, 255.

15. For a detailed discussion of women writers in the early postsocialist era, see Lingzhen Wang, "Chinese Gender Morality Tale."

16. See Li Xiaojiang's discussion of Zhang Jie's *The Ark* in *Eve's Exploration*, 295–301.

17. In chapter 6 I offer a brief discussion of personal, subject-oriented women's cinema in the early post-Mao era.

18. Li Xiaojiang, *Eve's Exploration*, 302–11.

19. Li gives similar answers in many of her publications. See *Eve's Exploration*, 3.

20. Li Xiaojiang, *Toward Women*, 7–9.

21. Li Xiaojiang, 8.

22. Li Xiaojiang, 9.

23. Zheng Wang, "Maoism, Feminism, and the UN Conference on Women."

24. Barlow, "Socialist Modernization."

25. Li Xiaojiang, "Progress of Humanity."

26. Li Xiaojiang; page references in internal citations hereafter are to the Chinese version of the article.

27. Barlow, *Question of Women*, 64–126.

28. See also Meng and Dai, *Emerging from the Historical*.

29. Li Xiaojiang, *Eve's Exploration*, 31.

30. Irigaray, *This Sex*.

31. Li Xiaojiang, "Women's Enlightenment," 282.

32. In chapter 5 I enter into great detail about the masculine nature of post-Mao mainstream discourse. For Li's critique of gender blindness in male intellectuals' works, see also Barlow, "Socialist Modernization," 281–82.

33. Chapter 1 includes a concentrated argument on the topic.

34. Geng, "Preliminary Research," 48.

35. Geng, 43–44, 48–49.

36. Geng, 45–48.

37. Barlow, "Socialist Modernization," 255.

38. Barlow, 258.

39. Geng, "Historical Examination," 83.

40. Lin, "Finding a Language," 15.

41. Geng, "Historical Examination," 83.

42. Lin, "Finding a Language," 11.

43. Lin, Liu, and Jin, "China," 108.

44. Lin, "Finding a Language," 12.

45. Lin, 11.

46. Min, "Awakening Again," 283.

47. Min, 283.

48. Min, 283.

49. Li Xiaojiang, "Responding to Tani Barlow," 175. I have slightly modified the translation.

50. Li Xiaojiang, *Eve's Exploration*, 32.

51. Deng, "Speech at Opening Ceremony," 11–12.

52. Although Hu Fuming's article "Practice Is the Sole Criterion for Measuring the Truth" was published on May 11, 1978, in the *Guangming Daily*, the initial discussion of the topic can be traced to an article published in the *People's Daily* on March 26 by Zhang Cheng: "There Is Only One Criterion."

53. Lin, Liu, and Jin, "China," 110; Barlow, "Socialist Modernization," 254.

54. Barlow, "Socialist Modernization," 269.

55. Barlow, 274.

56. Ma, "Notes," 63. See also my discussion of the topic in chapter 5.

57. Barlow, "Socialist Modernization," 271.

58. Barlow gives an in-depth analysis of Li Zehou's influence on Li Xiaojiang and their shared position, as well as their dialogues in the 1980s (Barlow, "Socialist Modernization," 268–95).

59. Li Xiaojiang, *Sex/Gender Gap*, 34. The quoted English translation is from Lin, Liu, and Jin, "China," 113.

60. Yuan, "Feminism." See also my discussion of Yuan Ying's essay in chapter 6.

61. Li Xiaojiang, *Eve's Exploration*, 1–3.

62. Meng and Dai, *Emerging from the Historical*, 268–69; translation by Dongchao Min. See Min, "Awakening Again," 285.

63. See Zheng, *On Paying a Price*, chap. 9.

64. Zheng, 69. See also Mayfair Mei-hui Yang's translation and discussion of the paragraph in "From Gender Erasure," 54.

65. Min, "Awakening Again."

66. Li Xiaojiang, "Responding to Tani Barlow," 176.

67. Li Xiaojiang, *Selected Works*.

68. Li Xiaojiang, "Progress of Humanity," 143.

69. Hartmann and Markusen, "Contemporary Marxist Theory"; Lin and Paczuska, "Socialism Needs Feminism."

70. See Kuhn and Wolpe, *Feminism and Materialism*; Sargent, *Women and Revolution*; Mitchell, *Women*. Additionally, Willis provides an in-depth discussion of radical feminism and its transformations (Willis, "Radical Feminism").

71. My chapter 1 discusses the radical feminist take on socialism and Chinese women's liberation extensively.

72. Willis, "Radical Feminism."

73. Harding, "From China, with Disdain," 258.

74. Harvey, *Brief History of Neoliberalism*.

75. See chapter 1 for a detailed discussion on the topic.

76. Zhong, "Why Reflections."

77. Li Xiaojiang, "The Progress of Humanity and Women's Liberation," 148–51.

78. Li Xiaojiang, "On the Characteristics," 28–29.

1. The "Gang of Four" refers to the group that rose to power during the Cultural Revolution to control most political propaganda and cultural production. The "Four" were Jiang Qing (Mao's wife), Zhang Chunqiao, Yao Wenyuan, and Wang Hongwen. They were arrested in October 1976 after Mao passed away.

2. Yingjin Zhang, *Chinese National Cinema*, 226.

3. Clark, "Two Hundred Flowers"; Xia Hong, "Film Theory," 36.

4. Xia Hong, "Film Theory," 36.

5. Xia Hong, 36.

6. Zhang and Li, "Modernization of Film Language."

7. I will discuss the conflicting ideas in the article and the different positions the two authors took in their cultural practices in chapter 6.

8. Li Suyuan, "Dialogues," 52.

9. Zhang and Li, "Modernization of Film Language," 52.

10. Luo, Li, and Xu, *Chinese Film Theory*, 2:3.

11. Xia Hong, "Film Theory," 43.

12. Xia Hong, 42–43.

13. See similar arguments in Hu, *Critical History*, 221.

14. Xia Hong, "Film Theory," 47–52.

15. Yuan, "Mainstream Trend," 29.

16. Ma, "Notes," 63.

17. For more recent scholarly works assessing the artistic innovation and creativity of cultural practices during the Cultural Revolution, see Clark, *Chinese Cultural Revolution*; Schmalzer, *People's Peking Man*; Andrews, "Cultural Revolution"; Roberts, *Maoist Model Theatre*; and Mittler, *Continuous Revolution*.

18. Eagleton, "From the Polis."

19. Chang, "Mechanics of State Propaganda," 9.

20. Geneviève Sellier particularly discusses the relationships among French film criticism, the New Wave, and the Cold War divisions in *Masculinity Singular*, 41.

21. Hess, "La politique."

22. Sellier, *Masculinity Singular*, 41.

23. Sellier, 42.

24. Sellier, 129.

25. Sellier, 2.

26. Sellier, 2.

27. Hess, "La politique."

28. See Sellier's discussion of other socioculturally oriented studies of the New Wave in *Masculinity Singular*, 4–6.

29. Sellier, 5.

30. Hess, "La politique."

31. A Soviet doctrine named after Andrei Aleksandrovich Zhdanov whose two main tenets were (1) stringent governmental control over the arts and (2) an uncompromising anti-Western disposition.

32. Sellier, *Masculinity Singular*, 5.

33. Sellier, 6.

34. Sellier, "French New Wave Cinema," 153.

35. Sellier, *Masculinity Singular*, 28–33.

36. Giroud, *La nouvelle vague*, 322.

37. Xueping Zhong discusses the related topics in *Masculinity Besieged?*, 155. See also chapter 4 of this book for a more detailed discussion.

38. Sellier, "French New Wave Cinema," 153.

39. Sellier, 158.

40. Sellier, *Masculinity Singular*, 5, 29.

41. Li Suyuan, "Dialogues," 53.

42. Hess, "La politique."

43. Sellier, *Masculinity Singular*, 27.

44. For a more detailed commentary on the Fourth Congress, see Hegel, "'Golden Age.'"

45. Hegel, 386.

46. Hegel, 386.

47. Yao, "Chinese New Cinema," 215.

48. Leenhouts, "Culture against Politics" (emphasis mine).

49. Yau, "*Yellow Earth*," 31 (emphasis mine).

50. Sun and Li, *One Hundred Years*, 66–68.

51. Derlic and Meisner's "Politics, Scholarship" offers a critical analysis of the wholesale condemnation of socialism in Chinese history in both post-Mao China and the United States.

52. Sun and Li, *One Hundred Years*, 66.

53. On privatization, see Yingjin Zhang, *Chinese National Cinema*, 238–39; on avant-gardism, see Sun and Li, *One Hundred Years of Chinese Cinema*, 66–67.

54. Sun and Li, *One Hundred Years of Chinese Cinema*, 67.

55. Sun and Li, 68.

56. Sun and Li, 68.

57. Dai Jinhua, in her discussion of Xie Jin's revolutionary melodrama *Oh Cradle!* (1978), insightfully points out that the film skillfully returns a female revolutionary fighter from the battlefront to a family setting, where maternal instincts and love prevail. See Dai, "Gender and Narration."

58. Dai, "Gender and Narration," 127.

59. Zhong, *Masculinity Besieged?*, 155.

60. According to Dai, these female characters have little to do with historical women, as they function mostly as empty signifiers for male intellectuals to contemplate China's cultural contradictions and problems. "Gender and Narration," 128–29.

61. See Rey Chow's discussion of Chen Kaige's films in *Primitive Passions*, 44–47.

62. Chow discusses Zhang Yimou's films in *Primitive Passions*, 47–48.

63. I discuss Pang's *Building a New China* in chapter 1.

64. For more discussions about the difference between Chinese cultural practice in the 1980s and the leftist cultural movement in 1930s Shanghai in terms of the relationship between politics and aesthetics, see Pang, *Building a New China*, 6–10.

65. Yao, "Chinese New Cinema," 208. See also Dai, "Severed Bridge."

66. On the film's success, see Dai, "Severed Bridge," 59; on the transition to commercial production, see Yao, "Chinese New Cinema," 199.

67. Yau, "*Yellow Earth*," 31.

68. Butler, *Women's Cinema*, 58–59; Karen Hollinger's discussion of Luis Buñuel's experimental film *Un chien andalou* (1929) in her *Feminist Film Studies*, 69; and Sellier, *Masculinity Singular*.

69. Yingjin Zhang, *Chinese National Cinema*, 240.

70. Yingjin Zhang, 240.

71. See chapter 7 for a related discussion.

Six. Alternative Experimental Cinema

1. See my discussion on this topic in chapter 5.

2. He and Xu, "Return to the 1980s." See also Zha, *Eighties*.

3. Wei, "Women's Trajectories."

4. For more information regarding the specific training Fourth Generation Chinese filmmakers received at the Beijing Film Academy in the 1950s and 1960s, see Yang, "Perseverance and Tranquility."

5. Zhang and Li, "Modernization of Film Language."

6. See chapter 5 for a detailed discussion.

7. Luo, Li, and Xu, *Chinese Film Theory*, 3.

8. Zhang and Li, "Modernization of Film Language," 46–47.

9. See my discussions on the connections between the rise of Western theory, the emergence of socially detached individual subjectivity, and the formation of a masculine aesthetic in chapter 5.

10. Zhou and Li, "Important Film Aesthetic." See also Hess, "La politique."

11. Li Tuo, "Cinematic Aesthetic of Screenplay."

12. Zhang Nuanxin, "Director's Notes on *Drive to Win*."

13. Ye, "Experimentation."

14. Zhang Nuanxin, "Let Historical Reality," 512.

15. Zhang Nuanxin, "Let Historical Reality," 512.

16. Zhang Nuanxin, "Let Historical Reality," 511.

17. Wu Guanping, "Experiencing Life."

18. Zhen, "Self-Consciousness to Self-Freedom," 129.

19. Hess, "La politique."

20. See the discussion of early post-Mao women's autobiographical stories in chapter 4.

21. See chapter 4 for my discussion of the gendered personal.

22. Hess, "La politique."

23. Berry, "China's New 'Women's Cinema.'"

24. Zhang Nuanxin, "Director's Notes on *Drive to Win*," 184–85.

25. Zhang Nuanxin, 183.

26. Zhang Nuanxin, "*Drive to Win*," 82–83.

27. Han, "Spark," 32–33.

28. Zhang Nuanxin, "*Drive to Win*," 82–83.

29. Zhang Nuanxin, "Director's Notes on *Drive to Win*," 190.

30. Han, "Spark," 33.

31. Han, 32–33.

32. Ye, "Experimentation," 64.

33. Ye, 64.

34. Zhou and Li, "Important Film Aesthetic"; Li Suyuan, "Dialogues," 53.

35. Berry, "China's New 'Women's Cinema,'" 13–19.

36. Kaplan, "Problematizing Cross-Cultural Analysis." This article was translated into Chinese by Yin Yao and published in *Contemporary Cinema* (当代电影), vol. 1 (1991).

37. Dai, "Invisible Women," 276–77 (page numbers refer to the English version).

38. Berry, "China's New 'Women's Cinema,'" 16–18; Dai, "Invisible Women," 276–77; Kaplan, "Problematizing Cross-Cultural Analysis," 49–50.

39. The study includes a short introduction, a research essay, and three interviews, all published in *Camera Obscura* 18 (1988): 4–41.

40. Berry, "China's New 'Women's Cinema,'" 5.

41. Berry, 6.

42. Berry, 5, 8.

43. Berry, 7 (emphasis added).

44. Berry, 8.

45. See my in-depth discussion of Judith Stacey and the influence of Western Cold War ideology on her works in chapter 1.

46. For a more detailed discussion of shot/reverse-shot in socialist cinema and Berry's argument, see chapter 3.

47. Berry, "China's New 'Women's Cinema,'" 16.

48. Berry, 16.

49. Berry, 17.

50. Berry, 17.

51. Berry, 15–16.

52. See my following discussion on Dai Jinhua in this chapter.

53. As quoted in Berry, "China's New 'Women's Cinema,'" 9.

54. See a related discussion on the socialist configuration of differences in chapter 2.

55. Kaplan, "Problematizing Cross-Cultural Analysis," 44.

56. Kaplan, 47.

57. Kaplan, 47.

58. Kaplan, 45.

59. Kaplan, 49.

60. Kaplan, 49.

61. Kaplan, 49.

62. Kaplan, 49.

63. Kaplan, 48.

64. Kaplan, 49.

65. Kaplan, 48.

66. Kaplan, 50.

67. Kaplan, 50.

68. Chen Juan, "'Feminism and New Era Films.'"

69. Yuan, "Feminism," 46.

70. Yuan, 49. Post-Mao feminist scholars like Li Xiaojiang had already made the argument about the Chinese women's liberation movement's dependency. See my discussion in chapter 4.

71. Yuan, 48.

72. Yuan, 46, 48.

73. See chapter 4 for an in-depth discussion of Li's ideas.

74. Yuan, "Feminism," 50–51.

75. Yuan, 47.

76. For a discussion of radical feminism, see chapter 1.

77. See the introduction and chapter 4 for a detailed discussion on this topic.

78. Yuan, "Feminism," 51.

79. Yuan, 52.

80. Yuan, 46–53.

81. Dai, "Invisible Women," 256.

82. Dai, "Gender and Narration," 100.

83. Kaplan, "Problematizing Cross-Cultural Analysis," 47.

84. See chapter 7 for a related discussion on Dai's theoretical position.

85. Dai, "Invisible Women," 270.

86. Dai, "Invisible Women," 260.

87. Dai also singles out Japanese-occupied Shanghai in the 1940s as another historical period and place in which female literary style and voice developed.

88. Emerging as a radically new feminist cultural theory at the end of the 1960s, cine-feminism and its early advocates like Laura Mulvey played an inestimable role in introducing poststructuralist, Lacanian psychoanalysis into cultural and film studies.

89. Dai, "Gender and Narration," 134.

90. Dai, "Invisible Women," 276.

91. Dai, 277.

92. Dai, 277

93. Dai, 277.

94. Zhang Yiwu, "Zhang Nuanxin."

95. For a more detailed discussion regarding the topic, see chapter 4.

96. See chapter 5 for a more specific discussion.

97. Zhang Manling, "Beautiful Place."

98. Lingzhen Wang, "Reproducing the Self."

99. This critique is voiced by one of the main characters in the story.

100. Zhang Manling, "Beautiful Place," 135.

101. Zhang Manling, 132.

102. Zhang Manling, 130–31.

103. See my detailed discussion of the influence of women's autobiographical literature on women's cinema in post-Mao China in Lingzhen Wang, "Female Cinematic Imaginary."

104. Zhang Nuanxin, "Director's Notes on *Sacrificed Youth*."

105. Zhang Nuanxin, "Director's Notes on *Sacrificed Youth*."

106. Zhang Nuanxin, 85.

107. Zhang Nuanxin, 85.

108. Ye, "Experimentation," 63.

109. Zhang Yiwu, "Zhang Nuanxin."

110. Zhang Yiwu, 46.

111. On repression, see Yuan, "Feminism"; on the girl's awakening, see Dai, "Invisible Women," 277.

112. Yang, "From Gender Erasure."

113. Han, "Three Theoretical Resources," 34.

114. Yao, "Chinese New Cinema," 214–15.

115. Yao, 215–16.

116. See Ba Jin's essays composed from 1978 to 1986 and collected in *Random Thoughts*.

117. It is no accident that in this scene Zhang also evokes Li Zehou, a well-known scholar of the early 1980s who paved the way for the theoretical and critical articulation of liberal and individual(istic) subjectivity in post-Mao China and who titled his influential 1981 essay "Go Your Own Way" (or "Let Others Talk"; 走自己的路).

118. Kuoshu, *Celluloid China*, 302.

119. Zhang Yiwu, "Zhang Nuanxin."

120. Zhang Nuanxin, "Getting Close to [Social] Reality."

121. Zhang Nuanxin, "Getting Close to [Social] Reality."

122. Wu Guanping, "Experiencing Life," 65.

123. Wu Guanping, 65.

124. Wu Guanping, 62.

125. Wu Guanping, 62.

126. Yang, "Perseverance and Tranquility," 40.

127. Wu Guanping, "Experiencing Life," 63–64.

128. Wu Guanping, 63.

Seven. The Black Velvet Aesthetic

1. Qu, "Female Image," 37.

2. Ren, "Return to Eden," 63.

3. Dai, "Invisible Women," 44.

4. Xie Fei made this comment in a group interview conducted by the editors of *Contemporary Cinema* on October 6, 2008. See Xie, "Filmmaking Trends," 6.

5. See my discussion of the debate in chapter 4.

6. Yao, "Chinese New Cinema," 219; Dai, "Broken Bridge."

7. Dai, "Broken Bridge," 59. See chapter 5 for a detailed discussion of the topic.

8. Chen and Zou, *Chinese Cinema*, 507–16.

9. Dai, "Invisible Women," 44.

10. Berry, "China's New 'Women's Cinema,'" 18.

11. See my discussion of the emergence of sexual difference in the China of the 1980s in chapter 4.

12. Wei, "Encoding of Female Subjectivity," 177–78.

13. Sun and Li, *One Hundred Years*, 68.

14. Yao, "Chinese New Cinema," 215. See also my discussion in chapter 5.

15. The title of this section, "Culture against Politics," is inspired by Mark Leenhouts's essay on Root-Seeking literature titled "Culture against Politics."

16. Zhang et al., "Ardent Pursuit of Art."

17. Huang Shuqin, "Female Director's (Self-)Statement," 69.

18. Shi Faming, "Life Perceived."

19. See chapter 4 for more on the rise of female consciousness in China in the mid-1980s.

20. Shao, "Agony of Suppressing."

21. See my detailed discussion of the essay in chapter 6.

22. Dai, "'Human, Woman, Demon.'"

23. See my discussion of Dai's poststructuralist approach to Chinese women's cinema and its problems in chapter 6.

24. The direct translation of the original Chinese term 女性电影 is "female film," but it means "women's cinema" in English, referring to films directed by female directors. The translator of Dai's article has translated it as "feminist film," which also makes sense because in Dai's article, other female directors' films cannot be counted as real female films. For Dai, it seems, a true female film is not simply a film by a woman; it also needs to contain feminist ideas.

25. This discrepancy is discussed by Ann E. Kaplan in her analysis of Hu Mei's *Army Nurse*. See the discussion of Kaplan's essay in chapter 6.

26. Laura Mulvey and Claire Johnston represent the two different approaches, respectively. See chapter 1 for a detailed discussion.

27. My translation here differs slightly from Kirk Denton's. Dai's article stresses the anti-male-pleasure character of Western feminist cinema rather than feminist pleasure derived in destruction.

28. See my discussion of Dai's position in chapters 2 and 6.

29. Dai, "Gender and Narration," 100.

30. Yuan Ying believes that female consciousness objectively exists and that social revolution does not help reveal or express it ("Feminism," 49).

31. See chapter 4 for a detailed discussion of post-Mao feminism.

32. Xu, "Fleeting Time," 18–19.

33. Xu, 18; Tong, "Another Discussion," 10–11.

34. Tong, "Another Discussion," 10. Tong also uses "the black screen effect" (黑布幕效果) to refer to the cinematic effect of *Woman Demon Human* on the silver screen (11).

35. Xu, "Fleeting Time," 18–19.

36. Xu, 7.

37. Huang Zuolin, "General Comments."

38. Chi, "Attempt of the Xieyi," 79.

39. Hu, *Chinese Opera*, 85.

40. Zhang and Gu, *Huang Shuqin*, 127.

41. Chi, "Attempt of the Xieyi," 79.

42. Huang Zuolin, "General Comments."

43. Huang Zuolin, "Full Story," 51.

44. Tian, "On Mr. Huang Zuolin's."

45. Tian, 22.

46. Xu, "Fleeting Time," 7–8.

47. Huang Shuqin, "Director's Reflections."

48. Huang Shuqin, 92.

49. The term "sedimented cultural mentality" comes from Li Zehou's concept of "historical sedimentation" (历史积淀说) as he discussed "cultural psychology" in the mid-1980s. See Li Zehou, "Regarding Confucianism."

50. Yang and Ge, "Quest for Self."

51. Zhou Xia, "Interview with Huang Shuqin," 88. See also Yang and Ge, "Quest for Self," 103.

52. The biographical sketch is based mostly on Wang Zhongde's published biography of Pei Yanling and Pei's interviews on TV. Wang got to know Pei in the early 1960s when he worked as a scriptwriter for Chinese opera. See Wang Zhongde, "Pei Yanling I Know."

53. Zeitlin, "Operatic Ghosts on Screen," 220.

54. Tian Ge's Beijing TV interview of Pei, "Sentimental Pei Yanling."

55. Wang Zhongde, "Pei Yanling I Know."

56. Wang Zhongde, "Pei Yanling I Know."

57. Huang Shuqin, "Annotated Film Script," 6, 10, 15, 16, 19.

58. Huang Shuqin, "Director's Reflections," 92.

59. Wang Zhongde, "Pei Yanling I Know."

60. Radical liberalism and individualism are usually traced back to the May Fourth Movement. In the post-Mao era, they are represented by intellectuals like Liu Xiaobo. See Liu Xiaobo, "Dialogue with Li Zehou," 54. Radical individualism critiques socialist collectivism by equating Chinese socialist ideology with traditional Chinese feudalism and superstitiousness.

61. Li Zehou best represents the rational liberalism of the 1980s through his philosophical and aesthetic theories. In the mid- and late 1980s, he advocated using the concept of "historical sedimentation" (历史积淀说) as a structure of "cultural psychology" (文化心理结构), promoted rational economic development and the renovation of Confucianism, and insisted on gradual reform rather than revolution as the way of moving forward. See Li Zehou, "Regarding Confucianism." For a critique of Li's repudiation of the concrete social reality of his time and his promotion of abstract ideas transcending historical time and space, see Zou, "Introversion and Unbalance."

62. The China Confucius Foundation was established in 1984, and *Confucius Studies* published its first issue in 1986. In 1986, Du Weiming (杜维明) began teaching Confucian philosophy at Peking University and contributed greatly to the revival

of Confucianism in China. Also in 1986, three influential scholarly articles were published: Li Zehou, "Regarding Confucianism"; Fang, "We Must Pay Attention"; and Bao, "Confucian Thought and Modernization." In winter 1986, "modern neo-Confucian thought" was established as a major national research project. In 1987, the China Confucius Foundation and the Institute of East Asian Philosophies in Singapore co-organized a large-scale international conference on Confucianism (儒学国际讨论会) in Qufu, the hometown of Confucius. See Li Zonggui, "Origin."

63. For a brief history of liberalism in modern China, particularly the argument for the similarities between liberalism and traditional world views like Confucianism, see Jenco, "Chinese Liberalism."

64. Dai, "Woman's Predicament," 161.

65. The critique of the Maoist "stronger women and weaker men" phenomenon was further developed in the 1990s. Zheng Yefu is best known for arguing for the return of gender difference and gendered division of labor in his article from 1994, "Sociological Reflection on Gender Equality." In 1995, he published *On Paying a Price* (代价论), approaching the issue from Western anthropological and free-market perspectives. See chapter 4 for a detailed discussion; see also Mayfair Mei-hui Yang's translation and discussion of the paragraph in "From Gender Erasure," 54.

66. Yang and Ge, "Quest for Self," 104.

67. Liu and Zhou, *Historical Materials*. The reference number for the first "Zhong Kui Marrying Off His Sister" opera show is 302·6.

68. Wang Zhongde, "Pei Yanling I Know."

69. Wang Zhongde, "Pei Yanling I Know."

70. Yang and Ge, "Quest for Self," 102.

71. Huang Shuqin, "From Silence to Expression."

72. Yang and Ge, "Quest for Self," 104–5.

73. Xu, "Fleeting Time," 18.

74. Yang and Ge, "Quest for Self," 104.

75. Huang Shuqin, "Annotated Film Script," 20.

76. Huang Shuqin, "Unique Perspective."

77. Huang Shuqin, 159–60.

78. Huang Shuqin, "Annotated Film Script," 21.

79. Zhu, *Chinese Cinema*, 76.

80. For a brief comparative study of the novel, the film, and a later TV series on Zhang Yuliang's life, see Sun, "From Biography to Film."

81. Shi Qing, "Disappointment."

82. Huang Shuqin, "Unique Perspective," 157.

83. Huang Shuqin, 157–58.

84. See chapter 5 for a specific examination of the linkage.

85. Yang and Ge, "Quest for Self," 112–13.

86. Yang and Ge, 113–14.

87. *Contemporary Cinema* (当代电影) 4 (1986): 111–14. For more discussions about the symposium, see chapter 4.

BIBLIOGRAPHY

Alexander, Sally, and Barbara Taylor. "In Defence of 'Patriarchy.'" *New Statesman*, February 1, 1980.

Althusser, Louis. "Ideology and Ideological State Apparatuses." In *Lenin and Philosophy and Other Essays*, edited by Louis Althusser, 127–88. New York: Monthly Review, 1971.

Andors, Phyllis. *The Unfinished Liberation of Chinese Women, 1949–1980*. Bloomington: Indiana University Press, 1983.

Andrews, Julia F. "The Art of the Cultural Revolution." In *Art in Turmoil: The Chinese Cultural Revolution, 1966–1976*, edited by Richard King, 27–57. Vancouver: University of British Columbia Press, 2010.

Anonymous. "Female Directors and Women's Cinema" [女导演与女性电影]. *Contemporary Cinema* [当代电影] 4 (1986): 111–14.

Bai, Ronnie. "Dances with Brecht: Huang Zuolin and His Xieyi Theater." *Comparative Drama* 33, no. 3 (1999): 339–64.

Ba Jin 巴金. *Random Thoughts* [随想录]. 5 vols. Beijing: Renmin chubanshe, 1986.

Bao Zunxin 包遵信. "Confucian Thought and Modernization" [儒家思想和现代化]. *Beijing Social Sciences* [北京社会科学] 3 (1986): 86–96.

Barlow, Tani. *The Question of Chinese Women in Chinese Feminism*. Durham, NC: Duke University Press, 2004.

———. "Socialist Modernization and the Market Feminism of Li Xiaojiang." In *The Question of Women in Chinese Feminism*, 253–301. Durham, NC: Duke University Press, 2004.

———. "Theorizing Woman: Funu, Guojia, Jiating [Chinese Women, Chinese State, Chinese Family]." *Genders* 10 (spring 1991): 132–60.

Baumbach, Nico, Damon R. Young, and Genevieve Yue, eds. "The Cultural Logic of Contemporary Capitalism," special issue, *Social Text* 34, no. 2 (2016).

———. "Introduction: For a Political Critique of Culture." *Social Text* 34, no. 2 (2016): 1–20.

Berry, Chris. "China's New 'Women's Cinema.'" *Camera Obscura* 18 (1988): 8–19.

———. *Postsocialist Cinema in Post-Mao China: The Cultural Revolution after the Cultural Revolution*. New York: Routledge, 2004.

———. "Sexual Difference and the Viewing Subject in *Li Shuangshuang* and *The In-Laws*." In *Perspectives on Chinese Cinema*, Cornell University East Asia Papers 39, edited by Chris Berry, 32–46. Ithaca, NY: China-Japan Program, Cornell University, 1985.

———. "Writing on Blank Paper: The Classical Cinema before 1976 as a Didactic Paradigm." In *Postsocialist Cinema in Post-Mao China*, edited by David Bordwell, 27–36. New York: Routledge, 2004.

Bordwell, David. *Narration in the Fiction Film*. Madison: University of Wisconsin Press, 1985.

Butler, Alison. *Women's Cinema: The Contested Screen*. London: Wallflower, 2002.

Cai, Xiang. *Revolution and Its Narratives: China's Socialist Literary and Cultural Imaginaries, 1949–1966*. Translated and edited by Rebecca E. Karl and Xueping Zhong. Durham, NC: Duke University Press, 2016. For original Chinese reference, see Cai Xiang 蔡翔. [革命/叙述：中国社会主义文学—文化想象 (1949–1966)]. Beijing: Peking University Press, 2010.

Chang, Julian. "The Mechanics of State Propaganda: The People's Republic of China and the Soviet Union in the 1950s." In *New Perspectives on State Socialism of China*, edited by Timothy Cheek and Tony Saich, 76–111. New York: M. E. Sharpe, 1997.

Cheek, Timothy. "Chinese Socialism as Vernacular Cosmopolitanism." *Frontiers of History in China* 9, no. 1 (2014): 102–24.

Chen Bo'er 陈波儿. "Screenwriting and Film Directing: The Preparation Work for Making Feature Films" [故事片从无到有的编导工作]. In *Research Materials for Chinese Film Studies, 1949–1979*, vol. 1 [中国电影研究资料，1949–1979，上], edited by Wu Di 吴迪, 58–66. Beijing: Wenhua yu yishu chubanshe, 2006.

Chen Huangmei 陈荒煤. "Striving for a Thriving Film Screenplay Production" [为繁荣电影剧本创作而奋斗]. In *Research Materials for Chinese Film Studies, 1949–1979*, vol. 2 [中国电影研究资料，1949–1979，中], edited by Wu Di 吴迪, 3–19. Beijing: Wenhua yu yishu chubanshe, 2006.

Chen Jingliang 陈景亮 and Zou Jianwen 邹建文. *Chinese Cinema of the New Era, II* [新时期中国电影，下]. Vol. 3 of *A Selection of Chinese Films Over One Hundred Years* [百年中国电影精选]. Beijing: Zhongguo shenhui kexue chubanshe, 2005.

Chen Juan 陈娟. "'Feminism and New Era Films': A Research Survey Essay" ["女性主义与新时期电影"：研究述评]. *Yunmeng Journal* [云梦学刊] 3 (2000): 27–29.

Chen Shan 陈山. "The Formation of Socialist Classical Cinema: The Maturation of Chinese Film Theory in the Fifties and Sixties" [经典的建构：五六十年代中国电影理论的成]. In *Fifty Years of New China Cinema* [新中国电影 50 年], edited by Li Suyuan 郦苏元, Hu Ke 胡克, and Yang Yuanying 杨远婴, 219–36. Beijing: Guangbo xueyuan chubanshe, 2000.

Chen, Tina Mai. "Female Icons, Feminist Iconography? Socialist Rhetoric and Women's Agency in 1950s China." *Gender and History* 15, no. 2 (2003): 268–95.

———. "Internationalism and Cultural Experience: Soviet Films and Popular Chinese Understandings of the Future in the 1950s." *Cultural Critique* 58 (2004): 82–114.

———. "Socialism, Aestheticized Bodies, and International Circuits of Gender: Soviet Female Film Stars in the People's Republic of China, 1949–1969." *Journal of the Canadian Historical Association* 18, no. 2 (2007): 53–80. https://doi.org/10.7202/018223ar.

———. "They Love Battle Array, Not Silks and Satins." In *Words and Their Stories: Essays on the Language of the Chinese Revolution*, edited by Wang Ban, 263–82. Leiden, Netherlands: Brill, 2011.

Cheng, Lucie. "Women and Class Analysis in the Chinese Land Revolution." *Berkeley Women's Law Journal* 4, no. 1 (1988): 62–93.

Chi, Yumei. "The Attempt of the Xieyi (Essentialist) Theatre 写意话剧 in the History of the Chinese Spoken Theatre." In *Intercultural Communication with China: Beyond (Reverse) Essentialism and Culturalism?*, edited by Red Dervin and Regis Machart, 79–90. Singapore: Springer Nature Singapore and Higher Education, 2017.

Chow, Rey. *Primitive Passions: Visuality, Sexuality, Ethnography, and Contemporary Chinese Cinema*. New York: Columbia University Press, 1995.

"Circular 85 of the Chinese Communist Party's Central Committee" [中共中央通告第 85 号], July 21, 1930. In *Historical Materials on Chinese Women's Movements* [中国妇女运动历史资料], 3:63–64. Beijing: Renmin chubanshe, 1988.

Clark, Paul. "Artists, Cadres, and Audiences: Chinese Socialist Cinema, 1949–1978." In *A Companion to Chinese Cinema*, edited by Yingjin Zhang, 42–56. Hoboken, NJ: Wiley-Blackwell, 2012.

———. *Chinese Cinema: Culture and Politics since 1949*. Cambridge: Cambridge University Press, 1988.

———. *The Chinese Cultural Revolution: A History*. Cambridge: Cambridge University Press, 2008.

———. "Two Hundred Flowers on China's Screens." In *Perspectives on Chinese Cinema*, edited by Chris Berry, 40–61. London: British Film Institute, 1991.

"Constitution of the Soviet Republic (November 7, 1931)." In *Fundamental Laws of the Chinese Soviet Republic*. New York: International Publishers, 1934.

Croll, Elisabeth. *Feminism and Socialism in China*. New York: Schocken Books, 1980.

Cui, Shuqin. *Women through the Lens: Gender and Nation in a Century of Chinese Cinema*. Honolulu: University of Hawai'i Press, 2003.

Dai Jinhua 戴锦华. *Cinema and Desire: Feminist Marxism and Cultural Politics in the Work of Dai Jinhua*. Edited by Jing Wang and Tani E. Barlow. London: Verso, 2002.

———. "Gender and Narration: Women in Contemporary Chinese Film." In *Cinema and Desire*, 99–150. London: Verso, 2002.

———. "'Human, Woman, Demon': A Woman's Predicament." In *Cinema and Desire*, 151–71. London: Verso, 2002. The original Chinese version of the essay,

[《人·鬼·情》: 一个女人的困境], was published in *Shanghai Literature* [上海文学] 4 (1990): 151–71.

———. "Invisible Women: Contemporary Chinese Women's Film" [不可见的女性: 当代中国电影中的女性与女性电影]. *Contemporary Cinema* [当代电影] 6 (1994): 37–45; English translation, *Positions: East Asian Cultures Critique* 3, no. 1 (1995): 255–80.

———. "Severed Bridge: The Art of the Sons' Generation" [断桥: 子一代的艺术]. In *A Scene in the Fog: Chinese Film Culture, 1978–1998* [雾中风景: 中国电影文化, 1978–1998], 23–60. Beijing: Peking University Press, 2006.

Davin, Delia. "Women in the Countryside of China." In *Women in Chinese Society*, edited by Margery Wolf and Roxane Witke, 243–73. Stanford, CA: Stanford University Press, 1975.

Deng, Xiaoping. "Speech at Opening Ceremony of National Science Conference (March 18, 1978)." *Peking Review* 21, no. 12 (1978): 9–18.

Derlic, Arif, and Maurice Meisner. "Politics, Scholarship, and Chinese Socialism." In *Marxism and the Chinese Experience*, edited by Arif Derlic and Maurice Meisner, 3–26. New York: M. E. Sharpe, 1989.

Diamant, Neil J. "Re-Examining the Impact of the 1950 Marriage Law: State Improvisation, Local Initiative and Rural Family Change." *China Quarterly* 16 (2000): 171–98.

———. *Revolutionizing the Family: Politics, Love, and Divorce in Urban and Rural China, 1949–1968.* Berkeley: University of California Press, 2000.

Diamond, Norma. "Review of *Women, the Family and Peasant Revolution in China* by Kay Ann Johnson." *China Quarterly* 103 (1985): 530–31.

Dong Kena 董克娜. "Film Art and Me" [我和电影艺术]. In *Their Voices: Self-Narration of Chinese Female Directors* [她们的声音: 中国女电影导演自述], edited by Yang Yuanying 杨远婴, 3–28. Beijing: Zhongguo shehui chubanshe, 1996.

Dong Limin 董丽敏. "Getting Organized: The Construction of the 'New Woman' and the 'New Society'—A Case Study of the Women's Textile Manufacture Movement in the Yan'an Period" [组织起来: "新妇女"与"新社会"的建构———以延安时期的妇女组织生产为中心的考察]. *Journal of Chinese Women's Studies* [妇女研究丛刊] 6 (2017): 10–22.

Dong Xuewen 董学文. "The Issue of Mainstream in the Development of Socialist Literature" [社会主义文学发展的主流问题]. *Beijing Social Sciences* [北京社会科学] 3 (1990): 4–10.

Dooling, Amy. *Women's Literary Feminism in Twentieth-Century China.* New York: Palgrave Macmillan, 2005.

Eagleton, Terry. "From the Polis to Postmodernism." In *The Ideology of the Aesthetic*, 369–420. Oxford: Basil Blackwell, 1990.

Eisenstein, Hester. "A Dangerous Liaison? Feminism and Corporate Globalization." *Science and Society* 69, no. 3 (2005): 487–518.

Evans, Harriet. "The Language of Liberation: Gender and *Jiefang* in Early Chinese Communist Party Discourse." *Intersections: Gender, History and Culture in*

the Asian Context 1 (1998). http://intersections.anu.edu.au/issue1/harriet
.html.

Fang Keli 方克立. "We Must Pay Attention to the Study of Modern Neo-
Confucianism" [要重视对现代新儒家的研究]. *Tianjin Social Sciences* [天津社
会科学] 5 (1986): 32–38.

Farquhar, Mary, and Chris Berry. "Shadow Opera: Toward a New Archaeology
of the Chinese Cinema." In *Chinese-Language Film: Historiography, Poetics,
Politics*, edited by Sheldon H. Lu and Emilie Yueh-yu Yeh, 27–51. Honolulu:
University of Hawai'i Press, 2005.

Foucault, Michel. "What Is an Author?" In *Language, Counter-Memory, Practice*,
edited by Donald F. Bouchard, translated by D. F. Bouchard and Sherry
Simon, 113–38. Ithaca, NY: Cornell University Press, 1977. Original: "Qu'est-ce
qu'un auteur?," *Bulletin de la société française de philosophie* 63, no. 3 (1969):
73–104.

Fraser, Nancy. *Fortunes of Feminism: From State-Managed Capitalism to Neoliberal
Crisis*. London: Verso, 2013.

Geng Huamin 耿化敏. "Historical Examination of the Transformation of ACWF
during the Cultural Revolution" [文革时期妇联组织演变的历史考察].
Contemporary China History Studies [当代中国史研究] 5 (2006): 76–84.

———. "Preliminary Research on the Organizational Crisis of ACWF and Its Cause
during the Cultural Revolution" [文革时期妇联组织危机与成因初探]. *Research
and Teaching on the Party's History* [党史研究与教学] 5 (2007): 43–50.

Gilmartin, Christina K. *Engendering the Chinese Revolution: Radical Women,
Communist Politics, and Mass Movements in the 1920s*. Berkeley: University
of California Press, 1995.

Giroud, Françoise. *La nouvelle vague: Portraits de la jeunesse*. Paris: Gallimard, 1958.

Glosser, Susan, ed. and trans. *Li Fengjin: How the New Marriage Law Helped
Chinese Women Stand Up*. Portland, OR: Opal Mogus Books, 2005. Original
Chinese edition: Shanghai: Xinchao, 1950.

Goodman, David S. G. "Revolutionary Women and Women in the Revolution:
The Chinese Communist Party and Women in the War of Resistance to
Japan, 1937–1945." *China Quarterly* 164 (2000): 915–42.

Grewal, Inderpal, and Caren Kaplan. "Postcolonial Studies and Transnational
Feminist Practices." *Jouvert: A Journal of Postcolonial Studies* 5, no. 1 (2000).
http://english.chass.ncsu.edu/jouvert/v5i1/grewal.htm.

Gu Zhengnan 顾征南. "China No Longer Has Women's Cinema" [interview with
Huang Shuqin] [中国如今已没有女性电影]. *Screen* [世界电影之窗] 11 (2007):
28–29.

Han Chen 韩琛. "Three Theoretical Resources for Chinese Female Film Discourse"
[中国女性电影话语的三个理论资源]. *Academic Journal of Zhejiang Media
College* [浙江传媒学院学报] 1 (2009): 32–37.

Han Xiaolei 韩小磊. "The Spark of a New Generation: On the Directing Art of
Drive to Win" [新一代的闪光：漫谈影片《沙鸥》的导演艺术]. *Art Film* [艺术
电影] 11 (1981): 29–35.

Harding, Harry. "From China, with Disdain: New Trends in the Study of China." In *America Views China: American Images of China Then and Now*, edited by Jonathan Goldstein, Jerry Israel, and Hilary Conroy, 244–72. London: Associated University Presses, 1991.

Hartmann, Heidi. "The Unhappy Marriage of Marxism and Feminism: Toward a More Progressive Union." In *Women and Revolution: A Discussion of the Unhappy Marriage of Marxism and Feminism*, edited by Lydia Sargent, 1–42. Boston: South End, 1981.

Hartmann, Heidi I., and Ann R. Markusen. "Contemporary Marxist Theory and Practice: A Feminist Critique." *Review of Radical Political Economics* 12, no. 2 (1980): 87–94.

Harvey, David. *A Brief History of Neoliberalism*. Oxford: Oxford University Press, 2005.

Hegel, Robert E. "A 'Golden Age' for Chinese Writers." *World Literature Today* 59, no. 3 (1985): 386–89.

He Guimei 贺桂梅 and Xu Zhiwei 徐志伟. "Return to the 1980s: Broaden China's Vision—Interview of He Guimei" [重返 80 年代: 打开中国视野—贺桂梅访谈]. *Journal of Modern Chinese Studies* [现代中文学刊] 3 (2012): 48–55.

Hennessy, Rosemary, and Chrys Ingraham. "Introduction: Reclaiming Anticapitalist Feminism." In *Materialist Feminism*, 1–14. New York: Routledge, 1997.

———. *Materialist Feminism: A Reader in Class, Difference, and Women's Lives*. New York: Routledge, 1997.

Hershatter, Gail. *The Gender of Memory: Rural Women and China's Collective Past*. Berkeley: University of California Press, 2011.

Hess, John. "La politique des auteurs (part one)." *Jump Cut* 1 (1974): 19–22.

Hird, Derek. "Making Class and Gender: White-Collar Men in Postsocialist China." In *Changing Chinese Masculinities: From Imperial Pillars of State to Global Real Men*, edited by Louie Kam, 137–56. Hong Kong: Hong Kong University Press, 2016.

Hollinger, Karen. *Feminist Film Studies*. London: Routledge, 2012.

Hong Hong 洪宏. *The Soviet Union's Influence and Seventeen Years of Chinese [Socialist] Cinema* [苏联影响与中国"十七年"电影]. Beijing: Zhongguo dianying chubanshe, 2008.

Hong, Xia. "Film Theory in the People's Republic of China: The New Era." In *Chinese Film: The State of the Art in the People's Republic*, edited by George Stephen Semsel, 35–62. New York: Praeger, 1987.

Honig, Emily. "Socialist Revolution and Women's Liberation in China—A Review Article." *Journal of Asian Studies* 44, no. 2 (1985): 329–36.

Honig, Emily, and Gail Hershatter. *Personal Voices: Chinese Women in the 1980s*. Stanford, CA: Stanford University Press, 1988.

Hsia, Adrian. "Bertolt Brecht in China and His Impact on Chinese Drama: A Preliminary Examination." *Comparative Literature Studies* 20, no. 2 (1983): 231–45.

Huang Huilin 黄会林 and Wang Yiwen 王宜文. "Exploration of the Cinematic Aesthetics of New China's First Seventeen Years" [新中国"十七年"电影美

学探论]. In *Fifty Years of New China Cinema* [新中国电影 50 年], edited by
Li Suyuan 郦苏元, Hu Ke 胡克, and Yang Yuanying 杨远婴, 211–18. Beijing:
Guangbo xueyuan chubanshe, 2000.

Huang Shuqin 黄蜀芹. "Director's Reflections on *Woman Demon Human*"
[影片《人鬼情》导演总结]. In *The Unique Beauty of the Eastern Light and
Shadow: Research Volume on Huang Shuqin* [东边光影独好：黄蜀芹研究文
集], edited by Wang Renyin 王人殷, 91–100. Beijing: Zhongguo dianying
chubanshe, 2002.

———. "A Female Director's (Self-)Statement" [女导演自白]. *Contemporary
Cinema* [当代电影] 5 (1995): 69–71.

———. "*Woman Demon Human*: The Annotated Film Script" [《人鬼情》导演评
注本]. *Selected Film Scripts* [电影选刊] 6 (1988): 2–21.

———. "Women's Cinema: A Unique Perspective" [女性电影：一个独特的视角].
In *The Unique Beauty of the Eastern Light and Shadow: Research Volume on
Huang Shuqin* [东边光影独好：黄蜀芹研究文集], edited by Wang Renyin 王
人殷, 151–60. Beijing: Zhongguo dianying chubanshe, 2002.

———. "Women's Cinema: From Silence to Expression" [女性电影：从沉默到表
达]. *Xinmin Evening News* [新民晚报], November 14, 2004.

Huang Zuolin 黄佐临. "The Full Story of the Birth of My Conception of *Xieyi*
Drama" [我的'写意戏剧观'诞生前前后后]. *China Drama* [中国戏剧] 7 (1991):
50–51.

———. "General Comments on the 'Conception of Drama'" [漫谈"戏剧观"].
People's Daily [人民日报], April 25, 1962.

Hu Fuming 胡福明. "Practice Is the Sole Criterion for Measuring the Truth" [实践
是检验真理的唯一标准]. *Guangming Daily* [光明日报], May 11, 1978.

Hu Ke 胡克. *A Critical History of Chinese Film Theory* [中国电影理论史评]. Beijing:
Zhongguo dianying chubanshe, 2005.

Hu Xingliang 胡星亮. *Chinese Opera and Spoken Drama* [中国戏曲与中国话剧].
Shanghai: Xuelin chubanshe, 2000.

Irigaray, Luce. *This Sex Which Is Not One*. Translated Catherine Porter with Caro-
lyn Burke. Ithaca, NY: Cornell University Press, 1985. Original French, 1977.

Jackal, Patricia Stranahan. "Changes in Policy for Yanan Women, 1935–1947."
Modern China 7, no. 1 (1981): 83–112.

Jameson, Fredric. *The Cultural Turn: Selected Writings on the Postmodern
1983–1998*. London: Verso, 1998.

Jenco, Leigh K. "Chinese Liberalism." In *Encyclopedia of Political Theory*, edited
by Mark Bevir, 164–66. London: Sage, 2010.

Jiang Zilong 蒋子龙. "A Boy with Long Hair" [长发男儿]. In *A Boy with Long Hair*
[长发男儿], 1–36. Beijing: Zhongguo shehui chubanshe, 2005.

Jin Fenglan 靳凤兰. *The Career Life of a Female Film Director* [一个女导演的电影生
活]. Beijing: Xueyuan chubanshe, 1994.

Johnson, Kay Ann. *Women, the Family and Peasant Revolution in China*. Chicago:
University of Chicago Press, 1983.

Johnston, Claire. "Dorothy Arzner: Critical Strategies." In *The Work of Dorothy
Arzner: Towards a Feminist Cinema*, 1–8. London: British Film Institute, 1975.

———. "Women's Cinema as Counter-Cinema." In *Feminism and Film*, edited by E. Ann Kaplan, 22–33. Oxford: Oxford University Press, 2000. Originally published in *Notes on Women's Cinema*. London: Society for Film and Television, 1973.

Juraga, Dubravka, and M. Keith Booker, eds. *Socialist Cultures East and West: A Post-Cold War Reassessment*. Westport, CT: Praeger, 2002.

Kaplan, E. Ann. "Problematizing Cross-Cultural Analysis: The Case of Women in the Recent Chinese Cinema." *Wide Angle* 11, no. 2 (1989): 40–50. Reprinted in *Perspectives on Chinese Cinema*, edited by Chris Berry, 141–54. London: BFI, 1991. Chinese translation, Yin Yao 尹尧. [令人困惑的跨文化分析: 近期中国电影中妇女的地位]. *Contemporary Cinema* [当代电影] 1 (1991): 35–43.

Khan, Naseem. "The Shared Space: Cultural Diversity and the Public Domain." Report from a working seminar held by the Arts Council of England and the Council of Europe, February 2002. London: Arts Council of England, 2002.

Korte, Barbara, and Claudia Sternberg. *Bidding for the Mainstream? Black and Asian British Film since the 1990s*. Amsterdam: Rodopi, 2004.

Kuhn, A., and A. Wolpe, eds. *Feminism and Materialism*. London: Routledge and Kegan Paul, 1978.

Kuoshu, Harry H. *Celluloid China: Cinematic Encounters with Culture and Society*. Carbondale: Southern Illinois University Press, 2002.

Leenhouts, Mark. "Culture against Politics: Roots-Seeking Literature." In *The Columbia Companion to Modern East Asian Literature*, edited by Joshua Mostow, 533–40. New York: Columbia University Press, 2003.

Lewis, Greg. "The History, Myth, and Memory of Maoist Chinese Cinema, 1949–1966." *Asian Cinema* 16, no. 1 (2005): 162–83.

Li Jingzhi 李静之. *Essays on Chinese Women's Movements* [中国妇女运动研究文集]. Beijing: Shehui kexue wenxian chubanshe, 2011.

Lin, Chun. "Finding a Language: Feminism and Women's Movements in Contemporary China." In *Transitions, Environments, Translations: Feminisms in International Politics*, edited by Joan W. Scott, Cora Kaplan, and Debra Keates, 11–20. New York: Routledge, 1997.

———. *The Transformation of Chinese Socialism*. Durham, NC: Duke University Press, 2006.

Lin, Chun, Bohong Liu, and Yihong Jin. "China." In *A Companion to Feminist Philosophy*, edited by Alison M. Jagger and Iris Marion Young, 108–17. Oxford: Blackwell, 1998.

Lin, James, and Anna Paczuska. "Socialism Needs Feminism." *International Socialism* 2, no. 14 (1981): 105–19.

Li Suyuan 郦苏元. "Dialogues between Modernism and Realism: Thoughts on Film Theory Debates in the New Era" [现代主义与现实主义的对话: 新时期之初电影理论讨论随想]. *Contemporary Cinema* [当代电影] 12 (2014): 51–55.

Li Tuo 李陀. "The Cinematic Aesthetic of Screenplay—Reflections on Composing the Film Script of *Drive to Win*" [电影剧作中电影美感—《沙鸥》剧本创作体会]. In *Drive to Win: From Screenplay to Film* [沙鸥: 从剧本到影片], 165–81. Beijing: Zhongguo dianying chubanshe, 1983.

Liu Bannong 刘半农 and Zhou Mingtai 周明泰. *Historical Materials for the Last Fifty Years of Opera Performances in Beijing* [五十年来北平戏剧史材]. Hong Kong: Huiwenge shudian, 1932.

Liu, Jianmei. *Revolution Plus Love: Literary History, Women's Bodies, and Thematic Repetition in Twentieth-Century Chinese Fiction*. Honolulu: University of Hawai'i Press, 2003.

Liu, Kang. "Subjectivity, Marxism, and Culture Theory in China." *Social Text* 31/32 (1992): 114–40.

Liu Xiaobo 刘晓波. "A Dialogue with Li Zehou: Sensibility, the Individual, and My Choice" [与李泽厚对话: 感性, 个人, 我的选择]. *China* [中国], October 1986: 52–74.

Liu Zaifu 刘再复. "On the Subjectivity of Literature" [论文学的主体性]. *Literary Review* [文学评论] 6 (1985): 11–26; 1 (1986): 1–15.

Li Xiaojiang 李小江. *Eve's Exploration* [夏娃的探索]. Zhengzhou: Henan renmin chubanshe, 1988.

———. "On the Characteristics and Road of Chinese Women's Liberation" [论中国妇女解放的特点和道路]. In *Contemporary Reflections on Women's Issues* [妇女问题在当代的思考], 11–30. Xi'an: Shanxi renmin chubanshe, 1988.

———. "The Progress of Humanity and Women's Liberation" [人类进步和妇女解放], originally published in *Marxist Studies* [马克思主义研究] 4 (1983): 142–66; English translation by Edward Gunn in "Other Genders, Other Sexualities: Chinese Differences," edited by Lingzhen Wang, special issue, *differences: A Journal of Feminist Cultural Studies* 24, no. 2 (2013): 22–50.

———. "Responding to Tani Barlow: Women's Studies in the 1980s." In "Other Genders, Other Sexualities: Chinese Differences," edited by Lingzhen Wang, special issue, *differences: A Journal of Feminist Cultural Studies* 24, no. 2 (2013): 172–81.

———. *Selected Works of the Foreign Feminist Movement* [外国女权运动文选]. Beijing: Chinese Women's Press, 1987.

———. *The Sex/Gender Gap* [性沟]. Beijing: Sanlian Publishing House, 1989.

———. *Toward Women* [走向女人]. 1993. Reprint, *Family, the State, and Women* [家国女人]. Nanjing: Nanjing Normal University Press, 2012.

———. "Women's Enlightenment and Political Price" [女性启蒙与政治代价]. *Women: Cross-Cultural Dialogues* [女人: 跨文化对话]. Nanjing: Jiangsu renmin chubanshe, 2006.

Li Zehou 李泽厚. "Regarding Confucianism and Modern Neo-Confucianism" [关于儒学与现代新儒学]. *Wenhui Daily* [文汇报], January 28, 1986.

Li Zonggui 李宗桂. "The Origin of the 'Study of Modern Neo-Confucian Thought' and the Debates at the Xuanzhou Conference" ["现代新儒家思潮研究"的由来和宣州会议的争鸣]. In *Collected Essays on Neo-Confucianism* [现代新儒学研究论文集], vol. 1, edited by Fang Keli 方克立 and Li Jinquan 李锦全, 332–40. Beijing: Zhongguo shehuikexue chubanshe, 1989.

Luo Yijun 罗艺军, Li Jinsheng 李晋生, and Xu Hong 徐虹, eds. *Chinese Film Theory: An Anthology, 1920–1989* [中国电影理论文选, 1920–1989]. Vol. 2. Beijing: Wenhua yishu chubanshe, 1992.

Lü Xiaoming 吕晓明. "A Study of Shanghai Film Dubbing Studio during 'the Seventeen Years'" [对"十七年"上海电影译制片的一种观察]. In *Fifty Years of New China Cinema* [新中国电影 50 年], edited by Li Suyuan 郦苏元, Hu Ke 胡克, and Yang Yuanying 杨远婴, 278–88. Beijing: Guangbo xueyuan chubanshe, 2000.

Lu Yan 陆岩. "On the Construction of Socialist Mainstream Culture" [论社会主义主流文化建设]. *Study and Exploration* [学习与探索] 2 (2007): 14–16.

Ma, Ning. "Notes on the New Filmmakers." In *Chinese Film: The State of the Art in the People's Republic*, edited by George Stephen Semsel, 35–62. New York: Praeger, 1987.

Mao, Zedong. "Report on an Investigation of the Peasant Movement in Hunan." In *Selected Works of Mao Tse-tung*, 1:23–62. Peking: Foreign Languages, 1967.

Marchetti, Gina. "Two Stage Sisters: The Blossoming of a Revolutionary Aesthetic." *Jump Cut* 34 (1989): 95–106.

Meisner, Maurice. "The Chinese Revolution and the Question of Capitalism." In *The Deng Xiaoping Era: An Inquiry into the Fate of Chinese Socialism, 1978–1994*, 3–24. New York: Hill and Wang, 1996.

——. *Mao's China and After: A History of the People's Republic*. 3rd ed. New York: Free Press, 1999.

——. "The Significance of the Chinese Revolution in World History." Working Paper. Asia Research Centre, London School of Economics and Political Science, London, 1999. The cited version is available at: http://eprints.lse.ac.uk/21309/.

Meng Liye 孟犁野. *Film Art of New China: 1949–1959* [新中国电影艺术: 1949–1959]. Beijing: Zhongguo dianying chubanshe, 2002.

Meng Yue 孟悦 and Dai Jinhua 戴锦华. *Emerging from the Historical Horizon* [浮出历史地表]. Henan: Henan renmin chubanshe, 1989.

Miller, Nancy. "Changing the Subject: Authorship, Writing, and the Reader." In *Feminist Studies / Critical Studies*, edited by Teresa de Lauretis, 102–20. Bloomington: Indiana University Press, 1986.

Min, Dongchao. "Awakening Again: Travelling Feminism in China in the 1980s." *Women's Studies International Forum* 28 (2005): 274–88.

Mitchell, Juliet. *Women: The Longest Revolution*. London: Virago, 1984.

Mittler, Barbara. *A Continuous Revolution: Making Sense of Cultural Revolution Culture*. Cambridge, MA: Harvard University Press, 2012.

Mohanty, Chandra Talpade. "Cartographies of Struggle—Third World Women and the Politics of Feminism." In *Third World Women and the Politics of Feminism*, edited by Chandra Talpade Mohanty, Ann Russo, and Lourdes Torres, 1–50. Indianapolis: Indiana University Press, 1991.

Moise, Edwin E. *Modern China: A History*. 3rd ed. New York: Longman, 2008.

Mulvey, Laura. "Film, Feminism and the Avant-Garde." *Framework* 10 (1979): 3–10.

Pang, Laikwan. *Building a New China in Cinema: The Chinese Left-Wing Cinema Movement, 1932–1937*. Lanham, MD: Rowman and Littlefield, 2002.

Petro, Patrice. *Aftershocks of the New: Feminism and Film History*. New Brunswick, NJ: Rutgers University Press, 2002.

Qu Yajun 屈雅君. "Female Image in 1990s Film Medium" [90 年代电影传媒中的女性形象]. *Contemporary Cinema* [当代电影] 2 (1998): 33–38.

Ren Zhonglun 任仲伦. "Return to Eden: Chinese Women's Film Practice in Transformation" [重返伊甸园：变迁中的中国女性导演创作]. *Journal of the Beijing Film Academy* [北京电影学院学报] 1 (1990): 52–67.

Roberts, Rosemary A. *Maoist Model Theatre: The Semiotics of Gender and Sexuality in the Chinese Cultural Revolution (1966–76)*. Leiden, Netherlands: Brill, 2010.

Rofel, Lisa. *Other Modernities: Gendered Yearnings in China after Socialism*. Berkeley: University of California Press, 1999.

Rubin, Gayle. "The Traffic in Women: Notes on the Political Economy of Sex." In *Toward an Anthropology of Women*, 157–210. New York: Monthly Review, 1975.

Saich, Tony. "Introduction." In *The Rise to Power of the Chinese Communist Party: Documents and Analysis*, edited by Tony Saich, xxxix–lxix. Armonk, NY: M. E. Sharpe, 1996.

Sargent, Lydia, ed. *Women and Revolution: A Discussion of the Unhappy Marriage of Marxism and Feminism*. Boston: South End, 1981.

Schmalzer, Sigrid. *The People's Peking Man: Popular Science and Human Identity in Twentieth-Century China*. Chicago: University of Chicago Press, 2008.

Scott, Hilda. *Does Socialism Liberate Women? Experiences from Eastern Europe*. Boston: Beacon Press, 1974.

Sellier, Geneviève. "French New Wave Cinema and the Legacy of Male Libertinage." *Cinema Journal* 49, no. 4 (2010): 152–58.

———. *Masculinity Singular: French New Wave Cinema*. Translated by Kristin Ross. Durham, NC: Duke University Press, 2008.

Shao Mujun 邵牧君. "The Agony of Suppressing Female Id: A Reading of *Woman Demon Human* [压抑女性本我的痛苦：对《人鬼情》的一点解读]. *Cinema Arts* [电影艺术] 8 (1988): 40–42.

Shi Faming 石发明. "Life Perceived through Female Consciousness: Watching *Woman Demon Human* and Discussing 'Women's Cinema'" [以女性意识关照生活：观《人鬼情》兼说"女性电影"]. *Film Criticism* [电影评介] 2 (1988): 4–5.

Shi Qing 石青. "The Disappointment of *A Soul Haunted by Painting*" [令人失望的《画魂》]. *Film Criticism* [电影评价] 10 (1994): 28.

Shi Yan 石言. "The Party, the Collective, and the Author—Thoughts after the Making of *The Story of Liubao Village*" [党·集体·作者—"柳堡的故事"创作的体会]. *Chinese Cinema* [中国电影] 10 (1958): 69–70.

Shi Yan 石言 and Huang Zongjiang 黄宗江. *The Story of Liubao Village* [柳堡的故事]. In *Chinese New Literature Series: Films, 1949–1966* [中国新文学大系：电影集, 1949–1966], vol. 1, edited by Luo Yijun 罗艺军, 601–26. Beijing: Zhongguo wenlian chuban gongsi, 1988.

So, Alvin Y., and Stephen W. K. Chiu. "Modern East Asia in World-Systems Analysis." In *A World-Systems Reader: New Perspectives on Gender, Urbanism, Cultures, Indigenous Peoples, and Ecology*, edited by Thomas D. Hall, 271–85. New York: Rowman and Littlefield, 2000.

Song Zhao 宋昭. *The Life of My Mother: Biography of Wang Ping* [妈妈的一生：王苹传]. Beijing: Zhongguo dianying chubanshe, 2007.

Stacey, Judith. *Patriarchy and Socialist Revolution in China*. Berkeley: University of California Press, 1983.

——. "When Patriarchy Kowtows: The Significance of the Chinese Family Revolution for Feminist Theory." *Feminist Studies* 2, no. 2/3 (1975): 64–112.

Sudo, Mizuyo. "Concepts of Women's Rights in Modern China." Translated by Michael G. Hill. *Gender and History* 18, no. 3 (2006): 472–89.

Suleiman, Susan. *Authoritarian Fictions: The Ideological Novel as a Literary Genre*. New York: Columbia University Press, 1983.

Sun Jimin 孙吉民. "From Biography to Film and TV Series: A Hermeneutic Analysis of the Three Versions of *A Soul Haunted by Painting* [从传记到影视：对《画魂》三个版本的阐释学分析]. *Journal of Chongqing Youdian University (Social Sciences)* [重庆邮电大学学报 (社会科学版)] 1 (2008): 95–99.

Sun Xiantao 孙献韬 and Li Duoyu 李多钰, eds. *One Hundred Years of Chinese Cinema*, vol. 2, 1977–2005 [中国电影百年, 下编, 1977–2005]. Beijing: Zhongguo guangbo chubanshe, 2006.

Tang Shuiqing 汤水清. "The Different Choices by Rural Women in the Soviet Revolution: An Investigation of the Central Soviet Area" [乡村妇女在苏维埃革命中的差异性选择—以中央苏区为中心的考察]. *Research on the History of the Chinese Communist Party* [中共党史研究] 11 (2012): 85–94.

Tang Xiaobing 唐小兵, ed. *Rereading: The People's Literature and Art and Its Ideology* [再解读：大众文艺与意识形态]. Hong Kong: Oxford University Press, 1993.

Tian Benxiang 田本相. "On Mr. Huang Zuolin's 'Conception of *Xieyi* Drama': Commemorating One Hundred Years of Chinese Spoken Drama" [论黄佐临先生的"写意戏剧观"：为中国话剧百年纪念而作]. *Nankai Journal (Philosophy, Literature, and Social Science Edition)* [南开学报 (哲学社会科学版)] 6 (2007): 22–27.

Tian Ge 田歌. "The Sentimental Pei Yanling Who Was Born for the Opera" [为戏而生的柔情裴艳玲]. TV interview, *Glorious Bloom* [光荣绽放], July 26, 2016.

Tong Daoming 童道明. "Another Discussion of Film and Opera/Drama" [再论电影与戏剧]. *Film Arts* [电影艺术] 5 (1991): 10–15.

Tong Hua 仝华 and Kang Peizhu 康沛竹, eds. *Historical Development of Marxist Feminist Theory* [马克思主义妇女理论发展史]. Beijing: Beijing daxue chubanshe, 2004.

Tuo Zuhai 庹祖海. "A Summary of Discussions of Literature, Human Nature, and Humanism" [关于文学与人性、人道主义的讨论综述]. *Theory and Criticism of Literature and Art* [文艺理论与批评] 3 (1991): 136–44.

Volland, Nicolai. *Socialist Cosmopolitanism: The Chinese Literary Universe, 1945–1965*. New York: Columbia University Press, 2017.

Walker, Kathy LeMons. "The Party and Peasant Women." In *Chinese Communists and Rural Society, 1927–1937*, edited by Philip Huang, Lynda Schaefer Bell, and Kathy LeMons Walker, 57–82. Berkeley: University of California Press, 1978.

Wang, Ban. "Desire and Pleasure in Revolutionary Cinema." In *The Sublime Figure of History*, 123–54. Stanford, CA: Stanford University Press, 1997.

Wang, Hui 汪晖. "Depoliticized Politics: From East to West." *New Left Review* 41 (2006): 29–45.

Wang, Lingzhen 王玲珍. "A Chinese Gender Morality Tale: Politics, Personal Voice, and Public Space in the Early Post-Mao Era." In *Personal Matters: Women's Autobiographical Practice in Twentieth-Century China*, 140–66. Stanford, CA: Stanford University Press, 2004.

———. "Chinese Women's Cinema." In *A Companion to Chinese Cinema*, edited by Yingjin Zhang, 299–317. Malden, MA: Blackwell, 2012.

———. *Chinese Women's Cinema: Transnational Contexts*. New York: Columbia University Press, 2011.

———. "Female Cinematic Imaginary: History, Gendered Subjectivity, and Ma Xiaoying's *Gone Is the One Who Held Me Dearest in the World*" [女性的境界：历史，性别，和主体建构—兼论马晓颖的《世界上最疼我的人去了》]. *Chung-Wai Literary Monthly* [中外文学] 34, no. 11 (April 2006): 27–52.

———. "Reproducing the Self: Consumption, Imaginary, and Identity in Chinese Women's Autobiographical Practice in the 1990s." In *Contested Modernities: Perspectives on Twentieth Century Chinese Literature*, edited by Charles Laughlin, 173–92. New York: Palgrave Macmillan, 2005.

———. "Socialist Cinema and Female Authorship: Overdetermination and Subjective Revisions in Dong Kena's *Small Grass Grows on the Kunlun Mountain* (1962)." In *Chinese Women's Cinema: Transnational Contexts*, edited by Lingzhen Wang, 47–65. New York: Columbia University Press, 2011.

———. "Transnational Feminist Reconfiguration of Film Discourse and Women's Cinema." In *Chinese Women's Cinema: Transnational Contexts*, edited by Lingzhen Wang, 1–44. New York: Columbia University Press, 2011.

———. "Wang Ping and Women's Cinema in Socialist China: Institutional Practice, Feminist Cultures, and Embedded Authorship." *Signs: Journal of Women in Culture and Society* 40, no. 3 (2015): 589–622.

Wang Ping 王苹. "Director's Notes on *The Story of Liubao Village*" [《柳堡的故事》导演阐述]. In *Collections of Film Directors' Notes* [电影导演阐述集], edited by Zuo Lin, Su Li, and Xu Tao 佐临，苏里，徐韬, 150–63. Beijing: China Film, 1959.

Wang, Zheng. "Chen Bo'er and the Feminist Paradigm of Socialist Film." In *Finding Women in the State: A Socialist Feminist Revolution in the People's Republic of China, 1949–1964*, 143–69. Berkeley: University of California Press, 2017.

———. "Creating a Socialist Feminist Cultural Front: Women of China (1949–1966)." *China Quarterly* 204 (2010): 827–49.

———. *Finding Women in the State: A Socialist Feminist Revolution in the People's Republic of China, 1949–1964*. Berkeley: University of California Press, 2016.

———. "Maoism, Feminism, and the UN Conference on Women: Women's Studies Research in Contemporary China." *Journal of Women's History* 8, no. 4 (1997): 126–52.

———. "'State Feminism?' Gender and Socialist Formation in Maoist China." *Feminist Studies* 31, no. 3 (2005): 519–51.

———. *Women in the Chinese Enlightenment: Oral and Textual Histories*. Berkeley: University of California Press, 1999.

Wang Zhongde 王仲德. "The Pei Yanling I Know" [我所认识的裴艳玲]. *Newspaper of Chinese Culture* [中国文化报], August 11, 2008.

Wei, S. Louisa (Wei Shiyu 魏时煜). "The Encoding of Female Subjectivity: Four Films by China's Fifth-Generation Women Directors." In *Chinese Women's Cinema: Transnational Contexts*, edited by Lingzhen Wang, 173–90. New York: Columbia University Press, 2011.

———. "Transformations of Women's Screen Images and Women's Cinema in the Last One Hundred Years" [百年银幕女性和女性电影传统的嬗变]. In *Study of Chinese Film History: Volume on Cinematic Culture* [中国电影专业史研究：电影文化卷], edited by Yang Yuanyin 杨远婴, 439–503. Beijing: Zhongguo dianying chubanshe, 2006.

———. "Women's Trajectories in Chinese and Japanese Cinemas: A Chronological Overview." In *Dekalog 4: On East Asian Filmmakers*, edited by Kate E. Taylor, 13–44. London: Wallflower, 2010.

Williams, Raymond. *Television: Technology and Cultural Form*. Hanover, NH: University Press of New England and Wesleyan University, 1992.

Willis, Ellen. "Radical Feminism and Feminist Radicalism." *Social Text* 9/10 (1984): 91–118.

Wolf, Margery. *Revolution Postponed: Women in Contemporary China*. Stanford, CA: Stanford University Press, 1985.

Wu Di 吴迪. "Exploration of 'People's Films': The First Wave of 'Nonmainstream' [Cinema] in the First Seventeen Years of Socialist China" ["人民电影"探讨：十七年中的第一波"非主流"]. *Film Arts* [电影艺术] 2 (2007): 80–84.

Wu Guanping 吴冠平. "Experiencing Life: Interview with Zhang Nuanxin" [感受生活：张暖忻采访录]. In *Their Voices: Self-Narrations by Chinese Women Directors* [她们的声音：中国女导演自述], edited by Yang Yuanying 杨远婴, 91–92. Beijing: Shehui chubanshe, 1996.

Xia Yan 夏衍. "Several Issues in Screenplay Writing" [写电影剧本的几个问题]. In *Essays on Film* [电影论文集], 93–181. Beijing: Zhongguo dianying chubanshe, 1963.

Xie Fei 谢飞. "Filmmaking Trends in the Early 1980s" [八十年代初期的电影创作思潮]. *Contemporary Cinema* [当代电影] 12 (2008): 4–12.

Xing Bensi 邢贲思. "How to Discern Humanism" [怎样识别人道主义]. *Encyclopedic Knowledge* [百科知识] 1 (1980): 22–24.

Xu Feng 徐峰. "Fleeting Time and Cultural Accumulation: Interview with Huang Shuqin" [流逝与沉积：黄蜀芹访谈录]. *Journal of the Beijing Film Academy* [北京电影学院报] 2 (1997): 3–21.

Xu Jianfei 徐建飞 and Shi Huiming 史慧明. "Path Selection in Socialist Mainstream Cultural Construction in the Early Period of Socialist New China" [新中国初期社会主义主流文化建构的路径选择]. *Guangxi Social Sciences* [广西社会科学] 8 (2014): 111–15.

Xu Mingqiang 徐明强 and Song Shaopeng 宋少鹏. "Collective Mutual Support and Women's Emancipation: The Rise of Neighborhood Public Day Care in Beijing, 1954–1957" [集体互助与妇女解放：北京地区街道托儿所的兴起, 1954–1957]. *Women's Studies Series* [妇女研究丛刊] 3 (2018): 67–82.

Yang, Mayfair Mei-hui. "From Gender Erasure to Gender Difference: State Feminism, Consumer Sexuality, and Women's Public Sphere in China." In *Spaces of Their Own: Women's Public Sphere in Transnational China*, edited by Mayfair Mei-hui Yang, 35–67. Minneapolis: University of Minnesota Press, 1998.

Yang Mayfair 杨美惠 and Ge Hua 戈铧 (戴锦华). "The Quest for Self" [interview with Huang Shuqin] [追问自我]. *Film Art* [电影艺术] 5 (1994): 101–15.

Yang Yuanying 杨远婴. "Perseverance and Tranquility: Interview with Director Wang Haowei" [坚守与淡定：王好为导演访谈录]. *Contemporary Cinema* [当代电影] 6 (2013): 33–41.

——. "Revolution and Resonance: Wang Ping" [革命与回响：王苹]. In *Film Auteur and Cultural Representation: Research on the Genealogy of Chinese Film Directors* [电影作者与文化再现：中国电影导演谱系研寻], edited by Yang Yuanying, 131–44. Beijing: Zhongguo dianying chubanshe, 2005.

Yao Xiaomeng 姚晓濛. "Chinese New Cinema: An Ideological Perspective" [中国新电影：从意识形态的观点看]. In *Cultural Consciousness of the 1980s* [八十年代文化意识], edited by Gan Yang 甘阳, 193–221. Hong Kong: Sanlian, 1989.

Yau, Esther C. M. "*Yellow Earth*: Western Analysis and a Non-Western Text." *Film Quarterly* 41, no. 2 (1987–1988): 22–33.

Ye Zhou 叶舟. "Experimentation—Still the Beginning Stage: A Dialogue with Zhang Nuanxin" [探索，还只是开始—与张暖忻对话]. *New Films* [电影新作] 3 (1987): 62–64, 69.

Young, Iris. "Beyond the Unhappy Marriage: A Critique of the Dual Systems Theory." In *Women and Revolution: A Discussion of the Unhappy Marriage of Marxism and Feminism*, edited by Lydia Sargent, 43–69. Boston: South End, 1981.

Yuan Ying 远婴. "Feminism and Chinese Women's Cinema" [女权主义与中国女性电影]. *Contemporary Cinema* [当代电影] 3 (1990): 46–53.

——. "History and Memory: On Director Wang Ping" [历史与记忆：论王苹导演]. *Film Art* [电影艺术] 2 (1991): 26–31.

——. "The Mainstream Trend of 1980s–1990s Chinese Film Theory Development" [八九十年代中国电影理论发展主潮]. In *Contemporary Chinese Film Theory: An Anthology* [当代电影理论文选], edited by Hu Ke 胡克, Zhang Wei 张卫, and Hu Zhifeng 胡智锋, 17–29. Beijing: Beijing guangbo xueyuan chubanshe, 2000.

——. *Their Voices: Self-Narrations of Chinese Female Directors* [她们的声音：中国女导演自述). Beijing: Zhonguo shehui chubanshe, 1996.

Zeitlin, Judith. "Operatic Ghosts on Screen: The Case of *A Test of Love* (1958)." *Opera Quarterly* 26, nos. 2–3 (2010): 220–55.

Zha Jianying. *The Eighties: Interviews* [八十年代访谈录]. Beijing: Sanlian shudian, 2006.

Zhang Cheng 张成. "There Is Only One Criterion" [标准只有一个]. *People's Daily* [人民日报], March 26, 1978.

Zhang Junxiang 张骏祥. *Special Ways of Cinematic Expression* [关于电影的特殊表现手法]. Beijing: China Film, 1958.

Zhang Junxiang 张骏祥 et al. "Ardent Pursuit of Art" [执着的艺术追求]. *New Films* [电影新作] 2 (1988): 54–62.

Zhang Manling 张曼菱. "A Beautiful Place" [有一个美丽的地方]. *Contemporary Time* [当代] 3 (1982): 130–50, 162.

Zhang Nuanxin 张暖忻. "Director's Notes on *Drive to Win*" [《沙鸥》导演阐述]. In *Drive to Win: From Screenplay to Film* [沙鸥：从剧本到影片], 182–94. Beijing: Zhongguo dianying chubanshe, 1983.

———. "Director's Notes on *Sacrificed Youth*" [《青春祭》导演阐述]. *Journal of the Beijing Film Academy* [北京电影学院学报] 3 (2005): 85–87.

———. "*Drive to Win*: From Screenplay to Film" [《沙鸥》从剧本到电影]. *Journal of the Beijing Film Academy* [北京电影学院学报] 3 (2005): 81–84.

———. "Getting Close to [Social] Reality: Selected Dialogues on *Good Morning, Beijing*" [贴近现实：关于《北京，你早》的对话摘录]. *Film Criticism* [电影评介] 12 (1990): 3.

———. "Let Historical Reality Return to the Silver Screen" (让历史真实回到银幕). First published in *People's Films* [人民电影] 10–11 (1978) and collected in *Research Materials for Chinese Film Studies, 1949–1979*, vol. 3 [中国电影研究资料, 1949–1979, 下], edited by Wu Di 吴迪, 508–12. Beijing: Wenhua yu yishu chubanshe, 2006.

Zhang Nuanxin 张暖忻 and Li Tuo 李陀. "On the Modernization of Film Language" [谈电影语言的现代化]. *Film Art* [电影艺术] 3 (1979): 40–52.

Zhang, Xudong. "On Some Motifs on the Chinese 'Cultural Fever' of the Late 1980s: Social Change, Ideology, and Theory." *Social Text* 39 (1994): 129–56.

Zhang, Yingjin. *Chinese National Cinema*. New York: Routledge, 2004.

Zhang Yiwu 张颐武. "Zhang Nuanxin: Chinese Dream, Film Dream" [张暖忻：中国梦·电影梦]. *Book City* [书城] 7 (2005): 45–48.

Zhang Zhongnian 张仲年 and Gu Chunfang 顾春芳. *Huang Shuqin and Her Films* [黄蜀芹和她的电影]. Shanghai: Renmin chubanshe, 2009.

Zhen Xin 震钦. "From 'Self-Consciousness' to 'Self-Freedom'" [从"自觉"到"自由"的求索]. In *Women behind the Silver Screen: Chinese Women Directors* [操纵银幕的女性：中国女导演], edited by Lu Le 鲁勒, 118–45. Changchun: Beifang funüertong chubanshe, 1989.

Zheng Yefu 郑也夫. *On Paying a Price* [代价论]. Beijing: Sanlian shudian, 1995.

———. "Sociological Reflection on Gender Equality" [男女平等的社会学思考]. *Sociological Research* [社会学研究] 4 (1994): 111–13.

Zhong Dafeng 钟大丰 and Shu Xiaomin 舒晓鸣. "Films of [Socialist] China's First Seventeen Years" [十七年中国电影]. In *Chinese Film History* [中国电影史], 84–99. Beijing: Zhongguo guangbo dianying chubanshe, 1995.

Zhong, Xueping 钟雪萍. *Masculinity Besieged? Issues of Modernity and Male Subjectivity in Chinese Literature of the Late Twentieth Century*. Durham, NC: Duke University Press, 2000.

———. "Why Reflections on 'Revolution and Women's Liberation' Become a Woman's Job" [为什么反思"革命与妇女解放"成了女性的专业]. *Journal of Chinese Women's Studies* [妇女研究论丛] 5 (2017): 8–13.

———. "Women Can Hold Up Half the Sky." In *Words and Their Stories: Essays on the Language of Chinese Revolution*, edited by Wang Ban, 227–48. Leiden, Netherlands: Brill, 2010.

Zhou Chuanji 周传基 and Li Tuo 李陀. "An Important Film Aesthetic: On Long Take Theory" [一个值得重视的电影美学学派—关于长镜头理论]. *Film Culture Studies* [电影文化丛刊] 1 (1980): 148–60.

Zhou Xia 周夏. "Interview with Huang Shuqin" [黄蜀芹访谈录]. *Contemporary Cinema* [当代电影] 3 (2015): 86–90.

Zhou Yang 周扬. "Exploration of Several Issues of Marxist Theory" [关于马克思主义的几个理论问题的探讨]. *People's Daily* [人民日报], June 3, 1983.

Zhu Guangqian 朱光潜. "On Human Nature, Humanism, Human Warmth, and Shared Sense of Beauty" [关于人性, 人道主义, 人情味和共同美问题]. *Literature and Art Studies* [文艺研究] 3 (1979): 39–42.

Zhu, Ying. *Chinese Cinema during the Era of Reform: The Ingenuity of the System.* Westport, CT: Praeger, 2003.

Zou Hua 邹华. "The Introversion and Unbalance of Historical Ontology: A Brief Discussion on Li Zehou's Aesthetics in His Later Period" [历史本体论的内转与失衡：李泽厚后期美学论析]. *Journal of Northwest Normal University (Social Sciences)* [西北师大学报(社会科学版)] 5 (2013): 28–33.

INDEX

aesthetics, 134, 144, 147, 153, 209–10; capitalist, 24, 138; documentary, 133; experimental, 52–53, 85, 142; and gender, 5–6, 59; feminist, 33; masculine, 132–33, 137, 148; masculine avant-garde, 19; principles of, 211; revolutionary, 53, 69; realist, 88; socialist, 1, 27, 53–54, 77, 139, 151, 155, 166; and socialist women's cinema, 57, 59, 69, 85; and socialist mass culture, 14, 47; universal, 139

agency: cultural, 165, 207; embedded feminist, 17, 56, 71, 81–82, 197, 242; historical, 17, 63; individual, 5, 57–59, 71, 124, 237; personal, 66, 79, 185; political, 77, 188; women's, 156, 188, 197, 207

alienation: and humanism, 109; liberal feminist, 239n52; and Marxism, 109; women's, 118–19, 129

All-China Congress, 38

All-China Federation of Democratic Women, 48

All-China Federation of Trade Unions, 121

All-China Women's Federation, 120–23; and National Conference on Women's Issues of the New Era, 122

Althusser, Louis, 244

Andors, Phyllis, 24

"art for art's sake," 139, 210

audience, mass, 1, 18, 54, 71, 77, 82, 101, 150; proletarian, 74, 85, 105

authorship, 17, 58–59, 81, 105, 190; cinematic, 6, 17–18, 57, 59–60, 71, 80, 81, 188; collective, 17, 105; cultural, 58–59; female, 60, 237; individual, 74, 105; socialist, 17, 59–60, 71

autobiographical literature, women's, 108, 111, 114, 116, 155, 170–75, 184, 187, 253; "A Beautiful Place," 170

avant-garde, 143, 145–47, 170, 236; aesthetic of, 2, 33; and commercial turn, 20, 146–47; as counter-cinema, 168; and Fifth Generation filmmakers, 15, 143, 212; films, male practice, 35, 199, 212; marginalization of, 10, 34, 167; Laura Mulvey, "Film, Feminism, and the Avant-Garde," 32; and women's cinema, 6

avant-gardism, 12, 19, 132–33, 135, 137, 139, 141, 143–47, 248–49

Bao Zhifang, 151, 199

Barlow, Tani E.: on the ACWF, 121; on Li Xiaojiang, 116; on post-Mao male intellectual, 110, 246n32, 247n58

Bazin, André, 135, 141, 153; *Cahiers du cinéma*, 139

beauty, 70, 100, 171–72, 175, 177–79, 203

Beijing, 213, 223, 250; CCP control of, 45; Chinese Writer's Association, 142; film academies, 133, 150–51, 189, 195, 242, 250; Deng Xiaoping address at National Science Conference, 124; Lu Xun talk at Women's Normal College, 63; as setting in films, 180, 188–89, 193; and state-run studios, 51, 66, 85; symposium on women's cinema, 107. *See also* film academies; Beijing; film studios

Berlin International Film Festival, 146, 196

Berry, Chris, 162, 197, 237, 242, 244–45; on apprenticeship structure, 244n4; "China's New 'Women's Cinema,'" 158, 235, 250–51, 254; on "consensus ideology," 157, 159–61; on flashback and memory, 86; on *Li Shuangshuang* and *The In-Laws*, 101–3; on memory, 86; on women's liberation, 25, 101–3

black velvet aesthetic, 195, 232, 253; as experimental technique, 208–9, 211, 229; and mainstream discourses, 207, 225; and *xieyi*, 21, 201, 211–12, 215

bourgeois, 7–8, 36, 162

Brecht, Bertolt, 210

Butler, Alison, 33, 239n49

Cai, Xiang, 97

Cai Chusheng, 53, 63

Camera Obscura (journal), 251n39

capitalism, 7, 14, 16, 28–29, 31, 34, 36, 233; bourgeois, 162; and feminism, 29, 40, 117, 129–30, 235, 239; geopolitics, 2; globalization of, 108; market, 190; modernity, 32, 193; society, 24, 107, 109, 117, 129, 138, 147, 160, 232; system of, 2, 11–12, 28, 32, 34, 83, 160, 162, 164; transnational, 192–93; Western, 4, 64, 130

CCP. *See* Chinese Communist Party

Central Film Bureau, 52–53

characters, female, 82, 145–46, 172, 188, 198, 249

Chen, Tina Mai, 48

Chen Bo'er, 51, 53, 241n122, 242n139

Chen Huangmei, 52, 53

Chen Kaige, 146, 179, 196, 249n61; *Yellow Earth*, 143, 180, 201

China: culture of, 15, 19, 143, 149, 174, 200, 207, 215, 221, 227; mainland of, 17, 30, 46, 55, 80; peasants in, 27, 40, 240; post-Mao, 10, 109–11, 113–14, 116, 125, 131–32, 143, 145, 149–50, 152–53, 155, 157–59, 170–71, 187, 189, 214, 216, 253, 255; rural, 31, 40, 42, 48–49, 67, 70, 102, 238; southern, 21, 39, 188; urban, 172, 184

—history, 56, 64, 82, 109, 149, 153, 198, 200, 208, 232, 238, 241, 243; Chinese women in, 123; critique of, 143; feminism in, 28, 116, 168, 204; feminist film in, 21, 34; film, of, 133–35, 141, 150, 196, 242; geopolitical, 4–5, 68; and historical legacies, 32; materialist, 44; modern, 124, 126, 163, 214; neoliberal, 156; revolutionary, 25, 29, 52, 97, 120, 130, 147; and revolutionary history films (genre), 99; socialism in, 14–15, 151, 169, 202, 211, 215–16, 223, 249; socialist feminism, 17, 37, 50, 84; (socio)political, 20, 69, 155, 159–60, 199, 225; women's cinema, of, 16, 58; and women's liberation, 38, 116; world, 30

—socialist, 54–58, 60, 67–69, 72, 87–88, 114, 145–46, 171, 199; and cinematic representation, 1, 51–52, 80, 211; construction of female subject in, 44–45, 47–48, 70, 103, 166; and cultural practice, 24, 177, 215, 242; female film directors in, 32, 32, 74, 81, 106, 150; and feminism, 2–3, 36–37, 44–45, 105, 236; and gender, 104, 121; gender roles in,

69, 72, 93, 96, 99, 112, 140, 202, 217, 226; geopolitics of, 9, 46; political history of, 160–62, 169; and institutional empowerment, 14, 58, 126; and mainstream culture, 11, 15, 50, 55, 57; Mao-era, 7, 56, 108, 123, 198, 233; national cinema, creation of, 53; post-Mao, 4; revolution, 10, 16, 26–31, 38, 41; women's equality in, 165, 172, 184, 213–14; and women's liberation, 25, 49, 60

China Film Art Research Center, 107, 233

Chinese Communist Party, 51–52, 66–67, 238, 240; in films, 86, 103, 198; leadership of, 108; members of, 38–39, 43, 53, 61, 64, 66, 120, 142, 191; and the party-state, 46; policies of, 44, 84; and post-Mao female intellectuals, 123; and rural peasants, 27; socialist period, 39, 45; and women, 31, 198; and women's labor, 25; and the women's movement, 36–37

Chongqing, 53, 57, 66

cinema, 19, 24, 34, 53, 243; anti-cinema, 34, 61, 167; art-house, 15–16; authorship of, 18, 55, 59–60, 71, 81; avant-garde, 33, 143, 146, 170, 236; commercial, 10, 20, 103, 133, 147, 187, 196, 206, 230, 232; counter-cinema, 32–35, 85, 168, 236, 239; directors of, 24, 55, 58, 239, 242; engaged, 187, 192–93, 199; Hollywood, 103; houses, 49; marginalized, 4, 61, 167; national, 53–55, 70; New Era, 19, 107, 110, 132–37, 144–45, 148, 152, 164, 187, 193, 233; proletarian, 70, 194; radical, 61, 65; style, 21, 75, 173–74, 179–80, 189–90, 193, 198; world, 53–54, 102, 134. *See also* women's cinema

—Chinese, 21, 150, 154, 195, 201, 214; National Cinema, 241, 248–50; socialist, 24, 51, 53–55, 85, 244; liberal turn of, 134; post-Mao, 102–3, 109, 112, 151

—experimental, 85, 145–48, 154, 167–70, 187, 250–53; engaged, 1, 192–93, 198–99; European, 133; and individualization, 179; mainstream, 17, 20, 24, 50, 106, 195; mainstream feminist, 55; New Era, 133, 135, 152; and popular cinema, 146; post-Mao, 20, 85, 133, 138, 148, 151, 187, 194, 242; socialist, 51–52, 57, 71, 106, 137, 244–45; subjective, 2, 88, 173; women's, 21, 35, 158, 167–69, 173, 192, 195

—feminist, 18, 21, 33–34, 55, 58, 60, 107, 169, 195, 254; genres, biographical, 111, 155, 212; transnational, 81

—mainstream, 1, 10, 16, 50, 70, 193; experimental, 17, 20, 195; and feminist practices, 6; mass-oriented, 69, 80; proletarian, 70, 73; socialist, 55, 70; women's, 57

—practices, 12, 50, 52–55, 61, 150–54, 157, 161, 187, 193, 201, 206, 230; Chinese, 134, 136; filmmakers, of, 18, 85; mainstream, 148–49, 168, 198–99; marginalized, 32; socialist, 17, 87–88; Western, 135; women's, 33, 145, 158, 169, 232–33

—socialist, 5, 17, 51–55, 59, 87–88, 94; aesthetics of, 99, 134; authorship of, 6, 18, 71, 80–81, 237; classical, 159, 242; experimental, 137, 145–47, 244–45; feature film production of, 69; and gender, 102–3, 110, 166; genre films, 144; mainstream, 13, 15, 21, 24, 57, 106, 167; melodrama, 193; national, 53, 55, 74, 80, 82; new, 20, 48, 138–39, 146–47, 151, 169, 179, 235, 241–42, 253–54; pedagogical, 87, 90, 105–6; proletarian, 194; women's, 11, 21, 23–25, 57, 60–61, 84–85, 167, 236

—techniques: amateur actors, 155, 173; camera work, 152; close-ups, 174–75, 177; direct sound recordings, 155, 173; filming, 232; filters, 174; flashback, 86–87, 90, 173, 228; individual reflection, 157; internal

cinema (continued)
    monologue, 71, 73, 171, 175; long
    shots, 174; long take, 87, 135, 152, 155,
    174; montage, 54, 152, 174; motion,
    174; narrative, 59, 74, 88–89, 93, 99,
    103, 151, 159–60, 173, 215; natural
    lighting, 155, 173; on-location shoot-
    ing, 155, 173; point-of-view, 99, 102;
    repetitions, 88; shot/reverse-shot,
    102–3, 159, 251; still shots, 174; sub-
    jective camera, 87–88, 94, 175; sub-
    jective perception, 157; suspensions,
    88; telephoto lenses, 174; voice-over,
    87, 89–90, 99, 157–58, 173, 175, 177,
    187; wide-angle, 174
class, economic, 1, 7–8, 40, 72, 86, 97,
    103, 138, 190–91
Cold War, 59, 83, 139–40, 236; and art,
    105, 137; context of, 140, 210, 236;
    and economic constraints, 47, 84;
    effects of, 15; end of, 4; environ-
    ment of, 53; ideology of, 2, 8, 18, 23–
    24, 27–28, 54, 84, 160, 237; ideology,
    Western, 138; paradigms of, 85, 137,
    238; Second, 1–2, 26, 129; as stance,
    17–18, 26, 29, 31–32, 45, 239
collectivization, 44, 46, 55, 57, 70
Combat Illiteracy Campaigns, 49.
    See also women: education of
commercialism, 10, 146–47, 232
Communist Party, 86, 93, 96
Communist Youth League, 121
Confucianism, 44, 48, 63, 104, 221,
    226–27, 230, 233, 255–56
consciousness, 2–3, 9, 127, 147, 164, 173,
    179, 212, 215, 221, 223, 226, 230, 245;
    cultural, 28, 119; individual, 197, 233;
    independent, 87, 125–26
Contemporary Cinema, symposium, 21,
    107, 201–2, 233, 256
control, political, 2, 134, 136, 152, 179, 210
cosmopolitanism, 14, 47, 50
critics, 61–62, 64, 135, 139, 151–52, 154,
    156, 163–64, 177, 179, 197, 201–3,
    209–10, 226–27, 230
cross-dressing, 178–79, 181–82, 223

Cui Shuqin, 60
cultural practice, 1–6, 10–14, 35, 113–14,
    138, 155, 179, 197, 233, 248–49;
    ahistorical, 129; detached, 141, 147;
    feminist, 6, 24, 33, 50, 71, 83, 106,
    108, 233, 233; feminist, Western,
    35; gendered, 184; mainstream, 14,
    16, 32, 141–42, 152, 196; marginal-
    ized, 12, 23, 64; mass-oriented, 57,
    215; pedagogical, 85; pluralist, 136;
    politicized, 132, 134, 137; post-Mao,
    111, 113–14, 157, 227; post-second-
    wave, 3; and sexual difference, 233;
    socialist, 13, 20, 46, 55, 59, 87, 95, 97,
    104, 147, 196, 208, 245; women's, 14,
    18, 108, 131, 156, 156, 166, 170, 226
cultural production, 12–13, 46–47,
    136–37, 158, 163, 170, 187, 192–94;
    "creative freedom," 142, 178–79,
    217; post-Mao, 132; socialist, 16, 23,
    59, 134
Cultural Revolution, 1–2, 8, 111–13,
    137–38, 150–52, 155–56, 168, 170–72,
    202; androgynous model of, 110;
    art of, 136; cultural practice of,
    19; denunciation of, 69, 136, 143;
    derailed, 5, 121; educated youth,
    67, 180, 185; and film academy stu-
    dents, 151; as historical context, 168,
    173, 175, 180–82, 186, 208; ideology
    of, 19–20, 54, 123–24; late period
    of, 114, 116, 184; and opera, 214,
    223; outbreak of, 69; persecution
    during, 109; policy of, 141; politics
    of, 132–33, 154; post-Mao reaction
    to, 60; radicalism of, 174, 177–78;
    scholarly reassessment of, 33; "sent
    down" youth, 142, 171, 173, 180;
    sexual difference, erasure of, 175,
    177; time before, 54, 56, 133, 150, 171
cultural unconsciousness, 2, 200
culture, 2, 127, 138, 143, 206–7, 213,
    215, 226; depoliticization of, 135;
    detached, 141, 147; differences of,
    160, 227; female/maternal, 60, 64,
    129, 131, 165, 204, 207, 228, 243;

feminist, 1, 13, 19, 25, 39, 71, 80–81, 150, 206; feminist, Western, 35; film, 51; folk, 75, 200; and global politics, 32, 35, 84–85; Han (majority), 171–72, 175, 177; liberal turn of, 134; mainstream, 3, 5–7, 14, 16, 34, 46, 60, 137, 149; mainstream, feminist, 10–12, 17, 48–50; mass, 11, 46, 104, 106, 213, 236; minority, 168, 172, 175, 177; patriarchal, 3, 23, 164, 199, 206, 232; popular, 12, 53–54, 150, 213; post-Mao, 111, 113–14, 125, 157, 227; and sexual difference, 167; socialist, 11, 18, 23–24, 49, 60, 64, 85–87, 97–99, 104–106, 111, 142, 208, 237, 245; socialist feminist, 4, 7, 19, 47, 49–50, 71; socialist mainstream, 10, 15, 19, 25, 34, 80, 93, 169, 195, 239, 242; traditional, 6, 21, 44, 213, 227; Western, 127

Curie, Marie Sklodowska, 171–72

Dai Jinhua, 174, 230, 239, 256; article "'Human, Woman, Demon': A Woman's Predicament," 205–7, 221; article "Invisible Women," 165, 235–36, 243–44, 249–54; and poststructuralism, 206–7; on revolution, 94; on women's liberation, 60. *See also* Huang Shuqin: *Woman Demon Human*

Dai people, beauty, 172, 175; community, 172–73, 180, 185; culture, 171–72, 175, 184–85; dress, 171–72, 176–77, 179–81; family, 172, 184; gender issues, 172, 174–75, 179, 183; minority, 171, 173, 185; village, 171, 173, 175, 183

Deng Xiaoping, 19, 101, 108–9, 115, 124, 132, 241n121

depoliticization, 124–25, 136–37, 198, 201, 211; of film production, 134, 136, 194; and sexual difference, 124–25

desire, female, 207, 221, 228

Diamant, Neil J., 25

difference: female, 205, 207, 224–25, 245; concealed, 60–61; essential,

3, 6, 8–9, 125, 164, 178–79, 187, 245; natural, 118–19, 153; post-Mao understanding of, 131; repression of, 18, 105, 165–66, 168, 177, 199; and reproduction, 114; and Western feminism, 167, 178, 197, 204–5; and socialist women's liberation, 68, 126. *See also* female consciousness; sexual difference

discourse, 2, 45, 102, 131, 133, 136, 166, 205, 222, 226–27, 246; cultural, 196, 199, 215; dominant mainstream, 46, 109; feminist, 36, 48, 215; and liberal humanism, 119; mainstream, 10–11, 13, 27, 35, 126, 216, 236; mainstream, 1980s, 133, 151, 170, 172–73, 184, 187, 207, 225, 227, 233; mainstream feminist, 48; mainstream intellectual, 19–20, 108, 124–25, 131, 147–49, 193, 199, 233; post-Mao, 246; and universal modernity, 148–49; Western, 11, 18, 160

Dong Kena, 6, 18–19, 55–56, 85, 87–101, 105, 150, 196, 245; experimental cinema, post-Mao, 85; Hua Ming, 89
—*Small Grass Grows on the Kunlun Mountains*, 14, 18, 55, 83, 85, 87–92, 94–105; characters: Hui sao, 85–87, 89, 92–93, 95–101, 103–5, 245; Lao Hui, 88, 93, 95–96; Li Wanli, 77, 86, 88–92, 94–95, 99–101, 103, 105, 185; Xiao Liu, 90, 93, 96, 98; Drivers' Home, 86, 94–97, 99–101; and socialist imaginary, 87, 94, 101, 103–4, 245; gender difference, 83, 85, 87, 89, 91, 93, 95, 97, 99, 101–6; intersubjective relationship, 19, 75, 82, 94–95, 99–101; socialist community, 86, 94–95, 101, 104–5

economic development, 84, 120, 122, 124, 133, 138, 221, 226–27; and feminism, 35, 41; Marxist theory of, 117–19, 128; post-Mao, 2–3; socialist, 45–47, 106; and women's labor, 25, 110 economic reform, 20, 109, 119–20, 127, 129, 153, 187–88; ideology of, 8; implementation of, 15, 19; literary representations of, 111–13, 115; mainstream discourses of, 13, 227; and open-door policy, 33; post-Mao, 1, 6, 16, 128–29, 137, 142, 145, 197; and post-Mao feminism, 108; and sexual difference, 119; state-initiated, 146–48; and thought liberation, 5; urgency of, 132

economy, commodity, 15, 232

emancipation: economic, 40, 46; and feminism, 41; Marxist view of, 45, 113; and socialism, 36, 120, 205, 207; and Soviet policy, 38; women's, 36, 38, 41, 45, 49, 83, 113, 205, 207, 224, 227

emotions: 81, 92, 142, 201; female, 198, 202; forbidden, 217; human, 117; individual, 72, 80; of the masses, 77; women's, 164, 225

endeavors, feminist, 4, 9, 35, 119, 123, 129–31, 161, 170

engagement, sociopolitical, 143, 155, 210, 227

Enlightenment, 110, 125, 166–67, 184, 186; Western, 64

environment, socialist, 1, 70, 103–5, 155

equality, social, 105, 226

essentialism, 3, 60, 119, 187, 194, 201, 206–11, 231

ethics, 1, 14, 18, 46, 112, 118–19, 127; revolutionary, 112; socialism, 14

experience, cultural, 69, 174, 241–42

experimentation, 54, 58, 250–51, 253; artistic, 1, 55, 88, 200. *See also* aesthetics: experimental

expression: cultural, 9, 147; subjective, 153, 155, 187, 201

family: bourgeois, 63, 90; happy, 217; proletarian, 78, 94; traditional, 64, 67, 114, 215, 222, 243; woman's, 212

father, 61–63, 78, 162, 173, 180, 209, 213–14, 225; nonbiological, 216–19, 224

female consciousness, 168, 195–97, 202–5, 207, 225, 227–28, 254; bourgeois, 164; and difference, 179; essential(ized), 127, 193, 231; and female inner world, 223; and feminism, 203–4; independent, 3, 7, 9, 126, 187, 216; linked to market economy, 230–33; suppressed, 18, 163–64, 177; and post-Mao feminist practice, 21–22; and self, 116, 123, 128, 221, 226, 227–29; universal, 131; and "women's cinema," 107–8, 159–60

female film, 202, 205, 254. *See also* women's cinema

feminism: antithetical to socialism, 8, 31; Chinese, 5, 17, 29, 32, 35–36, 47–50, 159–60, 241; cine-feminism, 18, 84–85, 103, 203, 205, 239, 252; film scholars, post-Mao, 6, 10, 68, 205; independent, 19, 115, 119–20, 122, 128, 131, 170, 197, 216, 239; institutionalized, 170; interdependent with socialism, 46; Lacanian, 167; left-wing, 48, 63; liberal, 28, 40, 130, 238; Marxist, 36, 128; policies of, 33, 37, 39, 41, 44; post-second-wave, 3–4, 8, 60, 84, 108, 129, 131, 150–51, 163, 207, 235; poststructuralist, 206, 230; practices, post-Mao, 11, 21, 115, 119, 123, 129, 170, 223; psychoanalytic, Western, 230; radical, 19, 28, 83–84, 128–30, 164, 168, 238–39, 247, 252; terminology, 164; theories of, post-Mao, 128; transnational, 4;
—cultural, 2, 8, 18, 28, 64, 129, 131, 164, 168, 200, 207, 227–28; post-Mao, 227–28, 233; universal, 21, 225, 230, 233
—post-Mao, 5, 108, 111, 113, 118, 120, 207, 230, 236, 254; 1980s, 3, 9, 19, 21; development of, 108, 119; early, 170, 227; and economic transformation, 131, 227; feminist scholars, 6, 8, 10, 60, 68–69, 93, 114, 116, 126–27, 158, 177, 227, 243, 252; film

studies, 34, 60, 84; and gender difference, 3, 104, 174, 207; and gender equality, 126; independent, 19, 115, 119–20, 122–24, 128, 148, 197, 239; late-1980s, 5, 21, 116, 131, 228; and mainstream intellectual discourses, 125–26; mid-1980s, 3, 108, 123; and sexual difference, 21, 227–28; and socialist feminism, 123, 130–31, 170; and socialist women's cinema, 11; and Western feminism, 104, 128–29, 164, 235; and women's cultural practice, 119; and women's liberation, 9

—practices of, 3–6, 35, 40, 81, 131, 215, 235–36; institutional, 32, 34–35, 40; post-Mao, 111, 113, 115, 119–20, 123, 129, 170; socialist, 108, 123, 126, 130–31, 178

—socialist, 3, 6, 49, 155, 169–70, 200, 238–40, 247; 1950s repudiation of, 20; 1980s dismissal of, 126; challenges to, 163–64; Chinese, 160, 241; and cultural practice, 104, 106; culture of, 13, 49; development of, 15, 47–48; early post-Mao era, in, 114–15; emergence of, 36; and first generation of female filmmakers, 80; and history, 84; integrated, 19, 31–32, 57, 82, 123, 125, 193, 242; Jiangxi Soviet, 39, 42; limitations of, 44, 69; mainstream, 4; and mainstream cinema, 5, 169; mainstream cultural, 14, 50; Marxist, 128; and other cultural movements, 46, 226; and proletarian women, 48; practice of, 4–6, 9, 16, 19, 32, 36, 46, 83–84, 108, 115, 119, 123, 126, 130–31, 155, 178, 226; renouncement of integrated, 131; state-sponsored, 59; theories, 116

—Western, 2, 58, 167, 203–4, 254; challenged, 33; cinefeminist, 32, 205; and cultural practice, 33; and film theory, 34; and gender erasure, 104; global spread of, 36; history of,

204; influence of, 197; and liberal ideas, 122; movements and theory of, 116, 127, 164, 227; nonmaterialist, 31; post-second-wave, 60, 108, 235; poststructuralist, 230; radical, 23–24, 27, 83–85, 105, 129, 168; socialist, 48; theories of, 158, 161–65; values of, 28

feminist studies, 1, 24, 32, 36, 39, 122, 147, 164, 206, 224, 227, 236

film academies, 51, 150, 192; Beijing Film Academy, 15, 133, 150–51, 189, 195, 242, 250; Central Academy of Drama, 150; Shanghai Professional Film School, 151

film critics, 33–34, 52–53, 59–60, 125, 134, 138–39, 151, 195, 197, 201–3, 230

film genres, 89, 94, 96, 133, 144, 152, 189, 193, 199, 230; revolutionary, 94

film industry, 16–17, 20, 24, 34, 51, 55, 57, 70, 144, 199, 206–7, 232

film language, 134, 136, 151–52, 174, 206, 248, 250

filmmakers, 81, 140–41, 190, 208; 1950s, 24, 70, 81; 1980s, 150, 158; denounced, 69; directors, 106, 135, 152, 242; and European film, 140–42, 152; and female intellectuals, 114; Fifth Generation, 15, 133, 142–46, 144, 151, 179, 196–98, 201, 212; Fourth Generation, 133–35, 145, 150, 152, 195, 201, 250; French New Wave (see French New Wave); post-Mao, 159; professional, lack of, 57; Sixth Generation, 148, 151, 188; socialist, 18, 24, 51–52, 57, 60, 81, 85, 99, 105, 153, 169; style of, 54–55, 59, 72, 157, 193, 208

—female, 5–6, 40, 84, 120, 148, 160, 199, 241, 245; and commercial cinema, 199, 232; emergence of, 60; first generation, 17, 24, 56–58, 69–70, 80–81, 150; individual agency of, 57, 59; institutional support of, 55, 150–51, 192; and mainstream experimental cinema, 151; and

filmmakers (continued)
  mainstream culture, 15–16, 25, 197,
    206; and production of culture, 1,
    18, 48, 158, 186–87; Mao-era, 3, 18,
    24–25, 56, 169, 204; marginaliza-
    tion of, 16, 20–21, 32–33, 144–45,
    232; New Era, 20, 144–45, 200; and
    post-Mao feminism, 10–11, 60,
    105, 254; publications on, 24, 107,
    165–68, 237; and women's cinema,
    88, 107, 158, 165–67, 169, 196–97.
    See also Dong Kena; Huang
    Shuqin; sexual difference; Wang
    Ping; Zhang Nuanxin
filmmaking, 52–54, 135, 153–57, 167, 196,
    199; and commercial production,
    146, 192; as cultural practice, 50;
    and cultural transformations, 11;
    experimental, 17, 170, 174; inde-
    pendent, 12; mainstream, chal-
    lenges to, 32; post-Mao, 151–52; and
    socialism, 59, 71, 81, 87, 133, 143, 158;
    women's, 1, 6; and women's sexual
    difference, 197
films: distribution of, 13, 16, 148, 230;
    experimental, 1, 81, 145, 174, 179–80,
    192, 196, 201, 250; feminist, 31, 34;
    mainstream, 18, 32, 34, 57, 61, 71,
    133, 167, 174, 199; and mobile pro-
    jection teams, 49; national awards,
    51; New Era, 133; and pluralism, 157;
    post-Mao production of, 143–46;
    production of, 15, 161, 212–13,
    241–42; progressive, 134–35; and the
    privatization of production, 16, 192;
    and sexual difference, 102; socialist,
    13, 34, 50–52, 59, 69, 87, 241; social-
    ist mainstream, 18, 55; soundtrack,
    174. See also cinema
film studies, 6, 23, 33, 58, 134, 136, 141,
    163, 168, 252; socialist, 23
film studios, 51, 57, 68; August First Lib-
    eration Army Film Studio, 57–58,
    68–69, 71, 82; Beijing Film Studio,
    85; Northeast Film Studio, 51, 66,
    242; Shanghai Dubbing Studio, 54;

Shanghai Film Studio, 201; social-
    ist, 5, 13, 58, 230; state, 13, 51, 55, 57,
    192, 230
film theory, 150, 248, 250; and depoliti-
    cization of Chinese film practice,
    135–37, 141, 143–44, 152–53; foreign,
    133–34, 139; and masculine avant-
    garde, 19; feminist, 33–35, 58, 205;
    Western, 55, 134, 204–5
folk culture, Chinese, 54, 77, 200
forces, sociopolitical, 28, 68, 120, 202,
    215, 232
Four Modernizations, 108–9, 156
Four Selfs, 122
France, 20, 138–40, 232
French Communist Party, 140
French New Wave, 20, 54–55, 133–35,
    138–41, 143, 145, 150–55, 236, 242,
    248–49; auteur theory, 138; ideol-
    ogy, 141; reception of, 141; tech-
    niques of, 155
Freud, Sigmund, 200, 202–3

Gang of Four, 132, 134, 248
gender, 30–31, 50, 66, 68–69, 170–71,
    202, 236–37; androgynous model,
    112–13, 115; avant-gardism, in, 145;
    blindness, 44, 104, 111, 119, 128, 246;
    and class, 2, 8, 36, 38, 43, 65, 136;
    concealing difference of, 61; and
    culture, 4; and the defeminization
    of women, 110, 126, 140, 222, 252,
    256; discourse, in, 80, 102, 139, 211;
    discrimination, 108, 111, 113, 115,
    128; and the division of labor, 110,
    127, 256; erasure of, 177, 245, 247,
    253, 256; essentialized, 106, 178,
    224; and experimental cinema,
    20; femininity, 75, 110, 112–14, 140,
    145, 165, 171, 175, 179, 198, 220, 222;
    formation, sociocultural nature of,
    105; hierarchy of, 7, 12, 30, 61, 69,
    104, 110, 115, 117, 128, 184; iden-
    tity, 60, 178; intersubjective, 95;
    and mainstream culture, 11; male
    masculinity, 110, 145, 186, 194, 222;

negotiations, 67–68, 74, 94, 97; as performance, 166–67, 178, 222–23; policy, 9, 221; post-Mao, 110, 222; and post-Mao Chinese feminism, 3; reconfiguration of, 5, 196, 200, 211, 231; relationships, 28, 46–47, 104, 140, 215, 222; roles, 44, 46–47, 55, 58, 155, 172, 190, 193, 217, 226; as a scientific category, 124–26; sex/gender gap, 113–14, 118, 125; sexual difference, 113, 178; and socialism, 5, 26, 28, 31, 48, 55, 58–59; studies of, 23–26, 116, 226; traditional, 46–47, 226; transformation of, 17, 145, 202, 215, 232; voice, 151

—difference, 18, 68, 83, 85, 87, 89, 91, 97, 99, 101, 103–5, 110; awakening to, 177; Cultural Revolution, in the, 175; erasure of, 99; essentialized, 197; natural, 118–19, 129; questioning a uniform model of, 179; psychological approach to, 203

—equality, 1–2, 6, 10, 13, 48–49, 55, 57–58, 77, 123, 131, 175, 179, 205; and class equality, 93, 103–4, 121; endorsed, 105; familial, 225; institutionalized, 70, 82, 120, 131, 150, 155, 171–72, 213; linked with political liberation, 110; socialist, 60, 68, 104, 110, 113–14, 126–27, 130, 145, 172, 213; and socialist feminism, 81–83; socialist policy on, 165; socioeconomic, 114, 119, 159–60; and women's liberation, 117, 207, 227

gendered personal, 19, 68, 87, 106, 108, 111, 114–15, 131, 153, 155, 250

geopolitics, 1, 5–7, 9, 18, 31, 40, 81, 83–85, 103

Golden Bear Award, 146, 196

government, nationalist, 42–43, 65, 198, 239

Great Leap Forward, 46

Han Chen, 178

happiness, women's, 204–7, 215, 225, 226

Harding, Harry, 26

Hartmann, Heidi, 128

Hershatter, Gail, 237n15

Hess, John, 139

history, socialist, 21, 119, 144, 151, 169, 202; socialist aesthetic approach, 214; sociopolitical, 211, 215, 225; women's, 58, 99, 117, 127, 129, 204–5, 249

Hollywood, 10, 35, 53–54, 103, 199, 206; films, 53–54, 103

Hong, Xia, 134

Hua Mulan, 61, 69, 166, 243n15

Huang Shuqin, 71–73, 195, 214–16, 218, 220–25; and commercial production, 206; essays, 227–33, 254–56; and essentialist theatre, 209; and film academies, 150, 192; film practice of, 227, 233; interviews, 208–9, 211, 224, 227, 232–33; as representative female director, 6; and *xieyi* aesthetic, 211

—*A Soul Haunted by Painting*, 230–32; characters: Pan Zanhua, 230; Zhang Yuliang, 231–32; commercial film, 230, 232; female consciousness, 231, 233

—*Woman Demon Human*, 16, 21, 195–96, 254; and "Ardent Pursuit of Art," 201, 231; characters: non-biological father, 216–19, 224–25; mother, 211, 213, 216–17, 219, 221–22, 228–29; Qiu Yun, 199, 201–5, 211–12, 214–22, 224–26, 228–31; Teacher Zhang, 205, 219–20; Zhong Kui, 199, 203, 205, 208, 212, 222–26, 228–30; and "Director's Reflections on Woman Demon Human," 211; female desire, 216, 219, 221; haystack scenes, 218–19; and neotraditionalism, 195, 208, 221, 224–26, 230, 232; self-salvation in, 206, 221–22, 224; sexual difference in, 196, 199, 202, 205

Huang Zongjiang, 71, 72–73

Huang Zuolin, 61, 209–10

humanism, 3, 109–11, 124, 135, 142, 145, 167, 207, 216, 231–32

Hu Mei, 151, 158, 162, 168, 196–97, 199; *Army Nurse*, 158–59, 161, 168, 197, 204, 254

Hundred Flower Film Festival, 56, 70

Hundred Flowers Campaign, 52, 71

Hu Shiyan, 71–73, 77–78, 142, 162; "The Story of Liubao Village," characters: Er meizi, 73, 77–80; Li Jin, 72–75, 77–79; Liu huzi, 77–78; Song Wei, 72–74, 77, 79

Ibsen, Henrik *A Doll's House*, 62–63. *See also* Wang Ping
—Nora, 62–64, 69, 241; left-wing Nora, 61–65, 69; Nanjing Nora, 62, 65; Shanghai Nora, 62

icons, female, 48, 237

identity, 178–79, 204, 207

ideology, 124, 136, 159–61, 169, 179, 221, 244; Cold War, 8, 84, 138, 237, 251; consensus, 157, 159–60; new, 8, 232; patriarchal, 47, 206; socialist, 3, 24, 57, 110, 120, 152; traditional, 142, 227

imperialism, 48; anti-imperialism, 29, 35; cultural, 161, 168; Japanese, 120; Western, 40, 64, 84, 120

independence, women's, 8, 25, 62, 101, 107, 122–25, 167, 190, 231

individualism, 8, 15, 34–35, 49, 181–82, 192, 255; abstract, 20, 174, 186–87, 189, 193; bourgeois, 7, 72; capitalist, 28–29; commercialized, 189, 191, 194; critical, 147; detached, 174, 184, 186–87, 189, 193–94; elitist, 15, 179, 187, 193; Enlightenment, 116, 167; Western, 166, 221

inner world, 214–15, 223–24, 231

intellectuals, Chinese, 109, 124, 132, 136, 163, 180, 210, 215, 243; female, 12, 109, 114–15, 123, 131; male, 110, 112, 119, 126–27, 140, 172, 186, 222, 246, 249; male, post-Mao, 145

intrinsicalism, 210. *See also* essentialism; *xieyi*

Italian neorealism, 54–55, 134, 141, 150–52; Rossellini, Roberto, 54

Jameson, Fredric, 235n1

Jiang Jieshi, 63; government of, 64–65

Jiang Qing, 62, 244n5, 248n1

Jiangxi Soviet, 38–42, 240; and Chinese women, 39

Jiang Zilong, 208, 223

Jin Fenglan, 87

Johnson, Kay Ann, 24, 238n24, 240n70

Johnston, Claire, 32, 56, 254n26

Jung, Carl, 143, 200; collective unconscious, 2, 143, 200

Kaplan, Ann E., 25, 161–62, 164–65, 167, 169, 237n6, 254n25

Kosmodemyanskaya, Zoya, 171–72

labor, and gender, 39, 44, 47, 110, 116, 126–27, 191, 256

Lacan, Jacques, 166; Lacanian feminism, 167; Lacanian theory, 166, 252n88; Western poststructuralism, 6, 58, 163, 166–67, 205, 252n88

land reform, 30–31, 43, 46

language: female, 207, 230; patriarchal, 207

Lan Ping, 62. *See also* Jiang Qing

left-wing, 28, 129, 134, 146, 236; activism, 65–66, 69, 71; artists, 17, 92; cultural productions, 134; drama, 61–62, 64–65, 82; feminists, 27, 48, 241; film movements, 53, 82, 133, 150; intellectuals, 18, 35, 72, 74, 80; movements, 8–9, 28, 48, 65, 68, 129, 146; Nora, 63 (*see also* Ibsen, Henrik); period, of biography, 60, 69–70 (*see also* Wang Ping); practices, repudiation of, 20; and socialism, 141; Western, 128, 131, 238

legal codes, new, 30, 38

liberalism, 168, 256

liberation, 9, 43, 45, 60, 116, 118, 120, 156, 165, 179, 207, 211; individual, 63, 67;

political, 110; proletarian, 36, 47; social, 38, 119, 204; socialist, 24, 29, 159–60, 163–64; thought, 2, 5, 108–9, 135, 137, 148, 155, 170, 193 —women's, 4, 7–8, 127–28, 236, 247; and CCP, 25, 40; Chinese, 2, 6, 17, 27, 42–43, 82, 164, 204, 252; Chinese socialist, 8, 24, 29, 83–84, 120, 159, 163, 243–44; and class, 29, 34, 41; constraints imposed on, 6; (socio) economic, 38, 47, 60, 113; emancipatory vision of, 4; independent, 85; institutional support for, 31; and Maoism, 121, 126; and Marxism, 36, 40, 44, 119–20, 127, 239; material, 38; of 1980s, 27, 83; post-Mao, 126; (socio)political, 60–61, 113, 125, 165, 207; rural, 30, 67; socialist, 9, 60, 68, 130, 160, 204, 207, 216, 235; as terminology, 7; ultimate, 9, 116–18, 129, 131; universal, 45, 83, 130; Western, 8–9, 85, 105, 128, 130. *See also* emancipation

Li Duoyu, 143–44

Lin, Chun, 122

Lin, James, 128

Li Shuangshuang, 101–3

literary practice, 111, 114

literature, avant-garde, 143; Chinese, 111, 114–15, 142, 244; engaged, 139–40, 143, 173; minor, 35; socialist, 24, 86, 97, 104

Li Tuo, 153, 154; "On the Modernization of Film Language," 134–36, 141, 151–53;

Liu Miaomiao, 151, 198, 212; *Hoofbeats*, 198; and sexual difference, 198

Li Xiaojiang, 114, 164, 227; *Eve's Exploration*, 125; and feminist independence, 123–26; and the gendered personal, 114, 115, 131; and post-Mao feminism, 8, 19, 115–16; "The Progress of Humanity and Women's Liberation," 116–17, 128, 130, 236n16; and revision of Marxist theory, 115–16, 119, 124, 128; sexual differ-

ence, 107, 110, 113–19, 124–27, 129, 131; universal model, 107, 110, 127, 130; and Western (radical) feminist theory, 8, 19, 127–31; and women's studies movement, 115, 123; and Zhang Jie, 114, 118, 246n16

Li Yunhe, 62. *See also* Jiang Qing

Li Zehou, 2, 110, 124, 143, 200, 247n58, 253n117, 255n60, 255n61, 256n62

Long March, 198

love, ideal, 112; romantic, 61, 63–64, 70–73, 96, 111, 156, 161, 171, 203

Lu Xiaoya, 196–97

Maeterlinck, Maurice, 208

mainstream, 127, 146–47, 152–53, 167–68, 197, 208–9, 212, 215, 236, 241; cinema, 16, 18, 21, 34, 54, 132–33, 136, 150, 174, 195, 206; experimental cinema, 17, 20, 151, 196, 245; cultural practice, New Era, 110–11; culture, 11–15, 19, 46, 242; feminist culture, 4, 24, 32, 45, 47, 49–50, 215; film practice, 5, 33, 84–85, 148–49, 168–69, 198; film production, 55, 167, 199; ideologies, 81; intellectual movements, 170, 193, 197; patriarchal culture, 23; proletarian cinema, 1, 70; socialist cinema, 25, 56–61, 70–71, 81, 86, 106; socialist culture, 10, 34, 87, 93, 142, 239; socialist feminism, 80; visual culture, 1; women's cinema, 6 —discourse, 27, 33, 119, 147, 216; 1980s, 126, 133, 136, 151, 170, 172–73, 184, 187, 207, 225, 227, 229; cultural, 16, 196, 215; feminist, 46, 48, 215; intellectual, 10, 19, 108–9, 124–25, 131, 152, 193; post-Mao, 148–49, 246; Western, 11, 18, 35

male-centered, 166, 221; avant-garde, 147; cinema, 145–46, 206; culture, 21, 145, 164, 232; pleasure principle, 206–7; society, 232; subjectivity, 146; values, 111, 147

Mao Zedong, 42, 46, 96, 107, 135, 210, 213, 236n31; era of, 10, 18, 21, 24, 33, 88, 101–3, 155, 222–23, 232–33; and female directors, 232; and filmmaking, 54; and Maoism, 121, 124, 142, 195, 208, 220, 246, 256; and Maoist Women's Federation, 121; and opera, 213–14; and reform period, 131; "Report on an Investigation of the Peasant Movement in Hunan, March 1927," 37; and revolutionary androgynous model, 115; socialist China, of, 7, 14, 56, 58, 71, 83, 102, 108–12, 162, 198, 204, 211; socialist China and feminist practice, 123; socialist film production, 167, 169; and socialist women's cinema, 25; wife, 62, 248 (*see also* Jiang Qing); and women, 42, 46, 108, 111, 233, 246; world cinema and the Mao era, 151

market, 197, 199, 226–27, 233; and capitalism, 13, 109, 190; capital, 188; commercialism, 15, 193; commodity, 189; consumption, 199; demand, 145, 187; development, 6, 121–23, 131, 137, 147, 169, 192, 221, 226–27, 232; economy, 15–16, 18–19, 108, 116, 122, 143, 148–49, 158, 163, 232–33; economy, France, 232; economy, United States, 232; era, 126, 225; feminism, 110; and film genres, 144; global, 4–5, 22, 129, 146, 168, 227; ideology, 35; individualism, 191, 193–94; liberalism, 221; and mainstream culture, 34, 46; post-Mao era, 11; progressive, 197; rationality, 221; and sexual difference, 127; society, 230; universal, 3, 84; value, 20

Markusen, Ann R., 128

marriage, 112, 205, 230–31, 238, 240; arranged, 21, 62–63, 66–67, 216–17, 225, 228; Confucian, 221, 225–26; conventional, 111, 115, 179, 222, 226, 231; and divorce, 216, 240; freedom of, 38, 63; marriage laws of 1950–53, 25, 46, 49; marriage policy, army's, 80; and women's destiny, 156, 206, 224, 231; and women's domestication, 172, 179, 184

Marx, Karl. *See* theory, Marxist

masses, 11, 14, 46, 82, 87, 215; proletariat, 50, 77, 97, 137, 142, 243

materialism, historical, 2, 109, 129, 154, 236

media, mass, 11–12, 50, 64, 102–3

Mei Lanfang, 210, 213

memory, 72, 86, 174, 206, 237, 241

mentality, cultural, 211–12, 215

Miller, Nancy, 58

modernism, 136, 162, 201

modernity, 3, 18, 33, 109, 133, 139, 152, 227; universal, 5, 148–49, 169, 184, 193

Mohanty, Chandra Talpade, 236n14

mother: character of, 156, 180, 186, 211, 213, 216, 218–19, 221–22, 228–29; Li Xiaojiang, in role as, 114, 117, 127; loss of, 78; mother-daughter bond, 112, 216, 217, 219, 221; mother-daughter disidentification, 217, 221; and Oedipal complex, 160; relationship with child, 119; and romantic love, 111–12; stepmother, 217; strong woman, 156; Wang Ping, in role as, 65–66, 69, 243; title, 31

movements: anticapitalist, 131, 162; Chinese women's, 36, 41, 163; cultural, 65, 110, 120, 168, 174, 186, 200, 235, 237, 249; feminist, 2, 8–9, 20, 29, 41, 111, 115, 127, 160, 163–64, 170, 204, 227; May Fourth, 25, 36, 40, 48, 60–61, 63–64, 67–68, 124, 135, 166–67, 216, 238–40, 243, 255; political, 8–9, 12, 28, 48, 53, 68–69, 125, 130, 146, 163–64, 201, 214–15; Root-Seeking, 2, 142–43, 145, 170, 200–201, 221; "Searching for Real Men," 145; socialist, 9; thought liberation, 108, 170; "Up to the Mountain and Down to the Countryside," 171, 173, 185 (*see also* Cultural Revolution)

—feminist, 111, 115, 160, 170, 204, 227; Chinese, compared to Western, 127, 164; and Chinese revolution, 29; and global changes, 2; independent, 20, 41; international socialist, 10; universal model for, 8; Western, 9, 116, 127, 163

—May Fourth: arranged marriage, target of, 67–68, 216; CCP's departure from, 25, 40, 238–40; feminist legacy of, 48; humanism in, 124; and left-wing, 48; and Marxism, 36; and New Woman, 60–61, 63; and Nora, 63–64 (*see also* Ibsen, Henrik); and radical liberalism, 243, 255; and Westernization, 135; and women's cultural practice, 166–67

—political, 201, 214–15; anti-imperial, 35–36; and cultural practice, 12, 237; disconnect from feminism, 120; and economic, 28, 30, 35, 241; left-wing, 9, 68–69, 129–30; problems of, 125; and women's movements, 163–64

—women's, 41–42, 105, 113, 121–23, 163–64, 240; and gender equality, 10, 46, 117; institutionalized, 32; peasant, 37, 39–40; and proletarian liberation, 36; "Resolution on the Women's Movement," 37; socialist, 23–24; and socialist revolution, 28, 44; Western, 107, 164; and women's liberation, 8–9, 125, 130, 252; women's studies, 115

Mulvey, Laura, 32, 34, 167, 252n88, 254n26

Nanjing, 61–62, 65; government, 62, 64; "Nanjing Nora," 62, 65. *See also* Wang Ping

nationalism, 50, 146; socialist, 50

National Science Conference, 124

New Era, 124, 130, 154–55, 193, 252; cinema of, 132, 133; Chinese women's cinema, symposium on, 107, 233; cultural pluralism in, 111, 132; and the Cultural Revolution, 109; and experimental cinema, 19–20, 135, 145, 152, 187; female directors, 144–45, 148, 200; and film theory, 134; and French New Wave, 138–41; and gender discrimination, 108; gender reconfiguration in, 115; and gender values, traditional, 155; individual subjectivity in, 114; love and marriage in, 112; mainstream cultural practice of, 110; National Conference on Women's Issues, 122; and sexual difference, 127

New Fourth Army, 72, 77–79

new woman, 60, 63–64, 217

objectivity, scientific, 8, 124

Oedipal complex, 160, 162, 164, 166

opera, 54, 199, 201, 208, 213–14, 256; artist, female, 208; child star, 208, 213; clapper opera, 213; films, 54, 208, 213; Hebei opera, 213–14, 223; Hebei, Great Leap Forward Youth Opera Troupe, 213; institutional endorsement, 214; *Lin Chong Flees at Night*, 54, 208–10, 214, 255; *Lotus Lantern*, 214; male characters, ideal, 199; male mentor, 217; masters, 213–15, 219, 224; *The Monkey King*, 214; performance, 213–14, 216–17, 223; Plum Performance Award, 214; regional, 223; Peking, 223; Sichuan, 223; repertoire, 223; revolutionary, 208; roles, male, 219–20, 223; roles, unconventional, 226; scholarship, Hu Xingliang, 255; singer, 219; stage, 223; teachers, 213–14; traditional, 150, 213; troupes, 213, 217, 223, 226; troupes, provincial, 213–14, 219–20

ownership, public, 46, 59, 118, 131

Paczuska, Anna, 128

party, 25, 36–37, 41–42, 52, 86, 95–96, 101–2, 120–23, 142, 189, 244; CCP, 25, 36–37, 44, 61, 93, 103, 108, 198; French Communist Party, 140; Nationalist, 37, 39, 64 party-state, 2, 8, 13, 46–47, 51, 122–23, 126

patriarchy: antipatriarchal space, 178; and capitalism, 11, 27, 44, 48, 103; characters, 21, 104, 222–24, 226, 228; and Chinese socialist revolution, 16–17, 23, 25, 27, 235–40; criticism on, 17, 24, 26–27, 31, 58, 166–67, 235–36; and family structure, 61, 63, 102; and ideology, 10–11, 47, 103, 143, 206; language of, 32; and radical feminism, 28, 129; rural, 29–30; socialist values combatting, 1, 46, 80; socioeconomic structures of, 8; transhistorical, 3, 128–29, 131, 197, 207, 230; universal, 69, 129, 207, 236; women's cinema, resisting, 35, 199; and women's movements, 117, 204

Pei Yanling, 208, 211–14, 216, 223–24, 226, 255; life, 208, 211–14, 216; mother, 213, 216; Zhong Kui, performance of, 223

Peking, 223; University of, 255n62

Peng Xiaolian, 151, 197, 199–200, 212; *Women's Stories*, 197

People's Daily, 85, 247

People's Liberation Army, 57, 66

People's Republic of China, 13, 27, 40, 45, 56–57

phallocentric, 102–3, 166, 204–6. *See also* male-centered

pluralism, cultural, 2, 109, 132, 149, 152–53, 156–57, 185, 190

post-Mao era, 1, 10, 54, 115, 121, 122–23, 159, 189, 200; early, 20, 109, 113–14, 116, 125, 131–32, 143, 145, 149–55, 157–58, 166, 170–71, 190; and gender discrimination, 111; market, 11; traditional family values, 102–3

poststructuralism, 6, 58–59, 163, 166–68, 205–7, 230, 252, 254. *See also* Lacan, Jacques

property rights, private, 45, 121

psychoanalysis, 2, 143, 200, 203–5, 252n88

psychocultural, 3, 211, 230; realm, 211–12, 215; space, 229

public space, feminist, 24, 32, 46, 125

Qinghai-Tibet Plateau, 86, 89–91

radicalism, 174, 178, 238; Western-influenced, 221

realism, 54, 111, 134, 141, 190, 201, 210, 212; conventions of, 208; documentary, 155–57, 188–89; "truthful state of the real," 141, 153–54; Western, *xieshi*, 209

reality, historical, 89, 152, 154;

Red Army, 38, 40, 198; soldiers, female, 198

relationships: emotional, 201; extramarital, 216; forbidden, 219; heterosexual, 179; personal, 215; social, 221; unhappy, 216

representation, cultural, 51, 53, 111, 216

reproduction, 44, 116, 129; role of, 114, 117, 129

Resnais, Alain, *Hiroshima mon amour*, 55

revolution: Chinese, 29, 56, 236–37, 239; Chinese socialist, 7–10, 16–17, 23–29, 31, 34, 38, 40–42, 46, 243; feminist, 42, 44; history of, 120; and love, 72, 244; narratives of, 245; proletarian, 8–9, 24, 26, 37, 40, 51, 240; social, 45, 163, 165, 204, 254; socialist, 16, 23–25, 27–29, 31, 41–45, 101; and women, 43–44, 81, 238, 240, 247. *See* Wang Ping: *The Story of Liubao Village*

revolutionary, 44, 53, 69–70, 74, 105

ritual, cultural, 222, 225; gender, 224; marriage, 21, 221, 224–26, 228; for self-representation, 208

Sartre, Jean-Paul, 139–40, 143

scholars, 40, 43, 50, 109, 114, 116, 124, 157, 178, 230; of China, 10, 25, 30–32, 47, 85, 236; Chinese, 33, 85, 122, 128, 149, 163; feminist, 4, 32, 44, 58, 99, 151, 158, 164–65, 203; feminist film, 3, 6, 11, 18, 20, 205; feminist film, post-Mao, 60, 68–69, 84, 226–27, 244, 252; film, 3, 151, 158, 230; international, 195; post-Mao, 93, 118, 123,

126–27, 158, 177, 243; scholarship, 23, 129, 169, 235n3; social science-oriented, 24, 238; Western, 8, 12, 27, 83, 130, 140, 159, 237, 240

science, 19, 24, 108–9, 116, 124–25

self, female, 68, 70, 82, 163, 204, 207, 215, 221–23, 226, 230

self-agency, 66, 156

self-commodification, 190–91; of women, 146, 190–91, 193. *See also* Zhang Nuanxin

self-consciousness, 117, 125, 228

self-redemption, 206, 226

self-representation, 221–22, 225, 229

self-salvation, female, 21, 221–22, 224

Sellier, Geneviève, 139–40, 236, 248–50

sex, 5, 29, 38, 43, 187, 246

sexual difference, 167, 196–99, 205, 245, 254; 1980s, 254; biologically defined, 21, 124–25, 219, 228, 233; capitalist, 178; discourse of, 102, 196; Enlightenment, 2; essential, 3, 103, 174, 187, 197, 207; and female self, 177, 207, 221; in films, 158, 161–62, 198, 216; Li Xiaojiang, writings on, 114–19, 127, 129; mainstreamed, 2, 193; as marker of post-Mao era, 110; natural, 20–21, 68, 116, 119, 164, 179, 199, 204, 220, 233; nonalienated, 115, 117–18, 127, 129; in post-Mao scholarship, 60, 131, 175, 177, 228; retheorization of, 85, 127; and scientism, 124–25, 227; and traditional femininity, 113–14, 178; transhistorical, 212; and universality, 107, 131, 147, 202, 221, 232; and women's oppression, 28

Shanghai, 51, 53, 57, 62–63, 65–66, 71, 86, 90, 146, 150, 243, 249; background, 54, 89; left-wing drama movement, 61–62; massacre, 64

Shanxi, 65–66, 92–93

Shao Mujun, 203–5; essay "The Agony of Suppressing Female Id: A Reading of Woman Demon Human," 203. *See also* Huang Shuqin, *Woman Demon Human*

Shi Faming, 202; "Life Perceived through Female Consciousness," 203. *See also* Huang Shuqin, *Woman Demon Human*

Shi Nan, *A Soul Haunted by Painting* (novel), 230

socialism, 44; and capitalism, 2, 29; and cosmopolitanism, 47, 50, 236, 241; cultural, 13; cultural practice, 13, 15, 20, 55, 59, 95, 97, 104, 141, 245; cultural production, 16, 23, 59, 106, 134; culture of, 10–11, 13–16, 23–24, 58–59, 87, 93, 101, 112; and economic development, 15, 31, 45; era of, 44, 48, 110, 114, 222; and feminism (*see* feminism; socialist); and gender, 26, 104, 111; gender equality, 82, 114, 213; history, 21, 249; ideology of, 3, 24; institutionalized, 242; institutional support, 31, 58, 68, 105, 150; mainstream culture of, 3, 14–16, 18, 34, 80, 239, 242; objectives of, 3; and patriarchy, 28; political aspects, 3, 13–14, 24, 46, 193; political endeavor, 13–14; post-Mao, 3; practice of, 3, 15, 46; system, 115, 130; transformations, 9, 13–14, 17, 24, 57

—and socialist revolution, 5–10, 14, 16–17, 128, 147, 221, 235–40, 243–244; cause, 79; and female consciousness, 80–82; and feminist revolution, 9; in films, 82, 85–86, 88–89, 94, 96, 101; and gender equality, 207; institutionalization of, 24, 32, 34; patriarchal character of, 23, 25, 27, 29; and rural peasants, 27, 37, 46, 80–81; practices of, 39; and proletarian class revolution, 29, 51, 72, 240; and radical feminism, 28; reassessed, 10; scholarship on, 17, 26–27, 29–31; and socialist cinema, 52; transformation of, 38, 40; and women's liberation, 36, 41–45, 83–84, 120, 130–31, 163, 165, 204

socialism (continued)
—and women, 8–11, 29, 117, 120–21,
236–37; liberation of, 2, 8, 128,
130–31, 160, 204, 207, 216; Maoist,
220; socialist women's movement,
9, 23–24, 26–28, 31, 36, 45
soldiers, female, 77, 198
Song Zhao, 62, 67–68
Song Zhidi, 65–68. *See also* Wang Ping
Soviet Republic, 38, 40; Soviet Republic
period, 39 (*see also* Jiangxi Soviet)
Soviet Union, 2, 48, 52–54, 84, 150–51,
171
space, interior, 224. *See also* inner
world
Stacey, Judith, 45, 159–61; *Patriarchy and
Socialist Revolution in China*, 17,
24–31, 161, 237n20, 238n22
Stanislavsky, Konstantin Sergeyevich,
208, 210
structure, patriarchal, 166, 207; phallocentric, 204. *See also* male-centered
structures, socioeconomic, 8, 28, 83,
105, 191
styles, film, 55, 75, 88, 134, 157, 174, 190;
melodramatic, 148, 187–90, 212,
230; representational, 190; subjective, 157
subjectivity, 245; and autonomy, 128;
bourgeois, 161–62; cultural, 60;
detached, 250; female, 158–59, 161,
167–68, 195, 197, 207; impossible,
162; independent, 109; and identity,
143; individual(istic), 2, 67–68,
114, 139, 156, 163, 182, 184, 227; and
liberal humanism, 111, 119; male,
102, 146; social, 188; socialist, 86;
and universal female difference, 68;
women's, and feminist endeavor,
165
Sun Xiantao, 143–44
systems, political-economic, 7, 11, 32, 35,
46, 83, 162

theater, distancing effect, 210. *See also*
Brecht, Bertolt

theory, 110, 154, 157–58, 161, 210–11; auteur, 139–40, 144, 155; cine-feminist,
33, 163, 167, 206; of experimental
cinema, 20, 145, 151; feminist, 25,
35, 58, 119, 125–26, 158, 195, 206,
236, 252; feminist film, 58; and film
practice, 53–55; Lacanian, 166, 252;
Maoist, 124; Marxist, 6, 8–9, 19, 37,
44, 50, 115–16, 124, 128, 247; Marxist, and class, 129; Marxist, and
Maoist, 124; Marxist, and women's
liberation, 27–28, 113, 119–20, 240;
poststructuralist, 163, 166–68, 206;
psychoanalytic, 206; of socialist
cinema, 55; of socialist feminism,
4; socialist, of women's liberation,
7; transnational feminist, 10, 23,
236; Western, 116, 130, 153, 206, 250;
Western feminist, 33–34, 127–28,
163, 165–66. *See also* film theory
thought liberation. *See* liberation
Tong Daoming, 208, 254n34
Toynbee, Arnold J., 2, 143, 200
transformations, 14, 58, 122, 149, 190, 193,
215, 233; cultural, 45, 145, 213, 215;
economic, 149, 227; gender, 69, 104,
202, 215, 232; of self, 95, 99; socialist, 9, 13–15, 19, 57, 104, 199, 202, 213,
215, 247; sociopolitical, 215, 232
transnational, 2, 7–8, 11, 14, 24, 29–30,
32; capitalism, 188, 190–93, 199
(*see also* Zhang Nuanxin); cinema,
55, 81; feminism, 4, 9–10, 19, 23, 45,
108, 119–20, 236, 239, 243; literature
and media, 5, 47, 50, 57
truth, 3, 47, 124–25, 135, 153–54, 180, 220,
225, 247

United States, 8, 24–26, 28, 47–48,
128–30, 138, 173, 180, 238, 249

values, patriarchal, 197, 232; socialist,
172, 178; traditional, 221–22, 226,
231; universal, 8, 20, 140, 200, 202,
206, 221
vision, socialist, 87, 93, 97, 101, 105–6, 149

women's cinema (continued)
125, 131, 158–60, 167–69, 237, 239, 242–43; experimental, 21, 34–35, 168–69, 173, 192; and female (self-) consciousness, 108; and feminism, 81, 204, 239; history of, 5, 55; mainstream, 16–17, 150; mainstream experimental, 20, 23, 57, 151, 195, 245; marginalized, 4; modernist, 158; post-Mao, 20, 88, 131, 157, 165; socialist, 10–11, 18, 23, 25, 60–61, 80, 84–85, 101; socially engaged, 192–93; studies of, 6–7, 24–25, 32–33, 125, 159, 161, 163, 167, 203–5, 208, 227, 235–37, 250–51; symposium on, 107; Western, 206
women's studies, 115–16, 120, 125–26
women's work, 42–44, 121, 128
workers, 38, 49, 51–52, 86, 96, 142, 191
Wu Guanping, 192

Xiang Jingyu, 37, 239n58. *See also* socialism: women's liberation
Xia Yan, 53, 241n122, 242n127
Xie Caizhen, 242n140
xieyi, 54, 210, 212–13, 215–17, 255; *xieyi* aesthetic, 21, 201, 208–9, 211, 215; *xieyi* scenes, 215–17. *See also* black velvet aesthetic
Xu Feng, 208, 224

Yan'an, 43, 51, 53, 236n31, 242n139
Yan Bili, 55–56, 150
Yang, Mayfair Mei-hui, 256n65
Yau, Esther, 143, 147
Yingjin Zhang, 147, 249n53
Yuan Ying, 235, 252; on female consciousness, 254n30; article "Feminism and Chinese Women's Cinema," 163–64, 204; on mainstream Chinese film, 136; and post-Mao film feminism, 125, 165, 227; and post-second-wave feminist theory, 163; on socialist women's liberation and gender equality, 207; on Wang Ping, 243n19, 44n32; and Western theory, 163

Zhang Jie, 111–14; "Love Must Not Be Forgotten," 111; and Li Xiaojiang, 114, 118, 246n16; *The Ark*, 113
Zhang Junxiang, 53, 201
Zhang Manling, 170–75, 178, 184; "A Beautiful Place" (novella), 171–73; "A Beautiful Place," characters: Big Brother, 172; Bilang, 172; Da-die, 184; Li Chun, 171–73, 175–76, 179–81, 183–84; Ren Jia, 173, 180, 182–84, 186–87; Ya, 172
Zhang Nuanxin, 6, 145–46, 165; article "On the Modernization of Film Language," 134–36, 141; cinematic style, 20, 190; critiquing the Cultural Revolution, 170, 173–75, 177–79, 184, 187, 232; and cultural pluralism, 132–33, 144, 149, 152–53, 156–57, 185, 190, 199; documentary style, 141, 151, 155, 157, 173, 187–90, 193; experimental cinema, 20, 180, 195; film practice of, 169, 177, 192; and institutional support, 150; and mainstream culture, 15; and mainstream intellectual movements, 170; as pioneer, 20, 145, 148, 151, 158, 173, 187, 204, 242; and realism, 154; studies of, 152–54, 161, 168; subjective camera, 155, 157, 174–75; and subjective experimental cinema, 88, 173
—*Drive to Win*, 151, 153, 155–57, 173, 193; "Director's Notes on Drive to Win," 153, 250–51
—*Good Morning, Beijing*, 188–89, 193; interviews, 153–54, 188–90, 192
—*Sacrificed Youth*, 20, 151, 158–59, 161, 165, 168–70, 173–83, 185, 189, 193, 204, 207, 227, 253; characters: Big Brother, 178, 185–86; Da-die, 175, 184–85; Li Chun, 151, 171–77, 179–86; Ren Jia, 173, 179–87, 253; detached individualism, 147, 174, 184, 186–87, 189, 193–94; "Director's Notes on Sacrificed Youth," 174, 253; Rousseau, Jean-Jacques, referencing, 180, 182; and Rousseau's *Confessions*,

180–82; sexual difference in, 177, 179, 193; uniformity, 20, 174, 178, 181, 190
—*South China*, 1994, 21, 188–93; <u>characters</u>: Jin Cuihua, 191; Liang Yifan, 190–91; Xu Jingfeng, 190–92; Yuan Fang, 191–92; Yu Jie, 191; main melody film, 16, 184, 189, 193; (socio) political melodrama, 21, 187–90, 193; transnational capitalism, 191–93
—*The Story of Yunnan*, 192

Zhang Xinxin, "Where Did I Miss You?," 111–12
Zhang Yimou, *Red Sorghum*, 146, 196
Zhong Kui, 199, 235, 237, 241; as alter-ego, 203, 212, 226, 228–30; demon, 203, 208, 223–24, 226, 228–30; as ideal man, 205, 222; opera "Zhong Kui Marries Off His Sister," 208–9, 223–25. *See also* Huang Shuqin, *Woman Demon Human*